Forging *the* Modern World

Forging *the* Modern World

SECOND EDITION

A HISTORY

James Carter
Richard Warren

New York Oxford
OXFORD UNIVERSITY PRESS

Oxford University Press is a department of the University of Oxford.
It furthers the University's objective of excellence in research, scholarship,
and education by publishing worldwide. Oxford is a registered trade mark of
Oxford University Press in the UK and certain other countries.

Published in the United States of America by Oxford University Press
198 Madison Avenue, New York, NY 10016, United States of America.

For titles covered by Section 112 of the US Higher Education
Opportunity Act, please visit www.oup.com/us/he for the latest
information about pricing and alternate formats.

CIP data is on file at the Library of Congress

ISBN: 978-0-19-090189-9

About the Cover

Sitting at the boundary between Europe and Asia, Istanbul (as it is now known) has long been a commercial, strategic, and military crossroads. This image of Istanbul, ca. 1900, is most likely a colorized photograph that was used as a postcard that tourists, including Europeans on the "Grand Tour," would have sent home. (Most Europeans would have known the city as Constantinople until the early 20th century.) The body of water here is the Golden Horn, an estuary that separated the oldest parts of Istanbul from the rest of the city, and was one of the most important harbors in the Mediterranean. The Galata Bridge in the foreground was itself an important market and was the third bridge to be built on this site, standing from 1875–1912.

9 8 7 6
Printed in Canada by Marquis

Brief Contents

Contents

List of Maps

Acknowledgments

We are fortunate to enjoy in our professional lives the generous encouragement and insightful intellectual support of many fellow teachers and scholars. We are particularly indebted to our past and present colleagues at Saint Joseph's University: Amber Abbas, Lisa Baglione, Melissa Chakars, Christopher Close, Emily Hage, Jane Hooper, Erik Huneke, Kazuya Fukuoka, Susan Liebell, Elizabeth Morgan, and Brian Yates all read numerous drafts in various stages of disarray. Thank you also to Brian Ulrich, Shippensburg University; Peter Worthing, Texas Christian University; Michael G. Vann, California State University, Sacramento; Erin E. O'Connor, Bridgewater State University; William E. Burns, George Washington University; James De Lorenzi, CUNY John Jay College; Bedross Der Matossian, University of Nebraska/Lincoln; Cecilia Miller, Wesleyan University; Isa Blumi, Centre for Area Studies, Leipzig University; Andrew D. Devenney, Grand Valley State University; Robert Cliver, Humboldt State University; Thomas Sanders, US Naval Academy; Chad Ross, East Carolina University; and the anonymous reviewers of the original manuscript. For help with particular queries, we'd like to thank Michael Chang, Jane Hooper, Jeffrey Hyson, Susan Liebell, Randall Miller, Bryan McCann, and Fritz Schwaller.

We are very grateful for the warm welcome that the first edition of *Forging* has received from many students and instructors. In particular, we have appreciated hearing about the ways in which the book has helped students understand better how historians work and how modern world history gets made. Several reviewers were especially generous with their time and provided valuable feedback on the first edition. These include J. Justin Castro, Arkansas State University; Christopher Ferguson, Auburn University; Christoph Strobel, University of Massachusetts Lowell; John Hepp, Wilkes University; and Suzanne Shoaf Smith, Cape Fear Community College. We hope their guidance is reflected in improvements to the current edition.

Administrative support from Susan McFadden and Denise Thomas helped make sure things got where they needed to go. Alex Gould and Jill O'Neil stepped in when we needed them for the second edition and sourcebook. Kelsey Kostelnik and Dale Pappas, both history majors at Saint Joseph's University, provided assistance during the research and writing phases of the book. The feedback from students and colleagues at Saint Joseph's University who used the first edition of the book has been very helpful. Matt Hanson and Ted Zeman, who have taught with us for may years, played important roles in bringing the second edition to fruition.

Charles Cavaliere, our editor at Oxford University Press, has been impassioned and enthusiastic about this project from its inception. It has been a delight to work with the entire staff at the press.

Finally, the lines between work and home are rarely bright these days, and this project has been no exception. Rich feels particularly thankful for the support he received from Suzanne Cohen and Ben, Rose, and Nate Warren, each of whom contributed to the completion of this book in many ways. Jay wants to thank Susan Liebell for contributing so much to this project both personally and professionally, Mariel and Charlotte for reminding him how important it is to teach and why it matters, and Adam, Julia, and Eli for many kinds of support.

Finally, and as always, any errors of fact or interpretation remain solely the authors' responsibility.

Changes to the Second Edition

1. Chapters were reorganized.

In the first edition, we found that the subheads and section breaks were uneven from chapter to chapter. Some chapters had six or seven subsections, whereas others had just two or three. This was confusing to students and made it more difficult for instructors to manage reading assignments and coordinate them with classroom discussion.

The new edition is more consistent. This should make it easier for students and instructors to learn from and teach the book.

2. We introduced new sections called "Historians Explore."

We added an entirely new feature called "Historians Explore," in which we introduce a historiographical debate, innovative new scholarship, or controversial approaches to historical events.

Although we incorporated some historiography in the first edition, this was not done in a systematic or consistent fashion. Some historiographical debates were pulled out in separate sections, but they were not identified clearly. Feedback from the first edition suggested that students were sometimes confused that these were the only, or most important, instances where historians disagreed or used innovative practices. By adding new sections, expanding existing ones, and labeling them all clearly and consistently, students and instructors can more easily find and discuss these examples of how historians work.

3. Introductory vignettes are now contextualized with discussion questions.

Each chapter begins with two vignettes. These were chosen to provide the opening and closing for each chapter, linked thematically to the subject of the chapter. Feedback from the first edition suggested that these introductory vignettes were sometimes confusing to students, who did not always understand how they were meant to relate to the rest of the chapter. Adding "Questions to Consider" after the vignettes will make the book more useful in the classroom and help to explain the structure of each chapter more clearly.

4. We updated discussion of topics to reflect new scholarship.

The new edition incorporates new scholarship to give students clearer understandings of some of the topics being addressed, including the following:

- the extent and causes of the depopulation of the Americas after 1492
- attempts at imperial reforms in the eighteenth century
- the lives of enslaved workers in the Americas
- the nature and limits of Reconstruction in the United States after the Civil War
- the First World War, reflecting the wave of new scholarship that attended the centennial of this conflict
- the Cold War, particularly its international aspects
- China's "reform and opening" era

5. We added new images.

Twelve new images have been incorporated into this edition to provide a broader visual representation of the topics being addressed.

6. We put together a companion sourcebook.

In response to many users who indicated that primary sources tied to *Forging the Modern World* would expand learning opportunities for their students, we have edited a document collection, entitled *Sources for Forging the Modern World*. The sourcebook follows the same organization as the parent text and includes approximately six sources per chapter. Sources are geographically and thematically diverse, and each is accompanied by an introduction and reading questions. For a listing of the sources, please see the Table of Contents at the back of book.

About the Authors

James Carter is a professor of history at Saint Joseph's University in Philadelphia and holds a PhD in modern Chinese history from Yale University. He is the author of *Creating a Chinese Harbin* (Cornell, 2002) and *Heart of Buddha, Heart of China* (Oxford, 2010), among other publications. When not teaching Forging the Modern World, he writes about the history of cultural interactions between China and the West.

Richard Warren is a professor of history at Saint Joseph's University, where he has served on the faculty since 1995. He is the author of numerous works on the political culture of modern Mexico, including *Vagrants and Citizens: Politics and the Masses in Mexico City from Colony to Republic* (Scholarly Resources, 2001).

Forging *the* Modern World

Introduction: Forging the Modern World

This is a book about history. It's important to point out from the start that when we say history, we don't mean the past. Despite science fiction plots and the musings of some physicists about the possibilities of time travel, we're comfortable saying that the earth's past cannot change: what happened once cannot be altered. History, however—our understanding of the past—changes all the time. New sources are found, new methodologies develop, and new concerns about the human experience emerge as subjects for investigation. New histories result, and this is one of them.

Forging the Modern World emerged from a question: if we had only one history course that we could teach every university student, what would that course look like? Our answer had two key parts. The first was to help students understand the development of the most important structures through which people around the world relate to each other (both the structures and the people who act within them are critical to the story we wanted to tell). The second was to pull back the curtain on what historical inquiry is so our students could better understand the distinction between the past and history and learn to analyze historical arguments (including those made by their instructors).

When we got the opportunity to design a course based on these ideas, we did not intend to write a book. However, conversations with colleagues and students led us to write one that would reflect the goals of the new course. This book is the result. It's a relatively short book with ambitious goals that tries to stick to some basic ideas: focus on a limited set of arguments based on the best available evidence; explain assumptions and terms clearly; and trust that readers will use this book as a starting point, rather than an endpoint, in the exploration of world history.

What Is This Book About?

The title is an important place to start understanding anything you read, watch, or hear. With that in mind, why do we call this book—and the course that produced it—*Forging the Modern World*? The last word, *world*, indicates that we are writing a history of the entire world, not of any particular place or group of places. We don't mention all areas evenly. Some places get more attention than others, and we leave out many important events. Nevertheless, the argument we try to make is one that applies to the entire globe.

Forging is the least common word in the title. We like it because it conveys the sense of active creation that applies to both historical actors and historians like ourselves. A smith in a forge takes raw materials and uses skill and hard work to shape them—within limits—into something new. In this same way, people in different times and places have shaped their world through their decisions and actions. Karl Marx, who we discuss later in this book, wrote in *The Eighteenth Brumaire of Louis Bonaparte* (1852) that people "make their own history, but they do not make it as they please; they do not make it under self-selected circumstances, but under circumstances existing already, given and transmitted from the past." In other words, everyone affects the world, but circumstances limit how and how much. This book looks at the decisions, actions, and contexts of people in the world and how those things created—*forged*—the modern world.

We, as authors, are forging something too: creating a history from sources, interpretations, our own experience and training, and the goals of the book. We're also limited in the tools that we have. We don't have access to every source, and we're not experts in every part of the world or every time period—not even close. Within these limits, we've crafted an argument and supported it with sources, forging our own modern world history. There are other ways it could have been created. You may not agree with every choice we have made in the way we present our evidence. If you're reading this in a class, your instructor, classmates, and you will disagree with some of the decisions we made and the conclusions we drew. We think our arguments are sound, but it's just as important to make the point that historical arguments are not received truths that exist outside of time and space: they are created by historians.

The Modern World

And what about *modern*? In everyday speech, this word means something like "newest" or "most current." With technology, for example, a radio in 1920, a television in 1940, or a desktop computer in 1980 might have exemplified modernity. The term modern in our title refers to something else, however. Starting sometime in the past few hundred years (exactly when is hard to pin down because it happened at different times in different places), the concept of modernity came to be used to define characteristics of certain societies that distinguished them from societies that existed in earlier eras and particular characteristics of the world as a whole that distinguished a new historical era from what came before. Coming up with a precise definition of modern that applies to all places and in all circumstances is impossible. We argue instead that there is a constellation of features that, taken as a whole, represents the modern world. Some are more, or less, present in any given place or time, but overall these seem to us a good list of what separates modern societies from what came before.

We ourselves, as authors, may be accused of *presentism*: seeing the past only through the lens of present outcomes. We'd respond in part by saying that the present is the only place where humans live—we're stuck here, at least for now! To be sure, many struggles and joys of the human experience endure across time and space, and there is value in studying them on their own terms. It does not diminish the grandeur, complexity, and variety of the past to say that in fundamental ways—politically, economically, and socially—human society looks very different today than it did only a short time ago and try to understand how those changes occurred. What, then, are some of these essential differences?

A Belief in Progress

A fundamental (and tricky) feature of modern societies is the belief among people, mostly elites, that they were thinking and acting in ways that were distinct—not just different but also fundamentally changed—from their predecessors. In societies that considered themselves modern, people have tended to believe that human action could, and with proper understanding of what needed to be done would, improve societies.

One way to make this clear is to think about the way the term *backward* came to be used to criticize other societies (or policies in one's own society). The belief in progress was tied to ideas about technology and material resources: modern societies had both the physical stuff and the ways of thinking to create progress, while *pre-modern* societies would not progress until they acquired these things. If you didn't have the right technology, or the right mindset, to move forward to the next stage, then you were behind, facing or moving backward. The idea that there is a single path and direction through history and toward the future, and that societies can move along it like pieces on a game board, is a common feature of how modern people view the world. This optimistic outlook overlooks many of the disastrous events and outcomes of world history over the past centuries. As we will explore in this book, those who possess political and economic power tend to overestimate the universality of their claims to truth and the justice of their decisions (calling both modern) while dismissing (perhaps as backward) those who disagree with them, especially those who are poor or culturally different.

Production of Knowledge

To support this position, modern people used particular forms of knowledge to assert that their ways of understanding the world were fundamentally different from, and superior to, the ways of earlier generations. Science became the quintessentially modern form of knowledge. Observation, hypothesis, and experiment produced results from which to better understand cause-and-effect relationships rooted in the natural world, not in the supernatural, spiritual, or religious realms that had been primary in earlier eras. Modern people came to think of themselves as rational, using the scientific method to solve all kinds of problems, while pre-modern peoples were superstitious, guided by custom. That isn't to say that modern people were always rational or even that they were more rational than people in the past, but rather that a general belief emerged that the world is governed by rules that can (in theory) be understood and applied equally to all things.

These ideas could be applied not only to the natural world but also to the social world. Egypt five thousand years ago, China three thousand years ago, and Greece twenty-five hundred years ago were technologically, socially, and politically sophisticated societies but they were not modern because those in power did not typically base their decisions—or justify their rule or political organization—on the methods and techniques of scientific inquiry. Explanations for the social order, government, or natural phenomena were often sought in supernatural authorities, in the inertia of custom or tradition, or in the private deliberations of an elite few. In contrast, by the middle of the nineteenth century, those with the greatest amount of economic and political power throughout most of the world tended to make political and economic decisions based on claims of progress and reason and a belief that the world is understandable through rational, scientific inquiry.

Global Interconnections

Connections between and among different parts of the world—even parts far away from one another—are not new. Ancient Rome and ancient China, for instance, traded with one another more than two thousand years ago. However, the quantity and quality of global connections have increased sharply in the past several centuries. In 1400, direct communication between China and North America was nonexistent. In 1600, letters from India to Europe took months to reach their destination, if they arrived at all. Just a few decades ago, communication beyond one's own town was frequently slow, expensive, or both.

Today, we receive emails, texts, and phone calls from around the world, all instantly delivered at low cost. This instant communication has enormous impact. Stock markets in New York rise and fall based on news from Beijing. Factory workers in Vietnam might be laid off because of an economic downturn in the United States or offered more work when reports arrive of a natural disaster in Indonesia. Gasoline prices in London can rise overnight on word of political unrest in Venezuela. In our global village, what happens anywhere can affect people and places everywhere.

Alongside increased global communication, patterns of mobility have fundamentally changed how people live. In one day, many of us travel farther than most people moved in their entire lives two centuries ago. This mobility matters: clothes at your local store cost less than they did a few decades ago because they can be produced at lower cost in other countries and shipped cheaply to the United States. Likewise, jobs at factories in the United States or Europe might disappear when their products can be made less expensively in another country. Workers may move thousands of miles in pursuit of new jobs. The effects of this great mobility can simultaneously increase economic productivity, degrade the natural environment, disrupt social relations, and rock the political order. Taken together, the movement of ideas, goods, and people across the globe is an essential part of how most people experience the modern world.

Production and Distribution of Resources

The interconnectedness of our world changes how resources are produced and distributed. Economic, social, cultural, and intellectual resources have never been evenly spread across the planet; we will analyze the reasons why. In 1400, material resources were arranged much differently than they are in the modern world. Because of differences in climate, geography, and technology, certain goods and commodities were only available in specific places. China was the main producer of silk and porcelain. The best cotton textiles came from India. Spices such as pepper and cinnamon were unique to Southeast Asia. Gold was concentrated in Africa and India. Europe was rich in some things, but lacked other valuable commodities and useful resources.

Reflecting this distribution of resources, the wealthiest parts of the world then were in East and South Asia; the world's richest man was probably the emperor of Mali in Africa. Trade routes crisscrossed the Indian Ocean to connect the unique products and commodities found along its rim with consumers. Overland trade routes brought the wealth of the Indian Ocean to the Asian, African, and European interiors. Other resources, too, were differently distributed than they are today. China had a distinct advantage over other regions in shipbuilding. Islamic empires in the Middle East and western Asia generated new insights in mathematics and astronomy. Indigenous societies in the Americas produced agricultural surpluses with ingenious engineering solutions.

By the twentieth century, that pattern had changed. Material wealth was concentrated in North America and western Europe, where the world's richest nations were found. The gap between the amounts of wealth controlled by residents of some regions compared to others had also increased dramatically so that the wealth of the average person in a rich country could be one hundred times that of an average person in a poor country. These same wealthy states exercised political control over much of the world and dominated scientific and cultural production as well. What changed? How? Why? Partly, political elites made decisions about how they wished to preserve their power. Partly, individuals and groups pursued their interests given the best information available to them. Both actions often led to unintended consequences in the long-term distribution of resources.

Technologies and economic productivity changed too, at different rates in different places, much of it having to do with circumstance. Although manufactured goods like porcelain or textiles were important to pre-modern long-distance trading networks, most economic production was locally generated and consumed. The power to grow crops, acquire commodities, finish goods, and transport it all to market was provided by human or animal muscle or wind or water power. Most producers were only indirectly linked to global, or even regional, economies. Barter was common; sophisticated economic transactions were not.

By the twentieth century, most goods—industrial and agricultural—were mass produced using machines powered by fossil fuels. Coal was of limited use in preindustrial societies, but once the use of steam engines spread, improving productivity, some coal-rich regions became economic powerhouses. Access to coal became a vital strategic and economic factor, although certainly not the only one, that explains where and how industrialization occurred.

For reasons and in ways we will demonstrate, political and economic elites in the industrializing zones of Europe and North America used emerging disparities in technology to redistribute wealth from other parts of the world to themselves and their countries. One feature of the modern era has been its coincidence with the dominance of western Europe and the North Atlantic, to the extent that some have argued that this part of the world is uniquely suited to be modern. Evaluating this claim is a central task of *Forging the Modern World.* India, Africa, and Southeast Asia still produced great wealth in the nineteenth century, but more of it came to be controlled by the populations of Europe and North America. Further shifts in the amount and distribution of the world's wealth characterized the twentieth century and this continues to our own day, as an accelerating pace of economic and technological change became one of the defining features of the modern world. Charting and explaining these shifts is thus another main aim of this book.

Political Organization

Try boarding a plane traveling from Atlanta to Tokyo without a passport: you'll fail. A valid passport, issued by a recognized nation-state, enables you to travel because citizenship—belonging to a nation-state—is an essential component of modern identity. Today, the landmass of the entire world is divided into nation-states. The only exception, Antarctica, is unclaimed by any nation . . . by an agreement among nations! The ability to live, work, travel, raise children, receive medical care, express yourself, and communicate with others is influenced by citizenship. Nearly every aspect of life on earth today depends on nation-states and the relations among them.

Six hundred years ago, there were no nation-states of the kind that exist in our time. Political organization in the world varied greatly, including large empires and kingdoms, smaller principalities or duchies, free cities, city states, and many others. Even if you lived in one of the large empires, like Ming China or Mali, connections to your family and village were still tangible in ways that more abstract associations to a larger political entity could never be. There is nothing natural or inevitable about the rise of nation-states, but they are a fundamental fixture of the modern world. Defining and understanding the characteristics, origins, development, and consequences of nation-states is essential to understanding modernity. This book traces the ebb and flow of political organization over several centuries, through waves of empire building and reorganization, and finally—and only in the twentieth century—to the domination of nation-states that characterizes the modern world.

Sources and Methods

This book is not *the* history of the modern world; it is one among many possible histories to be written on the topic. There are many different arguments to be made about the past, depending on an author's goals, perspectives, and sources. This is why so many books—so many histories—may be written about a single event. Thousands of books have been written about the US Civil War and each one is different. Books written today about the war differ from those written fifty or one hundred years ago. Some focus on military tactics, others on economics, or the causes of the war, or the experience of soldiers, or civilians. Even two books on the same subject, written at the same time, may be quite different. Can only one be "true" or "right"?

The differences among historical works come from how historians make history. (Yes, historians make history—though good ones do not make it up.) Historians combine raw materials and their own expertise to create histories. There are many ways to do this. Some are more interesting, more creative, and more sophisticated than others. Some approaches don't work at all. But they all require the historian to gather and interpret sources and to construct an argument about the past from them.

Before we go further, then, let's explain what we mean by evidence and by argument and look at some of the factors involved in putting them together. Historical evidence is anything that helps us understand the past. For the most part, historians work with two kinds of evidence: primary and secondary sources. (A third category, tertiary sources, usually refers to works like dictionaries, encyclopedias, or textbooks.) Primary and secondary sources are used differently, although they can overlap, and sometimes it can be hard to distinguish between them. In some cases, the same source can be either primary or secondary, depending on how it is used.

Primary and Secondary Sources

Primary sources are typically produced in the time being studied. Written documents are the most common, but photographs, paintings, sound recordings or music, buildings, and other objects can also be primary sources. Written primary sources include letters, government documents, memoirs, diaries, or any other document produced at, or near, the time of the events under scrutiny. A good rule of thumb for deciding what constitutes written primary sources is that they are generated by people who do not know how the subjects they are writing about will turn out at the moment they are writing. It is also important to understand that historians are limited by the availability of primary sources: a great idea about the past cannot be turned into history unless primary sources can be located and examined. Put another way, important questions about the past cannot be answered without relevant primary sources. Much of the human past has disappeared without a trace, and we can't write histories of it.

Like primary sources, secondary sources can be sounds, images, the printed word, or other kinds of objects. Usually these are produced not at the time being studied, but sometime later, and they typically use primary sources (and other secondary sources) to make their arguments. The most common of these are books or articles. Most of what you find in the history section of bookstores or online retailers are secondary sources: works of history that interpret primary sources to make an argument.

Historical arguments are made when researchers ask questions about the past. They then gather and analyze both primary and secondary sources and compare the results of their research to the work of others. Putting all this work together, historians offer conclusions about the best way to answer the question. An example illustrates how historical arguments get constructed. Let's take the sinking of the *Titanic* in 1912, an event that has been studied in many different ways for more than a century. A letter written by a passenger the night the ship sank or the captain's log of one of the rescue ships would be primary sources. So would the distress calls from *Titanic* and communications among different ships on the North Atlantic that night. Blueprints and plans for the vessel, weather reports, photographs of survivors, passenger lists, artifacts from the ship, and even the ship itself would be primary sources that can help us understand the events of that night, their causes, and their effects.

When historians gather sources and make arguments about what happened and why, they produce secondary sources. The first book about *Titanic* came out within a year of the sinking, and hundreds have been printed since then. Each uses some of the sources available to make an argument. No single work could use all the potential sources that exist at any given moment, and sometimes new sources are discovered. In addition, the interests of authors and the audience for books about history also change over time. Some authors and audiences are interested in the history of shipbuilding and technology, others in the social lives of the passengers, and still others in the cultural changes that *Titanic* represented. The discovery of the ship's wreckage in the 1990s led to new theories about how the ship sank. A 1997 movie about fictional passengers on the ship spurred a new round of historical research and writing.

To understand better the idea that sources might be either primary or secondary sources, depending on their use, let us take the example of books written about the history of Native Americans. These books might be used as secondary sources for understanding the expansion of the United States in the nineteenth century because these books use primary sources and the authors' analytical skills to make arguments about that topic. However, if we take a different topic—say, how portrayals of Native Americans changed over time—history books themselves could become primary sources.

Which are more useful for understanding the past, primary or secondary sources? The answer depends on what you are looking for. People sometimes assume that primary sources are better or more accurate than secondary sources and that is why they are called primary sources. This interpretation misunderstands the distinction between primary and secondary sources. Primary sources often convey immediacy and emotional power, but even the most detailed and beautifully written eyewitness accounts contain a limited perspective on events. They may lack important information unknown to the author and may even be untrue by design or unintended error.

As an example of the challenge of primary sources, let's think again about the US Civil War. If you were to read, as we did, the diary of a Confederate soldier who participated in the Battle of Gettysburg, you would discover that on July 1, 1863, his unit took three thousand prisoners and drove the Union soldiers out of the town. If you stopped your research here, you might conclude that the Confederate army was on its way to a quick victory (and many people did think this was the case at the end of the battle's first day). But this source gives only a brief portrait of events that this soldier believed to be true at the time, followed by a compelling description of what it was like for him to participate in battle. Despite what this source describes, the Union army won the battle, turning the tide of the war in its favor. This primary source might tell us many things of value about how a soldier lived and fought and thought, but this snapshot of one day's events does not reveal the bigger picture.

Using multiple primary sources and comparing them with one another helps get a more complete picture, but does not solve the problem of understanding the past in and of itself. To illustrate this limitation, let us imagine that you want to write the history of a college's sophomore class experience. If every person in that class—hundreds or thousands of students—kept a diary of what life at that university was like, they would produce a wealth of primary sources. Yet, even if they all tried to tell the truth, there would be major disagreements. What one student describes as the best part of college (location, food, social life, a particular course, sports), another may find unbearable. If you rely on just one of these sources, you may get a view of college life that is unrecognizable to another student. Yet these diaries would be eyewitness, first-person accounts: primary sources. What's more, they may all be true! The historian's challenge is deciding how to use these sources to answer questions that will help explain life at this college, assessing the collective experience of students, rather than trying to figure out which individual perspective is the singular historical truth.

The Question of Bias

The diaries of college sophomores would certainly include entries whose accuracy or objectivity you might doubt. There is much to think about in approaching this issue of bias in sources. The concept of bias is important but often misunderstood. Sometimes, a source will be clearly biased: skewed to a predetermined conclusion regardless of any consideration of the evidence. Adolf Hitler's writing about racial difference would be a clear example of this type of bias. If we understand Hitler's assumptions, we should know not to accept his opinions on Jewish culture at face value. More often, however, bias refers to unintentional assumptions and presuppositions that shape how an author interprets events. A newspaper report from the United States in the 1950s might contain observations or use assumptions—about different races, ethnicities, or political or social groups, for instance—that would seem odd or even outrageous in the twenty-first century, but they might have been typical for the time. In the same way, a French missionary's account of Native American society written in the 1600s would most certainly describe Huron social practices in ways that were influenced by the author's French and Catholic upbringing. These sources can be valuable for the historian, but to take advantage of them, one must work hard to account for how each author's worldview affects what was written and how it was written. In this way, a source might be less valuable for learning about Huron social organization than for understanding French missionary attitudes toward Native Americans. Bias is rarely a conscious attempt by an author to lie and more often the way in which deeply held perspectives and expectations shape the way an author writes.

All sources are biased. It is impossible to be human and not have presuppositions or a point of view. It's tempting, because of this, to throw up our hands and say that all sources are just opinions. But the fact that all sources contain bias does not make them invalid or useless . . . or equal. One of our jobs—our most important and most difficult job—as readers is to assess sources and their biases, how important those biases are, and how they affect what knowledge and information we can glean from the sources. We try always to learn as much as possible about who created sources and what their motivations were—goals, audience, background, worldview, and so forth. For primary sources, we often practice *close reading*, collecting everything possible from the sources themselves. For written sources, we take note of the organization, vocabulary, symbols, references, arguments, and suppositions. As we gather information about individual sources, we begin to compare them with other sources to build the base of evidence from which we will draw our own arguments and conclusions.

Just as all sources are biased, all readers are biased as well; and, as with sources, this bias is not necessarily a bad thing. Our biases are the sum of all the life experiences that we carry with us, including our ability to form thoughts with language. They are the things that allow us to learn in the first place. But reader bias can also affect how we evaluate sources in negative ways. For instance, if you know the race, gender, age, nationality, or social class of an author, do you take him or her less (or more) seriously? Should you? In the same way that we must make sure we understand the limits within which our sources are working, we need to undertake the (even harder) work of understanding our own limits as readers. Good historical inquiry means examining our own assumptions and preconceptions about the past and adjusting them if new evidence suggests that they need adjusting.

In this process, secondary sources become essential to historical inquiry. The authors of secondary sources benefit from hindsight, which can offer a perspective that primary sources lack. Secondary sources can combine, evaluate, and synthesize primary sources and weigh them against other secondary sources. A good secondary source provides balance, insight, and convincing analysis. Nonetheless, historians need to approach secondary sources with as much care as primary sources. They need to analyze the creator of the source and the context and motivations under which it was created. What do authors claim they are going to prove? Does the evidence they present adequately support the argument? For example, an author may present a portrait of life in the United States during the Great Depression using examples almost entirely from Chicago. The book may be a compelling analysis of life in Chicago, but we must be cautious about leaping to the conclusion that this study can apply to life in all cities during the same period, much less to other periods and places.

In secondary sources, we also look for transparency and reproducibility. Credible historical writing makes it easy for the reader to figure out what sources the author used, how they are used, and where those sources came from. Often that information is contained in notes, a bibliography, and perhaps even a separate discussion of how sources were located and used. Other researchers and readers can then track down the author's sources for themselves to confirm their content and verify that the author is using the sources responsibly. Casual readers often skip the documentation contained in notes and bibliographies, but they can be a key means to assess the value of secondary sources.

Practicing History

All these concerns and qualifications can overwhelm readers looking for an introduction to world history, so we decided to move much of the work we've done collecting, assessing, and interpreting sources to the background. Throughout the book, we provide readers with what we think are the best interpretations of all the evidence available, but we do not provide a very detailed roadmap of how we arrived at these conclusions. In the language of math tests, we haven't always shown our work and there are few footnotes in the book. This simplicity is important, but to emphasize that history is created by historians, we want to review for you some of the decisions that we've made in writing this book.

"Historians Explore . . ."

We devote one section of each chapter to a more detailed analysis of how historians explore a case, a theme, or different kinds of sources. Sometimes we highlight recent historical research that has challenged, changed, or enhanced our understanding of the past and thus made new history. For example, we present details about newly discovered sources (like data from slave cemeteries in the Caribbean or declassified documents from the Cold War) or especially innovative interpretations of sources. In these sections we cite the work of our colleagues, enabling readers to find their original research for more information or further explanation. In other places, we take an issue on which historians disagree and lay out the terms of the debate. We take a side in some of these debates; in others we just point out the different arguments and why historians disagree. Our goal here is to illustrate how even scholars with access to the same sources reach different conclusions on a topic. These tend to be big and controversial topics, often with contemporary political considerations and with great implications for our understanding of the past and the present: the reasons the Cold War ended or the nature of population decline after Europeans arrived in the Americas. In these cases, we present some of the competing arguments and cite books and articles where readers can learn more about them. These footnotes are not comprehensive but are designed to point readers to important original sources for the debates we describe.

You will also find footnotes in each chapter that reference specific secondary sources from which we drew information that we found innovative or particularly helpful in making a point. Please don't misunderstand our goals in proceeding this way. We don't intend to give the impression that these are the only areas where history is controversial or innovative—certainly not. Everything we know about the past is the product of historical research, and almost every sentence in the book could have been footnoted and expanded on. By highlighting instances of how historians practice their craft within the broader synthesis of this book, we hope to demonstrate that history is not a series of received truths while still writing a concise and readable introduction to a vast topic.

Labeling Time

In thinking about history, we often refer to memorable chronological markers—important years, days, generations, or epochs: 1492; 1776; December 7, 1941; and the sixties, for example. However, the study of world history challenges us to recognize both the power and the limits of convenient chronological markers. Let's take 1776 and the Declaration of Independence as an example. That summer day when the declaration was signed, it certainly didn't matter to the emperor of China or the sultan of the Ottoman Empire or even to many people living in North America. The declaration didn't even begin the American Revolution! This event clearly matters for world history, but knowing exactly how, for whom, and when means that our job barely begins with knowing that the US Declaration of Independence was signed in 1776.

And what is 1776 anyway? What most people in Philadelphia, where the declaration was signed, called 1776 AD—Anno Domini, Latin for "In the Year of Our Lord"—was the year 5536 in the Hebrew calendar, 1768 in Ethiopia, 1154 in Persia, 1189 by the Islamic calendar, 2320 by the Buddhist calendar, An'ei 5 in Japan, and Qianlong 41 (or the Wood Goat year 4472) in China, just to name a few alternative ways of marking time. Christian thinkers developed the designation Anno Domini about fifteen hundred years ago as a means of dating events from the presumed birth of Jesus Christ, adding this to a calendar system first adopted by the Romans. In English, dates preceding the presumed birth of Christ came to be designated BC: before Christ.

All calendars are frames of reference, marking the passage of time from some point in the past—perhaps the reign of a ruler, the mythical beginning of time, or a religious event. Most of the world, for most of its history, has not been Christian, so perhaps this calendar is not the optimal way to organize historical time. For that matter, not even all Christian calendars agree (and contemporary evidence suggests that Jesus was most likely born sometime between 3 BC and 1 AD).

To further complicate matters, different calendars measure the year differently. Many calendars measure the moon's orbit around the earth, but others keep track of the earth's orbit around the sun or a combination of the two. Years can last anywhere from (about) 354 days to (about) 365 days. Without agreement on how long a year is or when to start counting them, the seemingly simple question of when something happened becomes difficult to answer. Fortunately, we don't need to weigh in on any astronomical, mathematical, or theological debates about time. For this book, we consider the calendar a tool that allows us to establish when events happened in relation to each other. What is most important about the dates in this book is their usefulness to readers. So, how will we mark time in this book?

We have chosen to note dates throughout this book using the Gregorian calendar, a sixteenth-century revision of Julius Caesar's solar calendar, which has grown since the eighteenth century to become the most widely accepted calendar. As an acknowledgment of this shared past and common experience, we will refer to most dates in this book as belonging to the Common Era, abbreviated CE rather than AD (retaining the convenience of the Gregorian dating system without its religious overtones). However, in this book, because nearly all the dates we mention are from the Common Era, we will not typically use any letters after the numerical date. On those occasions when we refer to events prior to the Common Era, we will use the label BCE—before the Common Era. If you are accustomed to seeing dates with the labels AD and BC attached to them, keep in mind that it is not the dates themselves that are different, just the way they are labeled: it is an attempt to recognize difference while still embracing the links and shared experiences among people and places.

How Each Chapter Is Structured

A similar concern about the portability of dates across cultures and countries shapes the construction of the book's chapters. Periods like the Victorian era or the age of revolution depend on specific geographical, social, and cultural limits: they aren't universal. One way that we attempt to align our readers with the global context of this book is by creating less familiar starting and ending points for each chapter and overlapping them from chapter to chapter. Each chapter begins with a pair of vignettes, marking a start and end date for the chapter. The main importance of the events and people of those vignettes is symbolic, tying together the themes around which we have constructed that chapter. After these two vignettes, we provide questions that may prompt discussion in class or help you think about the themes we are trying to develop in the book. By overlapping the dates each chapter covers, we want to emphasize that history is not a linear progression of events but a series of interrelated and variable events that affect different parts of the world at different times and in different ways. The dates, and the vignettes that go with them, alert readers to themes that will be addressed and foreground our intention to move away from any effort to create in each chapter a self-contained historical epoch.

Places and Place Names

World history also challenges our ideas about geography. Different groups used different names to refer to the same place, place names changed over time, and even geographic markers that may appear objective are themselves historical artifacts injected with cultural and ideological meaning. Think about the term *Middle East*, for example, which is used daily in the US media to describe a vast and vaguely defined part of the world that is sometimes stretched from the eastern Mediterranean to the Arabian Sea and beyond. The term entered common usage only in the early twentieth century and only in some parts of the world. We have tried to balance historical accuracy in using place names with the need to help our readers find things on maps so that they may be compared over time. This means that, at times, we will use more than one term to refer to the same place or that we will use terms that carry heavy, even controversial, cultural and ideological meaning.

Generally, we use the current common Anglicized spellings of cities, countries, and other political geography, omitting accents and diacritics unless they are present in the English usage (for example, Mexico does not have an accent, but Potosí does). We have taken a similar approach to the labels we attach to people and things throughout the book. For proper names and transliterations, we have attempted to adhere to conventions that would make the text both acceptable to specialists and accessible to nonspecialists. But it would be fair for any of our readers to question the choices we made about naming and spelling and to decide whether they would have made different ones and, if so, why. Our hope is that questions about naming conventions proceed hand in hand with other discussions about the nature of historical events and processes.

Recommended Reading

Writing this book has reminded us of our limits as researchers and writers. We have read remarkable works by our colleagues, past and present, which push the boundaries of historical inquiry, from microhistory (the intensive study of a single place or issue) to *big* or *deep* history (which asks questions on enormous chronological and geographical scales). We have read masterful monographs and benefited from the ambitious projects of scholars who ask grand historical questions. We could not have finished this project were it not for the trust we place in our readers, especially the students and instructors who will use this book, knowing that they will understand that any individual text can only be a starting point. We assume that you will have ready access to the internet while you read this book. We encourage you to use it to find out more about the people, events, and arguments we present while you are working your way through the chapters that follow. We also want you to read what our colleagues have written, especially those who have different approaches and draw different conclusions from our own. To help with this, we end each chapter with a list of "a few good books" related to themes addressed in the chapter. By no means comprehensive, the lists are simply attempts to point out engaging, thought-provoking works so that you can continue the journey of historical inquiry.

Agency and Contingency

For us, being historians is an exercise in hope. Broad trends, covering large areas and long periods of time, are the stuff of world history. The enormous, abstract forces that shape history can make individual lives seem insignificant and individual actions appear irrelevant. Yet, a premise of this book is that historical outcomes happen because (but not *only* because) of human agency—people make choices. You will find in the pages that follow both analyses of large abstract processes and many stories about individual actions and decisions. Sometimes the actions of one individual can have enormous consequences. More often, groups of people bring about change. Human beings are not just passengers on a planet hurtling through space. The modern world is, within a set of material limits, a human creation.

In counterpoint, rarely are single human beings responsible for fundamental changes in world history. When Christopher Columbus (1451–1506) sailed from Spain to the Caribbean, he set in motion changes far beyond anyone's expectations at the time. The specific choices he made mattered enormously, but he was not the only person of similar background and motivation traveling in the Atlantic Ocean during that time. If Columbus had not embarked on, or survived, his transatlantic crossing, someone else would have, sooner or later. Columbus's actions changed the world, yet it would be wrong to conclude that had he not lived, the Americas and Afro-Eurasia would have remained unknown to one another. To take another aspect of this phenomenon, we can look at the case of Mohandas K. Gandhi (1869–1948), the activist for Indian independence. One of the most famous quotes about historical agency ever is attributed to Gandhi—"Be the change that you wish to see in the world"—and we can certainly say that the transition to independent nation-states in South Asia was shaped in large part by Gandhi's hand, but the thoughts and actions of millions of others also contributed to this particular historical outcome. A single person can change the world, to be sure, but always in the context of other events and other people.

This discussion of agency leads us to one last distinguishing characteristic of historical inquiry: the concept of contingency. We believe that our job as historians is to present the possibilities that existed in any given historical situation, not derive laws that can predict the future. We believe that the path that led to the predominant models of political organization and economic activity in the modern world could not have been predicted but that it can be explained. To do so requires us to consider the entire world, even if we do not cover all parts of it equally or equally well. It would be a fool's errand to try to account for every event that contributed to these outcomes. These pages don't detail every event—even every important event—that has occurred across the globe, nor do they emphasize equally each of the world's regions and distinct histories. Nonetheless, our scope is global. We are trying to explain how a world of distinct human traditions became increasingly interconnected, what the connections looked like, and why some connections, and not others, came to predominate in the modern world.

A Few Good Books

Joyce Oldham Appleby, Lynn Avery Hunt, and Margaret C. Jacob. *Telling the Truth about History*. New York: W. W. Norton, 1995.

Marc Bloch. *The Historian's Craft: Reflections on the Nature and Uses of History and the Techniques and Methods of Those Who Write It*. New York: Vintage, 1964.

R. G. Collingwood. *The Idea of History*. Reprint, Oxford: Oxford University Press, 2004.

Jared Diamond. *Guns, Germs, and Steel: The Fates of Human Societies*. New York: W. W. Norton, 1997.

Mark T. Gilderhus. *History and Historians: A Historiographical Introduction*. 7th ed. Upper Saddle River, NJ: Pearson, 2009.

J. R. McNeill and William H. McNeill. *The Human Web. A Bird's-Eye View of World History*. New York: W. W. Norton, 2003.

(RIGHT) Tribute Giraffe from Bengal with Keeper, China. The Chinese fleets led by Zheng He obtained a giraffe in India in 1414, but the transaction illustrates much wider trade networks connecting East Asia, South Asia, and East Africa. The animal had come originally from Malindi, in today's Kenya, as a gift to the court in Bengal. Zheng He purchased the animal and shipped it back to the Chinese emperor. Silk scroll paintings like this one memorialized the splendor of the royal menagerie.

(BOTTOM) Afonso De Albuquerque's Rhinoceros as Imagined by Albrecht Dürer. Albrecht Dürer (1471–1528) produced this woodcut in Nuremberg, in today's Germany, based on reports, and perhaps drawings, of the rhinoceros that Afonso de Albuquerque sent to Portugal from South Asia. Dürer never saw the live animal, yet for hundreds of years this drawing became the idea of what rhinos looked like for many Europeans.

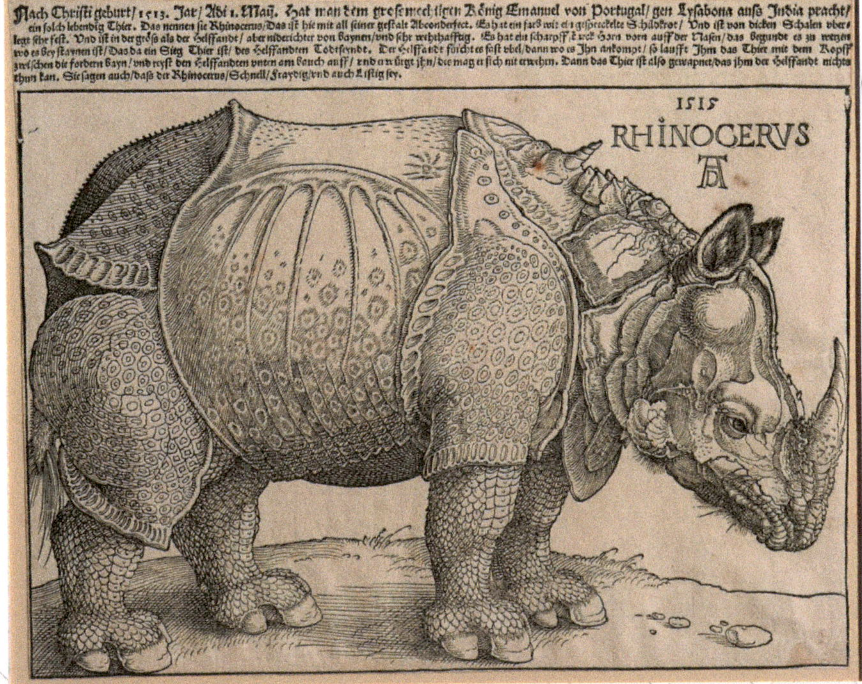

CHAPTER 1

The Many Worlds of the Fifteenth Century

1405–1510

On a hot July morning in 1405, a fleet of some three hundred vessels weighed anchor from the Chinese city of Nanjing, then the most populous city in the world. Sailing down the Yangzi River past Suzhou—a city that reminded the thirteenth-century merchant Marco Polo (1254–1324) of his home in Venice on the Italian Peninsula—this *treasure fleet* included the largest ships ever built, bigger than any humans would build for another five hundred years. Admiral Zheng He (1371–1433), a Muslim from the southwestern region of the empire, led the fleet into the South China Sea and across Southeast Asia before reaching the kingdom of Calicut in southwestern India, long a trade destination for the Chinese. The fleet returned to Calicut three years later when crew members witnessed the installation of a new hereditary Hindu ruler. Between 1405 and 1433, seven voyages brought thousands of Chinese sailors across the Indian Ocean as far as East Africa and Arabia. The voyages' commercial, diplomatic, and strategic accomplishments are symbolized by the gift of a giraffe for the emperor's menagerie, acquired in Bengal from African emissaries on their own trade mission. China's Yongle emperor (1360–1424) sponsored these impressive voyages to project the dynasty's political and economic authority, both within its own empire and abroad, but in the early 1430s, the voyages of the Chinese treasure fleets ceased.

During the same era, six thousand miles away on the western tip of Europe, Prince Henry (1394–1460), a son of the Portuguese king, financed a series of expeditions into the Atlantic Ocean. Over the course of the fifteenth century, Portuguese seafaring led to the establishment of plantations on islands in the Atlantic Ocean and trading posts on the west coast of Africa. The wealth these expeditions brought directly to Portugal, including gold from Africa and sugar from Madeira Island, inspired additional expeditions.

In 1497, four *caravels*—Portuguese vessels much smaller than their immense Chinese counterparts, but better able to maneuver in shallow coastal waters—left

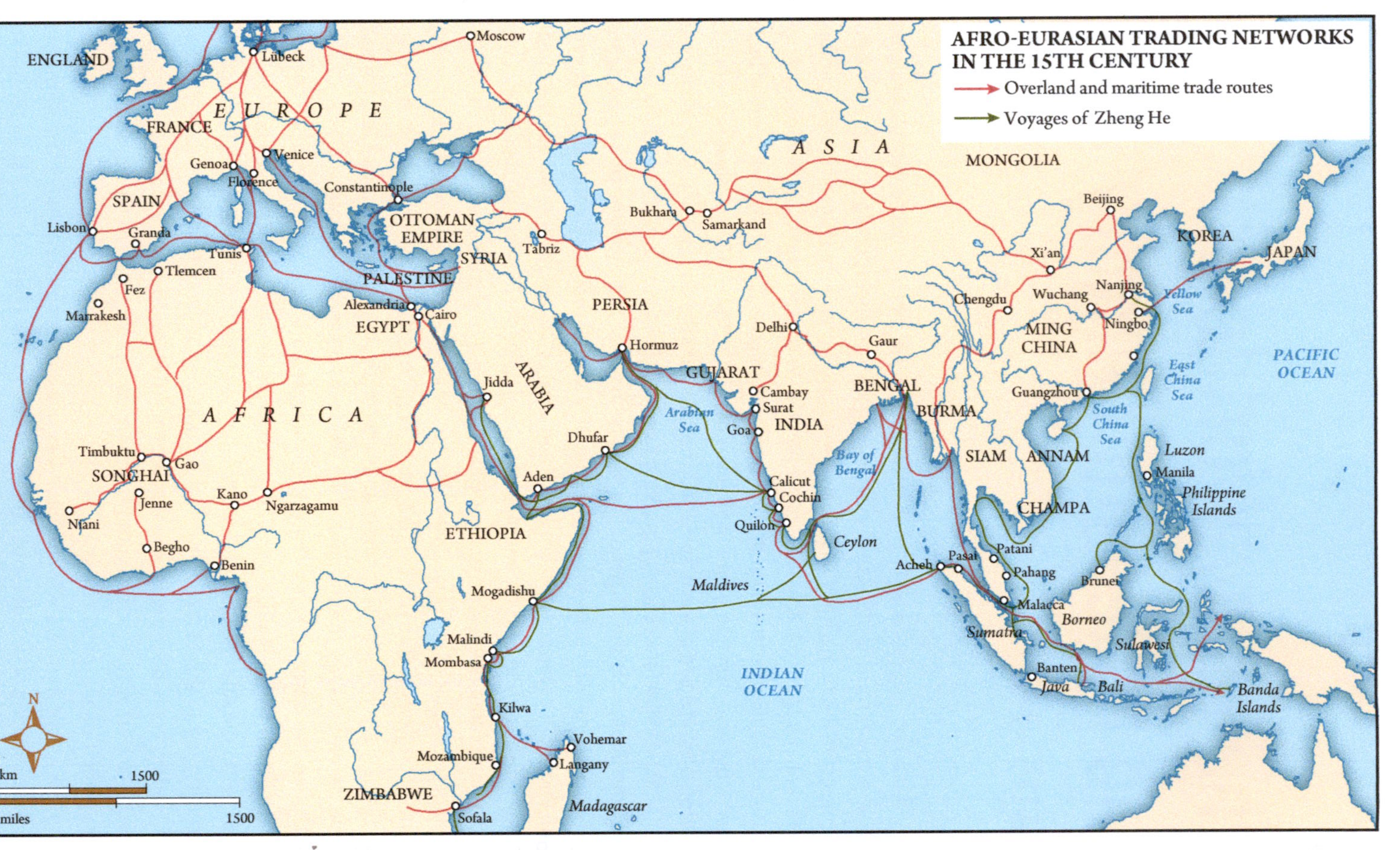

Map 1.1 Afro-Eurasian Trading Networks in the Fifteenth Century

Portugal under Vasco da Gama's command. These two hundred men became the first Europeans to round the Cape of Good Hope, Africa's southern tip, and cross from the Atlantic to the Indian Ocean. Over the following years, the Portuguese sailed this route regularly and hoped to establish a permanent outpost in the Indian Ocean. In 1510, the Portuguese nobleman Afonso de Albuquerque (1453–1515) seized Goa, north of Calicut, to become Portugal's base as it attempted to gain a greater share of wealth from the world's most lucrative commercial crossroads and to spread Christianity in Asia. Like Zheng He, Afonso de Albuquerque acquired animal gifts in exchanges with local rulers. The Muslim ruler of Cambay (in today's Gujarat, in India), Sultan Muzaffar II, provided him with a rhinoceros, which the Portuguese explorer sent back to Lisbon to demonstrate the scope of his endeavors. The rhino caused a great sensation when it arrived in Lisbon but died on the way to Rome when King Manuel attempted to regift the beast to Pope Leo X.

These stories of seafarers separated by decades converging on South Asia from opposite directions introduce key places, structures, events, and relationships among regional economies and political structures that we analyze in this chapter. Although it is common to divide the world's landmass into six or seven continents, we first explain why it makes historical sense to consider Europe, Asia, and Africa as a single Afro-Eurasian supercontinent across which ideas, commodities, and peoples flowed for thousands of years. We then detail some of the major political, military, and economic relationships on the supercontinent in the fifteenth century. In the last section of the chapter, we focus on the political and economic systems of the Western Hemisphere, which developed without any sustained or significant contact with the supercontinent until the very end of the fifteenth century.

Questions to Consider as You Read Chapter One:

1. What are the common characteristics that define the major political systems described in this chapter? What are some of the key differences among them?
2. How would you describe the distribution of different kinds of power—political, economic, social/cultural—within and between different regions of the world in the fifteenth century?

Political and Economic Order on the Afro-Eurasian Supercontinent

The Ming voyages were impressive—picture that huge ship on the high seas hauling a giraffe back to China—but their significance must not be misunderstood. They occurred in the context of a long history of interactions among peoples and cultures across the Afro-Eurasian landmass and its surrounding oceans. Trade networks traversed the South China Sea and Indian Ocean long before Zheng He sailed and survived long after he stopped. Chinese traders had first sailed the Indian Ocean as early as the seventh century and already dominated the South China Sea when the treasure fleet launched. Southeast Asian, Indian, and Arab merchants connected the Indian Ocean trade networks to the Mediterranean Sea and East African ports. Overland routes connected the long-distance oceanic trade to the interiors of Europe, Asia, and Africa and linked southern and northern seaborne trade as well.

Evidence of these connections includes written records and other primary sources going back many centuries. Roman coins, minted from precious metals mined in Britain, have been discovered on the coasts of South Asia. Records of the Roman senate include discussion of the trade in Chinese silks. Archaeologists have excavated stores of ivory in Roman ruins (and new techniques enable researchers to identify whether the ivory came from elephant, walrus, or hippopotamus). Roman authors from the first century of the Common Era, such as Juvenal and Pliny the Elder, describe ivory's use and status value. Artifacts found across Africa and Asia reveal extensive trade in precious metals, iron, pottery, lead, ivory, and other commodities between these regions. As we noted in our introduction, the unique technological, climatic, and geographical traits of different regions drove this trade, requiring traders to travel to China for silk and porcelain, Southeast Asia for spices, Africa for gold and ivory, and India for cotton textiles. Chroniclers like Abu al Hasan al Masudi (896–956), Muhammad al Idrisi (ca. 1100–1165), and others describe these networks. Sources like these suggest how the size, shape, and variety of political and social systems across Afro-Eurasia—as well as the trade that flowed through them—changed significantly over the course of centuries. Rather than attempt to convey their full scope and variety, the following sections define key terms and explain concepts of political and economic order generally before analyzing the fifteenth century more specifically.

Key Concepts of Political Order

Four key terms related to political order are used throughout this book: *state, sovereignty, legitimacy,* and *empire.* What we write here just scratches the surface of rich and complex issues, but these words are used so often and in so many contexts that it's essential to clarify how we plan to use them. Consider the word *state* first. A state is the organized exercise of power over a certain territory and the people who live in it. States take many forms, so it can be hard to see what they have in common. If you focus on what governments do—make and enforce laws, raise armies, declare wars, and collect taxes—rather than how any government does these things or claims the right to do them, then you've got the basic idea of what a state is. To think about and discuss states is to think about and discuss the accumulation, preservation, and use of the power to do these things.

Individuals or groups attempting to act like a state are claiming *sovereignty*; and if they succeed, they are exercising sovereignty. Sovereignty means an individual or group is making and enforcing rules for interactions within a given territory and/or among a group of people. Those who claim sovereignty (whether called emperor, shah, sultan, queen, or president) must strive continuously to maintain it against continuous threat—both from within the territory over which they claim sovereignty and from challengers who live in territory beyond a sovereign's current claims.

Although sovereigns wield power, power is not the same as sovereignty. Let's compare a sovereign state to the kinds of organized crime activities familiar to viewers of the *Godfather* movies of the 1970s or the television series *The Sopranos* (1999–2007). It's tempting to see sovereign governments as exercising power just like mobsters: both make rules, both enforce their will, both fend off challenges to their power. Both routinely exercise violence to maintain their power, against both internal and external rivals. Why are they not the same?

A third concept, *legitimacy*, matters here. Exercising sovereignty is about more than just enforcing your will through violence. To be legitimate, a ruler must not only show the ability to rule but also justify his or her claim. Relying on sheer physical force to subdue a territory and its residents is unsustainable over the long term for any ruler (which is why most mob bosses are, sooner or later, overthrown by their rivals or their lieutenants). States, therefore, tend to survive by delivering benefits to enough people to reduce the need for massive or constant physical violence imposed on the entire population. For example, enduring political systems such as Rome under the Five Good Emperors (96 CE–180 CE) or Han dynasty China (206 BCE–220 CE) made long-distance travel and commerce easier in many ways. The rulers of these states built infrastructure to collect and redistribute resources while maintaining control over territories and people through the use of legal systems as much as armies. Those who claim sovereignty link these demonstrations of how they *can* exercise power to claims of why they *should* be able to do so. This is a claim of legitimacy: the exercise of political power that is considered correct or appropriate.

Finally, across the centuries and around the world, the successful assertion of sovereignty over large expanses of territory in which ethnically, culturally, and religiously diverse peoples live has led to a particular kind of state—an *empire*. Empires are states in which those who rule act as if only practical considerations—oceans or mountain ranges, for instance—can limit their sovereignty and legitimacy.

They believe that, with the right combination of will, guile, military might, and/or divine providence, they can expand their control over territories almost without limit, regardless of the preexisting conditions in any of the territories over which the ruler wishes to exercise sovereignty.

Empires create imbalances among the various peoples and territories under the sovereign's authority, with some receiving greater benefits from the political and economic system than others. These others are often the most frequent target of the state's use of violence to maintain sovereignty. Empires have never been the only type of state but, as we shall see, they exerted an enormous amount of power for a very long time, in many different parts of the world. If we consider this book in two parts, the first part often focuses on the creation and expansion of empires, while the second part deals with their decay and destruction. Although this is too broad a pattern, it's worth thinking about how and why empires rise, and fall, as you read.

The Polycentric Supercontinent

No single region, state, individual, or group ever dominated the vast supercontinent—Africa, Asia, and Europe considered as one—entirely. Many ethnic, linguistic, and religious groups lived close together. Sometimes a large state, maybe an empire, exercised authority over many of them, but most people primarily experienced the power of regional or local states that made and enforced laws and distributed wealth in the form of resources such as land, gold, salt, wood, and human labor. Competition was fierce over the wealth of commercial centers.

States also competed over religious centers, which could confer legitimacy on states as they competed with rivals. This legitimating power made religion an important tool used by those who aspired to exercise sovereignty. This was especially true of Christianity and Islam, both because these religions were extraordinarily successful in attracting followers and (related to this) because both faiths encourage—some would say require—their followers to spread their religion by converting nonbelievers, an unusual trait among world religions. From the fourth century on, Christianity became important to empire builders as a faith tradition that could support claims of political authority; Islam emerged with similar characteristics during the seventh century.

Both Christianity and Islam held out the possibility of conversion to all peoples, yet neither religion was able to create a universal community of believers with a single authority, even among those who shared the same faith. Attempts to do so always foundered as spiritual and practical questions created enduring rifts among both Christians and Muslims. Claims of authority over all Christians or all Muslims persisted—leading to concepts like *Christendom* and *dar al-Islam*, which claimed to encompass the community of all believers—but neither Christians nor Muslims achieved consensus within their faiths on fundamental theological questions or on the channels through which faith should influence political order. As a result, we need to recognize that although Christians and Muslims carried on long and bloody wars against each other, it is also true that Muslims fought other Muslims and Christians other Christians in shifting alliances to control resources and territory.

Across the supercontinent, Christian and Muslim rulers also competed with political leaders who relied on other religious traditions—Hinduism and Buddhism were two of the largest, but dozens of others existed at regional and local levels—for their own claims to rule. Religious diversity, like linguistic and cultural diversity, characterized the physical space of Afro-Eurasia, complicating the ways sovereigns could use religion to claim and exercise power.

The Biological Old Regime

Even at moments of intense warfare or political fragmentation, ethnic and religious networks moved goods and people across Afro-Eurasia. Although most of the travelers along these networks are unknown to us today, a few left records, helping us see the connections among different parts of the supercontinent. One of these was a rabbi named Benjamin (1130–1173) from the town of Tudela (in today's Spain), who traveled across the Mediterranean world, down the Persian Gulf, into the Indian Ocean, and back again over the course of eight years. Almost two centuries later, Ibn Battuta (1304–ca. 1368) was born in Morocco, not far from Tudela by today's standards. Ibn Battuta traveled more than seventy thousand miles, over decades, throughout North Africa, across the Arabian Peninsula, through central and South Asia (including Calicut), and all the way to China. These travelers moved with the help of what might be called a cultural passport rather than the political one we are familiar with today. Benjamin sought out Jewish communities as he moved across the Mediterranean world. Ibn Battuta, trained as a scholar of Islamic law, found that his education, familiarity with the Arabic language, and religion opened doors and opportunities for him throughout his remarkable journey.

Although separated by almost two hundred years, many facets of life in Afro-Eurasia had changed little between the travels of Benjamin of Tudela and those of Ibn Battuta. It took Benjamin nine days to travel 150 miles from Al-Anbar to Baghdad (in present-day Iraq), one of the great centers of Islamic culture and home to forty thousand Jews. Two centuries later, Ibn Battuta could travel no faster. There had been few innovations in technology or major changes in the productivity of human labor in Afro-Eurasia in the intervening years. Many of the

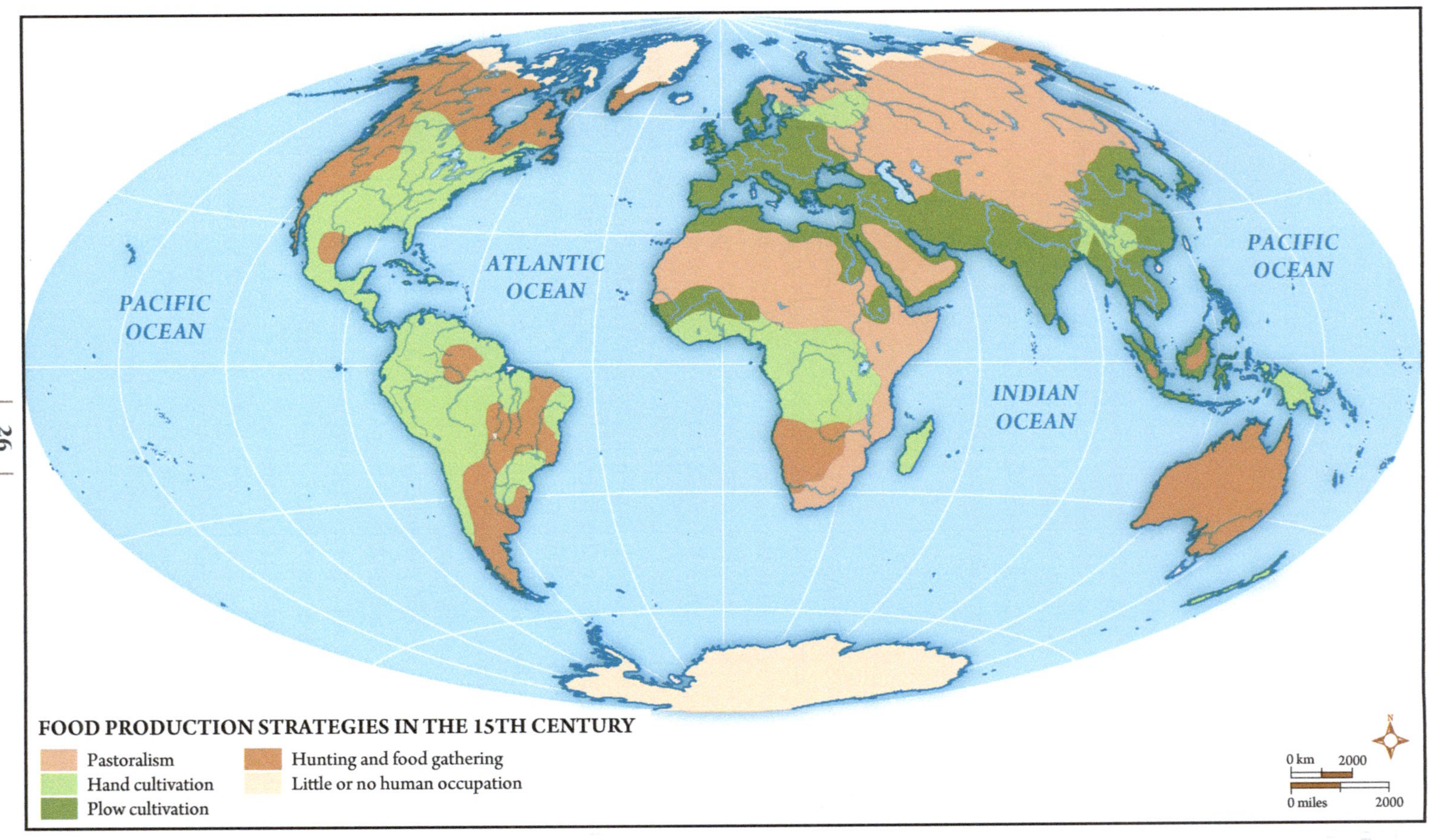

Map 1.2 Food Production Strategies in the Fifteenth Century

fundamental rhythms and constraints of daily life had remained steady, rooted in a relationship between energy and human productivity that had changed little since humans first began sedentary agricultural practices and domesticating animals thousands of years earlier.

Most human societies depended on agriculture, and agricultural output depended on the amount and quality of land under cultivation, the number of laborers working the land, climate, and weather. Few technological innovations had yielded significant growth in agricultural productivity. Techniques were not well developed for the long-term storage of food or for its rapid transit from places of plenty to places of need (although there were some impressive exceptions, like the Chinese state granary system that stored and distributed grain in times of famine). Most of the world's population devoted its time and energy to producing food. Bad harvests led to famine. Contagious diseases, of mysterious origin and unknown cure, attacked regularly. Scholars like Robert Marks refer to these realities, with their enduring constraints on population and productivity growth, as the biological old regime.[1] To call this the *old regime*, however, is hindsight. For the people who lived under its limits in the twelfth or fourteenth century, there was no foreshadowing that any *new regime* would ever replace their ways of life.

The Rise and Fall of States in Afro-Eurasia

The biological old regime's existence did not mean that things never changed. Elites of different religious and ethnic backgrounds struggled with each other to gain and control resources. The natural world, with earthquakes, unpredictable weather patterns, or epidemics, disrupted systems of production and resource distribution. In the sections that follow, we provide an overview of the changes in political structures and relationships that established the foundation for a major disruption of global relationships in the fifteenth and sixteenth centuries.

The Empire of the Mongols

In the early 1200s (between Benjamin of Tudela's death and Ibn Battuta's birth), the Mongol chieftain Chinggis Khan (ca. 1162–1227) and his heirs, descended from nomads of the Eurasian steppe, built the largest empire ever on the landmass of Afro-Eurasia. The imposition of Mongol authority over territories from Korea to central Europe came at a high price in lives and resources, and many works of history, particularly older publications, portray the Mongols as destroyers of order, ending the reign of the Islamic Abbasid caliphate in Baghdad in 1258

---

1 Robert Marks, *The Origins of the Modern World*, 3rd ed. (Lanham, MD: Rowman & Littlefield, 2015).

and overthrowing the Chinese Song dynasty in 1279. Because these societies kept more written records than did the Mongols, much of our understanding of the Mongol conquest came from these conquered peoples, who emphasized the destruction and disruption of the Mongols. More recent scholarship balances this view with what the Mongols built in its place. Some even use the term *Pax Mongolica* (Mongolian Peace) to characterize the Mongol Empire at its height, as people, goods, and ideas flowed back and forth across Eurasia, using routes protected by the Mongol military's highly skilled horsemen, but more importantly by the order imposed by the Mongol khan.

Unity across such a large and diverse empire did not endure, however. From one generation to the next, Mongol elites divided the empire into multiple states with different sovereigns. Over time, succession struggles within each dynasty and rebellion against the Mongols became more frequent. Baghdad, the great Muslim cultural center that attracted both Benjamin and Ibn Battuta, was sacked several times. The descendants of the Mongols who ended the Abbasid caliphate subsequently converted to Islam themselves and were trying to restore Baghdad to its former glory at the time of Ibn Battuta's visit in 1327. In China, rebel armies fought the Mongols, laying the groundwork for the rise of the Ming dynasty in the 1360s.

The Fourteenth-Century Crisis

Across the supercontinent, the fourteenth century brought a series of crises. The ruling elites of the kingdoms of England and France engaged in a seemingly endless cycle of battles that came to be known as the Hundred Years' War (1337–1453). Armies and leaders from across Europe joined the fighting intermittently. Unconnected to these military battles, but more important in shaping lives across a wider landscape, a cooling trend affected agricultural production. Ongoing warfare and the changing climate led to frequent and widespread food shortages in the fourteenth century. Deprivation, religious disputes, and discontent with rulers drove popular revolts across Europe.

In the middle of the century of crises arrived the most devastating of them all: the Black Death. Bubonic plague—known as the Black Death because of its symptoms and lethality—spread from China through oceanic and overland trade networks across much of Afro-Eurasia. It is difficult to tally the toll from the Black Death. In 1348, a landowner in Florence estimated ninety-six thousand plague-related deaths in his state between March and October of that year alone. Historians estimate that the population of Europe fell by one-quarter—from eighty to sixty million—during the era of the Black Death. Disease and warfare contributed to a population decline of as much as 40 percent in China between 1200 and 1400. Millions died across the rest of the supercontinent as well, although accurate numbers are impossible to acquire and the death toll varied widely from place to place. As we review the political, economic, and cultural geography of Afro-Eurasia in the fifteenth century, we need to keep in mind that both rulers and common people were responding to these multiple upheavals of the previous century.

The Ming Dynasty in China

Although it was also affected by the Black Death, China reigned as the wealthiest and most populous empire in the world in the fifteenth century. The ruling Ming dynasty had come to power in 1368 after defeating the Yuan dynasty, which had been established by the Mongol conquerors. The new dynasty was called *Ming*, meaning "bright," to proclaim that this was a new Chinese empire after two centuries of Mongol rule. Rebuilding after decades of war, plague, and political infighting at court, the Yongle Emperor moved the Ming capital to Beijing in the early 1400s. The imperial palace (still standing as the largest complex of its kind in the world) embodied the new dynasty's power. More than just a residence, the Forbidden City comprised one thousand buildings where tens of thousands of people could live and work, including all the offices of the central government as well as the imperial household.

Despite grand titles and projects, one must be careful not to overestimate the power of any ruler in this era, even the Ming emperor. The power of individual rulers and the strength of the empire varied over time, but there weren't enough government officials to regularly interact with the population across such a large landmass. More important to most people's lives than the imperial government was a local social hierarchy that regulated life according to age, gender, and occupational status. China's strength lay in its commercial vigor and regional autonomy, which yielded an economy that could produce and distribute staple foods within the empire as well as luxury goods like silk and porcelain. As long-distance trade routes recovered from the disruptions of the Black Death, porcelain bowls and silk robes from Chinese kilns and looms appeared again in grand residences, including royal palaces, across Afro-Eurasia.

Even with an inefficient tax system and an inadequate number of imperial officials, the expansive economy provided early Ming emperors with extraordinary resources. The scale and scope of Zheng He's maritime endeavors, introduced at the start of this chapter, reflect the wealth and ambition of the early Ming. The fleet featured the world's most advanced naval technology. The largest ships were four hundred feet long with four decks and luxury cabins for the officers and the merchants who accompanied the voyages. Capable of carrying five hundred tons, they were faster on the high seas, but less agile in shallow water, than the Spanish and Portuguese ships that would enter the Indian and Pacific Ocean trade in the next century. The Chinese vessels were double hulled—a feature of Chinese naval architecture since at least the Song dynasty (960–1279)—with as many as a dozen watertight compartments.

After Zheng He's first three voyages (1405–1412) had satisfied the Yongle Emperor that no rivals to the throne threatened him, later voyages proceeded beyond the tip of South Asia, reaching the Arabian Sea, the Persian Gulf, and East Africa. The Chinese fleets exchanged ambassadors and goods with states throughout. The fourth voyage (1413–1415) went as far as Aden and Hormuz on the Persian Gulf, as did the fifth. The seventh voyage, an armada of four hundred vessels and almost twenty-eight thousand men, traveled down the east coast of Africa as far south as Malindi (in modern Kenya), perhaps farther. A small expedition visited Mecca, the holy city of Islam on the Arabian Peninsula.

Historians Explore The Voyages of Zheng He

The Ming voyages, as they have come to be known, illustrate the extent of networks linking Africa, Europe, and Asia in the fifteenth century. In recent decades, scholars and governments have focused attention on these voyages and their meaning. Like all historical questions, political and economic interests shape how the past is interpreted. In our own time, Chinese government officials invoke Zheng He as a precedent for China's "peaceful rise" to great power status, emphasizing that during his "friendly diplomatic activities . . . Zheng He did not occupy a single piece of land, or seize any wealth from other countries."[2] Scholars who support this view include Tan Ta Sen, president of the International Zheng He Society, who has published widely in English and Chinese on the nonviolent nature of the treasure fleet. The possibility that this type of expansion, led by Chinese, might have shaped the world much differently than the often-violent colonial expansions that European nations—led first by Spain and Portugal—would undertake from the end of the fifteenth century onward has been picked up by many authors. Some even argue that Zheng He represents a cooperative approach to international relations that has lessons for today's business world.

Other historians, however, question this new depiction of Zheng He as a model of peaceful expansion, with some suggesting that the Ming voyages were not new and others indicating that they were not peaceful. Tansen Sen, among others, has established that rather than being a dramatic turn toward the oceans, Zheng He's voyages continued a trend of Chinese maritime ascendancy in the Indian Ocean

2 Xu Zuyuan (People's Republic of China Vice-Minister of Communications), July 2004, quoted in Geoff Wade, "The Zheng He Voyages: A Reassessment," *Journal of the Malaysian Branch of the Royal Asiatic Society* 78, no. 1 (2005): 38.

An Artist's Rendition Comparing the Vessels Commanded by Zheng He and Vasco Da Gama. China had the world's most advanced naval technology in the fifteenth century, capable of producing vessels far larger and faster than those made in Europe. The smaller European ships had some advantages, however, particularly in shallow coastal waters.

and South China Sea. Challenging their depiction as peaceful missions supporting trade and exploration, Geoff Wade, using evidence from Ming dynasty official histories, points to violence and intimidation by Zheng He's fleets in what is today Vietnam, Malaysia, Myanmar, Indonesia, Sri Lanka, Somalia, India, and Thailand. Wade sees the construction of Chinese garrisons and trading bases, as well as the imposition of Chinese will on Southeast Asian states, as similar to European expansion a century later. Other scholars stop short of the label *protocolonial* that Wade uses, suggesting that the Ming actions were focused on spreading the idea of a Chinese world order rather than occupying or controlling territory.[3]

[3] The standard account of Zheng He's voyages in English is Louise Levathes, *When China Ruled the Seas: The Treasure Fleet of the Dragon Throne, 1405–1433* (London: Oxford University Press, 1997). The views of Zheng He's voyages as expansionist and protoimperialist are expressed in Geoff Wade, "The Zheng He Voyages: A Reassessment," *Journal of the Malaysian Branch of the Royal Asiatic Society* 78, no. 1 (2005): 37–58; and Tansen Sen, "Maritime Interactions between China and India: Coastal India and the Ascendancy of Chinese Maritime Power in the Indian Ocean," *Journal of Central Eurasian Studies* 2 (May 2011): 41–82. Leading those supporting the view of Zheng He as a peaceful ambassador for trade is Tan Ta Sen, *Cheng Ho and Islam in Southeast Asia* (Singapore: Institute for Southeast Asian Studies, 2009), and Hum Sin Hoon, *Zheng He's Art of Collaboration: Understanding the Legendary Chinese Admiral from a Management Perspective* (Singapore: Institute for Southeast Asian Studies, 2012).

No primary source we have yet uncovered explains fully the decision to suspend the voyages in the 1420s and stop them for good in 1433 after one final voyage. No natural disaster destroyed the fleet or the resources that supported it. In the absence of direct evidence from primary sources, historians turn to context to find plausible explanations. Some scholars focus on the fact that the Ming's official ideology of Confucianism—named for the Chinese political philosopher Confucius (479–551 BCE)—mistrusted commercial motives. Confucian texts, knowledge of which was essential for serving in the imperial bureaucracy, declared that "the Great Man understands what is right; the Small Man understands what is profitable." These Confucian officials may also have been suspicious of Zheng He himself who, as a Muslim and eunuch, challenged Confucian expectations. Others, taking the opposite approach, see Zheng He's personal charisma as an important factor, so that when he died at sea returning from Africa in 1433, it was easier for opponents to scuttle the program. Other explanations focus on structural changes not related to the voyages themselves: the reconstruction of the Grand Canal, an interior waterway linking the Yangzi delta with North China, meant that costly seaborne excursions were no longer as important. As the fifteenth century went on, defensive priorities against the Mongols and other inner Asian groups took precedence over sea power. The practical challenges to maintaining a Chinese imperial presence in the Indian Ocean were exacerbated when the Ming dynasty relocated its capital from Nanjing to Beijing, further north and without direct access to the sea.

The end of the treasure fleet just decades before the arrival of Portuguese ships in the Indian Ocean leads to this question: What might have happened had the Chinese not retreated from their naval adventures? In her work on Zheng He's voyages, Louise Levathes writes, "Half the world was in China's grasp, and with such a formidable navy the other half was easily within reach, had China wanted it. China could have become the great colonial power, a hundred years before the great age of European exploration and expansion." If Zheng He had encountered Vasco da Gama, Levathes asks rhetorically, "seeing the battered Portuguese boats, would the Chinese admiral have been tempted to crush these snails in his path, preventing the Europeans from opening an east–west trade route?"[4] This question is a great parlor game, and we encourage you to imagine an answer if you are so inclined, but history is a web of contingent and interrelated events so that one cannot really ever know what would have happened had the treasure fleet voyages continued. Such speculation can draw one into the fallacy of predetermined outcomes, sometimes known as the historian's fallacy. In any historical event, there are too many variables at play to allow us to predict accurately what

[4] Levathes, *When China Ruled the Seas*, 20–21.

would have happened if we were to change only one of them. Using hindsight, it is tempting to make these predictions, but we have to remember that people at the time did not have the benefit of knowing what would happen next. (As one example, consider that people living in what we call the "interwar period" between World Wars I and II thought of themselves as living in the "postwar period," and they didn't think of World War I as "I" because there had been no World War II.) We can never really know what *would* have happened but only do our best to understand what *did* happen and why.

Although the Chinese state withdrew from its ambitious maritime program, Chinese merchants remained active in overseas trade and established communities in today's Vietnam, Indonesia, Thailand, Malaysia, and the Philippines. Although the end of the Ming dynasty's Indian Ocean fleet after Zheng He died changed the political and military profile of the region, robust overseas trade continued.

The Struggle over Central and South Asia

To the west and south of China during the fifteenth century, several key factors influenced political and economic events: the continued role of the Mongol rulers' descendants; the potential of Islam to build bridges across the region; the robust economic output of South and Southeast Asia; and the ability of Hindu and Buddhist institutions to underpin numerous states across South and Southeast Asia. Many of these factors shaped the history of the Timurid dynasty in southwest Asia, founded by Timur, also known as Tamerlane (1336–1405). A Muslim descendant of Mongol rulers, Timur built a vast empire populated by Mongols, Persians, Kazakhs, Turks, and others. Functionally, the empire was trilingual. Persian was the language of state and among urban dwellers, while many rural dwellers spoke Chagatai, a now-extinct Turkic language. Arabic, the language of the Qur`an, the holy book of Islam, was the language of literature and intellectual life.

Timur's ambitions led him into wars from China to eastern Europe and into South Asia, including conflicts with other Muslim rulers. The Indian subcontinent had been spared many of the effects of the Black Death; its dynamic economy, producing valuable textiles and spices, was an attractive target. The Muslim leaders of the Delhi sultanate had repulsed earlier Mongol raiders, but Timur's persistence, and the expense of fighting him off, proved too much. In 1398, Timur sacked the city of Delhi and temporarily annexed the entire region. The brutal summer heat dissuaded Timur from establishing a capital there, but incursions from the north became regular features of the South Asian political landscape during the next century. Timur's descendants could not hold the empire together; but in the sixteenth century, one of them (Babur) did succeed in creating a new South Asian Muslim empire, the Mughal, which would endure into the nineteenth century. Frequent disputes were common between and within the region's Islamic states.

From the fourteenth century through the seventeenth century, much of South Asia was ruled by a Hindu dynasty, the Vijayanagara, determined to keep the power of Muslim rulers from spreading south and to keep other Hindu kingdoms in check. In this multifaceted struggle, the Vijayanagara rulers were aided by Muslim mercenaries who trained Hindu warriors in new military strategies and tactics. This training would then be used against the (Christian) Portuguese incursions of the sixteenth century. These complex interactions illustrate the limitations of understanding conflict and expansion as primarily religious in nature.

The Ottoman Empire as a Key Afro-Eurasia Link

While one end of the Indian Ocean trade network was anchored in China, the other was on the eastern edge of the Mediterranean Sea, where land and sea routes linking this trade to the far reaches of western Eurasia and Africa came together. Beginning in the late thirteenth century, under the leadership of a sultan who claimed both secular and religious legitimacy, the Ottoman Turks began to expand and consolidate military and administrative control across Anatolia and the Balkans. Straddling the often-arbitrary dividing line between Asia and Europe, the Ottoman Empire is a good example of a new level of Afro-Eurasian statecraft, which we can see illustrated in the career of one of the Ottomans' most important sultans, Mehmed II, known as the Conqueror.

Mehmed II (1432–1481) was born a year before Zheng He's death. Like Zheng He, he was Muslim, but neither was Arab (neither was from the Arabian Peninsula or its surrounding territories, and neither spoke Arabic as his native language). The ethnic diversity within Islam reminds us that Islam, like Christianity, had evolved into a religion open to all rather than limited to a specific ethnic or linguistic group. As in Christianity at this time, followers of Islam were taught to spread and defend their faith, using force if necessary. Islam was essential to Mehmed's education as a ruler, and Mehmed embraced these roles of expanding and defending the faith. Indeed, his first challenge on ascending the Ottoman throne at age twelve was to defend his empire from invading Hungarian Christians. As sultan, Mehmed orchestrated the conquest of Constantinople, one of the world's largest cities and a center of Christian authority since the fourth century. Using superior weapons and naval technology, Mehmed's army and navy besieged the city, capturing it on May 29, 1453.

This is a good moment to remember that neither Islam nor Christianity was unified. The "Christian authority" in Constantinople did not recognize the pope in Rome—the Orthodox Church split from "Roman" Catholicism in 1054—and lacked a centrally organized hierarchy. On the Muslim side, the Ottomans laid claim to the traditions of Sunni Islam, which was the largest division within that faith, but by no means universal. Underscoring this point, Mehmed and his successors engaged in war against other Muslim kingdoms, emerging by the early sixteenth century as rulers of one of the largest and most powerful empires in the world and gaining control of the holiest sites of Islam, the cities of Mecca and Medina on the Arabian Peninsula. These military victories in the Muslim holy land also made the Ottoman sultan, beginning with Selim I (ca. 1465–1520), the caliph. According to Sunni tradition, the caliph is the successor to the Prophet Muhammad and the main interpreter and enforcer of Islamic law and practice for the entire community of believers. (Although their histories and traditions diverge considerably, a key difference between Sunni Islam and Shi`a Islam is that Shi`a Muslims believe that the Prophet Muhammad appointed his son-in-law and cousin, Ali, to be his successor and the first caliph. Shi`a Muslims would thus not recognize Sunni claims about a caliphate.)

Portrait of Sultan Mehmed II (1432–1481). Mehmed II became sultan of the Ottoman Empire in 1444. During his reign, the Ottomans conquered Constantinople (now Istanbul), which had once been the eastern capital of the Roman Empire. From this new imperial capital Mehmed continued the empire's expansion, earning renown among both admirers and detractors as Mehmed the Conqueror. This portrait of the sultan as *Victor Orbis* (Latin for "Conqueror of the World") is attributed to Venetian painter Gentile Bellini, who was sent to Istanbul on a diplomatic mission as part of a 1479 peace settlement between the Ottomans and the Venetian government.

As the Ottoman Empire expanded, its rulers considered the potential costs of enforcing religious authority across such a diverse landscape, even within the Islamic community, with its multiple traditions of belief and practice. Mehmed II established separate communities, called *millets*, organized by religious tradition, whether it be Muslim, Christian, or Jewish. For each community, a religious leader appointed by, and therefore most likely loyal to, the Ottoman government made most legal and political decisions, including those related to education and local administration. Mehmed's successors maintained this tradition.

As it grew in this strategic location linking South Asia, the eastern Mediterranean, and Europe, the Ottoman Empire could be either a bridge or a barrier for stitching together the northern regions of the supercontinent. The Ottomans participated actively in diplomatic and trade relations, as well as periodic wars, with Poland, Sweden, Finland, and others. Russia and the Ottoman Empire had a particularly contentious relationship because both were expanding, building up resources to defend new territories under imperial control, and focusing on their interests in the Black Sea. Between the sixteenth and nineteenth centuries, Russia was at war with the Ottoman Empire more than any other state.

The Hansa

The supercontinent's north introduces us to another type of economic and political organization. Starting in the mid-thirteenth century, much of the trade across the north—rich in timber, preserved fish, salt, grains, and other valuable commodities—was dominated by the members of the Hanseatic League, or Hansa, a commercial and defense arrangement among merchant guilds concentrated in central European cities, but with members as far away as modern-day England and Russia. In some ways, the Hansa acted like a state. For example, the league went to war with the kingdom of Denmark in the fourteenth century and England in the fifteenth century. Actions like these led to tensions between the Hansa and rulers (including England's Queen Elizabeth I [1533–1603] and Russia's Grand Prince Ivan III [1440–1505]) who claimed sovereignty over cities where these merchants operated. Over time, the merchants of the Hansa ceded their claims of sovereignty and focused on commerce or had their resources confiscated and destroyed. However, in central Europe especially, sovereignty contested among many groups, rather than concentrated under a single central authority, continued well beyond the sixteenth century.

Placing Africa within Afro-Eurasia

Peoples and resources of many African regions were essential components of the political and economic networks that spanned the supercontinent. North African cities like Tangier, Fez, Tunis, and Cairo connected the Mediterranean world and central Asia to an extensive commercial network in central and West Africa, and all were part of *dar al-Islam* (the "Abode of Islam"), territories in which Muslims resided and practiced their faith and where Arabic was understood by those with some education, including as a language of trade. The rulers of Mali, a large fourteenth-century empire in West Africa, claimed a lineage back to one of the Prophet Muhammad's early companions in the faith.

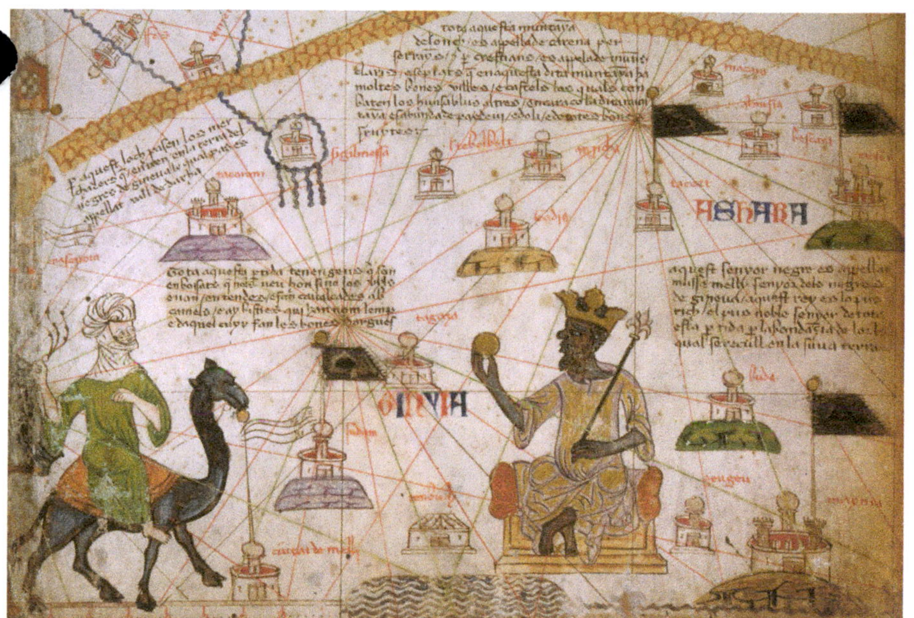

The Emperor of Mali. This image is found in the Catalan Atlas of 1375, created by Abraham Cresques, a Jew from the region of Catalonia. The text, in the Catalan language, identifies the image as that of the sovereign "Musse Melly" (perhaps Musa of Mali), "the richest and noblest of all these lands due to the abundance of gold" he controlled.

Like other Muslim rulers, Mali's Mansa Musa I (ca. 1280–ca. 1337) completed the *hajj*—the pilgrimage to Mecca that was a central feature of Islamic practice. Perhaps the wealthiest man in the world at the time due to Mali's extensive gold and salt reserves, some scholars believe that he spent so much during his 1325 hajj to Mecca that he single-handedly affected the price of goods across the super-continent during his travels. Because this pilgrimage was a pillar of Islamic faith, Mecca during the season of the hajj brought together people from across the Islamic world, from Spain to the South China Sea. Mansa Musa's wealth and the possibility of patronage helped invigorate the links of trade and scholarship between the Mediterranean and the states of the Sahara and West Africa. The open expanses of the Sahara, sometimes portrayed as a vast barrier separating peoples, can better be understood during this time as a highway linking different parts of Africa. The gold of Mali lured merchants and explorers much like the wealth of the Americas would two centuries later. New maps, produced in the 1300s, depicted the roads linking Mali and the Mediterranean coast, often with a gold nugget to represent Mali. Mansa Musa brought an Arabic library and religious scholars to the city of Timbuktu, as well as an architect to design mosques and a royal palace. Timbuktu became one of the world's most important commercial, religious, and political centers, linked by roads across the Sahara to the sea.

Although the neighboring Songhai Kingdom eclipsed Mali's power (and took control of Timbuktu) by 1400, the region remained a vital center of Islamic learning and scholarship. Sonni Ali (r. 1464–1492) expanded the Songhai Empire by conquering neighboring states, making it perhaps the largest West African empire to have ever existed, covering almost nine hundred thousand square miles (larger in land mass than all but about ten countries in the world today). The Songhai state revitalized Timbuktu, encouraging education, contemplation, and the production and collection of texts. Scholars from other Islamic kingdoms consulted with Timbuktu experts on key questions of Muslim belief and practice. The deep historical connections and dynamic relationship between Islam and Africa led some scholars to write of an Africanization of Islam as much as an Islamicization of Africa over the centuries.

As with many of the other empires we have seen, Songhai at its height (in the late fifteenth and early sixteenth centuries) exercised occasional bursts of power from the armies of the ruler, but local regions usually went about their business with little interference from the center. As long as tax revenue flowed to the central government and Songhai sovereignty was acknowledged (for example, when decisions about war and peace were to be made), the provinces of the empire were mostly self-governing. The empire thrived on the wealth of the goldfields and the trans-Saharan caravan trade until internal divisions and an invading military force from North Africa split the empire apart at the end of the sixteenth century.

No state as large as Mali or Songhai developed in East Africa. In these regions, multiple states actively participated in diverse trade networks across the Indian Ocean to South and East Asia. These were the regions visited first by Zheng He's fleets and then by the Portuguese in the 1400s. Trade in ivory, copper, and salt supported states like the Kingdom of Mutapa, but their ruling elites maintained religious traditions other than Islam. In the Horn of Africa, Christian dynasties continued to claim sovereignty over Ethiopia. From the late thirteenth century until the early sixteenth century, under the authority of a ruling dynasty that claimed a lineage back to King Solomon, Ethiopia enjoyed prosperous commercial relations with European merchants seeking alternatives to Islamic trading networks. In the rest of Africa, in the fifteenth century, most rulers made and enforced sovereignty claims over relatively small territories where production of surplus to be taxed or traded was much less than it was in these larger states.

The Changing Iberian Peninsula

Tangier, Ibn Battuta's birthplace, is a short boat ride across the narrowest point of the Mediterranean Sea to the westernmost territories of the European mainland on the Iberian Peninsula. Today divided between Spain and Portugal, fifteenth-century Iberia comprised five large states (and several smaller ones). Four of these states were ruled by Christian dynasties, but Muslims ruled the fifth. Many Muslims and Jews lived in the other four territories as well. A closer look at the history of this region can help us understand how a new political order emerged in Europe after the Black Death, with larger, more powerful and effective central states under the authority of hereditary monarchs.

King John I (1357–1433) and his successors are good examples of the monarchs who worked to change the relationships between territory, sovereignty, and material resources in the western regions of the supercontinent from the fourteenth into the sixteenth century. The Portuguese sovereigns used warfare, strategic marriages, increased revenue, and religious zeal to consolidate their power. They expanded long-distance commerce and oceangoing exploration in the fifteenth century. Establishing a presence in the North African city of Ceuta, seized from its Muslim ruler in 1415, the Portuguese then claimed several islands in the Atlantic Ocean in the 1430s and soon thereafter began to establish *feitorias*, fortified trading posts, on the west coast of Africa: first on an island off the coast of present-day Mauritania (1445) and then on the coast in present-day Ghana (1482), both close to the Songhai Empire. Over the course of the fifteenth and sixteenth centuries, the Portuguese established approximately fifty *feitorias* across Afro-Eurasia, from Ghana to Goa to Macau, just off the Chinese mainland.

The conquest of Constantinople by Ottoman sultan Mehmed II catalyzed the Christian rulers of Iberia to action. Over the second half of the fifteenth century, the rulers of the Christian kingdoms—Portugal, Castile, Aragon, and Navarre—declared a new round of warfare on Islam and each other. In 1469, Isabella I of Castile (1451–1504) and Ferdinand II of Aragon (1452–1516) married, beginning a long process of creating a new kingdom (Spain). Along with their well-known contributions to Christopher Columbus's sea voyages, they also declared a reconquest of the peninsula from Islamic rulers and demanded that all Muslims and Jews in their kingdoms convert to Christianity or leave. So it was with both religious fervor and commercial goals that Christopher Columbus and his crews set off into the Atlantic Ocean. What these men found in the last decade of the fifteenth century on the other side of the ocean was something no one on the supercontinent was prepared for.

American Empires of the Fifteenth Century

All the landmasses of the earth were at one time connected to each other, drifting apart about two hundred million years ago. Humans migrated to the landmass of North and South America relatively recently and the human, animal, and microbial populations there evolved in relative isolation from Afro-Eurasia for thousands of years. When the Americas rejoined Afro-Eurasia—metaphorically speaking—at the end of the fifteenth century, a remarkable new chapter in human history began.

Research Challenges

Although history did not begin for the Americas in 1492, several factors make it hard to study the hemisphere's past prior to that year using traditional historical research methods. First, the indigenous peoples of the Americas kept records in ways that were very different from the Afro-Eurasian empires. Only in the past few decades have scholars had any success in interpreting the evidence woven into the cloth memory devices of the Andes called *khipus* or the region's highly decorated drinking vessels called *keros*.

In addition, much of the material record of the indigenous past has been reclaimed by nature. New techniques, such as infrared aerial photography, have yielded many surprises about the dimensions and infrastructure of societies from Central America to the Amazon but scholars are still in the early stages of linking these to evidence gathered from oral histories, ethnographies, and archival work. Another factor is that the first Europeans who came to the Americas often destroyed the records and other artifacts that did exist. For example, in 1562, a Catholic priest named Diego de Landa (1524–1579) burned twenty handwritten books and thousands of artifacts of the Maya people of the Yucatán Peninsula, which he deemed to be the work of the devil. Despite these obstacles (which hold true for other parts of the earth as well), researchers have been able to piece together many aspects of life in the Americas prior to the arrival of Europeans, with significant growth over the past four decades in our understanding of these societies. Two important changes in the political organization of the Americas in the fifteenth century need attention in this chapter about empires, power, and trade in a polycentric world.

The Aztecs

Beginning in the early fourteenth century, a migrant group moving into the Valley of Mexico from the north transformed itself rapidly from mercenaries at the service of other city states to rulers of the most powerful empire in one of the most densely populated, culturally diverse, and economically productive regions in the hemisphere. In the first decades of the fourteenth century, the Mexica (often called Aztecs) founded a city called Tenochtitlan (today's Mexico City). By the 1370s, they were claiming their ruler was a descendant of a legendary leader from another central Mexican state of an earlier era. By the 1420s, Tenochtitlan was the dominant state in a powerful alliance of tribute collectors that spread its claims ever further across Mesoamerica.

Tenochtitlan grew into one of the world's largest cities with one of its greatest and most diverse markets for goods. The wide variety of products and significant supply were available to tributary states as well, but at a cost. As the Mexica increasingly relied on their war machine to generate wealth through tribute, internal hierarchies within Mexica society solidified. The ruler, known as the *tlatoani* or chief speaker, began to take on godlike aspects: he could not be touched or looked at directly. War became glorified and captured prisoners were sacrificed to the gods. Religious specialists rewrote Mexica history, burning records that contradicted the story they now wanted to tell about their society.

Over the course of the fifteenth century, the Mexica built a system of tributary states that supplied human and material resources, which in turn fed further expansion. Between 1440 and 1469, the *tlatoani* Moctezuma Ilhuicamina (Moctezuma I, 1398–1469) subjugated new tributary states while simultaneously consolidating the ruler's authority. Moctezuma's brother, Tlacaelel I (1398–1487), designed and enforced much of the new, more centralized, political system and would continue to serve as a trusted guide to Mexica rulers until his death in 1487.

The Mexica performed impressive feats of civil engineering, such as aqueducts to bring fresh water into their city and floating gardens to feed the population, but they did not invest significantly in infrastructure for the region as a whole. They did not offer to bring peace either. Instead, the Mexica offered something like endless conquest to other states and peoples in central Mexico, from the Gulf of Mexico to the Pacific Ocean, because the Mexica demanded that tributary states go regularly to war with them to ensure a steady supply of sacrificial victims, a key component of their ritual practices.

The Inca

Coincidentally, another new empire was emerging in the Andes Mountains of South America, eventually stretching over three thousand miles through a dramatic variety of ecosystems. Commonly known in English as the Inca (or Inka) Empire, these Quechua speakers, building from their power base in Cusco, called their realm Tahuantinsuyu ("land of the four parts"). The Inca date their arrival in Cusco to around 1200, gaining regional power in 1438 when the leader Pachacuti Inca Yupanqui (ruled 1438–1471) rallied troops in Cusco to defeat a powerful rival confederation. The Inca then invested in running an

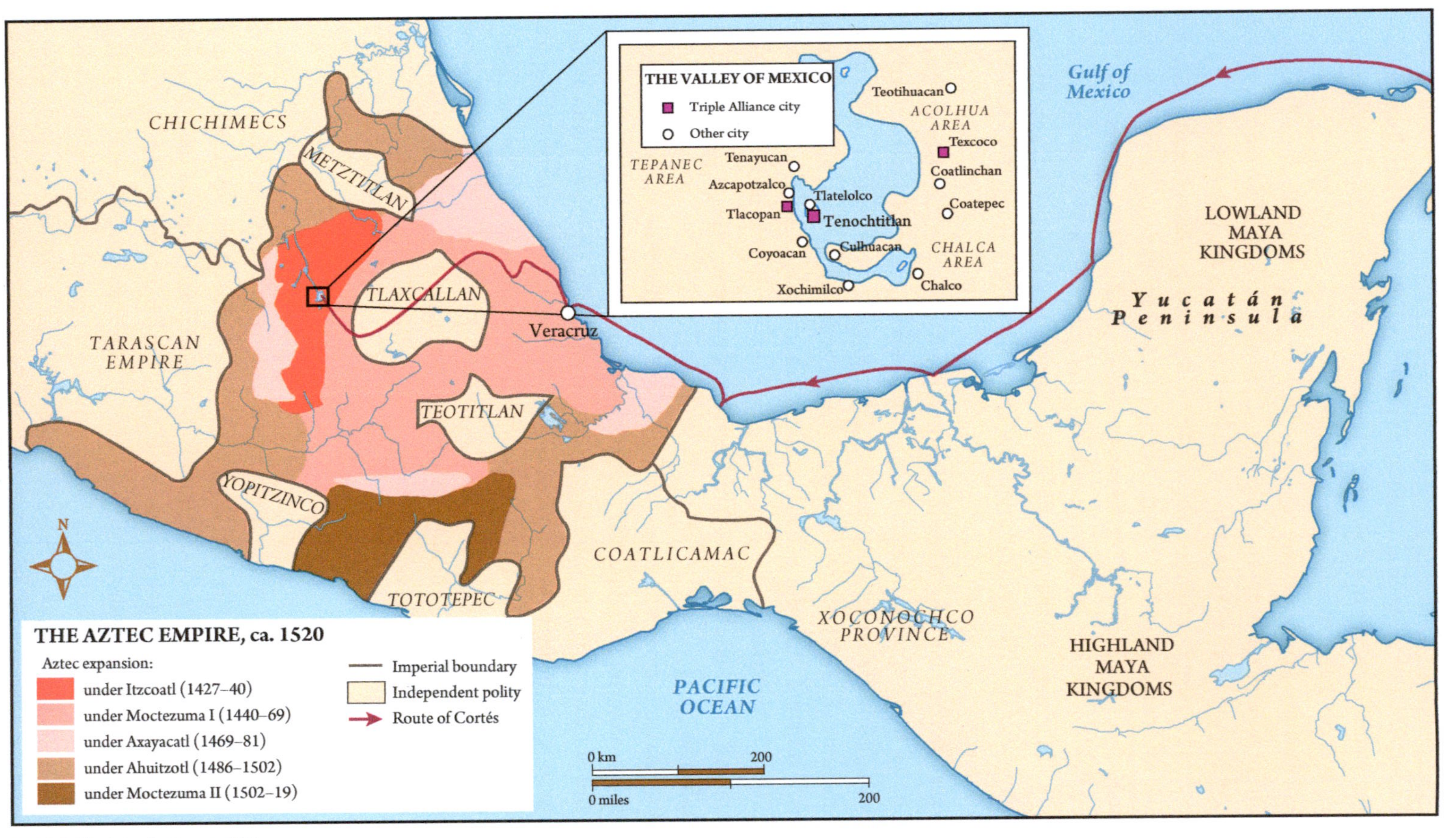
THE AZTEC EMPIRE, ca. 1520
Aztec expansion:
under Itzcoatl (1427–40)
under Moctezuma I (1440–69)
under Axayacatl (1469–81)
under Ahuitzotl (1486–1502)
under Moctezuma II (1502–19)
Imperial boundary
Independent polity
Route of Cortés
THE VALLEY OF MEXICO
Triple Alliance city
Other city
TEPANEC AREA
ACOLHUA AREA
CHALCA AREA
Teotihuacan
Texcoco
Coatlinchan
Coatepec
Tenayucan
Azcapotzalco
Tlatelolco
Tlacopan
Tenochtitlan
Coyoacan
Culhuacan
Xochimilco
Chalco
CHICHIMECS
METZTITLAN
TLAXCALLAN
TARASCAN EMPIRE
TEOTITLAN
YOPITZINCO
TOTOTEPEC
COATLICAMAC
Veracruz
XOCONOCHCO PROVINCE
Gulf of Mexico
PACIFIC OCEAN
LOWLAND MAYA KINGDOMS
Yucatán Peninsula
HIGHLAND MAYA KINGDOMS
N
0 km
200
0 miles
200

Map 1.3 The Aztec Empire, ca. 1520

Quito
Putumayo
Marañon
Juruá
Ucayali
Cajamarca
Huanuco Pampa
CHINCHAYSUYU
ANTISUYU
Cusco
Vilcas Huaman
Lake Titicaca
CUNTISUYU
COLLASUYU
PACIFIC OCEAN
Andes
Salado
NORTH AMERICA
ATLANTIC OCEAN
AZTEC EMPIRE
PACIFIC OCEAN
SOUTH AMERICA
INCA EMPIRE
0 km 2400
0 miles 2400
N
0 km 500
0 miles 500
THE INCA EMPIRE, ca. 1525
Imperial boundary
Boundary between the four quarters of the empire
Inca expansion:
to 1438
under Pachacuti 1438–63
under Pachacuti and Tupac Yupanqui 1463–71
under Tupac Yupanqui 1471–93
under Huayna Capac 1493–1525
Inca road
Imperial capital
Major Inca administrative center

Map 1.4 The Inca Empire, ca. 1525

empire, building roads and other infrastructure, and redistributing resources, including labor. Although some modern authors and audiences have romanticized the Inca state as a utopia, which it most certainly was not, records suggest that the state was able to do things like provide relief to the empire's population in times of food shortages. One very important thing that it did not achieve was a clear means of succession, which at times led to disputes, including warfare, over rulership.

Conclusion

As we noted in the introduction, this book does not catalog all—or even most—of the events of world history from 1400 to the present. Estimates of the global population at the end of the fifteenth century range from about four hundred million to five hundred million people. Missing from this chapter is an analysis of the political, social, and economic lives of most of them, with their own histories: village-dwelling agriculturalists of North America, pastoralists of the Eurasian steppes, hunter-gatherers of Africa and Australia. At times, further on in the book, we will include additional information about other peoples and places as they contribute to our analysis of how the structures that define the world we live in emerged. For now, we thought it most important to identify

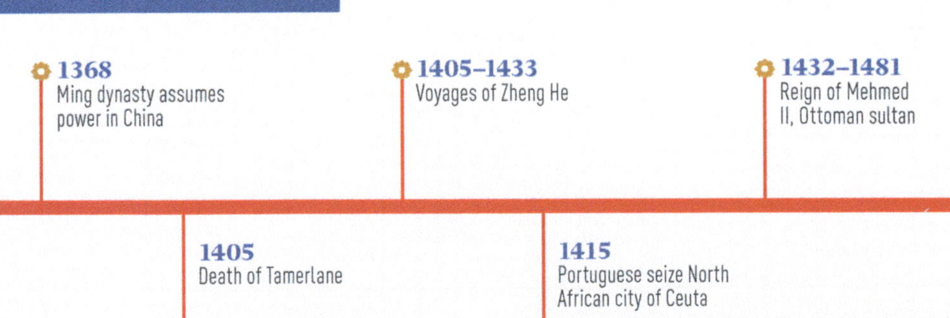
TIMELINE
1368
Ming dynasty assumes power in China
1405
Death of Tamerlane
1405–1433
Voyages of Zheng He
1415
Portuguese seize North African city of Ceuta
1432–1481
Reign of Mehmed II, Ottoman sultan

major circuits for the generation of surplus and long-distance exchange; explain the motivations and actions that brought the world's peoples to the edge of a new global interface in the late fifteenth century; and provide a context for understanding how that next chapter in world history would play out, to which we turn now.

A Few Good Books

Janet L. Abu-Lughod. *Before European Hegemony: The World System A.D. 1250–1350.* New York: Oxford University Press, 1989.

Ross Dunn. *The Adventures of Ibn Battuta: A Muslim Traveler of the Fourteenth Century.* Berkeley: University of California Press, 2012.

Halil Inalcik. *The Ottoman Empire: The Classical Age, 1300–1600.* New York: Phoenix Press, 1993.

Louise Levathes. *When China Ruled the Seas: The Treasure Fleet of the Dragon Throne, 1405–1433.* New York: Oxford University Press, 1997.

Charles Mann. *1491: New Revelations of the Americas before Columbus.* New York: Vintage, 2006.

Jack Weatherford. *Genghis Khan and the Making of the Modern World.* New York: Random House, 2004.

For instructional resources and study aids, please go to ***www.oup.com/us/carter****. For primary sources connected to this chapter, please see the table of contents for* Sources for Forging the Modern World *included at the back of the book.*

1438
Inca assume regional power in Andes

1453
Constantinople falls to the Ottomans; end of Hundred Years' War

1497
Vasco da Gama rounds Cape of Good Hope and reaches India

ca. 1500
Height of Songhai Empire, West Africa

1510
Portuguese seize South Asian trading center of Goa

(RIGHT) A Roster of City States Subjected by the Aztecs Under the Rule of Ahuitzotl. This is a page from the Codex Mendoza, which contains both pictograms and Spanish-language commentary. Produced in the 1540s, two decades after the Aztec Empire fell, this book, painted on indigenous paper, contains over seventy pages of text and images depicting the history and daily life of the Aztecs and their relationship to other peoples in central Mexico from the fourteenth to the sixteenth century.

(BOTTOM) A Japanese Perspective of Dejima, the Dutch Trading Post at Nagasaki. Japanese leaders restricted most overseas trade to a single port, at Nagasaki, from the seventeenth century to the nineteenth century. Dejima, an artificial island in Nagasaki harbor, served as the most important link between Japan and Europe for more than two hundred years. This painting, ca. 1800, is an example of *megane-e*, produced to be used in an optical device that would give viewers the illusion of depth in the picture. Originally made in Holland, these devices were most likely first imported through Nagasaki in the early eighteenth century.

CHAPTER 2

The New Global Interface

1486–1639

In 1486, a man named Ahuitzotl (r. 1486–1502) assumed power in the Mexica capital of Tenochtitlan. The following year, he presided over a rededication of the city's main temple, constructed to honor the gods of war and rain. Amid thousands of human sacrifices, Ahuitzotl—military, political, and religious leader—spilled some of his own blood as part of the rituals. Over the preceding half century, the Mexica had grown from their power base in the Valley of Mexico to gain supremacy in a triple alliance of city states that dominated one of the most densely populated and wealthiest regions in the Western Hemisphere. Driven by the same worldview that motivated his predecessors to military action, Ahuitzotl was determined to reignite Mexica expansion, which had stagnated in recent decades. He launched more than forty campaigns, subjugating new tributary states from the Gulf coast to the Pacific Ocean and south to the present-day border between Mexico and Guatemala.

Ahuitzotl was unaware that a Genoese navigator, looking for a sea passage to Asia, had landed on an island in the Caribbean Sea during his reign. No one could have predicted what would happen in the decades after this small group of Europeans made landfall in 1492. After Ahuitzotl's death in 1502, his successor, Moctezuma II (r. 1502–1520), came into contact for the first time with Europeans in 1519. Within two years, the mighty Aztec Empire had collapsed, as a new and cataclysmic era in world history unfolded.

Ahuitzotl was the last Aztec leader to rule in isolation from a rapidly accelerating, and profoundly disrupting, flow of goods and people. Over the subsequent century and a half, rulers around the world struggled with the mounting consequences of this wave of globalization. Continuing the search for greater access to Asia, European merchants and firearms first arrived in Japan in the early 1540s, followed soon after by Catholic missionaries. Over the following century, as complex alliances grew and fractured, Japanese leaders determined that contact with Europeans had to be severely limited. In 1639, the hereditary Tokugawa leader Iemitsu (1604–1651) banned Portuguese trade with Japan and expelled foreigners. A series

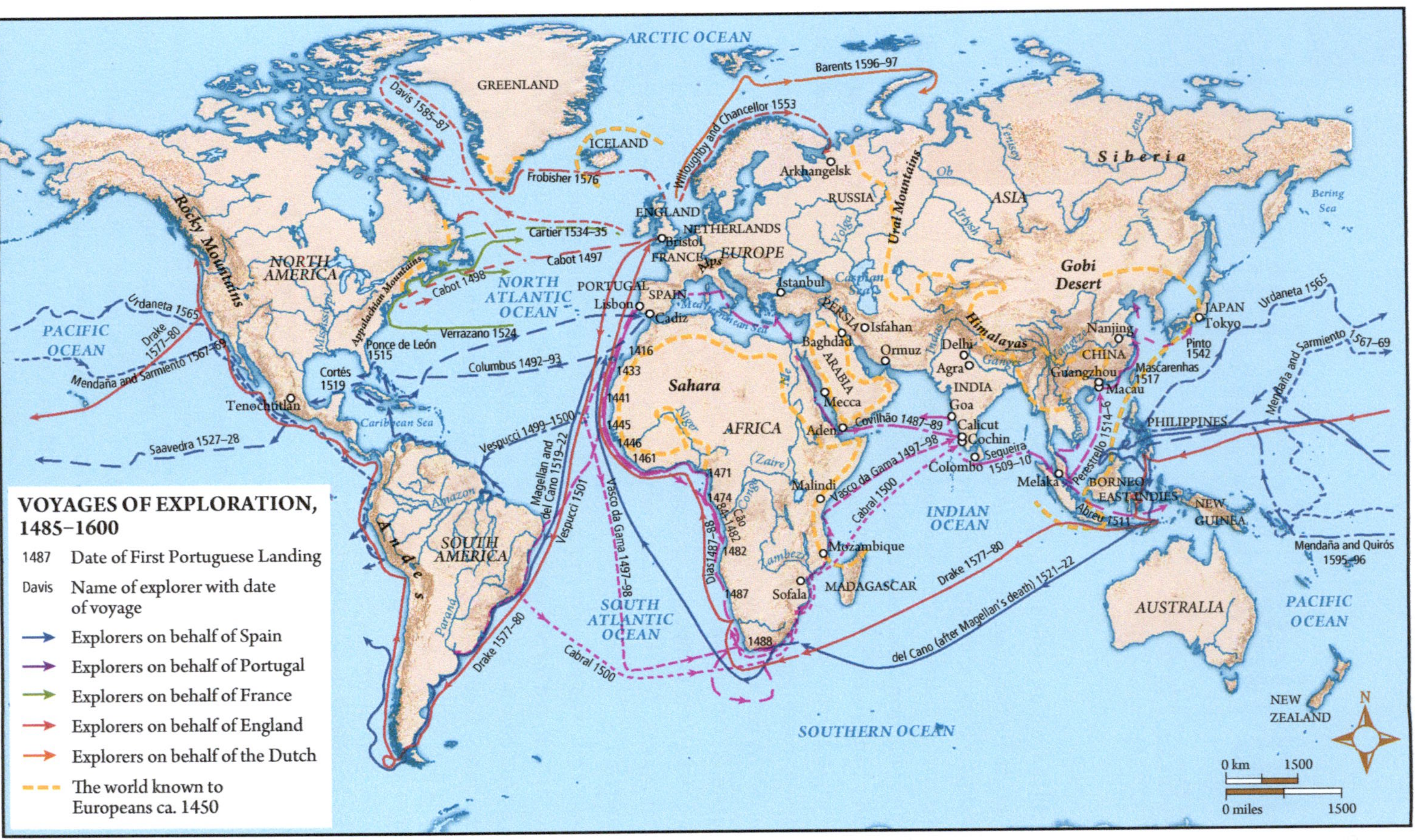

Map 2.1 Voyages of Exploration, 1485–1600

of other rulings around this time further tightened control over all contact between foreigners and Japanese. Japanese rulers continued to enforce strict limits on foreign interactions—commercial, religious, or otherwise—into the middle of the nineteenth century.

This chapter explains the emergence of, and responses to, the increasing flow of commodities, peoples, and ideas in all directions among the Americas, Europe, Africa, and Asia from the late fifteenth century to the middle of the seventeenth century. Although interactions among different parts of the world had long been a consistent feature of human societies, in the decades after Christopher Columbus (1451–1506) made landfall in the Caribbean in 1492, ideas, animals, germs, and commodities began to move around the world in unprecedented ways.

In the first section of the chapter, we present the interactions between indigenous peoples and invaders in the first decades after Europeans arrived in the Western Hemisphere. In the chapter's second part, we explain how different individuals and groups (beginning with the Spanish and Portuguese, followed by other Europeans) attempted to make sense of and use the resources of the Americas to their own advantage. In the last part of the chapter, we integrate events in other parts of the world to attain a broader perspective on the new global interface.

Questions to Consider as You Read Chapter Two:

1. In the early sixteenth century, Moctezuma II could not prevent Europeans from toppling the Aztec Empire. Almost 150 years later, the Tokugawa shoguns in Japan successfully limited European access to their land. What factors can help to account for these divergent outcomes?
2. Most historians emphasize that specific historical outcomes are often dependent on contingent events—the unexpected or unpredictable things that turn out to be truly important. What contingent events are most important in shaping the *new global interface* between 1492 and 1639?

The Conquest Era

In 1492, the expanding Mexica and Inca Empires had no contact with each other, nor did either have any contact with or understanding of myriad other societies of the Western Hemisphere, from the whale hunters of the Arctic Circle, to the people of the longhouse who live in today's New York State, to hunter-gatherers in the eastern Amazon basin. Europeans certainly had no detailed knowledge of the Western Hemisphere, its peoples, their economic and political structures, and their ideologies and religions. No one anywhere on the planet had a clue about the transformation that bringing these worlds together was about to set off.

First Encounters

The first contact with village-dwelling indigenous peoples living on islands off the coast of North America confused Christopher Columbus and his crew. Numerous sponsors, including merchants from his native Genoa and the Iberian monarchs Ferdinand and Isabella, thought they had financed a voyage to Asia to expand possibilities for trade and Christian evangelization there. It soon became apparent that what Columbus stumbled on challenged European conceptions of how the world fit together. Most Europeans who were interested in such things at the time believed that there was one great sea on the earth, with Europe on its eastern shore and Asia—China, Japan, and India—on its west. Columbus went to his grave believing that the Asian mainland was much closer to where he had landed than it actually was. Subsequent generations of seafarers continued to search for a western sea route to Asia.

When he returned to Spain, Columbus convinced Queen Isabella to sponsor additional voyages across the Atlantic. In 1493, he returned to the Caribbean to establish a fortified trading post with over one thousand sailors, artisans, and soldiers. This failed; the indigenous population had neither the interest nor the surplus to engage in commerce, and some Caribbean peoples resisted the strangers furiously. Those who arrived with Columbus grew impatient with promises of the future and began to look for ways to gain wealth more quickly. Borrowing from experiences, understandings, and self-serving interpretations of the Iberian and Christian traditions, they distributed among themselves mineral and land rights and implemented an *encomienda* system, similar in intent to European feudalism. Spanish *encomenderos* divided up the indigenous population and gave themselves the responsibility to Christianize and care for their charges in return for the right to exploit their labor. The potential profits to be gained from this access to indigenous labor power made the encomiendas immensely valuable. They became the primary reward sought by men expanding the Spanish presence in the Americas over the next half century.

Over time, Columbus lost favor with the Spanish monarchs. They appointed a new governor to oversee royal interests in the Americas, including the collection of tribute payments from indigenous taxpayers. Concern over the return on their investment, as well as the spiritual dimension of their claim to rule in the New World, led the Crown to instruct the governor to "ensure that the Indians are well treated" and to send more priests. As these decisions demonstrate, long before Europeans became aware that tens of millions of people lived on the American mainland, both Spaniards in the Americas and their rulers in Spain developed complex and competing goals for their relationships with the indigenous population. The indigenous peoples themselves had their own political, economic, and spiritual motivations, which impacted the nature of Spanish exploration and settlement.

The wealth of the Americas transformed European life, but the encounter between Old World and New devastated the people of North and South America. All manner of indigenous people, regardless of their rank or response to the Spaniards, began to die in numbers heartbreaking to contemplate. We know now that disease-causing microorganisms had been the conquerors' invisible cargo as they migrated to the Americas, but at the time no one was aware of the scientific explanation for the spread of the infectious diseases that decimated the indigenous population. The mounting death toll could not be ignored, however, and critics decried the terrible impact of the indigenous population's poor treatment. Early in the sixteenth century, priests like Antonio de Montesinos (ca. 1470–ca. 1545) and Bartolomé de las Casas (1474–1566) condemned the encomenderos' abuse of indigenous peoples.

In response, the Crown issued the Laws of Burgos (1512), which required those holding encomiendas to provide Catholic religious instruction, food, and clothing to their indigenous charges, and they banned certain types of corporal punishment. Around the same time, Spanish jurists also drew up a legal document known as the *Requerimiento* (Requirement). This text was to be read at the time of encounter with any new indigenous groups, offering the opportunity to accept Christianity and the authority of the Spanish Crown peacefully or refuse and jeopardize life, property, and freedom. Similar pronouncements were used during the long conflict between Christian and Muslim forces on the Iberian Peninsula.

Even at the time it was first issued, critics called the Requerimiento absurd because it presumed the indigenous people could understand the decree. It was supposed to be translated into the local language, but it was difficult, if not impossible, to translate the political and theological implications of the text adequately. Besides, it was often read in Latin or Spanish. In practice, even the barest threads of justice unraveled, as the Requerimiento was pronounced at times in the midst of empty villages, recited to trees, or accompanied by the burning of huts. The ritual may have assuaged the consciences of some Spaniards, but it did not offer the indigenous peoples genuine options.

Searching for additional resources and population centers, Spaniards established settlements across the Caribbean—Hispaniola, Jamaica, Puerto Rico, Cuba—and explored the coastline from present-day Venezuela to the Yucatán Peninsula to Florida. Encomiendas and land grants were distributed, while new arrivals and anxious veterans spurred further exploration and settlement. Disputes over chain of command were common, because the rights to move, explore, and conquer were in theory separate and controlled from above. Defiance was often the order of the day. In 1519, when the governor of Cuba decided that he did not want the encomendero Hernán Cortés (1485–1547) to lead an ambitious new expedition, Cortés simply left before the governor's agents could stop him. Cortés spent the rest of his life in disputes over the legitimacy of his subsequent actions in the Aztec Empire. When another group of adventurers subverted the Inca Empire over a decade later, they too argued with representatives of the Crown, leading to armed conflict and the assassination of royal officials by Spanish rebels.

The Fall of the Aztec and Inca Empires

Cortés, with about five hundred men, eleven ships, and thirteen horses, made landfall on the Yucatán coast of modern-day Mexico in February 1519. There, remarkably, he met a Spanish priest named Gerónimo de Aguilar, who had survived a shipwreck, washed ashore, and learned one of the Maya languages before escaping from an indigenous village. Soon thereafter, Cortés took several women from local villages after the Spaniards defeated an indigenous group in battle. One of these women, Malintzin, spoke Maya and Nahuatl, the language of the Mexica. Malintzin and Aguilar provided the links in a language chain that enabled Cortés to communicate with indigenous groups throughout the region. Working his way up the coast, Cortés founded the town of Veracruz in April 1519. From there, over the course of the coming months, he fought and negotiated his way into the center of the Aztec Empire. In November 1519, an uneasy encounter between Cortés and Moctezuma II, ruler of Tenochtitlan, soon broke down into open warfare that only ended two years later with Cortés in control of the city and its environs.

In the meantime, other Spanish expeditions were moving down the Pacific coast into South America. More than a decade after the fall of Tenochtitlan, the first Spaniards arrived at the heart of the Inca Empire high in the Andes on the Pacific coast of South America. With the indigenous population there in the midst of a civil war, the Spaniards kidnapped the Inca ruler Atahualpa (1497–1533) and later killed him. Like their counterparts in Mexico, this small group of Spaniards, led by the Pizarro brothers, swiftly undermined Inca authority in much of the Andes. From 1532 on, they began to reorganize the political, economic, and social structures of the region.

The falls of the Aztec and Inca Empires are most closely associated in our contemporary popular culture with the Spanish Conquest. They are also poorly understood and subject to great mythologizing, so we offer here several empirical observations about how and why things turned out as they did. By the time Cortés founded Veracruz in 1519, Spanish goals and motivations had shifted away from the trading-post model of the Portuguese *feitoria* to a more complete form of sovereignty that went well beyond the exchange of merchandise. In pursuing their goals, the Spanish had some advantages. Their guns were impressive noisemakers but they were inaccurate and slow to reload; the real battlefield advantages lay in steel swords and horses. Spanish motivations and limitations diverged from those

The Spaniards and Their Indigenous Allies Prepare to Take Tenochtitlan. This image is from a reproduction of the *Lienzo de Tlaxcala*, prepared by order of the indigenous city council of Tlaxcala in the 1550s. The council commissioned the work to demonstrate to Emperor Charles V the important role that the Spanish king's indigenous vassals played alongside Hernán Cortés in conquering the Aztecs.

of the indigenous populations. For indigenous leaders and warriors, concern for the survival of families and communities influenced their decisions; Spanish risk-takers did not include such factors in their calculations when preparing strategies and executing tactics. To remove the option of returning to their Caribbean home port, Cortés deliberately sank the ships that had transported his men to Mexico.

At least as important, this conflict was not simply one of Europeans on one side and indigenous Americans on the other. By the time the Spaniards made their final assaults on the power structures of the largest American empires, they had thousands of allies. Almost two years passed between Cortés's arrival at Tenochtitlan and the surrender of the city in August 1521. During the final siege of the city, which was nestled in the middle of a lake and crisscrossed by canals, the Spaniards had tens of thousands of laborers build more than a dozen ships, each over forty feet long. Squadrons of canoe-borne warriors enforced an embargo on food and other goods entering the capital city, and at least twenty-five thousand indigenous soldiers now thought of themselves as vassals of the Spanish Crown. In Peru, regional indigenous leaders, hostile to Inca expansion and sensitive to the shifting balance of military power in the Andes, made tense alliances with Spaniards, pursuing what they perceived to be their own best interests and those of their people by challenging Inca rule.

Smallpox and other diseases accompanied the arrival of Spaniards, devastating indigenous labor and military forces, undermining morale, and eliminating key leaders. Moctezuma's successor, Cuitlahuac (1476–1520), succumbed to one of these while the Spaniards were regrouping after a failed attack on Tenochtitlan. The succession crisis leading to civil war among the Inca that facilitated Spanish conquest of the Andes resulted when both the current ruler and his immediate heir died, leaving more distant claimants to power to fight for control of the empire. Spaniards were aware of their reliance on indigenous peoples, often for their very survival in unfamiliar environments. They neither planned nor pursued a strategy of genocide, but their war against Aztec and Inca authority exacerbated the conditions that spread disease and death, as depleted populations were congregated into new communities, encomiendas were allocated, and complex indigenous systems for the production and distribution of foodstuffs and other goods collapsed.

Historians Explore — Indigenous Population Decline

There is no question that the European conquest devastated the indigenous population of the Americas. Trying to understand the scope and scale of the cataclysmic changes in the population, scholars have focused on several connected issues: the size of the Western Hemisphere's population prior to the arrival of Europeans; the different causes of population decline; and how the causes and effects of population decline and recovery varied by region.

There is no direct evidence, even of questionable reliability, with which to start the task. Archives, one of the places historians usually look for primary sources about population, are of limited use. The comprehensive censuses and tax rolls that in modern states provide detailed records about population do not exist. The written record from the post-contact era, which includes the memoirs of conquistadors and priests, provides descriptions of indigenous populations from small villages to large cities in only vague and impressionistic ways. Indigenous documents, such as maps and tributary records, are fragmentary. Guessing and estimating from these traces, early twentieth-century scholars debated whether the total population of the Americas in 1492 reached even ten million. Subsequent researchers assailed these estimates as ridiculously low, but still varied widely in their methodologies and conclusions. To encourage additional scholarly inquiry into the matter, the journal

Current Anthropology published a special edition in 1966, "Estimating Aboriginal American Population," which featured more than two dozen contributions from scholars involved in the search for new ways to answer this vexing question.

Over the next decades, answers to the population question relied on growing confidence in interdisciplinary research methods that attempted to integrate things like estimates of the agricultural carrying capacity of land, anthropological interpretations of indigenous social organization and production techniques, statistical extrapolation, and the analysis of additional archival records, like those for births, baptisms, deaths, and burials in the early colonial period. Using these methods, some authors estimated a pre-contact population as high as one hundred million, although the most influential revisions were about half that number: forty to sixty million people. Scholarly critics of these new estimates suggested that the researchers who produced them were too optimistic in their assessments of things like the productive capacity of indigenous societies or too negative in their estimates of the spread and virulence of European diseases.

The debate continues. Why does this matter? One of the most important issues underlying this long debate over the size of the pre-contact population has been the effort to understand better the long-term impact of the arrival of Europeans. On this question, there will likely never be consensus on the exact scale of devastation, yet the overwhelming force of evidence subject to both qualitative and quantitative analysis leads to several conclusions. Almost the entire indigenous population of the Caribbean died within decades of the Europeans' arrival. On the mainland, the rates of population decline varied greatly from place to place. Most of the evidence points to disease and the disruption of indigenous political, economic, and social systems as the main causes of demographic decline. The overall indigenous population fell to perhaps four or five million during the first century after contact, a decline of some 90 percent from the most widely accepted estimates of the pre-contact population. Even if one were to accept the lowest pre-contact estimates (which we do not), the demographic decline of the indigenous population of the Americas after European contact remains one of the great catastrophes of human history.[1]

---

1 Henry F. Dobyns, "An Appraisal of Techniques with a New Hemispheric Estimate," *Current Anthropology* 7, no. 4 (1966): 395–416; H. Paul Thompson, "A Technique Using Anthropological and Biological Data," *Current Anthropology* 7, no. 4 (1966): 417–449; "Comments and Replies," *Current Anthropology* 7, no. 4 (1966): 425–499; Angel Rosenblat, *La población de América en 1492: Viejos y nuevos cálculos* (Mexico City: El Colegio de México, 1967); William M. Denevan, ed., *The Native Population of the Americas in 1492*, 2nd ed. (Madison: University of Wisconsin Press, 1992); Ann Ramenofsky, *Vectors of Death: The Archaeology of European Contact* (Albuquerque: University of New Mexico Press, 1988); David Henige, *Numbers from Nowhere: The American Indian Contact Population Debate* (Norman: University of Oklahoma Press, 1998); Massimo Livi Bacci. "The Depopulation of Hispanic America after the Conquest," *Population and Development Review* 32, no. 2 (June 2006): 199–232.

From Conquest to Colonialism

Focus on the actions of conquistadors like Cortés and Pizarro, dramatic as they were, suggests that Spanish control of the Western Hemisphere was completed with the fall of Cusco in the 1530s, but this is not the case. Vast expanses of the Americas and millions of people lay beyond central Mexico and the Andes. Much of North America remained outside the Spaniards' grasp, as did the interior regions of Central and South America. A remnant of the Inca Empire, based in the city of Vilcabamba, continued to fight the Spanish until 1572. Even places that Spaniards thought were under their control proved volatile: a 1541 revolt northwest of Mexico City (the Spanish capital, built on the ruins of Tenochtitlan) required the reconquest of the region, completed with indigenous forces loyal to the Spanish. In 1560, an Andean resistance movement (the *Taki Onqoy*) called for the complete elimination of Spaniards and their culture. Conflict and accommodation defined the next century and beyond, as the Spanish attempted to solidify their control over American resources, indigenous peoples devised strategies to survive, and the enduring impact of global integration reverberated.

The Columbian Exchange

A transfer of agricultural commodities originating in the Americas that would later be grown or consumed around the world began with Columbus's return to Europe and is often therefore called the Columbian exchange. The list of the agricultural products unknown in Afro-Eurasia prior to 1492 is long and stunning in its impact. Over time, many of these products even came to be associated with distinctive European, African, and Asian traditions. Consider, for example, that tomatoes didn't exist in Italy prior to the 1500s. Along with potatoes, peanuts, peppers, cassava, and corn, these are among the crops that originated in the Americas and then spread around the world to transform the diet of much of the world's population. Other plant products, such as chocolate, vanilla, and tobacco, changed consumption habits in similarly profound ways. The transformative power of American commodities can also be seen in the precious metals that began to flow out of the Americas to other parts of the world.

Things from the Old World also came to, and transformed, the New. Columbus himself brought Afro-Eurasian crops and seeds, including wheat, onions, radishes, and sugar cane, on his second voyage in 1493. By 1600, most of the major domesticated Afro-Eurasian crops were grown in the Americas. Rice, and the techniques for its production, arrived from Africa in the 1600s.

The Columbian exchange transformed demographic, economic, and environmental conditions around the world. New World crops did not simply enter Afro-Eurasian diets; they also fueled population growth and agricultural upheaval.

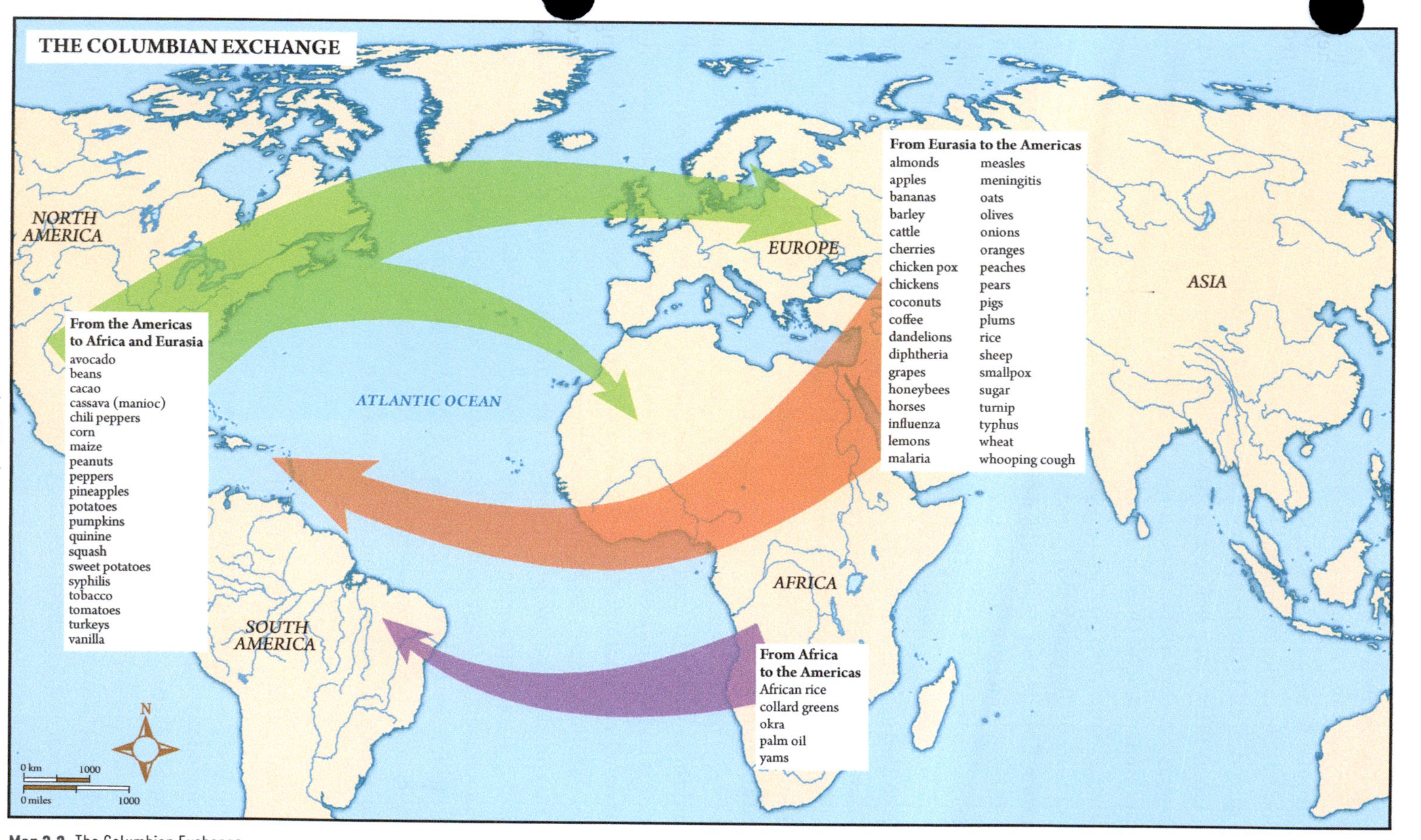
THE COLUMBIAN EXCHANGE
NORTH AMERICA
EUROPE
ASIA
AFRICA
SOUTH AMERICA
ATLANTIC OCEAN
From the Americas to Africa and Eurasia
avocado
beans
cacao
cassava (manioc)
chili peppers
corn
maize
peanuts
peppers
pineapples
potatoes
pumpkins
quinine
squash
sweet potatoes
syphilis
tobacco
tomatoes
turkeys
vanilla
From Eurasia to the Americas
almonds
apples
bananas
barley
cattle
cherries
chicken pox
chickens
coconuts
coffee
dandelions
diphtheria
grapes
honeybees
horses
influenza
lemons
malaria
measles
meningitis
oats
olives
onions
oranges
peaches
pears
pigs
plums
rice
sheep
smallpox
sugar
turnip
typhus
wheat
whooping cough
From Africa to the Americas
African rice
collard greens
okra
palm oil
yams
N
0 km
1000
0 miles
1000

Map 2.2 The Columbian Exchange

Sheep, pigs, and cows brought new sources of wool and protein to the Americas, but they were also a plague on the land, consuming native grasses and trampling the ground to bare wasteland. Horses were never supposed to get into the hands of the hostile indigenous groups on the northern edges of Spanish settlements, yet they did, and they transformed the society and politics of the North American Great Plains long before Europe's human settlers arrived in large numbers. Rats, earthworms, snakes, mosquitoes, honeybees, and all manner of other living things went along for the ride around the world.

The exchange also precipitated great demographic changes, including not only the decline of the indigenous population but also a great migration to the Americas from Europe and, especially, Africa. About 250,000 Europeans migrated to the Spanish Americas between 1492 and 1650, and similar numbers migrated to territory controlled by England. French migration to the Americas was only a trickle into the seventeenth century. During the same period, Brazil took a back seat to Portuguese interests in Asia, although the Portuguese developed sugar plantations along the Brazilian coast in the second half of the sixteenth century. By 1600 about 30,000 Europeans and 15,000 enslaved Africans resided in the territory claimed by Portugal, of a total population of perhaps 100,000. People of African origin arrived on the first vessels to reach the New World from the Old; but over time, the number of enslaved Africans in the New World far outnumbered those who arrived of their own volition. Overall, by 1600, about 275,000 Africans had been enslaved and transported to the Caribbean islands and mainland Americas. That number would skyrocket over the next two hundred years before declining again in the nineteenth century.

This immigration profoundly shaped the Americas. Despite moral, social, and religious proscriptions, the migrants, overwhelmingly men, reproduced with indigenous women. Their children formed their own relationships across ethnic and racial lines. Over time, cultures and societies combining features of distinct peoples and traditions—African, European, Asian, and indigenous—would become a signal characteristic of the Americas.

Colonial Authority and Competition

From the first moments of this encounter with indigenous peoples in the Americas, questions abounded for Europeans about what this New World meant, many of them reflecting the influence of Bible stories on their society during this era. The Bible stated that Christ's disciples had spread the gospel to the entire world, so which of them had brought the good news to the Americas, and why was there so little trace of that effort? Was the Garden of Eden upriver somewhere? Had the indigenous people's gold come from King Solomon's mines?

Questions such as these contributed to fierce disputes within Spain over how to relate to the Americas and its peoples. Like most of the rulers you have read about in this book so far, the Spanish monarchy based its authority on the contention that the will of the ruler aligned with divine objectives: What would God want someone ruling in his name to do? Trying to answer this question led to debates about the relationship among conquest, legitimacy, religion, and justice that began with Columbus's landfall in 1492. These debates focused on questions about the nature of indigenous societies and how to deal with them. Europeans had limited, but multiple, tools and techniques for answering these questions. St. Augustine (354–430), one of the pillars of medieval Christian political thought, wrote "remove justice, and what are kingdoms but bands of criminals on a large scale?"

During the first half of the sixteenth century, many voices with diverse interests argued over the meaning of justice as it related to the peoples of the Americas. Some, like the scholar Juan Ginés de Sepúlveda (1489–1573), asserted that the indigenous peoples were natural slaves and therefore the Spaniards had a right, even a duty, to subjugate them. Others, especially priests with some experience in the Caribbean, such as the former encomendero Bartolomé de las Casas, insisted that the mistreatment of the indigenous peoples jeopardized not only individual sinners but also the rule of sovereigns who implicitly or explicitly tolerated such behavior. However, even the most critical priests did not reject the Spanish monarchs' claim of sovereignty over the Americas. They just advocated a different kind of stewardship over the rich lands and peoples to which God had drawn them.

The Spanish Crown wrestled with how to balance justice, the riches of the conquest, and the maintenance of royal authority in distant lands among diverse peoples. In theory, all subjects of the Spanish Crown were subject to political and spiritual authorities (often the same person), but sixteenth-century transportation and communications systems made it difficult to bridge the great distances separating monarchs from their dominions. It could take four months to sail from Spain to the port city of Veracruz (founded by Cortés on the Mexican mainland in 1519). Movement within the vast expanses of the Americas claimed by the Spanish Crown was just as slow. Seven weeks of arduous travel were required to move silver from the Andean mines in present-day Bolivia to Portobelo (in Panama), the staging area for its movement across the Atlantic to the royal treasury. Decisions made in centers of power were rarely implemented quickly or as intended.

In an attempt to assert greater control over the Spanish dominions in the Americas, the Crown issued a set of "New Laws" in 1542 that created additional political infrastructure in the Americas, while banning the distribution of new encomiendas and the enslavement of indigenous persons. In effect, the Crown declared an end to the culture of conquest. Disgruntled encomenderos assassinated the first viceroy to arrive in Peru with this news. Lacking support among settlers and the ability to impose reforms from above, the Crown backed off on many of the reform's key features. Throughout the subsequent 250 years of Spanish rule in the Americas, Spanish monarchs and their advisers strove to balance material interests, royal dependence on local power brokers in the Americas, and a sense of religious obligation.

As soon as word of Columbus's voyages reached Europe, rivals hotly contested Spain's claims to dominion over the peoples, territories, and resources of the New World. Pope Alexander VI (1431–1503) brokered the Treaty of Tordesillas in 1494, drawing an imaginary line from north to south in the middle of the Atlantic Ocean, giving that which fell to the east to Portugal and that which fell to the west to Spain (the line crosses the South American mainland, explaining why Portugal claimed Brazil and Spain claimed the rest of South America). Although both England and France explored and made claims in North America in the sixteenth century, neither kingdom paid the New World much attention at that time. For a century after Columbus's voyage, it was primarily the people of Spain and their monarchs who invested time, energy, and resources connecting the New World to the Old. Their great maritime rivals were the Portuguese, who focused on protecting their trade routes to West Africa and around the Cape of Good Hope to the Indian Ocean.

As the sixteenth century gave way to the seventeenth, however, the English, French, and Dutch began to challenge the Spanish and Portuguese in global oceanic trade. They also employed a new model of enterprise—the joint stock company—that spread the high risks of global commerce among investors who would purchase from their sovereign the exclusive right to trade in a region. English companies received charters to trade, explore, and settle Jamestown (1607) and the Plymouth Colony (1620) on the east coast of North America. The French, trading guns for furs in the northern reaches of the continent, established Québec in 1608. The Dutch chartered the West India Company in the 1620s and built Fort Amsterdam on the tip of Manhattan Island to defend their interests. Even the Swedes established short-lived New Sweden, building Fort Christina (in today's Wilmington, Delaware) to defend their interests. From these points of entry, contact, alliances, and conflicts developed among various combinations of Europeans and indigenous groups.

By 1546, when rebel encomenderos beheaded the first viceroy of Peru, interactions among Europeans and between Europeans and the broader world had gained greater volatility and complexity as disputes over fundamental issues of Christian faith and practice fragmented the world of Christian believers. Those who remained supportive of and loyal to the traditions and teachings advocated by the papacy became known as Roman Catholics. The protesters (hence *Protestants*), drawn to the ideas of Martin Luther (1483–1546), Huldrych Zwingli

The Port at Calicut. This 1572 image shows Portuguese and other vessels in the harbor. Elephants, like the one on the right side of the image, were used for heavy lifting, such as moving timber for ship repairs. Calicut (not to be confused with Calcutta) had been an important trading hub in southern India since at least the twelfth century. Zheng He's Chinese fleet and Vasco da Gama's Portuguese ships both landed there in the fifteenth century, about ninety years apart. Portugal, France, Britain, and the Netherlands competed with Indian states for control of the city, which gave its name to the popular calico cloths (see Chapter 4, p. 94 [Figure 2]).

(1484–1531), John Calvin (1509–1564), and others, rejected the structures and practices of Roman Catholic tradition. The link between religion and claims to political sovereignty led to wars and rebellions that disrupted relationships between sovereigns and subjects in territories ruled by Christians. We will discuss the impact of this upheaval on the formation of early modern states in a subsequent chapter; but for now, it is important to note the extent to which these conflicts affected emerging globalization and European migration. First, religious groups out of favor with political power holders left Europe for other parts of the world, from southern Africa (French Protestants in the Dutch Cape colony) to New England (the Puritans). Second, the emergence of Protestant Christianity spurred a reforming spirit within Roman Catholicism, inspiring new generations of missionaries—especially Dominican, Franciscan, and Jesuit priests—who believed that God had bestowed the fruits of the world on them for the express purpose of providing the means to save millions of souls, whether from heathenism; rival religions like Islam; or, now, Protestantism.

A World Connected

Asia was the goal that brought Europeans to the Americas, so it should be no surprise that the pursuit of an increased presence there continued in the sixteenth century. However, the interactions between Europeans and Asians both intensified and changed direction as a result of the European conquest and colonization of the Western Hemisphere. The type and volume of commodities available for global consumption increased dramatically, as did competition over lucrative trade networks and markets.

Commodities and Contested Sovereignties

All manner of global interactions deepened in the sixteenth century. In the realm of production, consumption, and trade, the spread of plants around the world—sugar to the west, peppers to the east—is only one piece of a more comprehensive transformation of the global economy. China and India devoured American silver. The mines of Spanish America produced 85 percent of the world's silver between 1500 and 1800, and China alone absorbed 40 percent of that. In exchange, Chinese goods were shipped to the port of Acapulco, on the Pacific coast of Mexico (New Spain), on a regular basis beginning in the 1570s. By the 1580s, Asian products were the main commodities exchanged between the two Spanish viceroyalties in the Americas. At this same time, both free and unfree migrants from Asia, although fewer than those from Europe and Africa, had a substantial impact in the Americas. The Spanish Crown struggled to control the burgeoning direct trade between Asia and the Americas, while local subjects on both sides of the Pacific Ocean undermined the efforts of the distant monarchs. The struggle among priests, settlers, merchants, and royal officials over the management of and profit from the Americas accelerated over the course of the sixteenth century.

In southern India, Portuguese forces pushed out from their anchorage at Goa and in 1511 took control of Malacca, a key point of exchange between Chinese and Islamic trading networks. Through the middle decades of the sixteenth century, Portuguese traders engaged in the vibrant commerce of the Indian Ocean and South China Sea, contending with smugglers, pirates, and Chinese imperial policy. During the sixteenth century, trade through Southeast Asia grew rapidly. The rulers of *port-states*—safe harbors for trade in the places known today as the Philippines, Indonesia, Vietnam, Cambodia, Thailand, Myanmar, and Malaysia—collected taxes on the goods passing through their realms and used these revenues to assert their power, purchasing gunships and muskets and hiring both Muslim and Christian mercenaries. Contending with the Portuguese for control of trading routes and resources, some Muslim sultans of Southeast Asia turned to Suleiman, ruler of the Ottomans and protector of the Islamic faith, who sent materiel and perhaps even supported a military academy in the sultanate of Aceh, on the Indonesian island of Sumatra.

The promise of much-desired American silver prompted Chinese officials to open trade with the Europeans, leading in 1557 to the establishment of a

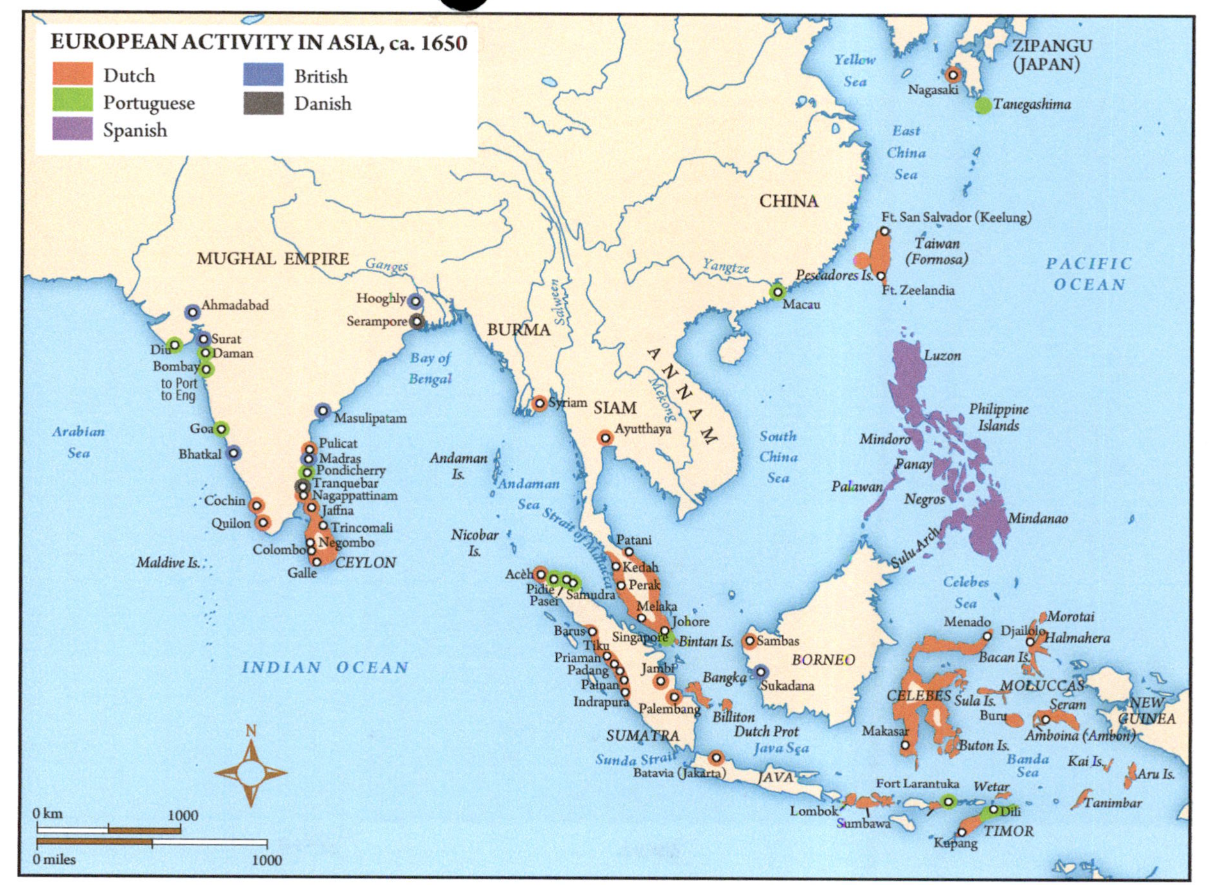

Map 2.3 European Activity in Asia, ca. 1650

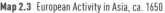

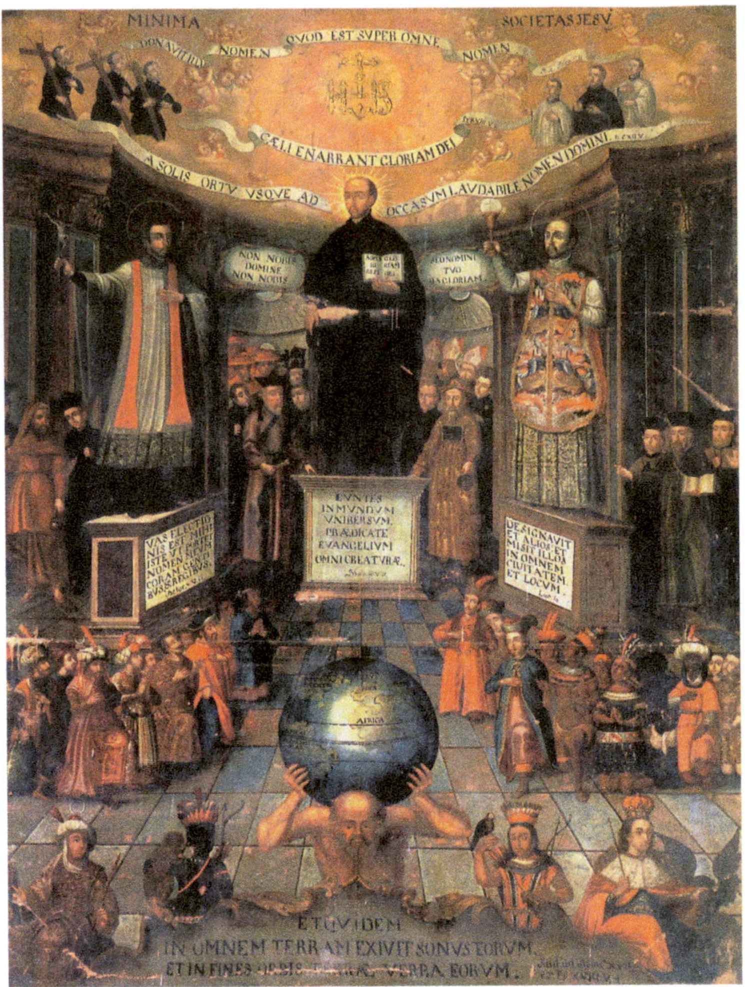

An Artist's Rendering of the Global Missionary Initiatives of the Society of Jesus (Jesuits). The Society of Jesus commissioned this painting in the seventeenth century for the Church of San Pedro in Lima (Peru). The Jesuits used art as a key means to convey their image as a global Catholic missionary enterprise. Notice the variety of clothes and phenotypes portrayed. The Jesuit missionaries, displayed in the center of the painting, bring the New Testament message, excerpted in Latin from the Gospels of Mark and Luke and the Acts of the Apostles.

permanent Portuguese settlement at Macau, on the south China coast. In the 1560s, a Spanish expedition, launched from the Pacific coast of Mexico, founded a commercial and administrative settlement on one of the islands they called the Philippines, named after the Spanish monarch Philip II (1527–1598). From these bases, the Spanish and Portuguese conducted trade throughout maritime Asia. With the merchants and sailors came priests, who, as in the Americas, attempted Roman Catholic evangelization of the region's peoples.

The Asian Powers and Limits on European Expansion

The great diversity of political and social power structures both provided opportunities for and placed limits on European action in Asia. Miguel López de Legazpi (1502–1572), leader of the Spanish expedition to the Philippines, remarked that "the inhabitants of these islands are not subjected to any law, king or lord," which meant that the islands lacked a political and military organization that could prevent Spanish dominion over them. His sovereign, Philip II, wanted to use this island base as the foundation for a new diplomatic relationship with the Chinese emperor. Chinese pirates, captured by the Spanish, were returned to Chinese imperial officials, priestly emissaries were dispatched, and gifts were exchanged; but officials in Mexico and the Philippines who advocated military intimidation rather than negotiation undermined Philip's efforts. Sovereign-to-sovereign diplomacy did not materialize, although Jesuit missionaries were ultimately permitted to enter Beijing, the imperial capital.

The Jesuit Matteo Ricci (1552–1610) became the first European invited to the Forbidden City, although he never met the emperor. The Jesuits, through their strategies of adopting local customs, learning local languages, and interpreting Christian doctrine in the context of local practices, converted tens of thousands to Catholicism in the early 1600s, including some members of the imperial court. Still, this was a tiny fraction of the total population, and any momentum these Christian missionaries had at the Ming court flagged as the dynasty declined into rebellion and disorder in the 1640s. As the new Qing imperial dynasty consolidated power in the middle of the seventeenth century, its rulers chose to regulate interactions with foreigners carefully. The same was true for Korea, although neither kingdom limited the presence of foreigners to the extent that Japan would.

In an effort to limit foreign influence and consolidate authority around a single ruler, the Japanese imperial regent Toyotomi Hideyoshi (1536–1598) expelled Christian missionaries and limited the spread of Christianity by regional authorities. When the Tokugawa clan acquired the title of shogun—the supreme military ruler in Japan—in the early 1600s, successive Tokugawa leaders extended these limitations with a series of proclamations. First, the Portuguese were isolated on an artificial island (Dejima) built in the harbor at Nagasaki. Then, after the Shimabara Rebellion (1637–1638), a large-scale uprising of mostly Catholic peasants, Shogun Tokugawa Iemitsu (1604–1651) began to implement the Sakoku Rei (Closed Country Edict), barring the Portuguese, banning evangelization, and forbidding Japanese from leaving the islands (and from returning to the islands if they did leave). In 1641, the Dutch received permission to serve as the only European merchants legally empowered to import goods to Japan through Dejima. The Dutch commercial privileges in Japan were given in part because

Dutch Protestants were not committed to Christian evangelization as part of their global engagements the way the Catholic Spanish and Portuguese Crowns were.

The Dutch success illustrates how competition for trade among European powers strengthened the position of Asian rulers against the Spanish and Portuguese and contributed to the decline of the Iberian powers in relation to other kingdoms. From this period forward, British, French, and Dutch merchants and seafarers would be the most important Europeans in the region. The British and Dutch East India Companies, both established in the first decade of the seventeenth century, would dominate European–Asian economic relations over the next 150 years, particularly in South and Southeast Asia. The French, too, established trading posts in West Africa (Senegal), South Asia (Pondicherry), and the Indian Ocean (Île de Bourbon) during this period.

Conclusion

First setting eyes on Tenochtitlan, Bernal Díaz del Castillo wondered if he was seeing a mirage. Arriving with Cortés, Díaz cast his gaze on a city that appeared to him straight out of medieval legends. His memoir of the conquest, written as an old man back in Spain, continued to couch the activities of Cortés and his band in the terms of these epic tales. Understanding the full scope of this era, and its importance, requires overcoming enduring misconceptions that emerge from relying on the perspective of conquistadors like Bernal Díaz or those who place these men as the only protagonists who mattered in shaping historical outcomes. In this chapter, we have tried to provide a broader perspective. Even so, through much of the sixteenth century, Spanish and Portuguese institutions, individuals, and ideas mediated the connection between the Western Hemisphere and the rest of the world. Because Iberia—Spain and Portugal—was already part of the European–Asian–African network, the Western Hemisphere was immediately

TIMELINE

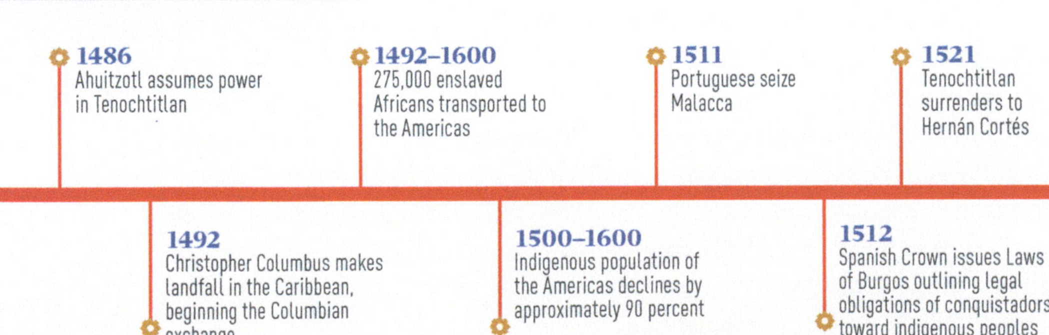
1486
Ahuitzotl assumes power in Tenochtitlan
1492
Christopher Columbus makes landfall in the Caribbean, beginning the Columbian exchange
1492–1600
275,000 enslaved Africans transported to the Americas
1500–1600
Indigenous population of the Americas declines by approximately 90 percent
1511
Portuguese seize Malacca
1512
Spanish Crown issues Laws of Burgos outlining legal obligations of conquistadors toward indigenous peoples
1521
Tenochtitlan surrenders to Hernán Cortés

linked into that complex. Yet, this joining of the hemispheres with Iberian political, economic, and cultural thread is not the whole story. Other changes of global significance in the sixteenth and seventeenth centuries also wove the globe together. German and English religious dissidents, Chinese potters, Islamic sultans, Hindu textile workers, Japanese officials, and Dutch merchants joined Spanish priests, Portuguese sailors, Aztec warriors, and Inca mine workers in the new era of globalization, to which we will devote further attention in the following two chapters. First, we will describe how this emerging global economy worked. Then, we will see the ways in which rulers attempted to muster both old and new resources to gain and maintain power.

A Few Good Books

Giancarlo Casale. *The Ottoman Age of Exploration*. New York: Oxford University Press, 2010.

Inga Clendinnen. *Ambivalent Conquests: Maya and Spaniard in Yucatán*. 2nd ed. Cambridge: Cambridge University Press, 2003.

Alfred W. Crosby Jr. *The Columbian Exchange: Biological and Cultural Consequences of 1492*. 30th anniversary ed. Westport, CT: Praeger, 2003.

Roger Crowley. *Conquerors: How Portugal Forged the First Global Empire*. New York: Random House, 2009.

Douglas Hunter. *Half Moon: Henry Hudson and the Voyage That Redrew the Map of the New World*. New York: Bloomsbury, 2009.

Charles Mann. *1493: Uncovering the New World Columbus Created*. New York: Alfred A. Knopf, 2011.

Matthew Restall. *Seven Myths of the Spanish Conquest*. New York: Oxford University Press, 2003.

Jonathan D. Spence. *The Memory Palace of Matteo Ricci*. New York: Penguin, 1985.

For instructional resources and study aids, please go to **www.oup.com/us/carter**. *For primary sources connected to this chapter, please see the table of contents for* Sources for Forging the Modern World *included at the back of the book.*

1533 Spanish conquistadors execute Inca ruler Atahualpa

1542 Spanish Crown attempts to assert greater control over the Americas with "New Laws"

1557 Portuguese establish permanent trading port at Macau, China

1607 Jamestown colony founded by English

1639 Portuguese banned from Japan

1641 Dutch become only European merchants legally permitted to import goods to Japan

(TOP) Masjid-i-Shah, Isfahan, Persia (Iran). Begun by Shah Abbas in the early seventeenth century, the mosque was a testament to the ambitions and wealth of the Safavid rulers who built the capital of their empire at Isfahan. This photograph, ca. 1900, was taken by Percy Molesworth Sykes, a British military officer and diplomat stationed in the region.

(RIGHT) The Kangxi Emperor of Qing Dynasty China. Seen here in a formal imperial portrait painted on silk, the Kangxi Emperor ruled from 1661 to 1722, longer than any other emperor of China up to that time. Under his rule, the Manchu Qing dynasty consolidated its conquest of China and expanded its borders in central and Southeast Asia.

CHAPTER 3

The Paradoxes of Early Modern Empire

1501–1661

In 1501, the army of a young religious visionary named Ismail (1487–1524) captured the city of Tabriz, about four hundred miles northeast of Tehran (in present-day Iran). Just fourteen years old, Ismail rose to power with the military aid of the *Qizilbash*, warrior horsemen with roots in Azerbaijan and Anatolia. Ismail believed he was the "Shadow of God," divinely ordained to impose and spread the practices of Shi`a Islam, and his warriors adopted the battle cry, "My spiritual leader and master, for whom I sacrifice myself!" Assuming the title shah, a Persian title that dated back almost two thousand years, Ismail established the Safavid Empire. Under Ismail and his descendants, who also embraced the principle of divinely inspired rule, the empire survived for over two centuries. Royal workshops produced high-quality textiles for the imperial court but also for export, delivering income to the royal treasury. A sophisticated administrative structure maintained the imperial court's power. At the end of the sixteenth century, Ismail's descendant Shah Abbas (1571–1629) moved the capital to Isfahan and added an entirely new city to the existing urban complex, building a grand mosque, an imperial palace, and a giant commercial center (bazaar). Isfahan grew into one of the most dynamic economic and cultural hubs of the early modern world.

One hundred sixty years after Ismail captured Tabriz, a Manchu prince who would rule as the Kangxi Emperor (1654–1722) succeeded to the throne in China, beginning the longest individual reign in China's history. Every new ruler faces challenges, but these circumstances were particularly difficult. When he took the throne in 1661, Kangxi was only seven years old. He began ruling in his own right (without supervising regents) just six years later. Like all rulers of the Qing (pronounced "ching") dynasty, he was not Chinese but Manchu, a linguistically and culturally distinct people who had conquered China from the north only two decades before. Many Chinese, especially those loyal to the preceding Ming dynasty, still

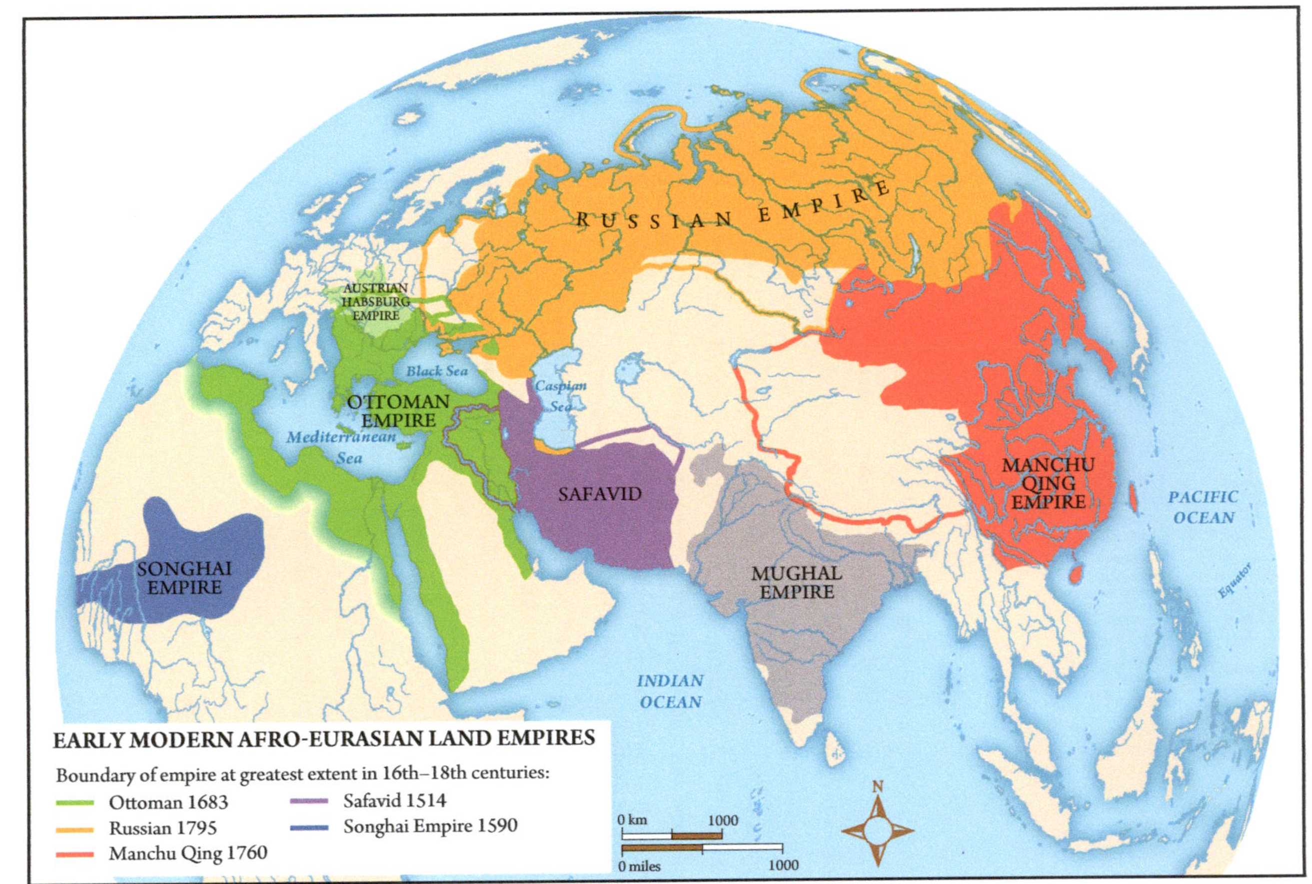

Map 3.1 Early Modern Afro-Eurasian Land Empires

regarded the Manchus with hostility, and the Kangxi Emperor worked hard to establish and maintain his legitimacy. He made six tours of the south (for centuries the traditional center of Chinese culture) so he could learn about local conditions and demonstrate his active leadership, but also so that he could impress the population with the scale and grandeur of this still-new dynasty. He also issued a "Sacred Edict"—to be read in every village by local officials—that encouraged filial respect, generosity, frugality, and loyalty. These were Confucian principles that had been the official foundation of Chinese statecraft for centuries, showing that although the Qing rulers were Manchu, they were familiar with the values that Chinese emperors had invoked for centuries to maintain a stable and well-ordered society. The Kangxi Emperor also worked to win over the Chinese scholars needed to run the bureaucracy. He sponsored a special examination to select authors to write the history of the Ming dynasty and set others to work compiling a dictionary (still used today) and an encyclopedia of five thousand volumes. Combined with military expansion into Tibet and Mongolia, the emperor's actions solidified the Qing claim to sovereignty.

The actions of Shah Ismail and the Kangxi Emperor illustrate many of the ways rulers and their peoples related to one another during the sixteenth and seventeenth centuries. Leaders made increasingly audacious claims to rule great expanses of territory and resources. To turn claims into action, they created laws and constructed rituals to unify diverse ethnic, religious, linguistic, and social groups into political bodies loyal to only one head. They deployed religious, military, and judicial enforcers and distributed material rewards and harsh punishments to reinforce their claims. In this chapter, we analyze the actions of different claimants to power and explain how and why some succeeded and others failed during this time. We will explain first how the era's new economic and technological landscape altered the way elites made war and built states. Then we will analyze the ways competing groups and individuals justified these new forms of power philosophically, religiously, and culturally. Our goal for this chapter is to show how material conditions, ideas, and individual agency influenced the practices of rulership, the relationships among rulers, and the tensions that could emerge between rulers and the peoples over whom they claimed sovereignty during this era of empire building.

Questions to Consider as You Read Chapter Three:

1. Rulers use many different tools—armies, weapons, jails, laws, ideas—to assert and maintain control. How would you compare and contrast the tools available to the different empire builders who emerged during this era?
2. How did rulers during this era relate to those over whom they ruled? What were some of the risks or advantages of different relationships between ruler and ruled?

The Words and Deeds of Empire Building

During the sixteenth and seventeenth centuries, the ability of rulers to use their power changed dramatically. Improved weaponry changed the way states prepared for and conducted war. Strategies and tactics changed to accommodate new technologies. Larger and more heavily armed ships traversed the world's waterways. New features of warfare held the promise that those who mastered their techniques could conquer more territory.

No technological innovation transformed warfare more than gunpowder, which originated in ninth-century China. Weapons based on it spread through Afro-Eurasia over the subsequent centuries. The significant transformation of the sixteenth and seventeenth centuries was not the invention of gunpowder, but the changing scale of weapons and the means to acquire and use them. Rulers across the supercontinent—Safavids, Mughals, French, Spanish, Russians, English, Japanese, Ottomans, Qing, Asante, Dahomey, and others—turned revenues into firearms and soldiers. New weapons and ammunition, and their innovative use, could help determine victory and defeat, but not alone. Enduring factors like the economic resources available to supply a war effort, decisions made in the heat of battle, and the commitment of troops to their cause could still determine their outcomes.

In Chapter 4, we will examine the early modern global economy in detail. For now, just keep in mind that the resources used to support larger, more expensive armed forces and military campaigns varied in their specific origins, but could all be traced to the processes of globalization we have already described. More material resources for state building were now available, as were larger and higher-quality weapons for use on land and sea. Merchants and manufacturers filled government coffers in exchange for the right to bring goods to markets around the globe. Innovations in finance lubricated global commerce and allowed states to wage larger wars on the promise that they would pay for them with the spoils of victory.

How to Be a Ruler

The changing stakes were not lost on those seeking power in the sixteenth century. Niccolò Machiavelli (1469–1527) was a keen observer of political and military affairs who served as an official of the city-state of Florence on the Italian Peninsula. Machiavelli concluded that no overarching or universal set of religious or ethical rules guided or constrained political interactions, so understanding and using power was the essential component of political leadership. Machiavelli's advice on how to act on this insight is contained in his most famous work, *The Prince*, but Machiavelli produced other works that contain observations on both conceptual and practical matters, such as *The Art of War* and *A Discourse about the Provision of Money*.

Machiavelli is sometimes portrayed as a ruthless calculator who advised that any action was acceptable if it led to a positive outcome for the ruler. But what truly set Machiavelli's political philosophy apart from that of most of his contemporaries was that God was not at the center of the political world he described. Few people at the time shared this view; most assertions about political legitimacy and sovereignty connected rulers with supernatural or divine powers beyond the scope of human comprehension. As a result, disputes over theology and religious practice linked the geographic spread of different religious traditions and empire building.

Machiavelli was not alone in trying to understand what states were and how they worked at this time, nor was this process limited to Europe. The historical sociologist Charles Tilly (1929–2008) described this process as the achievement of *stateness*, a process that Linda Darling notes is one of the defining features of this early modern era across Afro-Eurasia. The emergence of stable, larger, centralized states was accompanied by the proliferation of political advice literature on how states work, which appeared not only in Christian Europe but also in Islamic kingdoms, written in Arabic, Persian, and Turkish. For example, both *The Jalalian Ethics* by Jalal al-Din al-Dawani (ca. 1427–1503) and *The Conduct of Kings*, by his student Fazlullah ibn Ruzbihan, elaborate on the connection between power and action in ways similar to Machiavelli and others, analyzing both the conceptual foundations of the state and the practical applications of those concepts.[1]

Of course, rulers, groups, or institutions exercising power—and writing and thinking about it—were not new in the 1500s. Armies, taxes, and courts of law did not originate in this period. However, from the end of the fifteenth century to the middle of the seventeenth century, individuals and groups tended to claim greater control over more material resources and more aspects of more lives in greater expanses of territory, even across open ocean. Creating these ambitious states exposed a set of paradoxes. These new states often aspired to be highly centralized, with a single, strong leader. But, to organize the material and human resources needed to construct these larger states required cooperation among many groups, increasing the chances of conflict between the central leadership and potential rivals, often thousands of miles from their rulers' ancestral homelands but sometimes in the

1 Charles Tilly developed his analysis over the course of a long career and many publications, including *Coercion, Capital, and European States: AD 990–1992* (Cambridge, MA: Blackwell, 1990). See also Charles Tilly, "War Making and State Making as Organized Crime" in *Bringing the State Back In*, ed. Peter B. Evans et al. (Cambridge: Cambridge University Press, 1985), 169–191. This essay inspired our use of *The Godfather* reference earlier in this book. For discussions of the broader Afro-Eurasian context of state making and political philosophy during this era, see Linda Darling, *A History of Social Justice and Political Power in the Middle East: The Circle of Justice from Mesopotamia to Globalization* (London: Routledge, 2013); and Adeeb Khalid, *Islam after Communism: Religion and Politics in Central Asia* (Berkeley: University of California Press, 2014).

The Battle of Bundi, 1577. This miniature painting presents the Mughal army on the battlefield in northwest India. It was completed to accompany the Akbarnama (*Book of Akbar*), a chronicle of the achievements of the Mughal emperor Akbar the Great (1542–1605). These kinds of illustrations were often the work of multiple artists contributing to both the design and the application of paints. Note the variety of weapons, warriors, and animals used in battle during this era of changing military technologies and strategies.

rulers' strongholds themselves. Finally, the construction of, and conflict among, empires during this era reminds us that every claim to sovereignty invites questions about legitimacy: Is a claim to power recognized and accepted by people and institutions other than yourself? Can the claim be defended—logically and militarily—against challengers? For most people living at the time, the answers to such questions remained rooted in divine order. In the sections that follow, we examine these trends in several regional variations. The full scope of religious transformation in this era is dizzying, so we will limit our discussion here primarily to the question of its relationship to state building.

Consolidation and Struggle in the Islamic World

Over the centuries, Islam spread far beyond its geographic origins in the Arabian Peninsula. Along with a commercial and political network based on the Arabic language, Islam linked believers to a larger world of commerce and learning. Muslim rulers could use this broader world to support themselves against challengers who claimed the right to rule based on other religious traditions. For example, as we saw in Chapter 2, the sultan of Aceh (in today's Indonesia) sent an ambassador more than five thousand miles to the Ottoman Empire during the reign of Suleiman I to negotiate an alliance. The sultan of Aceh (like many, but as we shall see not all, Muslims) recognized the ruler of the Ottoman Empire as the caliph, the successor to the Prophet Muhammad and therefore leader of all the Islamic faithful. The sultan also recognized that the Ottoman Empire was seeking allies in its multifront war against some of the world's other major military and economic powers.

In the Mediterranean region, the city of Constantinople, conquered by Sultan Mehmed II (1432–1481), had provided a strategic base for subsequent expansion. Mehmed and his successors continued to spread Ottoman influence from the outskirts of Vienna (Austria) in the west, south through Egypt, across the Red Sea to the holy Muslim cities of Medina and Mecca (in Arabia), and east to the

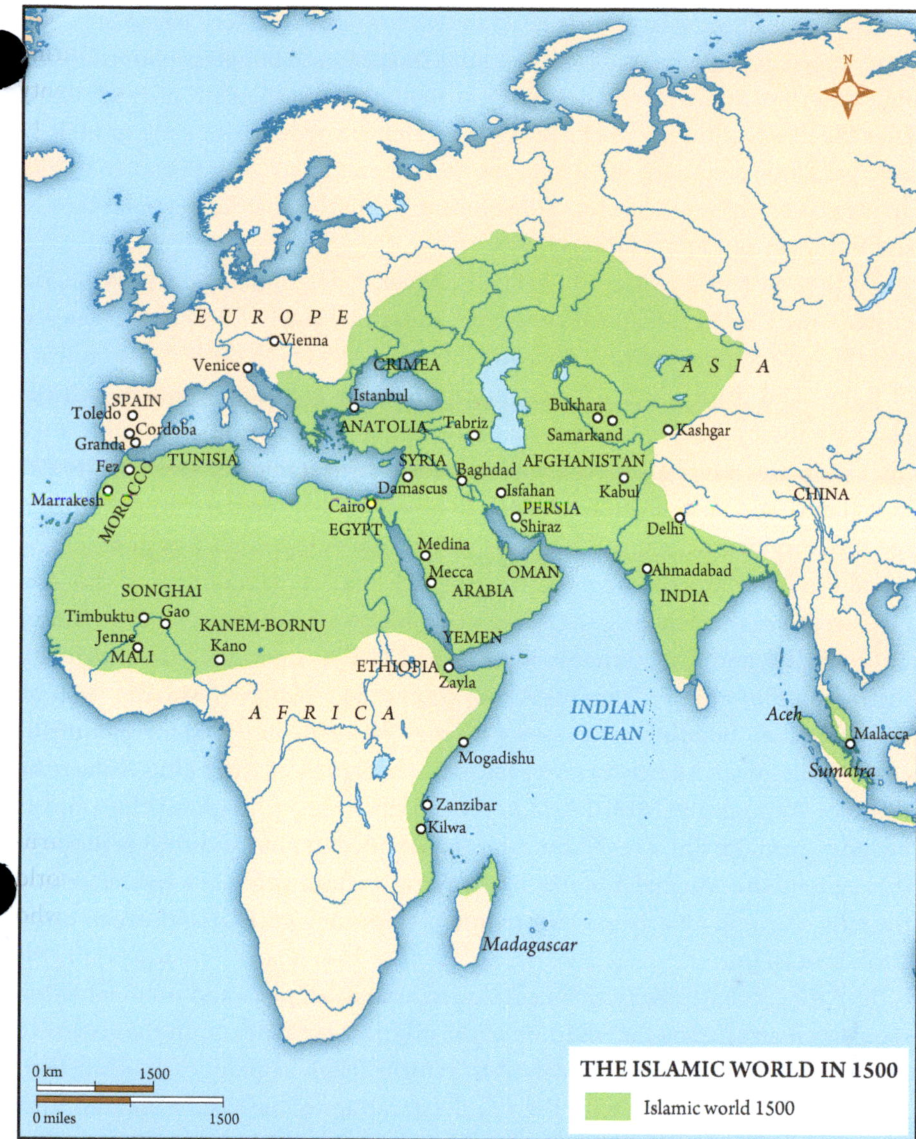

Map 3.2 The Islamic World in 1500

Persian Gulf, reaching the lucrative Indian Ocean trading routes. As the empire grew, Ottoman sultans continued to tolerate communities of religious minorities within the empire under the millet system. Although composed of many religions, languages, and ethnicities, a Sunni Islamic legal and administrative system held the empire together, with government funds supporting Islamic education and the training of the Sunni religious hierarchy.

Unlike the Ottomans, Shah Ismail I and his Safavid successors, based in Persia, were rooted in the Shi`a tradition. The long-standing and important Sunni–Shi`a split had roots in the seventh-century struggles over leadership of the faithful after the death of the Prophet Muhammad and had grown over time to include divergent interpretations of Islamic law and other matters. This Sunni and Shi`a divide was one of several factors contributing to multiple battles between successive Ottoman and Safavid rulers.

To the south and east of the Safavids, Muslim descendants of the Mongols united much of the Indian subcontinent under the Mughal Empire. In the sixteenth century, an ambitious and skillful ruler, Akbar (1542–1605), grandson of Babur and third Mughal ruler, emerged in the sixteenth century and deployed military, political, social, and cultural tactics to build an empire. Like the Ottomans, Mughal rulers embraced the Sunni tradition. The question of how the dynasty would view religious diversity was particularly important for the territory over which the Mughals claimed to rule, which was perhaps the world's most productive economy during this era. Large numbers of this empire's residents—including many wealthy and powerful ones—were Hindus or Buddhists, and Christian missionaries and traders moved regularly through the region. For a time, Emperor Akbar promoted a fusion of Muslim, Hindu, Christian, and Buddhist traditions with himself as the unifying force, but this cosmopolitanism did not survive past Akbar's reign. A century after Akbar, the emperor Aurangzeb (1618–1707) provoked uprisings throughout the empire, including a major Shi`a rebellion, when he decided to impose Sunni orthodoxy throughout the Mughal Empire by banning certain practices and attacking the holy sites and objects of other religious traditions, including those of other strands of Islam.

In Africa, robust interactions continued among scholars and political elites, regularly nourished by the tradition of the pilgrimage to Mecca. In the sixteenth century, many African rulers vowed to reform religious practices within their kingdoms, aligning them with their understandings of how Islam should function and how they, as Islamic rulers, could maintain their legitimacy. In the Horn of Africa, a Somali Muslim named Ahmad ibn Ibrahim al-Ghazi (ca. 1504–1543), supported by the Ottoman Empire, conquered most of Ethiopia at the end of the 1520s; but this initiative began to collapse when he was killed in a battle with the Portuguese in 1543. Imam Ahmad's death did not bring peace or political stability, however, because fighting for control of Ethiopia and the entire Horn of Africa continued among local groups and empire builders, including the Ottomans and the Portuguese.

Christian Reformation

About the same time as Machiavelli was writing, a young Roman Catholic priest named Martin Luther (1483–1546) also offered some advice. A theology professor in the German city of Wittenberg, Luther wrote about how God's will was reflected in human practice. He concluded that the Christian institutions of his day were out of whack and reported his findings—ninety-five observations in all, usually called the Ninety-Five Theses—on Halloween 1517. Luther's critique outraged his superiors, but Luther refused to back down. Instead, he expanded on his critiques in three pamphlets challenging the church's entire hierarchy, up to and including the pope, as corrupt and immoral and challenged its right to rule over Christians and interpret Holy Scripture.

From the perspective of western Europe, Luther appeared to be questioning a monolithic Christendom dominated by the Roman Catholic Church, but Christianity was already—like Islam, Hinduism, or Buddhism—riven by differences among the faithful. Although the church based in Rome was the largest, distinct Christian hierarchies and practices existed in Russia, Ethiopia, and elsewhere.

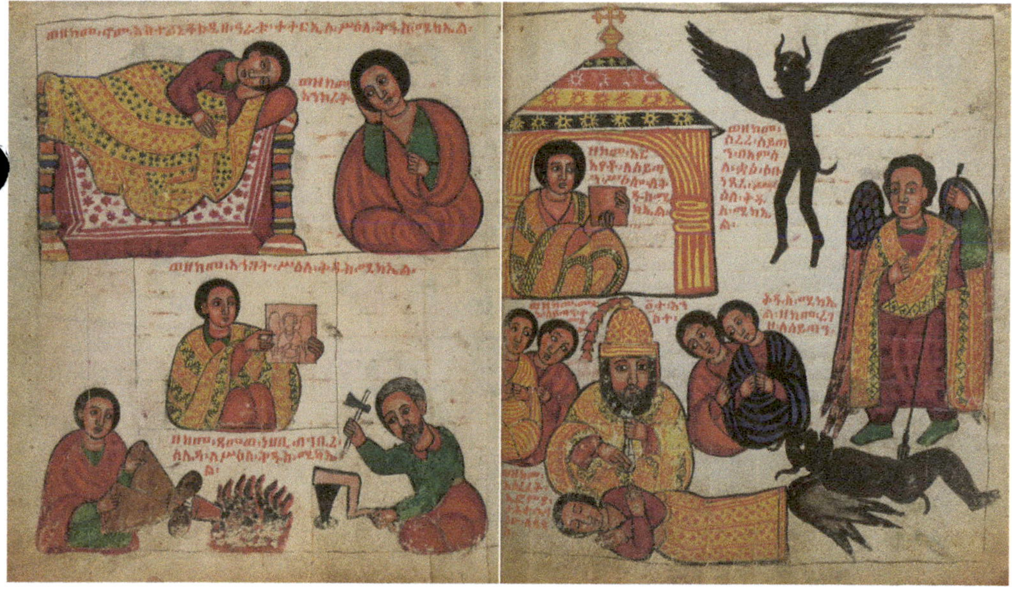

The Miracles of the Archangel Michael, from a Homilary from Gondar, Ethiopia. Late Seventeenth Century. This book, a collection of inspirational stories of miracles performed by the archangel Michael, was most likely commissioned by members of the Ethiopian imperial court for use during feast days in the capital. The Ethiopian royal court used such tools to reinforce the cultural connection between Christian traditions and its authority.

In these places, political leaders of the sixteenth and seventeenth centuries used Christian traditions as a fulcrum to move people and resources to their causes.

In Ethiopia, leaders invoked an Orthodox Christian tradition as the element of Ethiopian identity that could rally forces of resistance against Islamic warriors but also expel missionaries who tried to bring the Ethiopian church in line with the Roman hierarchy and tenets of the faith. In Russia, Ivan IV, the grand prince of Moscow (1530–1584) and first person to be called "Tsar of all the Russians," did many of the things the other empire builders we discuss in this chapter were doing. He armed the first permanent Russian military force with an early form of rifle, conceded monopoly trading rights to gain revenue from merchant groups, and developed a policy to secure an adequate labor supply for the empire's rural estates. He also commissioned elaborate Orthodox cathedrals to commemorate his victories over Islamic foes and supported the Orthodox Church in myriad other ways. The clerical hierarchy reciprocated by supporting Ivan's growing territorial claims of sovereignty.

So, while Martin Luther's protests did not bring an end to a single universal Christian faith—he could not destroy something that did not exist—they did challenge religious and political authorities in western Europe at an important moment. Luther's target, the clerical hierarchy, was in many ways the most powerful institution in this part of the world at the time. In addition to guiding the spiritual lives of Europe's overwhelmingly Christian population, church leaders controlled great wealth and often served as political advisers or even as de facto rulers themselves. In the region where Luther lived, to advocate or practice Christianity in ways that the Roman hierarchy did not sanction was subject to both religious and political punishment: public penance, excommunication, exile, imprisonment, and even execution. Luther and other "Protestants" (protesters against church teachings or the clerical hierarchy) therefore challenged both religious and secular authority in Europe. Both the pope and the Holy Roman emperor, who claimed authority over the lands where Luther lived, leveled charges against him. In the spring of 1521, a special court condemned Luther as a heretic and criminal.

But Luther was never turned over to these authorities to face punishment. He was protected by the powerful Frederick III, elector of Saxony (1463–1525), who had founded the university where Luther had worked. That Luther could be publicly condemned by leading political and religious authorities yet remain unpunished demonstrates the limits to the real power of both the pope and the Holy Roman emperor. This is crucial to understanding this moment. Power in Europe—political, economic, and now religious—appeared to be up for grabs and a violent sorting-out process erupted.

The "Reformation" that Luther precipitated transcended religion. Over the coming months and years, supporters and interpreters of Luther's ideas launched rebellions from below against authorities throughout German-speaking lands and beyond. More than one hundred thousand people died in what became known as the German Peasants' War, a bloody conflict that illustrates the complex interactions of religion and politics at the time. In 1525, one group of rebels demanded the right to choose their own pastors and have more control over church funds, clearly reflecting the anticorruption rhetoric of Luther's protests. But the rebels went further, demanding that local elites respect their rights to hunt and gather wood and to limit their labor contributions to their landlords. Finally, they demanded fairness in the creation and enforcement of laws.

The rebels justified their demands with multiple and specific references to the Bible, based on Luther's assertion that the Bible was the ultimate source of all authority. But rather than being pleased by this interpretation of his call for reform, Luther condemned the rebels as "murdering, thieving hordes" and encouraged the rulers of central Europe to simultaneously reform the practice of Christianity in their realms and put to death for their blasphemies those who challenged political authority.

The Power of the Printed Word

In the ensuing war of words and deeds among Christians, all sides made use of a new and powerful weapon: the printing press. The importance of the printing press was appropriate given that the written word had been at the center of reform movements in Christianity for many decades. Like earlier reformers, including Englishman John Wycliffe (ca. 1328–1384) and Bohemian Jan Hus (1369–1415), Luther insisted that the Mass—the central ceremony in Christian religious life—and the Bible be presented in languages that most churchgoers could understand rather than Latin, the language of clergy and the educated. This was politically, socially, and religiously radical. Placing Holy Scripture directly into the hands of many more people—like the German-speaking rebels of the Peasants' War—would greatly diminish the power of the clergy, who were freer to interpret Scripture if it were available only in Latin.

For earlier generations, the cost of translating and reproducing new Bibles helped keep their protests largely theoretical but, by Luther's day, new technology made printing and distributing texts easier and less expensive. While in hiding after his trial, Luther set to work translating the Bible into German, arranging to publish his translation of the New Testament in 1522 and the Old Testament thirteen years later. This made the basic religious texts of Christianity accessible in new ways to millions of people and shaped the modern German language. Translations of the Bible into English and other languages would have the same effect. Printing presses with moveable type dramatically lowered the costs of reproducing all types of information, not just the Bible. Written commentary on

Matthias Gerung, "Apocalypse and Satirical Allegories on the Church" (1546). This woodcut print was commissioned by a Protestant nobleman in central Europe to illustrate an anti-Catholic pamphlet. The upper half of the image contrasts the rectitude of Protestant forms of worship with the corrupt practices of Roman Catholicism in the lower half.

Luther's grievances spread quickly across Europe and beyond. Some of the thousands of texts published during this era lampooned the pope; others demonized Luther.

Printing demonstrated the relationship between power and ideas in shaping the world. Using carved wood blocks, printing had first developed in China, probably in the early centuries of the Common Era. In those first presses, an entire page would be carved (in reverse) into a piece of wood. Movable type, with individual characters that could be rearranged to print different content, did not develop until about 1300, using first porcelain and then metal, in China and Korea. But printing did not become widespread, perhaps because the thousands of characters needed to print in classical Chinese—the elite language in both places—made a complete set of type expensive to produce and cumbersome to use. European presses, however, needed just a few dozen characters—the letters of the alphabet—that could be rearranged to print each page. A Bible, printed in Latin by Johannes Gutenberg (ca. 1398–1468) in the 1450s, was the first major printed work in Europe.

Presses spread across Europe during the late fifteenth century, and their products flowed across the continent and beyond. European colonizers and explorers from the sixteenth century carried books to help accomplish their goals of conversion and domination. Presses arrived in Mexico City (1539), Goa (1557), Macau (1588), and Nagasaki (1590). Jesuit missionaries first arrived in China around this time, and Matteo Ricci carried books with him as part of his attempt to convert the top layers of society to Christianity when he finally received permission to enter Beijing in 1601.

In Europe, the circulation of books promoted the standardization of languages that served the needs both of rulers and of printers who needed a large enough marketplace to sell their goods. More books began to be published in languages other than Latin, especially French and Italian. Before 1500, most books published in Europe were in Latin (about ten times more than any other language) and nearly half of them were on religious topics. During the sixteenth century, religious texts continued to dominate, but their share of all published works fell as interest in the Greek and Roman classics grew. Books on history also became very popular, often printed both in Latin and in other languages.

Politics, religion, and culture were clearly and closely entangled. Languages often assumed to be ancient and unchanging coalesced in this period as ruling groups saw the political importance of language. Antonio de Nebrija (1441–1522), who compiled and published the first book of Spanish grammar in 1492, asserted in the prologue that the book was important because history had proven that a proper language has always been the companion of empire. French was established as the official language of the courts of justice in the kingdom of France in 1539. Luther himself wrote his political pamphlet, "To the Christian Nobility of the German Nation" (1520), in German, not Latin, revealing both his confidence in the marketplace for publications in that language and his target audience: literate but not scholarly. Recognizing the political potential of the written word, rulers attempted to control it both by promoting languages, literatures, and histories that supported their claims to rule and by censoring and suppressing the printed word in efforts to guard state secrets.[2]

Tangled Loyalties and the European Wars of Religion

Given these complex interconnections, you may not find it surprising that the bitter Wars of Religion that dominated the sixteenth century in Europe were about much more than religion. When Luther wrote his controversial theses, the Holy Roman emperor Charles V—also at the time king of Spain and the most powerful ruler in Europe—held him accountable. Charles's grandparents, Ferdinand and Isabella, had supported Columbus's voyages and driven from the Iberian Peninsula Muslims and Jews who refused to convert to Christianity. The Spanish Inquisition, designed to enforce Christian thinking that supported royal power throughout the empire, reflected in its operations the roots of a modern state bureaucracy. Charles controlled a large, land-based empire as well as vast

---

2 Lucien Febvre and Henri-Jean Martin, *The Coming of the Book: The Impact of Printing, 1450–1800*, 3rd ed. (London: Verso, 2010); Elizabeth Eisenstein, *The Printing Revolution in Early Modern Europe* (New York: Cambridge University Press, 1983); R. A. Houston, *Literacy in Early Modern Europe: Culture and Education, 1500–1800* (New York: Longman, 1988); Julie Greer Johnson, *The Book in the Americas: The Role of Books and Printing in the Development of Culture and Society in Colonial Latin America* (Providence: John Carter Brown Library, 1988); Tessa Watt, *Cheap Print and Popular Piety, 1550–1640* (Cambridge: Cambridge University Press, 1991); Robert W. Scribner, *For the Sake of Simple Folk: Popular Propaganda for the German Reformation* (Oxford: Oxford University Press, 1994); María M. Portuondo, *Secret Science: Spanish Cosmography and the New World* (Chicago: University of Chicago Press, 2009).

seaborne wealth and a fearsome crew of enforcers. Yet, he could not silence a German monk who dared challenge his authority.

Fragmentation of the Empire of Charles V

Emperor Charles V claimed sovereignty over four million square miles of territory on three continents. When Charles abdicated in 1556, his titles and territories were divided between his brother and son. One got Austrian and German lands and became Holy Roman emperor. The other inherited claims to the Netherlands, the Italian Peninsula, Spain, and its New World territories. The son, Philip II (1527–1598), still ruled what was by many measures the strongest empire in Europe, but Philip overplayed his hand trying to tighten his control over the Netherlands. Consisting of seventeen distinct political entities covering today's Netherlands, Belgium, and Luxembourg, this was an economically and culturally diverse region, prosperous from commerce and manufacturing. Philip, seeking to finance the expansion of his empire and secure its unity, increased the tax burden on the Netherlands and worked to stamp out Protestantism. In 1567, Philip sent ten thousand troops in response to resistance, including vandalism of churches. Brutal suppression, including thousands of public executions, temporarily stalled the revolt, but ultimately the rulers of Spain could not control the Netherlands, which emerged independent in the 1580s.

Independence did not mean peace. Sporadic armed struggle continued between Spanish forces and those of the United Provinces of the Netherlands, part of a continent-wide conflict in the early seventeenth century known as the Thirty Years' War (1618–1648). This is often seen as a fight between the Roman Catholic south, led by Spain and the Holy Roman Empire, and the Protestant north, including many German states, led by the empire of Sweden. But the war had just as many political and economic aspects as religious ones. For example, France, under a Catholic sovereign, fought on the side of Protestant Sweden and the Netherlands; the Muslim Ottoman Empire made an alliance with the (Protestant) Christian prince of Transylvania. In Europe, as we had seen in other parts of the supercontinent, strategic and economic interests guided sixteenth- and seventeenth-century empire builders, complicating, and sometimes overriding, religious conflicts.

In 1648, the Peace of Westphalia ended the Thirty Years' War. The peace settlement attempted to address some of the root causes of conflict and establish some new grounds for relations between and among states. For example, the treaties established that religious difference alone could not justify war among Christian rulers and that religious practices within any state were the sole business of the ruler and not the rulers of other states. Reflecting new circumstances in

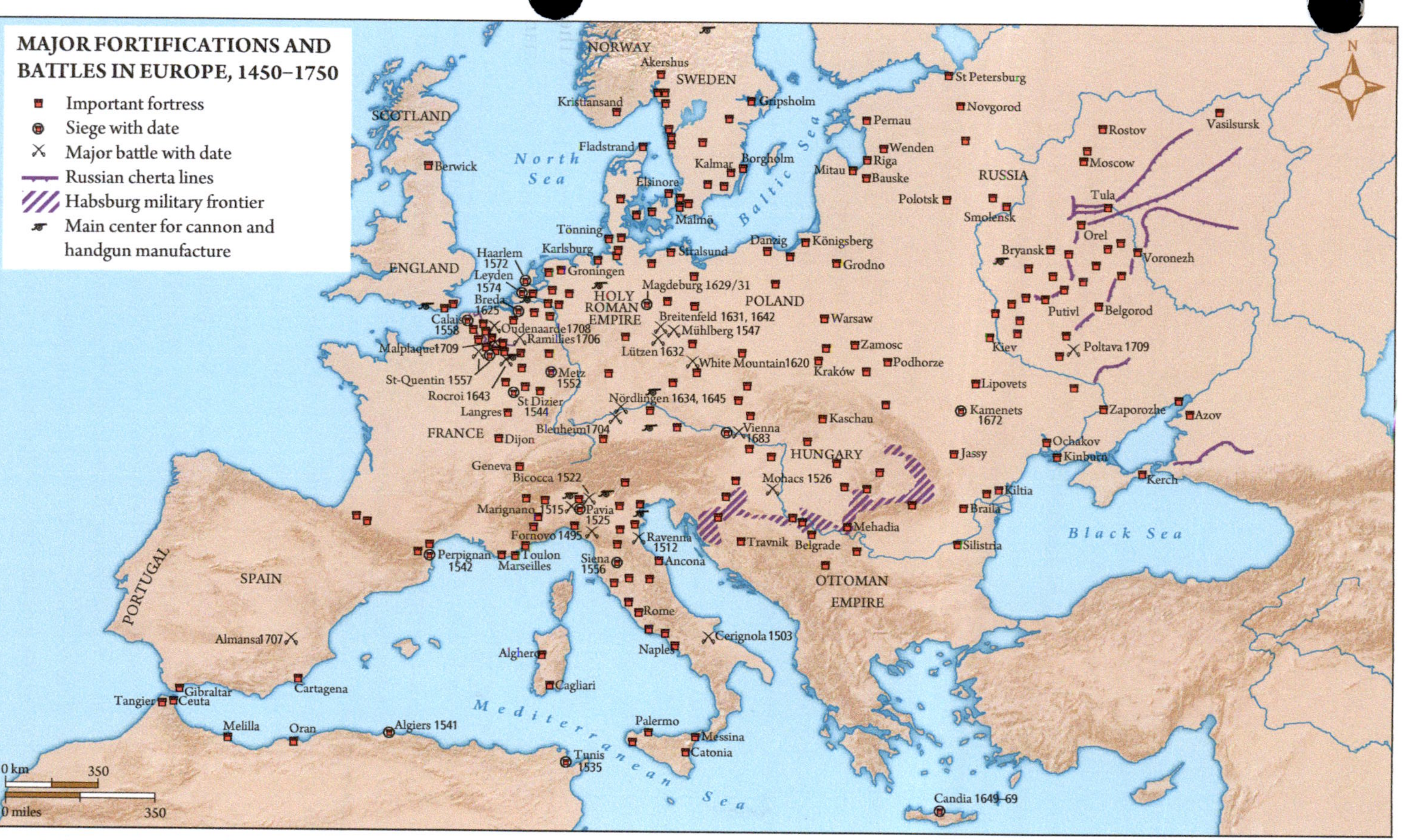

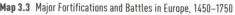

Map 3.3 Major Fortifications and Battles in Europe, 1450–1750

international relations, the pope played virtually no role in the peace settlement. The outcome of conflict within another Afro-Eurasian kingdom will further aid our understanding of political change during this era.

Civil War in England

Within the vast expanse of Afro-Eurasia, tiny England seems an unlikely place for a fundamental shift of political organization to have global repercussions. It appeared a small theater of the Wars of Religion in the mid-sixteenth century. Henry VIII (1491–1547) had established the Church of England when the pope refused to bend to Henry's wishes, but Henry's successor, Mary I (1516–1558), was Catholic and furthermore married Philip of Spain, making England an important ally to Spain's Catholic order. Catholic hopes for England were dashed, however, when Mary died and the English throne passed to Elizabeth I (1533–1603), a Protestant. Elizabeth sought to privilege the Church of England and Philip tried to resist, branding Elizabeth a heretic and seeking to replace her with her Catholic cousin (confusingly, also named Mary). Elizabeth in turn aided Protestant rebels in the Netherlands and even attacked Spanish shipping, demonstrating both England's naval power and the growing importance of maritime trade. When Elizabeth had her cousin Mary (who was already queen of the Scots) executed for plotting to take the throne in 1587, Philip launched his navy, known as the *Armada Invencible* (Invincible Fleet), to overthrow Elizabeth. Bad luck, bad strategy, and English tactics destroyed the Spanish fleet in 1588. Although Spain and England continued to fight for decades, the defeat of the armada opened the door for England's rise as a seafaring kingdom and Spain's decline, with consequences across the globe.

In the sixteenth century, commercial revolution and religious reformation transformed—and destabilized—Europe. Both had important political implications, but the nature and direction of political change were not clear. Across Europe, owning land was usually the basis of political power, so merchants and other non-noble classes could become rich but, unless they could acquire land, they had limited political power. At the same time, the most extensive landholder of all—the Roman Catholic Church—was fragmenting, leaving many of its resources to be redistributed and fought over. New political thought emerged in the struggle to make sense of this new era. As an island kingdom, England could not rely on contiguous overland expansion of wealth or sovereignty, but it could take advantage of the growing Atlantic maritime trade. Geography does not always determine the political development of states, but it is noteworthy that this kingdom whose borders were enforced by the sea would develop in theory and practice lasting and comprehensive limits on the powers of its monarchs.

During the first half of the seventeenth century, political tensions grew in England. The ruling Stuart dynasty did not wish to be constrained in its ability to levy taxes and raise an army. Opponents of the monarchs' assertion of greater power argued that English tradition gave a consultative body—the Parliament—an important role in these decisions. To complicate matters, some influential members of Parliament were also interested in transforming religious practices in England and saw the king as an obstacle to that. In 1642, this conflict erupted in civil wars that devastated England, Scotland, Wales, and Ireland (where as much as 40 percent of the population died as a result of the war). In 1649, parliamentary forces executed King Charles I (1600–1649) for treason and abolished the monarchy. For more than a decade, the country had no king and struggled to establish a sovereign state with internal and external legitimacy. Under pressure from an army invading from Scotland, in 1660 a beleaguered Parliament restored the monarchy and invited the son of the beheaded king to take the throne.

Thinking Anew about Sovereignty

In the shadow of the king's execution, Thomas Hobbes (1588–1679) published a book called *Leviathan*, subtitled *The Matter, Form and Power of a Commonwealth, Ecclesiastical and Civil.* Hobbes developed political theories that supported absolute government but argued that sovereign authority was based on the consent of the people and not on divine providence or natural order. Like Machiavelli, Hobbes wrote that a ruler was entitled to take extreme measures in defense of his power and his state but that these measures should serve the goal of a flourishing society—orderly and rich in culture—not the king's own interests or personal wealth. While acknowledging that people had to surrender many freedoms to a powerful sovereign—or suffer the "nasty, brutish, and short" life that plagued people in a state of nature without government—Hobbes also insisted that the legitimacy of the sovereign came from the consent of the governed in doing so, preserving for the people certain inalienable rights.

Hobbes was among the first to present a "social contract" theory of legitimacy. Later writers, especially John Locke (1632–1704) and Jean-Jacques Rousseau (1712–1778), would develop this idea in greater detail and draw some different conclusions, but the basic principles Hobbes suggested remained: in the state of nature (i.e., the time before society and government), people were perfectly free but also absolutely vulnerable. Everyone could do as they pleased, but—because of this—there was no security, no safety. The freedom of the state of nature was false; one was not even free to live in peace. In response, people could agree to give up some of their freedoms in exchange for security. Consider it this way:

by giving up the right to take anything I want, I surrender some freedom. In exchange, I gain security because others have also given up the right to take whatever *they* want. We agree to live in a society with a social contract. We designate certain people to make rules—laws—by which everyone agrees to live and others to enforce those laws, but only so long as they preserve the public peace and protect the public interest. Together these people—the government—preside over society in a way that benefits its members.

Hobbes's views troubled all sides in England's conflict and continued to vex future generations. On the one hand, he insisted that power to govern derived from the consent of the governed, angering those who argued that God, not the people, empower a ruler. On the other hand, he vested nearly limitless power in the state once it was formed, unsettling those wary of too powerful a sovereign. Nonetheless, his idea that a government's legitimacy comes from the people, and from its ability to protect the people's interests and well-being, ultimately emerged as the basis for many theories of the state in subsequent generations.

Collapse and Restoration of Empire in China

While Hobbes was contemplating Leviathan and war was brewing in England, war was also imminent on the eastern edge of the supercontinent where China's Ming dynasty, in power since 1368, faced financial and political crises on a scale that matched or exceeded that in Europe during the Wars of Religion. Indeed, it may be useful to think of China as akin to Europe because of its size and the diversity of languages, religions, and cultures found within territory claimed by China's imperial dynasties.

Like their counterparts around the world, Chinese rulers grappled with questions of legitimacy, authority, and sovereignty. Judaism, Christianity, and Islam all look to the God of the Hebrews as the Creator, so rulers across much of Afro-Eurasia had often used this idea of God (who was believed to speak to people directly through earthly prophets and holy texts) as a source of legitimacy. In China, however, this was not an option for political elites. A key difference was the lack, throughout most of East Asian history, of any anthropomorphic idea of God, and certainly not one who spoke directly to people. As far back as 1000 BCE, rulers in China had appealed to the Mandate of Heaven (*tianming*) to justify their rule. Like the European idea of divine right, this notion of legitimacy derived from a supernatural source, but in China, the well-being of the people indicated the holder of the mandate. If the people didn't prosper, the mandate could pass to another steward. This was not an idea like the *consent of the governed* constructed by Hobbes or other social contract theorists, but the suffering of the empire's subjects could indicate a ruler who had lost the mandate, a prelude to being swept away. A ruler didn't need the people's consent to rule, but he (and it was almost always he) did need to rule over them well to maintain his power.

From Ming to Qing

Within this framework, China developed a complex and sophisticated statecraft. The size and diversity of Chinese empires was a challenge even in good times, and natural or manmade disasters strained even the most capable of leaders. The Mongols, who had swept across most of Asia in the 1200s, established a sophisticated hierarchy and implemented some key financial innovations as part of their Yuan dynasty in China, yet could only maintain their dynasty for a century. That was when a peasant rebel named Zhu Yuanzhang (1328–1398) overthrew the Mongols and established the Ming dynasty. Under Ming rule, China prospered politically, economically, and culturally, expanding its borders in all directions and knitting society together with an intensive commercial network. The early Ming emperors oversaw a state based on Confucian precepts of loyalty, benevolence, and propriety. As we saw in Chapter 1, Ming ships sailed the Indian Ocean as far as the Middle East and East Africa, maintaining diplomatic and trade ties across the supercontinent.

By the late 1500s, however, the Ming state was in decline. Corruption at court and an inadequate tax structure undermined effective governance. Even the wars between Spain and England played a role: New World silver had been flowing into the Chinese economy, but English and Dutch raiders disrupted the supply. As the silver supply dwindled, its value increased. The Ming government required that taxes be paid in silver but did not mint it into coins. As a result, Chinese peasants conducted most of their daily business in copper coins—silver was too valuable to be practical for ordinary expenses—and had to buy silver to pay their taxes (the Chinese word for bank, *yinhang*, means literally "silver shop"). As silver became more valuable, more copper was needed to buy the same amount of silver, impoverishing the peasantry, dragging down the entire economy, and further reducing government revenues. Civil servants, including the military, were paid poorly, sometimes not at all. Public works projects, a traditional measure of a dynasty's effectiveness, were neglected. The Yellow River levees fell into disrepair; grain stored to ward off famine rotted. For a state with its legitimacy rooted in the well-being of its people, these were potent dangers. Several would-be rebels, including an unemployed post-station attendant named Li Zicheng (1606–1645), mobilized popular discontent against the Ming and initiated a rebellion in the 1630s.

Li and other rebellious peasants were not the only challenge facing the Ming. The Manchus—people who were distinct linguistically and culturally from China's Han majority—had built their own empire starting in the 1500s to the northeast, in a region (Manchuria) that is a part of China today bounded by

Russia and North Korea. Modeling their state largely on Chinese precedents, the Manchus expanded their territory until they were at the Ming's northern border. The Manchu Empire was more stable and prosperous than China under the failing Ming. In the spring of 1644 (the same era as the English Civil War, six thousand miles away), Manchu armies prepared to march on Beijing from the east, even as Li Zicheng's peasant army bore down on the capital from the west. The last Ming emperor hanged himself upon hearing the news. With a rebel army occupying the capital and Manchu soldiers on the doorstep, the Mandate of Heaven seemed about to pass, but to whom?

The Ming's top general, Wu Sangui (1612–1678), remained in a position to play kingmaker between the two sides. The Manchu regent and Wu Sangui exchanged letters. Wu asked the Manchus to help him fight Li Zicheng's rebels. Manchu leaders argued for their legitimacy using Chinese political logic: they would take up the Mandate of Heaven by restoring order to the empire and its people. Maybe Wu believed this; maybe his calculus was more cynical. Perhaps he thought the Manchus simply had the resources to win and he would benefit if he backed the right side. Whatever his reasons, Wu Sangui supported the Manchu claim to the throne, although his actions were not universally admired. Many Ming generals, officials, and subjects rallied against the Manchu as illegitimate usurpers. The Manchu conquest of China was bitter and bloody, taking decades to complete. Some Ming princes attempted to maintain governments in exile, and many Chinese scholars remained loyal to the Ming dynasty, some choosing suicide or exile rather than aiding the Qing.

Historians Explore The Qing Conquest

Debates over the Qing conquest provide a good example of the way scholarship evolves based on new sources and new political contexts. For decades, scholars contended that the Manchus conquered China militarily, but were themselves overwhelmed by Chinese cultural superiority and assimilated into Chinese culture. This view is shaped by traditional Chinese historiography that has viewed these *conquest dynasties* (i.e., dynasties led by non-Han rulers) as militarily capable but culturally weak. Confucian scholars wrote history, and these men—actively or unconsciously—were biased in favor of classical Chinese practices and attitudes. It was impossible to deny that non-Chinese peoples had conquered China, but they could argue that the ongoing and more valuable elements of Chinese culture outlasted these "uncivilized" invaders.

Recent scholarship, based largely on new sources, has challenged this view of the Qing. The Manchus employed Han Chinese scholars and officials alongside

Manchu ones, producing documents in both Chinese and Manchu (a language unrelated to Chinese and written in a completely different script). Few scholars, even in China, could read the Manchu documents, and many had assumed that the twin sets of correspondence were versions of the same information in different languages. Because few historians were reading Manchu (in part because few people believed it said anything new or interesting), this assumption went unquestioned.

Then, in the 1980s and 1990s, a movement called the New Qing History gathered momentum. More scholars began learning Manchu and looking at the records. What they found was that the Manchus retained aspects of their culture and identity for much longer than people had supposed. The Manchus did employ many aspects of Chinese statecraft, but that did not mean that they simply became Chinese. Similar to the way Habsburg monarchs ruled Germans and Slavs, or Catholics and Muslims, differently, or as the Ottomans preserved religious autonomy through the millet system, Qing monarchs presented their rule differently to different parts of the empire. To the Han Chinese—who wrote imperial history as part of their own tradition—they adopted the air of Han Chinese emperors. But in central Asia, or Tibet, or Manchuria, they behaved quite differently. And what of the "duplicate" correspondence written in Manchu and Chinese? Sometimes they were just translations for the use of non-Chinese speakers, but other times they were audits of Chinese officials or documents designed for direct use by the emperor and kept secret from the Chinese bureaucrats who could not read Manchu.

Other scholars downplay the importance of the Manchus to understanding early modern China. In their view, even if the Manchu language can reveal nuances of policy debates and decisions, hundreds of millions of Chinese during this period lived their lives with little direct influence from the imperial government—regardless of their ethnicity. And even if the Qing emperors presented themselves differently in Tibet or Mongolia, the great majority of the Qing Empire's population was Han Chinese. To this view, too much focus on the Manchus distorts the picture. The New Qing History is ongoing, a project involving thousands of scholars to move our knowledge forward based on further exploration of primary sources.[3]

---

[3] Prominent examples of the New Qing History include Pamela K. Crossley, *A Translucent Mirror* (Berkeley: University of California Press, 1999); Mark C. Elliott, *The Manchu Way* (Stanford, CA: Stanford University Press, 2001); Laura Hostetler, *Qing Colonial Enterprise* (Chicago: University of Chicago Press, 2001); James P. Millward, *Beyond the Pass* (Stanford, CA: Stanford University Press, 1998); and Evelyn S. Rawski, *The Last Emperors* (Berkeley: University of California Press, 1998).

How to Govern? "Seek Truth from Facts"

As they consolidated their rule, the Manchus, like other new governments, struggled to establish their legitimacy while they asserted their sovereignty. Although the Mandate of Heaven is an enduring idea, Chinese thinkers regularly revisited the foundations of imperial legitimacy. One of them, Gu Yanwu (1613–1682), looked at the collapsing Ming dynasty and blamed its weakness on its unreflective adherence to ancient ways. According to Gu, scholarly obsession with the writings of Confucius, who lived two thousand years prior to the rise of the Qing dynasty, or even his later interpreters like Zhu Xi (1130–1200), had led to an inefficient and impractical state. Although Gu refused to serve the new Manchu rulers, remaining loyal to the fallen Ming dynasty, he did seek ways for China to strengthen itself. Gu traveled and observed widely and wrote about what he saw during his travels, on subjects ranging from geography to statecraft. Gu urged people to understand and act based on rigorous analysis, convincing evidence, and clear reasoning to "seek truth from facts." To promote these ends, he wrote practical studies of mining, banking, farming, and government, insisting on natural explanations for phenomena, rejecting the metaphysical speculation common in much Ming scholarship, which he blamed for the Ming's decay. Gu's methods exemplified *inductive reasoning*, which leads to generalizations about the world based on observation.

Gu's emphasis on observation had parallels across the supercontinent at this time, part of a stream of changes to the ways humans perceived and understood the natural world. Observations about the cosmos accumulated across Afro-Eurasia. The Indian astronomer Nilakantha Somayaji (1444–1544) determined that the planets Mercury, Venus, and Mars orbited the sun, observations confirmed by the Danish astronomer Tycho Brahe (1546–1601). At about the same time, Galileo Galilei (1564–1642) and Johannes Kepler (1571–1630) built on work by Nicolaus Copernicus (1473–1543) to reimagine the earth's place in the solar system. These men, like Gu Yanwu, practiced inductive reasoning, a key part of what the Englishman Francis Bacon (1561–1626) called the scientific method.

Induction relies on observation and building conclusions from observed phenomena. Like *deductive reasoning*, it attempts to prove its conclusions based on premises, but there are differences. Deductive reasoning relies on premises devised in one's mind that would then be applied to the world, a process that, Bacon felt, limited understanding because it fitted observations into preexisting theories. Like Gu Yanwu, who praised observation and experimentation rather than abstract application of Confucian principles, Bacon suggested an understanding of the world that was based on what one perceived rather than on what one believed to be true.

Bacon's key work, *Novum Organum Scientiarum* (New Instrument of Science), depicted a vessel sailing out beyond the known waters to explore and understand the unknown. Symbolically, this represents his method, which he saw as enabling a more accurate and complete understanding of the world. His method was not entirely new—across Europe, China, India, and the Middle East, scholars were developing models based on experimentation—but Bacon's methods resonated strongly amid the upheaval in Europe at this time. Luther, remember, challenged received wisdom about the Bible and its interpretation by clergy alone. He advocated a "priesthood of all believers" who could read the Bible for themselves so that they could observe and draw conclusions. These ideas rippled through to the political order, suggesting that the legitimacy of government might be determined by observing its effects rather than deriving from abstract premises, and that political truths, as biblical truths, might be assessed by ordinary people.

Conclusion

Studying the past forces us to examine carefully things we misunderstand or take for granted about our own times. This certainly holds true for states. Understanding states lies at the heart of this chapter. Over the course of the sixteenth and seventeenth centuries, different states gained, wielded, and lost sovereignty and legitimacy as they acquired and lost material resources. Conflicts broke out as rivals for power tried to supplant or suppress each other, leading to new ways of claiming and establishing legitimacy. The ferment of this period dislodged some long-standing relationships and understandings of the world, creating both new opportunities and constraints in the world of politics. Yet no one could have predicted that several centuries later, the idea and practice of the nation-state—where state sovereignty aligns with the construction of certain kinds of equality of identity and consent of the governed—would become dominant. In fact, in many ways, Afro-Eurasia's hereditary empires appeared stronger at the end of the seventeenth century than they did at the beginning of the sixteenth century. After the upheaval of the civil war, monarchy was restored in England in 1660. China under the Qing, after the civil war surrounding the fall of the Ming, was as stable, prosperous, and expansive as any ruling dynasty in China had ever been.

In many ways, empire building under the constraints of the biological old regime reached its apogee in the late seventeenth century. States rose and fell, but the new global stakes created opportunities on a broader stage of action, changing the very idea of what a state and its rulers were and could be. Controlling ever greater resources came to be imperative for the survival of political systems in this new global game of empire. So it is worth asking, how did the global economy work during this era? We turn to this subject in Chapter 4.

A Few Good Books

Liam Matthew Brockey. *The Visitor: Andre Palmeiro and the Jesuits in Asia*. Cambridge, MA: Harvard University Press, 2014.

Jane Dunn. *Elizabeth and Mary: Cousins, Rivals, Queens*. New York: Vintage, 2007.

Lucien Febvre and Henri-Jean Martin. *The Coming of the Book: The Impact of Printing, 1450–1800*. 3rd ed. London: Verso, 2010.

Steven Ozment. *The Serpent and the Lamb. Cranach, Luther and the Making of the Reformation*. New Haven, CT: Yale University Press, 2012.

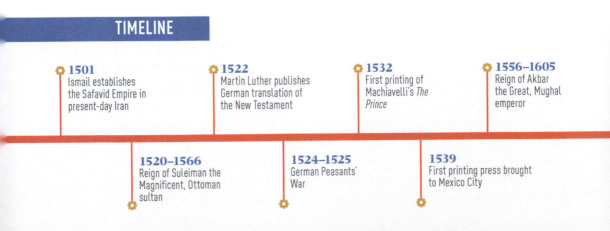

TIMELINE

1501
Ismail establishes the Safavid Empire in present-day Iran

1520–1566
Reign of Suleiman the Magnificent, Ottoman sultan

1522
Martin Luther publishes German translation of the New Testament

1524–1525
German Peasants' War

1532
First printing of Machiavelli's *The Prince*

1539
First printing press brought to Mexico City

1556–1605
Reign of Akbar the Great, Mughal emperor

María M. Portuondo. *Secret Science: Spanish Cosmography and the New World*. Chicago: University of Chicago Press, 2009.

Diane Purkiss. *The English Civil War: Papists, Gentlewomen, Soldiers, and Witchfinders in the Birth of Modern Britain*. New York: Basic Books, 2007.

Sarah Schneewind. *A Tale of Two Melons: Emperor and Subject in Ming China*. Indianapolis: Hackett, 2006.

Douglas Streusand. *The Islamic Gunpowder Empires: Ottomans, Safavids, and Mughals*. Boulder, CO: Westview Press, 2010.

For instructional resources and study aids, please go to ***www.oup.com/us/carter****.* *For primary sources connected to this chapter, please see the table of contents for* Sources for Forging the Modern World *included at the back of the book.*

1601
Matteo Ricci receives permission to enter the Ming capital of Beijing

1613–1682
Life of Gu Yanwu, Chinese scholar of political order

1620
Novum Organum by Francis Bacon

1644
Last Ming emperor commits suicide; Qing dynasty begins reign over China

1649
Charles I executed for treason, England

1651
Thomas Hobbes publishes *Leviathan*

1661
The Kangxi emperor assumes throne of Qing dynasty

(TOP) Silver Mining at Potosí. This painting, ca. 1585 by an anonymous artist, provides one of the earliest visual records of the silver industry at Potosí. In the background, one can see miners and pack animals ascending the Cerro Rico to the mines. The refining works and counting house are in the foreground.

(RIGHT) Indian Calico. Brightly colored cotton cloth imported from India, calico became popular in Europe in the seventeenth century. Trying to protect domestic textile manufacturers, the English Parliament banned calico imports in the early eighteenth century. The fabrics take their name from the city of Calicut, where they were first manufactured (see page 106).

CHAPTER 4

Production and Consumption in the First Global Economy

1571–1700

More than twelve thousand feet high in the Peruvian Andes, the village of Huancavelica was a small agricultural community in the sixteenth century. Although the arrival of Spaniards in the Inca Empire in the 1530s disrupted many aspects of Andean life, decades later the few thousand indigenous inhabitants of Huancavelica and its surrounding areas still mostly farmed and herded in ways that would have been familiar to their ancestors. In the hills surrounding the village, however, a key to unlocking the tremendous mineral wealth of the Andes would soon help transform both the local and the global economies. In 1571, just outside Huancavelica, Spanish colonizers began mining mercury—also called quicksilver—a highly toxic metal that flowed as liquid through the veins of the earth. The use of mercury in the silver refining process permitted the extraction of more silver from lower-quality ore. The fortuitous proximity of abundant mercury supplies to silver ore, coupled with a Spanish imperial policy that focused on providing a steady labor supply to the mines, fueled a surge in production. Soon, Potosí produced much of the world's silver. The subsequent discovery of rich silver deposits elsewhere in Spanish America, also refined with mercury, further increased the global silver supply.

In 1700, the British Parliament passed legislation designed to curtail the use of Asian textiles in England. In passing this law, legislators were especially concerned with rising demand for the cloth from India known as calico. This fabric was less expensive, more comfortable, and considered by many more beautiful and of higher quality than anything produced in Britain. Surging imports of Asian textiles in the seventeenth century had triggered a crisis for the British textile industry, pressed

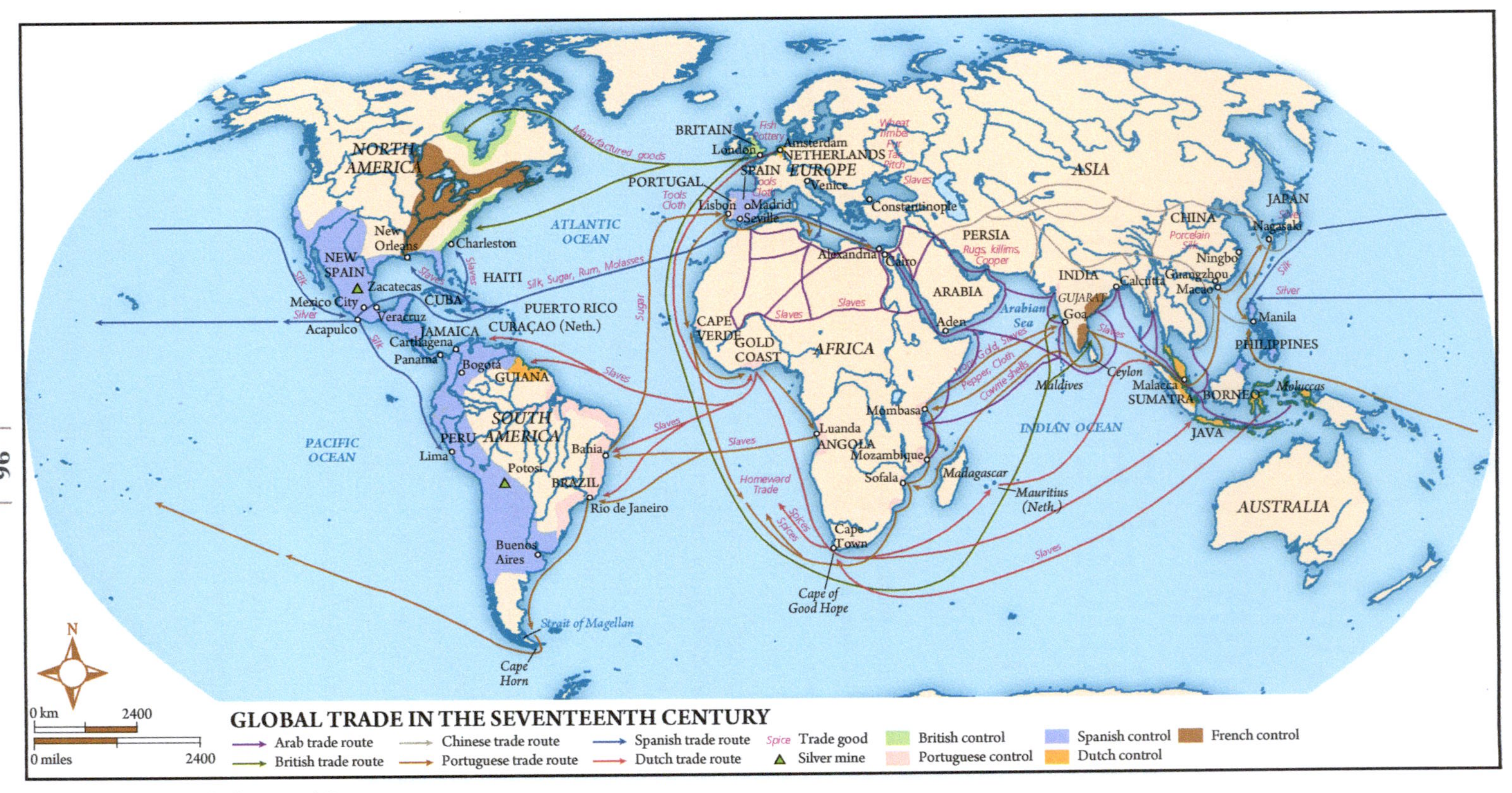

Map 4.1 Global Trade in the Seventeenth Century

to compete with the higher-quality, lower-cost imports. Under pressure from wool producers, legislators passed this law, which banned the use in England of most calico, while permitting its re-export to the rest of the British Empire. The results were mixed, as a market in contraband cloth thrived. Prompted by ongoing pressure, including riots by local weavers, additional legislation over the next two decades culminated with the Calico Act of 1721, which attempted to ban entirely the use of calicoes in clothing and household goods. Despite these measures, Britain's textile industry continued to struggle to match that of India.

These two cases illustrate the unpredictable outcomes that accompanied the emergence of a global economy. In this chapter, we explain in greater detail the production, distribution, and consumption of material resources during this era. We will pay particular attention to both changes resulting from globalization and the enduring realities of a world where some key factors in economic life changed little despite increasing interconnectedness.

In the first section of this chapter, we survey the nature of the world's agricultural economies; we then turn to manufactured goods, made in a wide variety of work settings. With mass production still in the future, most commodities (anything that can be exchanged in a marketplace, including food) were produced and distributed locally. In contrast, some goods, such as fine ceramics, quality textiles, firearms, silver, and some agricultural commodities, such as spices, tea, coffee, and sugar, were used far from where they originated. After discussing these fundamental aspects of production and consumption in the early modern world, we end the chapter with an analysis of the ways in which political leaders attempted to manage their relationships to a new and volatile global economy.

Questions to Consider as You Read Chapter Four:

1. The supply of silver and gold in the world expanded dramatically in the sixteenth century. What role does this play in the early modern global economy? Why?
2. In the stories in the introduction to this chapter, the Spanish and British governments tried to push economic activity in particular directions. What were the crucial assumptions that different rulers made about the way the global economy worked during this era? How did this influence their actions?

Agricultural Production

In the early 1500s, about 80 percent of the world's population tilled the soil or tended livestock to feed their families and passed some part of their production on as taxes to political, military, and religious authorities. Rural, agrarian peoples produced and distributed their bounty in diverse ways, often relying on long-standing traditions that governed their work. At the same time, multiple disruptions roiled rural life during this era. The Columbian exchange affected every aspect of what people around the world grew and ate. The increase in the enslavement and forced migration of Africans to work in tropical agricultural production also transformed economies, cultures, societies, and politics across the entire world.

Staple Foods

Most agricultural products were consumed very close to where they were grown. If they grew enough, rural producers exchanged some of their surplus for tools, beasts of burden, and maybe even some luxuries produced in distant locations. Beyond these broad brushstrokes, sweeping claims about how the agricultural sector worked unravel quickly, even within a single empire. Local judicial and religious conventions, access to markets, community practices, and even the characteristics of the land itself make it nearly impossible to generalize. Allowing for this immense local variety, let us suggest some ideas about what life was like for most of the world's rural peoples in the sixteenth and seventeenth centuries. First, the idea of individual ownership of land would have made no sense to most agricultural laborers. People often had a close personal relationship to the land they lived on and worked, but that relationship was not about their ability to do whatever they wished with a specific piece of the planet, whether to buy it, sell it, or change the way they used it. They would apply the same logic to the claims that anyone else had to the land, even elites. A web of political, cultural, and religious relationships influenced decisions about how to use land. The term *peasant* usually refers to those rural commoners who worked according to terms that granted them access to land for agricultural production and often other rights (e.g., hunting, gathering wood, grazing) but did not necessarily grant them the rights to sell the land, inherit it, or divide it among their heirs. Serfs were bound to the land they worked and by law or tradition were unable to relocate or change jobs.

Rural elites—those who controlled the land but did not work it directly—balanced prestige, political power, and religious obligation against risk, potential profit, and other economic calculations. The same was true for the rural common folk who produced staple foods not only for themselves and their political, religious, and ethnic overlords, but also for a broader marketplace. Although they rarely owned land outright, agrarian workers still made decisions about what they produced and participated in markets for both goods and labor. In the vast Chinese Empire, where ownership of land was widespread relative to other regions, approximately 80 percent of the population lived within one day's journey of a market town where they could sell their produce. Similar opportunities existed in many parts of the world. A robust market for rice existed throughout Southeast Asia, with thousands of tons of grain shipped through major port cities each year. In Spanish America, indigenous villagers' collective claims to agricultural land existed alongside—and conflicted with—large agricultural enterprises that focused primarily on production for urban markets. Many rural people with access to communal lands still performed wage labor for others at least part of the year.

It is tempting to think of explorers, merchants, generals, and kings as agents who move history forward, while rural common folk resist, clinging to traditional ways of life as long as possible. The diverse and dynamic patterns of early modern agricultural life underscore that this is not true. In the Russian Empire, for example, serfdom—legally binding rural workers to the land they tilled—expanded in the seventeenth century by imperial decree, but so did resistance to the tsar's new agricultural labor laws. Most rural populations across western and central Europe had witnessed the demise of serfdom long before, but these regions also experienced repeated and violent confrontations between commoners and the authorities over their own changing rural relationships, like what land was available to them and how taxes were levied and paid. As we saw with the German Peasants' War in Chapter 3, rural peoples might even use revolutionary ideas and methods while at the same time claiming a desire to restore tradition.

Changing Foodways around the Globe

Over time, the new global interface spurred economic changes for rural peoples as much as for merchants and rulers. Indigenous peoples of the Americas faced challenges to their ways of life from European settlers who brought competing notions of property, spatial organization, and agricultural production. European conquerors discouraged cultivation of some common indigenous staple foods (like amaranth, a starchy grain that had been cultivated in the Americas for millennia) because of associations with pre-conquest religious practices. New domestic animals, including pigs, sheep, and cows, degraded the environment, simultaneously increasing the supply of animal protein and diminishing the overall supply of food directly available for human consumption. The introduction of wheat, rice, and other staple Afro-Eurasian food crops remade the diets of both immigrants and indigenous peoples of the Americas.

Conversely, Western Hemisphere crops that spread to other parts of the world became essential to the diet of Afro-Eurasian peoples. We've already mentioned tomatoes in Italy, but "Irish" potatoes and "Thai" chili peppers are also imports from the Americas. The potato, brought to Europe from South America, became the primary staple to allay hunger and enable population growth across northern Europe from Ireland to Russia. In China, American crops like sweet potatoes, maize, chili peppers, and others enhanced the diet, provided staple crops for regions where rice and wheat did not thrive, and helped the empire's population grow and spread.

Western Hemisphere transplants also changed the food landscape of Africa. Maize entered Africa from all directions. It was already established in West Africa by 1540, where in addition to meeting local demand, it was exported to feed transatlantic maritime traffic. People in parts of East Africa associated maize with Muslims who brought kernels back from their pilgrimage to Mecca. In South Africa, Portuguese traders planted maize to provision their ships; residents of the southeast coast believed maize to have originated in India. African port cities cultivated the grain, along with chickpeas and other crops, to sell to vessels sailing the long-distance routes from East Asia across the Indian Ocean and around the Cape of Good Hope to western Europe.

While staple crops were sometimes traded in long-distance commerce, most of the agricultural products that traversed the globe were luxury items that had higher value relative to their weight. Spices like pepper, cloves, nutmeg, and mace remained coveted rarities. Trade brought American crops like cacao (from which chocolate is made) and vanilla, African and Arabian coffee, and Asian tea to places where they could not be produced. Coffee, tea, and chocolate all first arrived in Europe around 1650, illustrating increased global commerce as well as the growing disposable income of some portion of the world's population, mostly in urban commercial centers. By the eighteenth century, coffee and tea houses in cities like Amsterdam, London, and Paris became places to socialize and exchange information about business—ship arrivals, supply and demand for various commodities, who needed a loan, and who had money to lend. The search for new ways to produce and distribute such luxury goods led to a significant expansion of the sugar–slave plantation system in the seventeenth century.

The Sugar–Slave Plantation System

Sugar cane is picky. It requires substantial water and average daily temperatures around 80 degrees Fahrenheit to thrive. Planting and especially harvesting are labor and fuel intensive. Until 1500, much of the world's sugar was produced in the Arab world, where prisoners of war often worked the cane fields. Sovereigns and merchants regulated its supply to other parts of the world. As a result, we need to think of sugar prior to 1500 as a spice—perhaps of great abundance (at least to the wealthy) in one part of the world, but a costly thing and generally in short supply in others. When the Columbian exchange brought together this plant indigenous to New Guinea, American land, African labor, and European capital, the relationship between humans and sugar changed. As a result, the global supply of sugar exploded; some men grew rich, but many more were enslaved.

The Caribbean islands did not have the spices Columbus had been seeking, but parts of the Americas did have the climate needed to grow sugar. By 1600, northeastern Brazil, controlled by the Portuguese, was the largest sugar producer in the world. At first, indigenous peoples did much of the work, but disease and harsh treatment depleted this labor force within decades. Over the course of the seventeenth century, the Brazilian sugar industry grew as a destination for enslaved Africans. Spanish, French, and British producers in the Caribbean soon competed against their Portuguese counterparts.

Sugar production on the Caribbean islands grew after the mid-seventeenth century. In British Barbados, for example, the enslaved population increased almost seven times over between 1645 and 1680, by which time almost forty thousand slaves worked 350 sugar estates and produced eight thousand tons of sugar annually. Over time, competing empires attempted to incorporate sugar production, along with as many other activities as they could, within self-contained imperial economic circuits. Control of sugar-producing areas and the slave trade therefore featured in war strategies and treaty negotiations, as in the Treaty of Ryswick (1697), which ceded control of the western part of the island of Hispaniola to the French. The French considered Saint-Domingue, as they called this part of the island, the economic jewel of their overseas empire. As such, it became one of the most productive, brutal slave regimes in the world. Over time, the use of enslaved Africans expanded in other sectors of the economy as well, including mining, crafts production, and domestic labor.

In Africa, the growth of the international slave trade made some men rich and powerful, while undermining the continent's economic productivity overall. Imported firearms became one of the principal commodities purchased on the African side of the slave exchange; those individuals and states that participated in the trade accumulated weapons and other wealth, which disrupted existing relationships of production and power. In addition, we must remember that the primary form of productive energy in the early modern world was human labor. The slave trade removed much of the continent's productive population from the local economy, forcing them to produce wealth for others. In the next chapter, we will investigate further the changes that ensued as the slave trade accelerated through the eighteenth century.

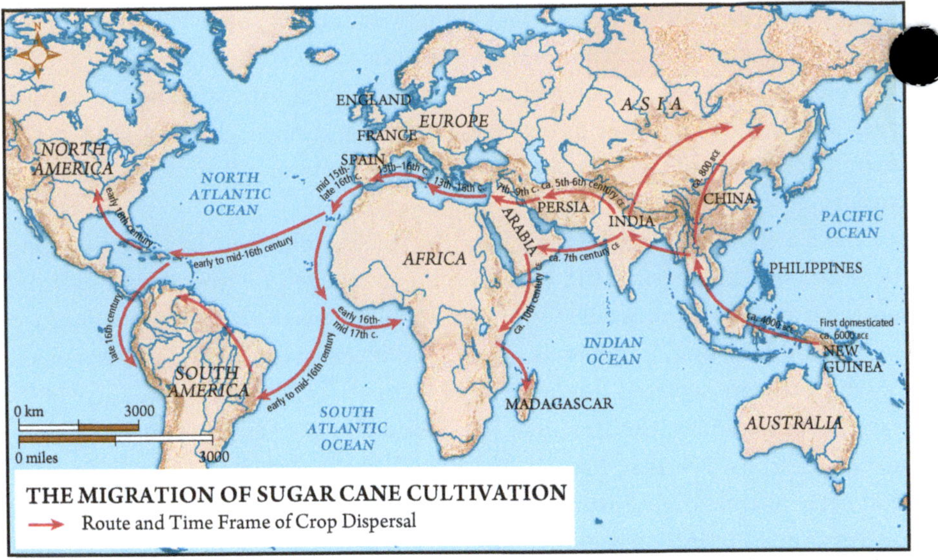

Map 4.2 The Migration of Sugar Cane Cultivation

Enslaved Africans and Early Plantation Society

As historians struggle to understand this overwhelming phenomenon, one of the major threads that ties recent investigations together is an increasing focus on the African perspective itself, from the role of African political elites in shaping the slave trade at its geographic origins to strategies of resistance and self-manumission. None of these studies diminishes the horrible reality of the practice—the unnecessary deaths of millions caught up in the trade, the daily cruelty inflicted on those who survived the passage from Africa, and the denial of the fundamental humanity of millions of people over the course of centuries.

Historians struggle to convey what it was like to be enslaved on a sugar plantation in the seventeenth century. First, we must dispose of the idea of a sugar plantation as just a big farm. The Portuguese word for sugar plantation was *engenho* (factory), a good way for us to think of these agroindustrial production facilities. Enslaved Africans did hard labor, suffering routine abuse, for many hours a day. Sugar cane takes up to eighteen months to mature, but the same field can then yield a new crop in nine months without replanting. Harvesting a single crop could take six months of nonstop activity. Working a sugar plantation was some of the most difficult work a human could do, both because of its location—the low-lying, often marshy, fields were exposed to relentless sun, heat, and insects—and because of the nature of the field work. In addition to planting and fertilizing the cane with manure, enslaved Africans used machetes to hack the cane stalks, which are similar to bamboo in diameter (about two to three

Sugar Mill, French West Indies. This illustration, from a late seventeenth-century history of the Caribbean, identifies the various phases of sugar production. Fortunes were made and lost in the sugar business, as mass production on plantations like this transformed the global sugar supply. Plantation work was dangerous and difficult, built on the enslaved labor that sustained the sugar economy.

inches per stalk). Once they had cut the cane, laborers (mostly enslaved, but in some cases free) loaded it on carts and hauled it to the on-site refinery, where other workers crushed, cleaned, boiled, and cooled the final product. The most physically demanding work was assigned to adult men, while women and those too young or too old to work the fields were given other jobs like cleaning equipment or keeping pests from damaging the crops.

Discovering more about the lives of enslaved Africans in the Americas is especially challenging because most of the sources commonly used by historians were generated by slave traders and slave owners, who viewed enslaved people as commodities to be bought and sold. The records they kept reflect this view of people as property: detailed records exist about the transportation of enslaved Africans from the African coast—where African slave traders dealt with European ones—to their arrival and sale to plantation owners in the Americas. As for slave life on plantations, most records were generated by slave owners rather than those enslaved. Some records written by the enslaved exist, but many slaves were not literate or not permitted to write. The sources that do exist are rich; additional evidence helps to paint a fuller picture. Some researchers have even studied the physical remains of enslaved peoples from Caribbean plantations. Physical anthropologist Kristrina Shuler, working in a cemetery in Barbados, found a high death rate from infectious diseases like measles, leprosy, tuberculosis, and dysentery. Skeletons showed evidence of injuries to limbs—apparently caused by machetes—and accompanying infections. The average life expectancy at birth for enslaved Africans in this sample was about eighteen years.[1] Other sources suggest that the average life expectancy for an enslaved laborer was about seven to nine years after arriving on a plantation.

Global Trade Networks

The plantation–slave system is one illustration of the new global economy, but it is by no means the only one. A blue-and-white ceramic jar that now sits in the Philadelphia Museum of Art can also tell us about changing patterns of production, consumption, and exchange. At first glance, it reminds many people of a Chinese object, because of its design and color pattern. Ming dynasty ceramics were the most advanced and coveted in the early modern world (the reason the word *china* became synonymous with fine ceramics in English). But the jar is not from China at all; it was produced in the city of Puebla (in present-day Mexico) around the year 1650. The potter, trained in a Spanish style of ceramic making, used local materials and added a variety of Iberian design motifs (including some from the Islamic tradition) to the obvious influence of Ming ceramics.

Jar with Handles, Puebla (Mexico), Early Seventeenth Century. Attributed to the potter Damián Hernández. With Chinese, Italian, Spanish, and Islamic influences, this ceramic object, discussed in the text, shows the rich and complex commercial and cultural ties connecting Asia, Europe, and the Americas in the early modern world.

How can we explain this seventeenth-century combination of Spanish technique, Mexican

1 Kristrina A. Shuler, "Life and Death on a Barbadian Sugar Plantation: Historic and Bioarchaeological Views of Infection and Mortality at Newton Plantation," *International Journal of Osteoarchaeology* 21 (2011): 66–81.

materials, and Chinese aesthetics? Puebla was one of Spanish America's largest centers of textile and ceramic production. Its prosperity was tied closely to the global economy. Precious metals from New Spain were exported not only to Europe, but also to China, the largest market for American silver. This jar shows that the exchange was more than just American silver for Chinese manufactured goods. Ideas, goods, and manufacturing techniques flowed in all directions across the globe.

Supply and Demand for Manufactured Goods

The story of ceramics helps us to understand the importance of maintaining a global perspective on economic developments in this era. Direct trade between Asia and Spanish America began in the 1570s. This Manila galleon system, named for the type of ship and its destination, moved a breathtaking volume of silks, porcelain, ivory, pearls, and furniture despite legal limitations on trade imposed by the Spanish Crown. Most of these goods remained in Spanish America, distributed throughout the region and paid for with shipments of silver and cochineal, a brilliant red dye made from an insect reliant on a specific variety of Mexican cactus. The growth of manufacturing in Puebla for local consumption was one indication that the empire's economic dynamism resided outside of Spain itself. Much of the wealth generated never found its way to the imperial center.

In the Portuguese Empire, the Brazilian cities of Salvador and Rio de Janeiro were ports of call on both ends of a commercial circuit that linked Lisbon to Goa, Malacca, and Macau. Millions of Chinese porcelain objects were sold in Brazil between the sixteenth and nineteenth centuries. Consumers in all European empires coveted ceramics produced in China, Korea, and Japan. In the seventeenth century, potters in other places tried to compete with Chinese ceramics, leading to distinctive cultural hybrids like the Puebla vase in the Philadelphia Museum of Art. Imitating Ming ceramics was a growing industry in the seventeenth century. In and around the city of Delft in the Netherlands, just as in New Spain, a robust industry developed to produce ceramics for Dutch consumers who desired, but could not afford, true Chinese porcelains. Like seventeenth-century Puebla pottery, Delftware of the same vintage is now coveted in its own right by museums and private collectors. However, although European porcelain manufacturers often imitated design and color, they could not compete with Chinese technical and aesthetic standards.

No single state had the political, military, or economic power to dominate global manufacturing or trade during this era. Ships flying the French, Dutch, and British flags challenged, and then supplanted, Spain and Portugal in trade with the Americas and they increasingly competed to move goods within Asia and between Asia and Europe. There, they alternately cooperated with and

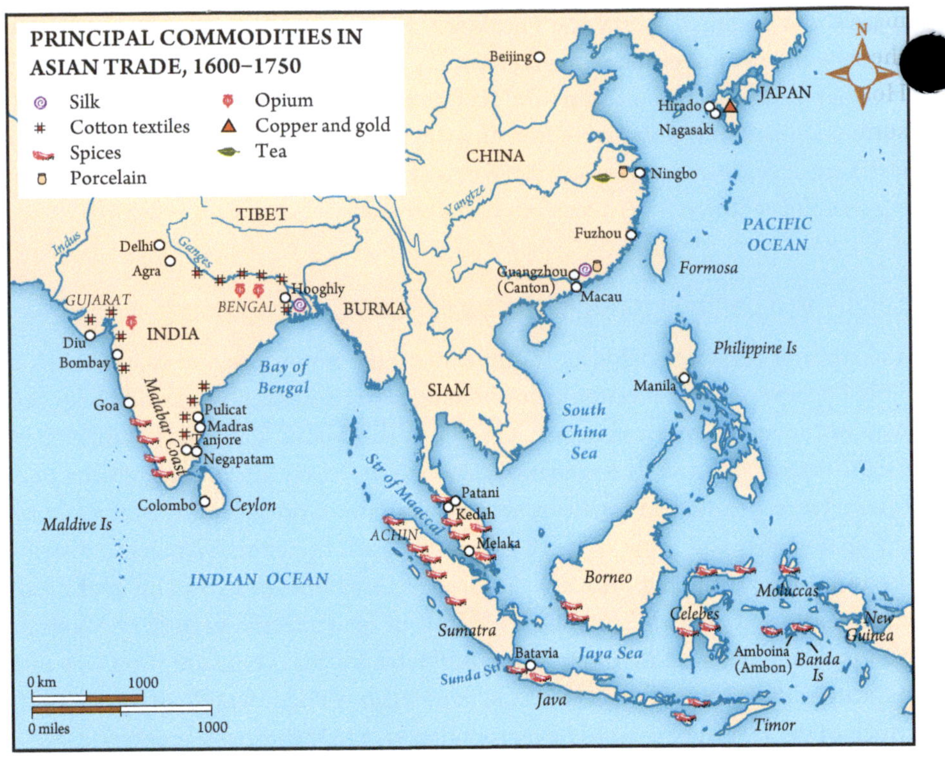

Map 4.3 Principal Commodities in Asian Trade, 1600–1750

fought against Islamic, ethnic Chinese, and other regional merchant groups for access to those lucrative markets. You are probably already familiar with the idea that the search for spices motivated these European sojourns into Asia. Pepper, cinnamon, and other spices unique to this part of the world were extraordinarily valuable and—like sugar—became precious additions to European tables. We have now introduced the idea that much of the global trade in manufactured goods from the sixteenth through the eighteenth centuries also revolved around products made in Asia. What exactly did European merchants exchange for these commodities? To answer this question, in the following sections we will discuss the role that textiles and silver played in driving global trade.

The Textile Trade

Textiles, the most important manufactured items traded in the early modern global marketplace, can tell us more about the relationships between trade, place, and power. The textiles most in demand in the global market at this time were manufactured in India. European merchants learned that to trade for spices in the islands of the South China Sea, they needed to bring Indian cotton cloth. How was India able to produce high-quality textiles at a reasonable cost to consumers in distant places? Indian workers had the flexibility to move from place to place in search of better conditions or wages. Merchants had sophisticated means of finance and distribution at their disposal. Combined with a productive agriculture sector that supplied high-quality raw materials, the Indian textile industry produced goods of a quality and price for the Asian market that other manufacturers could not match. As a result, some historians estimate that India had the world's most productive economy during this era.

Europeans did not create Asian trade networks, but they joined and helped to expand them. European outposts in Asia—notably Goa, Malacca, and Batavia—were different from European settlements in most of the Americas. These Asian settlements were primarily ports through which negotiations could be conducted with indigenous merchant networks and political systems, not the steppingstones for vast claims of sovereignty over land and people more typical in the Americas. Robust trade continued within Islamic trade networks from Anatolia through Southeast Asia and across the religious divide between Islamic and Christian networks in the Mediterranean world. The Dutch East India Company, for example, brought cloth from India to Southeast Asia and rice from Siam to Taiwan, moving with other merchants along existing trade routes. Only when the timing was right, enabled by the twice-yearly shift in the monsoon winds, did Dutch ships return to Europe, laden with spices and other luxuries for the European market. Over time, European merchants began to seek textiles from South Asia not only because they were trying to trade them for spices and other agricultural goods but also to bring them back for sale in Europe.[2] Demand in Europe and the Americas for silks and calicoes skyrocketed in the seventeenth century. The most valuable commodity that left European sources in exchange for all these Asian goods was silver.

Silver and the Global Economy

The Spanish Conquest of the Americas did not affect the global silver supply immediately. Far from the front lines of the Spanish assault on the Aztec and Inca, Japanese silver production experienced a boom in the sixteenth century. Japan was the most important source of silver imports in China through the

[2] On this topic see, for example, numerous articles in Giorgio Riello and Tirthankar Roy, eds., *How India Clothed the World: The World of South Asian Textiles, 1500–1850* (Leiden, the Netherlands: Brill, 2009), especially contributions by Anthony Reid, Om Prakash, and Ian Wendt. Also, Robert Parthesius, *Dutch Ships in Tropical Waters: The Development of the Dutch East India Company (VOC) Shipping Network in Asia 1595–1660* (Amsterdam: University of Amsterdam Press, 2010).

1570s, when American silver began to arrive via Manila. Spanish conquistadors spent substantial time looking for precious metals in the Americas, and what they ultimately found surpassed their wildest expectations. The transfer of mineral wealth from the Americas into the global economy was profoundly important to the history of the modern world, but we can only understand how if we view this new source of wealth in context.

Silver and gold had long been valued across the globe, and of course the mines of the Americas were not the world's only source of silver. In addition to the Japanese industry noted previously, European silver production had grown significantly prior to the discovery of the vast American reserves. This was the source of wealth for some of the most successful commercial enterprises in Europe, but an increased silver supply also led to inflation that caused popular unrest in parts of Europe in the early sixteenth century.

Understanding where silver went helps illustrate the global trade networks and interconnections that are so vital to this period, but how do we know what became of all that silver? Here, too, researchers have used innovative methods to understand the past. Using the knowledge that silver from different sources carries a unique chemical signature, researchers can analyze objects made from silver to determine the original sources of the metal, even when silver from different sources is mixed together. These chemical signatures tell us that English coins from 1550 to 1650 contain significant amounts of silver from Mexico and Europe but almost none from Potosí. And coins minted in Spain during the early seventeenth century contain virtually no American silver. This tells us several important things about silver generally and about American silver in particular. First, it tells us that one important use of silver was as coin. Second, it tells us that American silver at this time did not stay in Spain to be minted into coin by the Spanish Crown (in the eighteenth century, because of changes in imperial policies, more American silver did make it into Spanish coins). Overall, approximately 20 percent of American silver wealth remained in the Western Hemisphere; 10 percent went directly to Asia; and perhaps 15 percent leaked to pirates and smugglers. Most of the rest moved through Spain quickly, often to pay off imperial loans or to bear the costs of imperial armies fighting elsewhere in Europe. Chinese demand for silver drew much of the world's supply there. Japanese rulers in this era, in addition to asserting more direct government control over foreign trade as we have already described, implemented currency systems based on silver as a tactic designed to strengthen their regime.[3]

3 Anne-Marie Desaulty and Francis Albarede, "Copper, Lead, and Silver Isotopes Solve a Major Economic Conundrum of Tudor and Early Stuart Europe," *Geology* 41, no. 2 (February 2013): 135–138; Dennis O. Flynn and Arturo Giráldez, "Cycles of Silver: Global Economic Unity through the Mid-Eighteenth Century," *Journal of World History* 13, no. 2 (Fall 2002): 391–427.

Historians Explore Silver Mining in Spanish America

Given the importance of silver to this era, it should be no surprise that historians have worked hard to understand the local and global effects of its production and distribution. The American silver industry did not spring up immediately with the arrival of Europeans. At first, Europeans simply took the silver stock of indigenous societies; over time, this gave way to a more complex plan to extract the hemisphere's silver from the earth itself. This required a labor force as well as raw materials and other inputs: tools, timber for support beams for the mines, leather to make sacks for ore, and animals to haul them. Food for the populations of the silver mining regions also had to be produced and distributed. The two most important silver mining sites in the Western Hemisphere—one in the central Andes and the other in today's Mexico—had different human and natural resource bases, but both followed the same general pattern of a dramatic increase in production during the first century of European control followed by a stagnation of production after 1650.

Potosí, the most famous and productive silver city in the Americas, lies high in the Andes Mountains of what is today Bolivia. It is one of the highest human settlements in the world, at twice the altitude of Denver, Colorado. Spaniards first tapped into its veins in 1545. By the end of the 1560s, the richest ore and local fuel sources for ore-smelting furnaces began to run out. Just twenty years after Europeans began exploiting Potosí's silver, it seemed poised to decline.

Producing precious metals in the Americas was vital to the Spanish Crown, which claimed a monopoly on the output of some mines and claimed a tax of 20 percent—the *quinto* or "royal fifth"—on all precious metals produced in the empire. Enormous revenue was at stake if the mines closed, so the Spanish tried to revive them. Supported by the Crown, mine operators in the Andes changed the production process with profound repercussions for the local population and for world history. The first change was a new technique to extract silver from a toxic sludge of crushed ore, mercury, copper sulfate, and water. Using a newly discovered, local source of mercury at Huancavelica, silver production in Peru grew to over three thousand tons per year in the 1590s. The new production process also left a legacy of poisonous mercury runoff in the local environment that survives to this day.

The second change involved the labor working the mines. To maximize profits, mine operators were unwilling to pay wages sufficient to attract enough free laborers, so the colonial state helped them with the force of law. The government imposed a labor tax, called the *mita*, on the indigenous villages of the Andes. Systems like this (called corvée) in which a tax was assessed, not in cash or goods, but in labor, were common in the early modern world and remain so in some societies.

Under the mita system, more than eleven thousand indigenous workers from the Andean highlands were forced into the mines and refineries. This forced labor impoverished local communities to enrich mine operators and landowners, with lasting consequences for colonial society. Even as the costs of other factors of production increased and ore quality decreased, cheap labor enabled mine owners to continue squeezing a profit. Some indigenous people chose to avoid the onerous—often deadly—labor obligations by migrating, making the painful decision to permanently leave their communities. Others made cash payments to mine operators who could use the money to hire workers or simply keep the profit. As the city's silver production skyrocketed, so did its population, exceeding 150,000 by 1610. By the mid-seventeenth century, Potosí was one of the world's largest cities, about the same size as the Dutch capital, Amsterdam.

Other parts of Spanish America relied on different systems, using indigenous communal labor, enslaved Africans, indentured workers, and free labor. Between 1550 and 1650, these workers produced three hundred thousand tons of silver, dwarfing the production of the rest of the world combined. New Spain over the long run produced even more silver than Peru. From the beginning of the sixteenth century to the end of the eighteenth, American silver probably accounted for more than three-quarters of the world's supply.[4]

As the example of Potosí illustrates, states and their rulers made important decisions about how wealth could be created and maintained and about the relationships between states and the economy. In the next section, we explore the assumptions behind those decisions, the actions that flowed from them, and the repercussions that ensued.

States and Economic Activity

In 1615, a Frenchman by the name of Antoine de Montchrestien (1575–1621) wrote *A Tract on Political Economy*, introducing to western European readers this new term that reflected a growing sense among philosophers, financiers, and rulers that the acquisition and distribution of wealth were intimately related to

[4] Excellent and accessible overviews of silver mining in colonial Spanish America include Peter Bakewell, "Mining in Colonial Spanish America," *The Cambridge History of Latin America*, vol. 2, *Colonial Latin America*, ed. Leslie Bethell (New York: Cambridge University Press, 1984), 105–152; D. A. Brading and Harry E. Cross, "Colonial Silver Mining: Mexico and Peru," *Hispanic American Historical Review* 52, no. 4 (1972): 545–579; and Richard L. Garner, "Long-Term Silver Mining Trends in Spanish America: A Comparative Analysis of Peru and Mexico," *American Historical Review* 93, no. 4 (October 1988): 898–935. Studies of the role of indigenous labor in the Andes silver mines include Peter Bakewell, *Miners of the Red Mountain: Indian Labor of Potosí, 1545–1650* (Albuquerque: University of New Mexico Press, 1984); Jeffrey A. Cole, *The Potosí Mita, 1573–1700* (Stanford, CA: Stanford University Press, 1985); and Enrique Tandeter, *Coercion and Market: Silver Mining in Colonial Potosí, 1692–1826* (Albuquerque: University of New Mexico Press, 1993).

what states were and how they worked. Tight restrictions on economic activity, both within and across political boundaries, were long-standing and commonplace around the world. During this era, it was still a common idea that the amount of wealth in the world was limited, and therefore economic activity was a zero-sum game: one person or state's economic gain was another person or state's economic loss. Rulers, as a result, generally saw the role of the state in economic activity as granting and enforcing limits on how big the slices of the economic pie would be and who would be served.

While the idea that economic activity was zero sum persisted, the emergence of a truly global economy shook other pillars of long-standing belief about wealth generation and maintenance. By the late sixteenth century, the global economic pie was much larger than anyone would have believed one hundred years before. And the rules seemed different: the Netherlands, a small land poor in natural resources, was growing rich on trade. Montchrestien was part of a group of thinkers who developed theories of *mercantilism* as a solution to this new economic puzzle. In mercantilist thinking, a state's economic health could be measured by the amount of precious metals in its treasury. The surest way to do this, so the thinking went, was to maintain a positive balance of trade with one's rivals. The role of the state, then, would be to create policies that encouraged exports and discouraged imports, disrupted the economic activities of other states, and expanded control over as many natural resources as possible. These assumptions guided the decisions made by many early modern states attempting to manage the accumulation and preservation of wealth.

Economic Privileges and Restrictions

The idea that states must tightly control the flow of material and human resources within its territory was neither new nor limited to European thinkers. The Edo regime's policy of *sakoku* in Japan not only limited trade with Europeans; it also strictly controlled economic interactions with all foreign entities, including China, Korea, and other regional states. The Chinese Empire organized an elaborate, tightly controlled system in which commerce was accompanied by ritual recognition of the Chinese emperor's power. Dozens of states conducted trade with China through this so-called tribute system, including much of East and South Asia as well as European states. All claimants to sovereignty were trying to manage increasing global commerce and its unanticipated consequences.

In many states, including the European and Ottoman Empires, most products were manufactured by members of guilds, which were organizations sanctioned by the government to limit the number of producers, set prices, and train the next generation of artisans. Merchant guilds existed as well. As Europeans expanded their participation in long-distance commerce and overseas colonization, guilds moved with them, as did other kinds of monopoly practices. For instance, in 1506 the Portuguese Crown attempted to make the spice trade a Crown monopoly, meaning all profits from the import and sale of spices in the Portuguese Empire would accrue to the royal treasury. In other cases, rulers sold monopolies to produce or distribute certain goods in certain places—brandy, ice, playing cards—to the highest bidder. In still other cases, rulers granted licenses to a group of investors, who formed a joint stock company, for a monopoly on trade or other economic activities in certain parts of the globe. The Dutch East India Company, mentioned earlier, and the British East India Company (founded in 1600) are two examples. Other examples initiated the earliest attempts at English settlements in North America, such as the Plymouth Company in Massachusetts and the Virginia Company. In nearly all cases, these companies—or individual merchants—paid fees to their rulers for economic privileges, ensuring that the state would accumulate wealth.

The Role of Currency

In addition to regulatory practices, states affected economic activity through tax and monetary policies, which were often interconnected. In our own time, we take for granted the existence of money—currency—issued by governments. Although the early modern period is not the first era in which currency was being used (government-issued paper money first circulated in China in the 1100s), the extent to which the world's growing silver supply was being turned into currency, and the extent to which states attempted to turn this into tax revenue, is noteworthy.

Currency is a search for economic liquidity. What does this mean? Consider a fundamental question in economics—how do you get things that you don't (or can't) make for yourself? One way is to barter. You and I can exchange things we produce with each other and figure out their value in direct exchange—how many of my tomatoes are you willing to take in exchange for your strawberries? The barter system is straightforward but presents problems for more complex transactions that involve things like delayed consumption (I don't want to eat strawberries today), a poor fit between producer and consumer (I want shoes but the shoemaker doesn't want tomatoes), long-distance exchange (I want tea but not strawberries), or large-scale transactions (I want to raise and equip an army to go to war with my enemies next month rather than eat my dinner tonight). Such dilemmas over the exchange of goods led societies around the world at different times to develop ways to make these transactions easier, using money (currency) and credit. Both practices enable a wider variety of transactions to take place, but also introduce additional complications to the world of production and consumption.

Currency is a tool for storing and transporting value. The challenge is convincing people that currency has real value in an economic exchange—if I give you cash for food, I can eat the food. Will you be able to exchange that cash for food when *you* need to eat? To solve this problem, some kinds of currencies consist of something seen to have high intrinsic value, like precious metals. One important role that rulers increasingly claimed in the global economy was as an issuer of currency in which buyers and sellers could have confidence. For example, if a coin were issued from a government mint with the ruler's seal on it, the state was claiming that users could be confident that the coin would really contain the amount of silver stamped on it. If this were true, one would always have a valuable amount of precious metal to exchange.

Other currency systems are based on a promise that sellers will be able to obtain things of value at a later date. These promises could be letters of credit or paper money. Open your wallet or purse: if you pull out cash from the United States, you have in your hand a Federal Reserve note that the Treasury of the United States guarantees can be used to reduce or eliminate "all debts public or private." In the past, *promissory notes* were most often commitments that the issuer, whether an emperor or a merchant house, had a reserve of precious metal to make good on the promise being made. In fact, as recently as the 1970s, US currency (and that of most other countries) were based on this system of precious metal reserves held in government treasuries.

Taxes and Unrest

The infusion of New World silver into the global economy permitted greater liquidity in the global economy, but also led rulers to reform their tax systems in an attempt to increase the amount of precious metals in their treasuries. In India, for instance, the emperor Akbar reformed the tax code in the 1580s so that rather than taking an annual percentage of agricultural production from a region, peasants would pay, in currency, the equivalent of some portion of the average value of the last ten years' production. China's Ming dynasty accomplished something similar around the same time with its Single Whip reforms, making all taxes (previously collected throughout the year in a variety of forms, including produce and labor) payable once per year in silver. These reforms rationalized imperial accounting but also exposed agricultural populations to the global market in new ways. Silver currency was too valuable to be practical for most everyday transactions, where it would be like trying to use a one hundred dollar bill to buy a pack of gum. Instead, peasants in China (and India as well) continued to use copper coins for most purposes, acquiring silver when they needed to pay taxes. As the silver supply fluctuated, determined in large measure by production levels in the mines of Spanish America and the economic networks that moved silver across the globe, the value of silver (and therefore the tax burden) rose and fell relative to other costs.

A similar tax reform initiative in the Ottoman Empire helped to spark widespread revolt. Ottoman rulers determined a tax quota for each region of the empire, but relied on local leaders who controlled the land and the labor of those who worked it to deliver this amount to the imperial government. In turn, these feudal lords collected taxes from the community, often more than what the region owed, keeping the difference as a profit. Ottoman rulers, after expanding their empire through a series of expensive military campaigns during this time, raised their tax demands. Attempts to collect additional revenue produced a backlash. In central Anatolia (the heart of what today is Turkey), a rebellion broke out in 1595, called the Celali Rebellion. Named for its leader, Celal—a preacher in a Muslim sect called Alevism—the rebellion brought tens of thousands of people to the regional capital, demanding relief from taxation and the corruption of local landlords. Although imperial troops soon captured and killed Celal, the rebellion continued for fifteen years. Periodic rebellions continued through the seventeenth century. Although none of these rebellions overthrew the empire, scholars have argued that they did weaken it.

Although similar strains existed in other regions—Chinese and Indian tax reforms increased pressure on rural populations—the results were different in the Ottoman Empire. Why do we see rebellion in one case and not in the others? As always, historians assess different kinds of evidence to debate an answer. One factor may have been religious and ethnic difference, but China and India were no less diverse than the Ottoman Empire. Of course, individual actions and decisions matter, so the charisma of Celal or the intransigence of local lords may have played a role.

Historian Sam White offered an alternative explanation, pointing to climate change as the key factor.[5] The seventeenth century marked the height of a Little Ice Age, when average temperatures in many parts of the world were markedly lower than immediately before or after. Global climate change does not affect all places in the same way, of course. The Little Ice Age hit Anatolia with severe drought, much more drastic than what occurred in India or China. The pressures of famine in one of the empire's most fertile regions may have driven peasants to desperation and revolt. If we add to this rising pressures on subsistence from fluctuations in the tax burden and the international silver market, we have a compelling illustration of how global processes interact with local conditions.

---

5 Sam White, *The Climate of Rebellion in the Early Modern Ottoman Empire* (New York: Cambridge University Press, 2011).

The changing global economy produced other kinds of dislocations and upheaval. The increase in the global silver supply increased opportunities for long-distance trade by bringing a much greater amount of a broadly accepted and easily transferred standard of value into the global marketplace. New opportunities for the expansion of relationships between producers and consumers, within and between states, empires, and regions, proliferated. Conversely, it also helped to throw off perceptions of how much things were worth (in relation to silver and therefore in relation to each other), contributing to a long-term rise in the cost of living accompanied by periodic economic booms and busts. One extreme and infamous instance of unstable perceptions of an item's worth occurred with a tulip craze in the Netherlands in the 1630s.

Tulipmania!

Native to central Asia, tulips had long been cultivated and bred there, resulting in spectacular varieties. In Turkey, they attained great popularity, particularly at the Ottoman Court, as a favorite landscaping feature of many sultans. Turkish tulip gardens earned great admiration from visiting dignitaries, and according to most accounts, tulips were first cultivated in Europe from bulbs obtained by the Austrian ambassador to the Ottoman Empire in the 1550s.

Within a few decades of arrival, tulips had been bred and adapted to withstand the harsher climate of the Netherlands. Remember that Dutch merchants were becoming rich on global trade with fortunes earned in Southeast Asia. Tulips, a riot of color against the gray Dutch skies, were a perfect way to display new wealth and power. "Broken" tulips—solid tulips of one color with the insurgence of a second color—were considered most valuable. The Semper Augustus (a blood-red and white variety) was the most desired and rare. A Semper Augustus bulb could cost thirty times more than the average Dutch worker earned in a year. At the height of Tulipmania, one tulip sold for as much as the grandest homes in Amsterdam: perhaps ten million dollars today!

Early in 1637, investments in tulip deals amounted to more than six times the total currency available in the Netherlands—those who made these deals were making financial promises (or bets) about the future value of tulips with little actual money backing them up at the time they were made. Moreover, the tulips themselves were not being bought and sold at the moment of these transactions. The Dutch were using an economic instrument called a futures contract. An investor could buy a contract for tulips to be delivered in the future at a certain price, hoping that the price in the marketplace would go up as the time came closer for the flowers to be delivered. The contract could then be sold to someone else for more than its original cost, making a profit. Sometimes, part

Flora's Wagon of Fools, ca. 1637. Hendrik Gerritsz Pot (1580–1657) was a Dutch artist well known for his portraits of the wealthy and powerful of the seventeenth century. In the midst of Tulipmania, Pot produced this satirical painting of Dutch society gone mad. Flora is the goddess of flowers, speeding off in a tulip-laden ship, powered by the wind. The Dutch word for speculative trade is *windhandel* ("trade in the wind"). Holland's productive classes—prominent among the figures following the ship are weavers—have abandoned their work to follow Flora's temptation of easy money to their doom.

or even all of the initial investment to purchase a contract was borrowed against the promise of future profits, to be repaid after the shipment of goods arrived and was sold.

Of course, there is a risk. You might buy a contract (i.e., make a promise) to receive tulips at $100, hoping to sell the tulips (or resell the contract) for $200, in which case you would make a tidy profit. But these were guesses, not guarantees. You might only be able to sell the tulips (or resell the contract) for $50, in which case you would lose half of your investment. In 1637, rumors of what the next deliveries of tulips to Amsterdam would be worth ran rampant, and robust reselling of contracts drove contract prices to astronomical heights.

Perhaps you have already guessed how the Tulipmania story ended. Brokers expected huge profits when the first auctions of actual tulip bulbs began in the winter of 1637, but in fact there were no bids at all. People who had invested vast sums, planning to get rich reselling their bulbs, found that what they had bought was worthless. Prices are hard to verify, but it seems that between early February and early May of 1637, the average prices of tulip bulbs fell 99.5 percent from their height. Imagine thinking you could sell a flower for more than $200 and being able to sell it for only $1. Now imagine that you had plans to sell a nursery full of them with the same expectation, with the same result. Investors were ruined, including many common people seduced by the "guarantee" of easy money.

The Dutch tulip bubble was not typical. Most people in the world remained far from that kind of speculative finance. However, this story points out that in this increasingly connected world, prosperity and poverty, economic growth and decline, became more closely linked to new economic factors, often far beyond the control of individuals or local authorities. These factors included the global supply and distribution of commodities and the ability of individuals and institutions to evaluate new kinds of risks and to make and keep longer-term promises about credit and debt. This new environment also challenged models for how rulers make decisions about the relationship between their states and economic activity.

Conclusion

Despite all the changes we have described in this book so far, agrarian concerns continued to dominate human activity across the globe through the seventeenth century. A compelling case can be made that a cooling trend over the course of this era reduced agricultural productivity in much of the world. Fears over scarcity—remember the zero-sum model—drove bellicose political decisions. Wars between nations were seen as a way to acquire more resources, and the wealth flowing out the Americas or across the Indian Ocean was seen not as a way for all parties to benefit but as an opportunity to acquire more at the expense of rivals. Expensive imperial wars, designed to alleviate strains on resources, exacerbated suffering. Popular revolts spread. A loss of up to one-third of the world's population may have ensued. Not all regions and peoples were affected equally, but turmoil in some of the largest and most powerful of the early modern empires—including the Chinese, Ottoman, and Russian Empires as well as France, Spain, and England—must be placed in this material context.

Whereas most modern economic understandings reject the theories of wealth creation and preservation that prevailed during this era, there is no doubt that this was a world of strict limits, made clear by a convergence of multiple factors that contributed to a crisis across much of the globe in the seventeenth century. This was an understandable conclusion looking at a world dominated by the rules of the biological old regime. It was, perhaps, a conclusion reinforced by scandals like Tulipmania in which fortunes appeared and disappeared as if by magic, leaving some to wonder whether they ever really existed.

Most rulers certainly perceived power to be meted out in a zero-sum system. For any state to gain resources, another state would have to lose them. Sometimes the competitors erected legal or financial barriers, like the Calico Acts that banned Indian textile imports to Britain. In other cases, they sponsored violence, using privateers—essentially, state-approved pirates—to steal another state's wealth. Frequently, the answer was direct war. As the eighteenth century dawned, war, like trade and travel, became global in its reach.

A Few Good Books

Timothy Brook. *Vermeer's Hat: The Seventeenth Century and the Dawn of the Global World.* New York: Bloomsbury, 2008.

Randy M. Browne. *Surviving Slavery in the British Caribbean.* Philadelphia: University of Pennsylvania Press, 2017.

Jonathan Eacott. *Selling Empire: India in the Making of Britain and America, 1600–1830.* Chapel Hill: University of North Carolina Press, 2016.

Jane T. Merritt. *The Trouble with Tea: The Politics of Consumption in the Eighteenth-Century*

TIMELINE

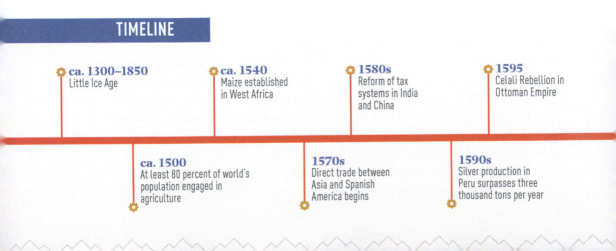

ca. 1300–1850
Little Ice Age

ca. 1500
At least 80 percent of world's population engaged in agriculture

ca. 1540
Maize established in West Africa

1570s
Direct trade between Asia and Spanish America begins

1580s
Reform of tax systems in India and China

1590s
Silver production in Peru surpasses three thousand tons per year

1595
Celali Rebellion in Ottoman Empire

Global Economy. Baltimore: Johns Hopkins University Press, 2016.

Geoffrey Parker. *Global Crisis: War, Climate Change and Catastrophe in the Seventeenth Century*. New Haven, CT: Yale University Press, 2013.

Om Prakash. *Bullion for Goods: European and Indian Merchants in the Indian Ocean Trade, 1500–1800*. New Delhi: Manohar, 2004.

Jane Whittle and Elizabeth Griffiths. *Consumption and Gender in the Early Seventeenth-Century Household: The World of Alice Le Strange*. New York: Oxford University Press, 2012.

For instructional resources and study aids, please go to ***www.oup.com/us/carter****. For primary sources connected to this chapter, please see the table of contents for* Sources for Forging the Modern World *included at the back of the book.*

ca. 1600
Brazil is largest sugar producer in the world

1602
Dutch East India Company established

1615
Antoine de Montchrestien, *A Tract on Political Economy*

1636–1637
Tulipmania in the Netherlands

1645–1680
Enslaved population of Barbados increases by a factor of seven, to forty thousand

1701
First Calico Act limits imports of Indian cotton cloth to England

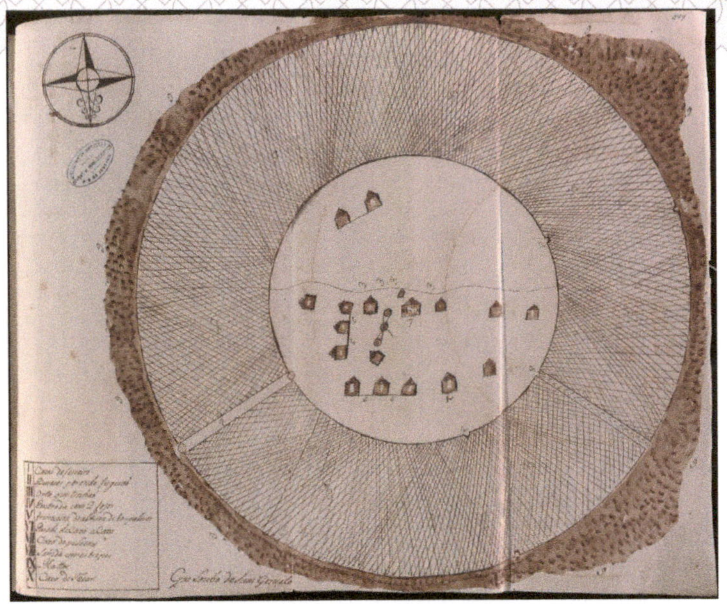

(TOP) Map of a Quilombo, ca. 1769. This sketch of the quilombo of Sao Gonçalo, Brazil, shows artisan workshops, including a blacksmith, gardens, and defense works surrounding the settlement. Over time, European settlers and imperial officials increasingly saw these independent Afro-Brazilian settlements as a threat to their plans for Brazil and worked to eliminate them.

(BOTTOM) Shah Alam, Mughal Emperor, Conveying the Grant of the Diwani to Lord Clive, August 1765. This is the second version of the same painting by Benjamin West (1738–1820), a well-known artist. The painting depicts the moment at which the Mughal emperor granted the British East India Company the right to collect taxes and administer civil justice in his realm. The first version of this painting was commissioned by Lord Clive himself. This copy, ca. 1818, was created by West for Lord Clive's son, who donated it to the British East India Company. The image itself is a fantasy because it portrays real people in the scene who were not present when these events took place.

CHAPTER 5

Global War and Imperial Reform

1655–1765

Zumbi dos Palmares—"Zumbi of Palmares" (1655–1695)—was born in northeastern Brazil, in a settlement of free people of African descent. Palmares was ruled neither by the Portuguese, who dominated most of Brazil, nor by the Dutch, who were at war with the Portuguese across the globe, including in Brazil. It was a *quilombo*, an independent community under the leadership of Africans who had freed themselves from slavery in the sugar plantations on the coast. At its height, more than thirty thousand people—some born in Africa and some in Brazil—lived in Palmares, which some historians argue was governed along the lines of the African kingdoms from which many of its residents had been taken. Portuguese raiders captured Zumbi when he was six years old and gave him as a slave to a Catholic priest, who educated him in Latin and Portuguese. Escaping and returning to Palmares in 1670, he proved his military and political skill, and upon the death of his uncle, Zumbi became the *quilombo*'s leader. Under his leadership, Palmares fought, negotiated treaties, and traded with indigenous peoples and the Portuguese until 1695, when the Portuguese captured Zumbi and beheaded him. Today, Brazil observes a national holiday on the date of Zumbi's death, which is known as Black Consciousness Day, but in the late seventeenth century, the Portuguese Crown granted the land Palmares had occupied to settlers who worked to ensure that the region's population would resist the encroachment of other European powers and return former slaves to those who had claimed them as property.

A century later, in 1765, representatives of the Mughal emperor Shah Alam II signed the Treaty of Allahabad with Lord Clive, an agent of the British East India Company. Britain had defeated France during the Seven Years' War, fought on land and sea across the globe between 1756 and 1763. In the years after the war, a tightening commercial embrace between Britain and South Asia became one of the important forces driving global change. The Treaty of Allahabad granted the company

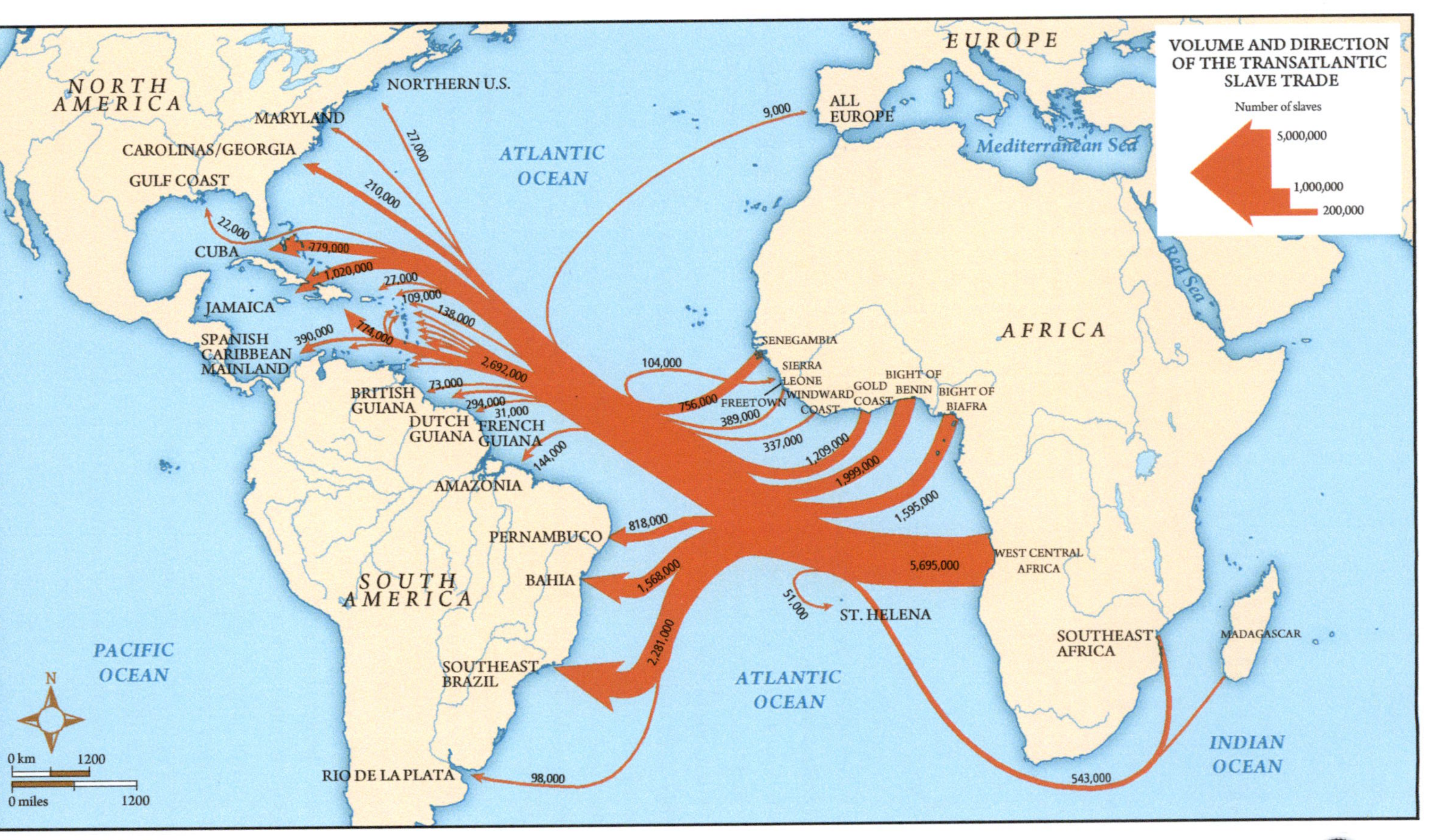

Map 5.1 Volume and Direction of the Transatlantic Slave Trade

the right to collect and administer tax revenue across a large area of the Indian subcontinent as well as the right to engage in duty-free commerce in the same region. This treaty culminated decades of unrest among indigenous rulers and their European merchant allies struggling to control parts of the Mughal Empire as it began to fragment following the death of Emperor Aurangzeb in 1707. With this treaty, the British East India Company asserted itself as an economic and military force in South Asia. In the following decades, it served as a party to additional treaties and even placed some sovereign rulers on the company payroll, initiating a new and much more ambitious undertaking for British subjects in Asia.

These encounters in Brazil and India bookend a multilayered global struggle over resources, commerce, labor, and territory in the seventeenth and eighteenth centuries. During this era, many imperial rulers sought more direct control over their territories so that they could extract greater value from their subjects and protect their interests against internal and external threats. At the same time, the people and places from whom the early modern empires sought tribute developed according to their own political, economic, and social dynamics. In the 1750s, these two trends led to global war that altered the shapes of empires, political and economic policies, and how people related to their governments. This war has several names, the Seven Years' War (1756–1763) being most common in European history books, although the French and Indian War may be more familiar to students of US history. In other parts of the world, it is called the Third Silesian War, the Third Carnatic War, or the Pomeranian War. In this book, we're calling it World War Zero and using it to illustrate the colossal scope and consequences of conflict and European expansion during this time.

In the first section of this chapter, we compare different practices of sovereignty across Eurasia from the mid-seventeenth to the mid-eighteenth centuries. We then examine the growth of the slave economy and tensions between European and indigenous political and economic systems, two factors driving conflict in the Americas and the Atlantic world. Following this, we survey additional factors in the competition among rulers on the Afro-Eurasian supercontinent, as the pursuit of advantages over rivals became entangled in shifting diplomatic and military alliances. These different trajectories overlapped just after the mid-century in military confrontations in the Americas, Europe, Asia, and on the seas: World War Zero.

Questions to Consider as You Read Chapter Five:

1. As we see in the two vignettes above, very different kinds of entities—the Mughal, British, and Portuguese Empires, the free state of Palmares, the British East India Company—were conducting wars and signing treaties in this era. How does your understanding of the past change when you consider this wider variety of political organization and conduct, rather than just thinking about "countries"?

2. The concept of World War Zero takes a phrase from the twentieth century—World War I and World War II—and applies it to an earlier one. No one in the seventeenth or eighteenth centuries used this phrase. What are the advantages and disadvantages of using an idea from one era to try to understand an earlier period?

Consolidating the Center: Modernizing Monarchies

Important ideas about the nature of political power that would fuel debate and conflict for centuries emerged from seventeenth-century experiences. At the time, which of those ideas would become influential and which would fade into obscurity was impossible to predict. In 1688–1689, England's *Glorious Revolution* (a name applied by its winners) forced the monarchy to accept clear limits on its power. In retrospect, this is often seen as the start of a trend away from absolute royal power, but limits on English royal power did not inspire universal acclaim or immediate imitation. Most states remained autocratic hereditary imperial states (in theory, if not always in reality) into the nineteenth century. In many other empires, royal power continued to grow in the decades after the Glorious Revolution in England. In this vein, the regimes of three other rulers—King Louis XIV of France (1638–1715), Tsar Peter the Great of Russia (1672–1725), and the Kangxi Emperor of Qing dynasty China (1654–1722)—can be fruitfully compared to England and to each other. Each of these monarchs ruled for at least four decades, and although no ruler single-handedly managed an empire, the representation and exercise of royal power in these regimes helps us to understand the variety of ways sovereignty was constructed and sustained.

Limiting the Power of the Monarch: England

John Locke attended Oxford University in the 1650s and found himself bored with the classical curriculum that had been in place for generations. Experimental and applied science, particularly chemistry and medicine—the practice of inductive reasoning—interested him in ways that memorizing ancient texts did not. After completing his degrees, Locke pursued his eclectic interests with the help of powerful patrons who employed him in various ways, often as a secretary. These positions provided Locke opportunities to travel. These trips exposed him more directly to the political issues of his day and led him to change his thinking about fundamental questions of political order still roiling England in the aftermath of the Civil War and restoration of the monarchy described in Chapter 3. At one point, Locke fled to the Netherlands out of fear he might be arrested as a conspirator against the Crown. Locke returned to England in the entourage of

Mary Henrietta Stuart (1631–1660), who, along with her husband, William of Orange (1650–1702), was offered the English throne in 1688. Although Locke wrote many of his most important works on political philosophy in the 1670s and 1680s, they were not published until he returned to England.

Influenced by the recent history of his homeland—civil war, military rule, the abolition of monarchy, continued tensions between Parliament and Crown after the restoration of monarchy—Locke's most important writings search for principles to understand how states come into being, what their purposes are, the circumstances under which they can be altered, and to what end. Locke shared his countryman Thomas Hobbes's vision of life before government: human beings in a state of nature are free, and all individuals are sovereigns, that is, responsible for protecting their own lives and possessions. But what does that freedom mean? Consider squirrels, completely free to constantly search for food: gathering, hiding, digging up, moving, and fighting over acorns, all while hoping to avoid being devoured by a hawk or a fox. The absolute freedom of the state of nature can be a horrible freedom, a squirrel's freedom. States are formed when individuals try to move beyond this by creating a social contract for their mutual protection, which means giving up absolute freedom (and the idea of every individual as sovereign) for the enjoyment of greater security of person and property. However, unlike Hobbes, Locke asserted that those who rule—those to whom portions of individual sovereignty are entrusted—are bound by the same social contract. Rulers do not have absolute freedom of action either. If rulers impinge on the essential freedoms of their people, then there is tyranny, and that can be grounds for removing the officeholder from power. For Locke, any claim of absolute power violated the social contract that creates a state in the first place.

The agreement that King William and Queen Mary made with Parliament in 1689 reflected aspects of Locke's thinking on government. The English Bill of Rights, resulting from this agreement, confirmed that English monarchs could not arbitrarily suspend the enforcement of laws and that Parliament must participate in decisions about raising public revenues through taxation. As we have seen, such things are key components in the exercise of sovereignty and the maintenance of state power. The Bill of Rights also stipulated that the monarchy would not interfere with parliamentary deliberations or with judicial proceedings. Finally, it recognized that individuals had certain rights that must be safeguarded against state power, for example, protections against cruel and unusual punishment or excessive fines. In short, England's new king and queen agreed that the sovereign's power was neither absolute nor resident in the person(s) of the monarch(s). Sovereignty was a relationship between ruler and ruled that did not require the ruled to sacrifice all political power.

Absolutism in France and Russia

When William and Mary came to power in England, the French Estates General, a consultative body with some similarities to the English Parliament, had not met in decades. In contrast to England, the French monarchy had defeated seventeenth-century revolts against increasing royal power. King Louis XIV strengthened provincial officials called *intendants,* appointed by the monarch. Intendants had administrative, judicial, fiscal, and military authority as the local base of a bureaucratic pyramid designed to enforce the will of the monarch. Ideologically, Louis's supporters reinforced the idea of royal absolutism. Bishop Jacques-Bénigne Bossuet (1627–1704), a renowned theologian in Louis's court, described royal authority as sacred, paternal, and absolute. In sharp contrast to the limited monarchy in England, Bossuet wrote in *Politics Drawn from the Very Words of Holy Scripture* that the French monarch "need render account to no one for what he orders."

King Louis's Russian contemporary Tsar Peter also claimed expansive personal powers, and as in France, his claims of greater authority were challenged. The Cossacks, a multiethnic group made up of peoples from across Eurasia (from Ukrainians to Turks to Buryats), remained hostile to the idea that a distant ruler could impose restrictions on them. Stenka Razin (1630–1671) led the largest uprising of the era in 1670, when thousands of troops, under the leadership of Cossack military veterans with experience in both land and naval warfare, took numerous towns and sought to establish an independent state along the Volga River. By no means universally popular or respected, Razin faced resistance from other Cossacks and was condemned by the Orthodox Christian hierarchy. Troops loyal to the tsar captured him in 1671 and brought him to Moscow, where he was tortured and put to death.

Peter, like Louis, attempted to consolidate military victories with administrative reforms. Peter terminated the Boyar Duma, an aristocratic consultative body, and replaced it with a governing senate. These reforms were couched within a claim of absolute power for the sovereign. The senate, the highest organ of state, was appointed by the tsar to be his council of advisers and top administrators. Peter delegated administrative responsibility on a model largely borrowed from Sweden, but did not wish to diminish the tsar's personal power. Peter remained suspicious of the government institutions that he created. An imperial official called the sovereign's eye presided over the senate, and other officials monitored and reported directly to Peter on the workings of various government ministries. The Russian Imperial Code stated that the sovereign's power was absolute. Peter himself sought—through imperial decrees—to govern even how people could dress and what kind of facial hair men could grow. Scholarly research from many

Peter the Great Inspects a Ship at Amsterdam. This painting, ca. 1700 by an unidentified artist, is another imaginary depiction of a real event that occurred during Tsar Peter I's 1697–1698 diplomatic tour of Europe. Peter, who built up the Russian navy, took a personal interest in naval engineering and military matters. While in Amsterdam, he was treated to a parade of ships and a mock sea battle, depicted here.

cultures and periods suggests that laws like these were impossible to enforce, but they are important indicators of a political system in which it is the sovereign's prerogative to make such rules in the first place.

The Qing Consolidation in China

A decree on hairstyle also played a role in the efforts of Qing rulers to establish their authority in China. In 1645, the chief advisor to the first Qing emperor—Manchu, remember, not Chinese—decreed that Chinese men had to adopt the Manchu hairstyle called the queue. By shaving the fronts of their heads and braiding the hair in back in a long ponytail, Qing subjects would acknowledge the new regime's authority. At first, many Chinese rejected the hairstyle and the acceptance of Manchu rule it represented; resistance to the Manchu conquest was fierce and persistent. Over time, however, the Qing dynasty stabilized, real incomes increased for most people, and both commercial activity and agricultural production expanded. A vast civil service, including over fifteen hundred county magistrates, selected (at least

Map 5.2 China from the Ming to the Qing Dynasties

in theory) by examination rather than heredity, enforced laws, adapted from the Ming Code, for the entire empire. There were other ways to gain office, including buying titles and taking special exams, with quotas designated for ethnic, regional, or social groups, but government by meritocracy—based on merit and competence rather than social or familial privilege—remained a powerful ideal.

During a long and stable era that followed this early turbulence, the Qing expanded rapidly, doubling the territory of its Ming predecessor. A growing population and economy appeared to signal that the dynasty was fulfilling the Mandate of Heaven to provide for the empire's prosperity, an impression the Kangxi Emperor showcased during the six grand inspection tours we described in Chapter 3. These journeys were designed to legitimate the emperor by demonstrating his power over a large, diverse, and at times rebellious population. The tours reinforced the association between central authority and public works, as when the entourage traveled along the Grand Canal through the commercial centers of the empire to the silk manufacturing city of Suzhou. The tradition continued under the Qianlong

Emperor (1711–1799), who visited, among other sites, the flood prevention network that protected southern China's agricultural heartland. These emperors managed their images carefully, portraying themselves in the guise of Buddhist priests, shamans, Confucian officials, or powerful warriors, depending on their audience.

With its economic expansion, rising affluence, population growth, and political stability, China appeared to many a model of imperial rule worth emulating. Some European political philosophers wrote admiringly of China's political and economic system, and the (often idealized) principles and practices of the Chinese civil service had real influence elsewhere. Over time, the idea of a merit-based system to replace patronage appointments or hereditary government service attracted adherents in many countries. Indeed, managers of the British East India Company used the Chinese system to advocate modernization of their own company's training and appointment policies.

Of course, none of these rulers had truly absolute power. In comparison to the English monarchy, most Eurasian rulers made decisions with far fewer restrictions on them, but they all still relied on the advice and abilities of powerful individuals and groups within their empires. They also faced structural limits on the economic, military, and cultural resources available to carry out their programs. These leaders—Manchu, French, English, and Russian—incorporated in their decisions understandings of how the world was changing (or not changing), from economic activity to warfare, and all of them acted within constraints imposed by the availability of resources and the strength of other domestic or international actors and institutions.

The Question of Control in the Atlantic Seaborne Empires

The sovereigns of seaborne empires could not travel their realms the way Qing emperors did. The distances and dangers of open ocean were too great, so they projected their power through symbols and subordinates. These monarchs claimed vast areas, yet no Spanish, English, or Portuguese ruler ever set foot in those territories. Viceroys and governors represented royal authority. Numerous and often overlapping political and ecclesiastical divisions further divided space and population, with religious and political officials sometimes cooperating and sometimes competing, all claiming to act on behalf of the sovereign.

Resistance and Rebellion in the Americas

Complex and intertwined structures of political, economic, and spiritual power evolved. Although in theory (and mostly in practice), European-origin peoples dominated all these hierarchies, the indigenous, African, and mixed-race populations had power of their own. The Spanish record contains many complaints against local officials, including public protests accompanied by cries of "Long Live the King, Death to Bad Government." These demonstrations led to investigations into the cause of upheaval (and the accompanying revenue shortfall) and in some cases the removal of officials. Indigenous and mestizo communities and individuals also used the imperial legal system to pursue their interests, often with success. Government officials, from local magistrates and judges to viceroys themselves, had great flexibility in implementing imperial policy because of the distance from Spain, the size of the empire, and the inability to communicate speedily. Officials in the Americas could provisionally reject an order from Spain using the formulaic response, "I obey, but I do not comply," which would trigger an automatic review of the law back in Spain. This reply acknowledged the Crown's legitimacy (I obey my sovereign) while also asserting its ignorance of local matters (there's no way this law could work here).

In some places, Spanish authority was so weak that it could be totally reversed, at least temporarily. This happened in a region that today is part of the US state of New Mexico, where Spaniards first arrived at the end of the sixteenth century. Franciscan priests established a mission to convert to Christianity the urban-dwelling indigenous population, who came to be known as the Pueblo (Village) people to distinguish them from the nomadic groups that also lived in the region. For decades, an uneasy relationship existed between the Pueblo people and the recent European arrivals, made even more complex by the threat posed to both by other indigenous groups. In the 1670s, a drought prompted Pueblo medicine men to perform rituals designed to bring back the water. When the Franciscans condemned the practice as sorcery, the Pueblo people revolted in 1680, killing several hundred Spaniards and driving the surviving two thousand from the region for a decade.

The abrupt Spanish withdrawal transformed the region even more dramatically than their rule had. Fleeing the Pueblo, the Spanish were forced to leave behind their horses and sheep. Taking over the herds, the Pueblo began raising and trading these horses. Quickly, indigenous populations made use of the horses to transform their societies as completely as any new technology has ever done. Horses, acquired through war and trade by indigenous peoples across North America, enabled greater mobility and increased hunting efficiency. Firearms, another import from Iberia that Europeans did not wish indigenous peoples to acquire, also entered their possession through trade and confiscation. One indigenous group, the Comanches, made especially effective use of horses in building an empire across the southern plains—the Spaniards called it *Comancheria*—that covered much of today's Texas, New Mexico, and Oklahoma. Across North America, territorial conflicts between indigenous and European settlements endured through the nineteenth century. Some Spaniards on the northern frontiers of New Spain were so convinced of the superior numbers and firepower of hostile indigenous warriors that they warned repeatedly of the potential collapse of the entire European enterprise in that part of the world.

Europeans and indigenous peoples also clashed in eastern North America. From Virginia to Canada, French, English, and Dutch settlers, with their rivalries, diseases, and economies, challenged indigenous populations. Indigenous governments adopted diverse strategies for dealing with the new arrivals. Alliances shifted; conflicts were common. In New England, King Philips' War broke out in 1675 and lasted until 1678. The conviction in an English court of three Native Americans for the murder of another indigenous man who had converted to Christianity set off this clash between English settlers and the Algonquians, who attacked more than half of the towns in New England. Led by Metacomet (also known as King Philip), the Algonquians fought on multiple fronts, both against the English and their indigenous allies and against the Mohawks, their long-standing rivals from the Iroquois Confederation. Disease, starvation, and bullets all took their toll. The Algonquians lost. King Philip himself was killed and beheaded, his head (like Zumbi's in Brazil) put on display, a sign of the hardening relationship between Europeans and North American indigenous peoples.

Enslaved People and the Slave Trade

Conflict between indigenous and European-origin peoples was one factor shaping European endeavors in the Americas during this time. The growing importance of slavery, especially in the Caribbean and Brazil, was another. There are complex explanations for the rapid growth of Atlantic-world slavery during this era. The expansion of Europe into global trade routes had spurred European demand for tropical commodities, and this demand continued to rise. Unable to grow these products in Europe or control these commodities at their sources in Africa and Asia, Europeans eyed tropical regions of the Americas, but if they were to produce the commodities they wanted, they needed human labor (remember that as much as 90 percent of the New World's population had died in the sixteenth century because of disease and war).

A complex web of factors led to the enslavement of human beings on an unprecedented scale, including the European demand for plantation labor in the Americas, the potential profits to be made, African political practices and rivalries, and the individual decisions of countless people across the globe. In the century and a half between Columbus's landfall and 1650, an estimated three hundred thousand Africans were transported to the Americas to be enslaved. In the century that followed, the figure was ten times higher: almost three million people embarked. The number continued to grow over the subsequent decades before declining in the nineteenth century. Europeans did not yet lay extensive claims to territorial sovereignty in Africa but negotiated instead with regional and local political leaders.

During this era, some African states paralleled developments in other parts of the world, replacing hereditary posts, reforming tax schemes and military organization, and fighting and negotiating with other states. The history of African slavery is intertwined with these transformations. For the most part, Europeans did not simply arrive and abduct tens of thousands of Africans. Enslavement was a common practice in Africa, as it was in many parts of the world, usually involving prisoners of war. Enslaving human beings is abhorrent, but the nature of slavery in Africa differed in important ways from the slavery that came to dominate the Americas. In Africa, servitude was often for a limited term, at the end of which people could expect to be freed and return to their homes. The children of enslaved people were usually considered free.

The growth of transatlantic slavery changed these terms, as the people enslaved were treated as commodities to be owned and traded. West Africa was the region most affected by these changes in the seventeenth and eighteenth centuries. This region was a crucial part of the early modern trade network linking Africa, Europe, and Asia, contributing gold and other products. This wealth drew the first Portuguese and Dutch traders, who named their ports of call after the riches they sought to acquire, for example, the Gold Coast (today's Ghana) or the Ivory Coast (Côte d'Ivoire). When Europeans arrived, different ethnic and political groups were already competing for power, much like the rest of the supercontinent. In this context, Europeans could be powerful allies in local conflicts, much as they had been in the Americas. Many African rulers at first did not trade in slaves with Europeans, instead trading local commodities for desired imports. European firearms—one area in which European technology was at the forefront of global manufacturing—were especially desired because they could be key in defeating local rivals. Enslaving one's rivals could also change military and economic power relationships. The slave trade provides an interesting and paradoxical example of one of the disadvantages of stateness: African regions without effective centralized sovereign states appear to have been less subject to the depredations of the slave trade.

In the calculation of some smaller states, with fewer commodities or resources to trade, exchanging human beings for firearms appeared a sound strategy. These considerations combined with the burgeoning European demand for labor in their American colonies; the slave trade accelerated. Some African states, like Benin, refused to participate in this emerging traffic in human beings. Others gained and maintained control of greater territory and resources, in part as a result of participation in the slave trade (for example, Dahomey).

Slavery, and the long-distance trade in enslaved Africans, did not originate with Europeans, but Europeans transformed the practice. Once sold into bondage—usually at West African ports—enslaved people by the millions were taken across the Atlantic Ocean on ships flying the Portuguese, British, Spanish, Dutch, and even Polish flags. This Middle Passage of the triangular trade linking Africa, the Americas, and Europe was three to four months of hell for the newly enslaved Africans. No longer prisoners of war or temporary bondservants, to satisfy European demand for labor led these men and women were taken into *chattel slavery*: the enslaved person became property for life, a commodity that could be controlled, inherited, bought, sold, or otherwise disposed of as the owner saw fit. Children of the enslaved also became the property of the parent's owner. The seemingly endless appetite for labor in the Americas transformed the scale at which the system operated.

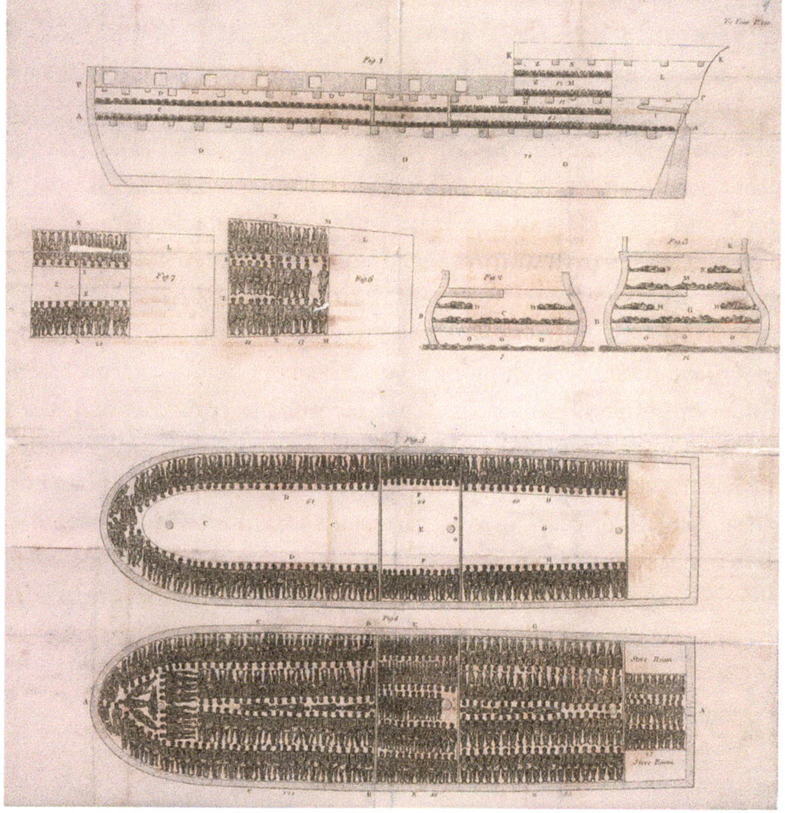

Plan of a Slave Ship, Showing Conditions of the Middle Passage between Africa and the Americas. From the seventeenth to the nineteenth century, more than eleven million Africans were transported to the Americas under horrific conditions. This image depicts the way human beings were packed onto vessels to carry as many people as possible, maximizing potential profits for the traders. In the late eighteenth century, antislavery activists began to use illustrations like this in their literature to demonstrate the cruelty of the slave trade.

Historians Explore The Slave Trade

Firsthand accounts of the Middle Passage are rare. By far the most widely circulated and well-known description of the experience comes from a memoir by Olaudah Equiano (1745–1797), who describes himself as having been born in what is now Nigeria before being enslaved and transported against his will across the Atlantic. Equiano's account provides another chance to see the challenges of historical inquiry. Scholar Vincent Carretta found evidence suggesting that Equiano may have been born not in Africa, but in South Carolina. If this is the case, then Equiano may not have experienced firsthand the Middle Passage, which he describes in rich and horrible detail, but instead used information that he had read or heard from others. Historians disagree about this kind of evidence. If Equiano was not born in Africa (there is no consensus on this), is Equiano's description of the Middle Passage rendered useless? Most historians would argue that all sources are flawed, incomplete, or compromised in some way, so we need to approach them all with care. If there is reason to question some details of Equiano's memoir, then we must examine it more closely rather than discard it. Carretta's research went on to show that other sources confirm most details in Equiano's book. The evidence also shows that Equiano's description of the Middle Passage is consistent with other narratives, even if it is not from firsthand experience. Olaudah Equiano's account of the Middle Passage may or may not be a personal recollection, but we have every reason to think it is an accurate depiction of the experience.[1]

There are other sources for understanding the slave trade. In the United States, you can find records of slaves in tax documents because they were reported as property. Slave traders and shipping companies kept detailed records, reflecting the business of human trafficking. These records are spread around the world, principally in archives of the countries that dominated the movement of enslaved Africans across the Atlantic Ocean. Although scholars had been working with these records for years, in 1990 historians David Eltis and Steven Behrendt started to collect all available records into a single database. Combing collections from France, Britain, the United States, the Netherlands, Spain, Portugal, Brazil, and elsewhere, a comprehensive and detailed portrait of the slave trade became more accessible. Now hosted at Emory University, the Trans-Atlantic Slave Trade Database (www.slavevoyages.org) brings together records from more than

---

1 Vincent Carretta, *Equiano, the African: Biography of a Self-Made Man* (Athens: University of Georgia Press, 2005). A thorough, and critical, review of Carretta's book is Douglas Chambers, "Review of Carretta, Vincent, *Equiano the African: Biography of a Self-Made Man*." *H-Atlantic, H-Net Reviews*, November 2007, http://www.h-net.org/reviews/showrev.php?id=13855. For a good overview of the debate, see "Olaudah Equiano: African or American?" in *1650–1850: Ideas, Aesthetics, and Inquiries in the Early Modern Era* 17 (2008): 229–248.

thirty-five thousand voyages that carried more than twelve million Africans between 1514 and 1866. The database reveals both the vast scope of the slave trade and the details of many individual lives, including the age, gender, and origin of millions of Africans. Nearly one hundred thousand people are identified by name.

The Trans-Atlantic Slave Trade Database also reveals the importance of resistance and shipboard revolts. Escapes, daily acts of defiance, and outright rebellions characterized slave societies. As we saw at the start of this chapter, enslaved Africans, brought to labor on sugar plantations, freed themselves and intermingled with indigenous populations, forming the *quilombos* of Brazil. Escaped Africans also formed and ruled communities in northern Colombia, Cuba, Jamaica, and Dominica, putting down roots alongside the autonomous indigenous states throughout the Americas that survived well beyond the first century of the European invasion. In addition, conspiracies were endemic, for example, among the plantation slaves of the Virginia colony in the late seventeenth and early eighteenth centuries. Revolts also rocked the mining communities of New Spain and Peru. These actions, along with those of Europeans and indigenous peoples, shaped the flow of resources and the ways in which claims and exercises of sovereignty in the Western Hemisphere developed in this era.

The Path to World War Zero

Over the course of decades, the Eurasian empires skirmished on a regular basis, building to a protracted war on three continents in the middle of the eighteenth century. The British and French Empires began the war in 1754; shifting alliances brought additional European powers into the conflict in 1756. Seven years later, the major European protagonists brokered a series of treaties. This sequence of events is the origin of the name Seven Years' War, but these battles were only a part of larger, ongoing hostilities. Little European territory changed hands as a result of the Seven Years' War, but recent research on the war and its consequences has taken a broader perspective, showing the significant shifts it produced in global power relationships. We are using the name *World War Zero* to emphasize the global context of the conflict.

The term World War Zero invites comparisons with the conflict of 1914–1918 that came to be known as World War I. Both were preceded by a global arms race and a series of limited regional wars that political leaders considered useful in the pursuit of their interests. In both cases, fear of (or desire for) changes in the balance of power in the eastern Mediterranean and central Europe fueled conflicts that preceded the larger conflagration, which played out on a global canvas with shifting alliances among European and non-European armies determining the outcome. After each war, the reallocation of territories and other concessions made to end the war led in short order to further violence, exposing the short-sightedness of the peace settlement. In the aftermath of war, leaders of the main protagonist empires, their treasuries depleted, decreed changes within their realms that precipitated additional conflict.

Competition and Conflict among the Seaborne Empires

The Atlantic slave trade expanded rapidly in the seventeenth century. The morality of owning other human beings, or the concerns over the suffering slavery caused, remained primarily in the background as empires tried to ensure revenues and compete with rivals in a rapidly changing global economy. Empires vied with one another to gain the economic upper hand, including the right to control the flow of slave labor. Rights over enslaved people were negotiated as lucrative contracts or as pieces of international agreements, as when the British gained control of the slave trade to Spanish America in 1713. Valuable plantation territories also traded hands, as the Dutch–Portuguese rivalry in Brazil or the French seizure of Saint-Domingue in the second half of the seventeenth century demonstrated. In the period 1679–1700, in the early years of French control, around 5,000 slaves disembarked in Saint-Domingue. In the next twenty-five years, the number passed 40,000; and in the twenty-five years after that, it exceeded 140,000. Saint-Domingue became the tropical economic gem of the French Empire, built on the expansion of human misery. In 1685, King Louis XIV issued an edict, commonly known as the *Black Code*, regarding the French dominions in the Americas. Its provisions clarified Crown policy regarding slave life, denying enslaved people rights in court, in the marketplace, and even to control the fate of their own progeny. The code also expelled Jews from the French Caribbean and suppressed the practice of any religion other than Roman Catholicism, even among slaves (an interesting provision that seemed to affirm the enslaved people's humanity even as fundamental human dignities were denied).

In its Caribbean and North America territories, the British Crown also asserted more direct control over colonial life and commerce. It established a board of trade and plantations and pushed legislation both to raise the cost of commodities produced by rival empires and to require that goods shipped from Europe to British colonies had to pass through England. The Spanish and Portuguese followed similar practices. Events of the early 1700s confirmed for these empires that they needed to defend their imperial interests even more aggressively.

War constantly accompanied European maritime empires during this era. Spain was at war with another European power on average three of every four years. The size of armies and navies grew; weapons became more powerful, and the costs of preparing and conducting war grew with them. The main armies in the Thirty Years' War (1618–1648) had approximately one hundred thousand soldiers each. By 1710, King Louis XIV could put over three hundred thousand French troops in the field and had the world's largest navy: about two hundred warships. England claimed approximately the same number as it emerged as the primary naval power in the world.[2]

The War of the Spanish Succession

The eighteenth century began with a dynastic crisis in Europe when the Spanish Empire passed to a member of the Bourbon family, which also controlled the French Crown. Fearing that this might lead to a unification of both empires, creating a continental superpower, England led an alliance into a decade-long war over this issue. Only after accommodating English demands, including a commitment to maintain separate kingdoms in perpetuity, did the Bourbon family finally win the Spanish throne. These new Spanish royals launched a series of reforms in hopes of reviving the empire's fortunes after decades of stagnation. Borrowing from their French cousins, the Spanish Bourbons created a system of intendancies, with imperial officials reporting directly to the Crown from throughout the empire. They also added new viceroyalties, courts, and military infrastructure to their Western Hemisphere enterprise and initiated sweeping economic and social reforms.

The Netherlands also had interests in the War of Spanish Succession. They allied with the English because both opposed France and Spain. However, the war also confirmed England's military and commercial primacy on the world's oceans, threatening the Netherlands, which relied on maritime commerce for its prosperity. In the 1680s, the Dutch East India Company may have been the largest private employer on the planet, with almost twenty-two thousand employees. During the first half of the eighteenth century, however, the burdens of warfare, increasing encroachments on Dutch commerce from larger territorial empires, and a faltering domestic economy took their toll. The Netherlands remained prosperous by comparative global standards, but the golden age of Dutch commercial power came to an end during these decades.

The Land-Based Empires of Central Eurasia

Important changes in the balance of power in central and eastern Europe, particularly the interventions of Russia and Prussia in regional affairs, also led to war among these traditionally land-based empires during the middle of the

2 Frank Tallett, *War and Society in Early Modern Europe: 1495–1715* (New York: Routledge, 2010).

eighteenth century. Russia was at war almost constantly during the reign of Peter the Great, who had set out to build not only a successful army but also a navy, taking a personal interest in nautical science and shipbuilding. With the help of British expertise, he built a navy of approximately thirty thousand sailors and almost fifty large ships, but it came at a high price: military expenditures consumed up to 85 percent of government revenues. Peter's neighbors and rivals in Prussia (the state surrounding Berlin in what is now Germany) consolidated a powerful monarchy in the decades after the Thirty Years' War, introducing a system of permanent taxation to increase state revenue significantly. These revenues built a formidable army. By 1740, under the "Soldier-King" Frederick William I (1688–1740), Prussia had the fourth largest army in Europe even though it ranked only twelfth in population.

In the 1730s and 1740s, succession disputes in Poland and Austria precipitated more war. Prussia and Russia, having invested so heavily to develop their militaries, aggressively asserted their interests. They also engaged repeatedly in territorial disputes to the west, east, and south. Russia, for example, went to war with the Ottoman Empire in the 1670s, 1680s, 1710s, and 1730s. The reversal of Ottoman fortunes contributed to major changes in the Middle East and South Asia in the eighteenth century, but the Ottoman Empire managed to survive into the twentieth century. The same cannot be said for the Safavid Empire, which collapsed in the eighteenth century, or the Mughal Empire, which survived, but saw its power decline greatly over the same period.

The Safavid Empire fought over territory and other resources with the Russian, Ottoman, and Mughal Empires. Its trading network—and the accompanying tax revenue—contracted at the hands of competition from European maritime commerce. Ongoing disputes over the alignment between political power and religious practice among different Islamic traditions also weakened Safavid claims of sovereignty. Sunni Afghans forced the Safavid ruler Shah Sultan Husayn (1668–1726) to abdicate in the 1720s.

As the Safavid dynasty collapsed, Nadir Shah (1688–1747) proclaimed a new empire, the Afsharid, which lasted only a few decades. The son of Turkmen pastoralists from northwestern Iran, Nadir Shah attempted to resolve regional ethnic and sectarian disputes not only within the historical limits of the Safavid regime but also across the wider Islamic world. In 1736, he gathered religious, political, and military leaders from throughout the fractured empire and asked them to choose a new ruler who could unify them. Probably inspired and intimidated in equal measure, the group selected him. Fashioning himself in the tradition of Timur (Tamerlane), the famous unifier of the region from an earlier era, he used war and diplomacy to claim an empire stretching from the Indus River to the Caucasus. Economic development, religious initiatives, and strategic marriages cemented his relationships with local groups and other regional powerhouses, particularly the Ottomans, with whom he repeatedly attempted to reconcile by promoting an innovative solution to the Sunni–Shi`a rift in Islam. Nadir Shah was a brilliant military leader but not a diplomat, imam, or economist. He died at the hands of his own guards in 1747, leaving a legacy of increased vulnerability in the region rather than a shoring up of its resources around a central sovereign authority.

The Mughal Empire experienced similar pressures in the eighteenth century. The Mughal emperor Aurangzeb may have been the wealthiest man in the world when he died in 1707, but after his demise regional power holders grew less willing to sacrifice sovereignty and material wealth to an imperial center returning uncertain benefits. European merchant groups, mostly French and English, established fortified trading posts and formed alliances with regional leaders that brought in resources, including weapons, which accelerated trends toward ethnic, religious, and economic regionalism. Like Europe, South Asia moved quickly from one war to the next through the first half of the eighteenth century.

The Seven Years' War and Its Aftermath

In 1754, British troops attacked French territorial claims in North America and seized French ships. Within two years, the other European empires had entered the war. Prussia, Great Britain, and Portugal fought on one side; France, Spain, Russia, Austria, and Sweden on the other. Smaller principalities in central Europe joined on both sides, as did indigenous states and peoples in North America and South Asia. Sea battles involved dozens of ships firing hundreds of cannons. Ports were seized, forts constructed, and trade disrupted. States entered and left the conflict at different times, and at least four different treaties ended hostilities.

When the war finally ended in 1763, Great Britain (England and Wales were now united with Scotland as Great Britain, although England dominated political decision-making) appeared as the biggest winner and France the loser. After victories at Québec (1759) and Pondicherry (1760), Britain was the dominant European power in North America and South Asia, respectively. Territory changing hands was not the war's only consequence. Both England and France doubled their public debt. Other European powers also accumulated significant financial burdens fighting the war. The war led Europe's political elites to conclude that a permanent war footing was essential. This combination of debt and constant preparation for the next war contributed to further changes in imperial policies, with many consequences, some by design and others a complete shock.

For the British Empire, the Peace of 1763 carried great opportunity at a high cost. The size of British North America doubled; political elites in Britain debated how to make this vast territory best serve the empire's interests. Should the imperial center focus on managing commerce and tax revenues, or should more effort be expended to govern the territories themselves? Advocates of a more intensive approach to the overseas empire won the day, and Britain began to build what historians call its *New Imperial System*. On the revenue side, Parliament passed new taxes with the Sugar Act and the Stamp Act. In addition, the government increased efforts to curtail the flow of untaxed merchandise (contraband) through the empire and to stimulate trade between the Americas and Great Britain rather than simply within its Western Hemisphere territories. In the short term, the plan appeared to work. Revenue to the Crown from its colonial enterprises increased significantly. But negative consequences also accompanied these policy changes, exacerbated by further decisions about how the empire was to be managed.

Emerging from the war, the British government decided to station imperial troops permanently in North America and prohibit the movement of colonists west of the Allegheny Mountains, hoping to avoid conflict with indigenous states in the region, such as the Iroquois, that might drag Britain into another expensive war. These decisions affected some individuals and communities that had expected access to this territory. The changes in tax policies stirred even wider resentment. Some in the colonies also felt that the way these decisions were made violated both the letter of the law and the implied social contract—think back to John Locke's writing presented at the start of this chapter—under which all Englishmen lived. However, the colonies were divided regionally, socially, politically, and economically. Despite tensions with Britain, few in the colonies could agree on how to respond. Collective action was not universally supported, and even those who agreed it was necessary did not agree on how to proceed.

One must be careful, therefore, not to assume that the seeds of an inevitable uprising were planted in British North America at this time. Most residents, although aggravated by certain imperial policies, did not advocate independence. They felt a deep and abiding connection with the empire, even if they had never set foot in England. The 1765 Stamp Act, which created a new tax on legal documents to pay for a British army in North America, provoked widespread protests, but rarely did they spill over into violence or extensive property damage. The repeal of the Stamp Act in 1766 did not heal a growing sentiment toward republicanism in certain sectors of British North American colonial society, but one should note that widespread organized violence against the empire did not erupt until well into the next decade, and significant portions of the colonial population remained loyal to the crown throughout the subsequent war for independence, which lasted more than seven years.

Spain neither gained nor lost significantly in World War Zero, but it responded to its lessons, accelerating a reform program under King Charles III (1716–1788).

(a)

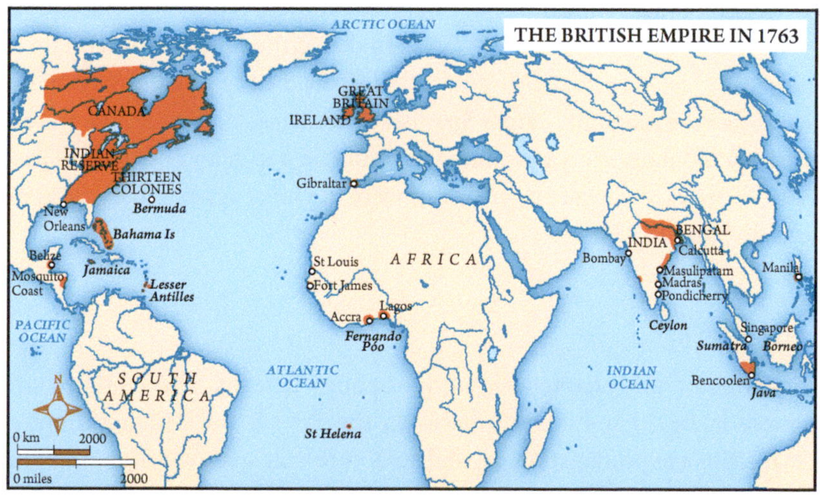

(b)

Map 5.3 (a) The Seven Years' War; (b) The British Empire in 1763

Kangxi Emperor Mounted on Horseback. The Kangxi Emperor ruled the Manchu Qing dynasty from 1661 to 1722. He was the first Qing emperor to be born south of the Great Wall and presided over the expansion of the Qing Empire and the consolidation of Qing rule over China. This painting depicts him as a martial ruler, in full armor. In other contexts, he appeared quite differently, as a Confucian scholar, a Chinese monarch, or a Buddhist devotee, depending on the audience being addressed.

Spain imposed new taxes, new monopolies, and more colonial officials to enforce the royal will, creating a fourth viceroyalty (with its capital in Buenos Aires) and increasing military spending. As in British North America, imperial reforms sparked protests. In 1765, tax reforms designed to increase revenue flow to Spain triggered an unprecedented rebellion against Spanish rule in the city of Quito (Ecuador) on the Pacific coast of northern South America. In this event, which came to be known as the Rebellion of the Barrios, elite petitions and meetings to devise bureaucratic maneuvers to overturn royal decrees gave way to popular rioting, culminating in attacks on the tax collector's office and the royal brandy distillery. As indigenous peoples from the surrounding countryside descended on the city to add their own grievances to the protests, rumors circulated that they were planning the mass murder of white people. Threatened, Quito's elite closed ranks to defeat the rebellion and retain their place at the top of colonial society. In the years after the rebellion, across Spanish America, social and economic cleavages within colonial society continued to limit the depth and breadth of protest activities even in areas where populations were the most aggrieved by royal interventions in American life.

Conclusion

The vignettes of this chapter—fighting among Africans, the Dutch, and the Portuguese in Brazil and a treaty between the British and Mughal Empires—mark transitions of power, strategy, and structure that spanned the world during the period between 1655 and 1765. At the start of this era, a handful of large land-based empires dominated the Afro-Eurasian landmass. These included three large Islamic states (the Ottoman, Safavid, and Mughal Empires) and two new dynasties governing established polities (Romanov Russia and Qing China). At the western edge of the supercontinent, maritime empires competed over resources and power, especially France, Britain, the Netherlands, Spain, and Portugal. By 1765, the fortunes of these states had diverged. The Safavid Empire was gone. Spain, Portugal, the Netherlands, and the Mughal Empire remained, but greatly diminished, relying increasingly on the resources and goodwill of other states to maintain their places in the global order.

Some states, especially Britain, China, and Russia, appeared stronger at the end of this period than when it began. In England, a "glorious" revolution had retained the monarchy but limited its power, part of a broad reconception of sovereignty that made its government more responsible to the governed. This did not mean democracy in the sense of broad participation in the selection of government officials, but the principle that legitimacy derived from consent of the governed was an important innovation. The French, Russian, Chinese, and Ottoman Empires, among others, retained the principle of absolutism, claiming that rule was ordained by a supernatural power, but even there, competition from other stakeholders was increasing. In the Americas, indigenous peoples resisted the expansion of European-derived states, challenging the terms by which non-European, or mixed-race, people could exercise control over their own territories or have meaningful input into decisions about the imperial political, social, and economic order.

Increasing investment in human bondage unified the world's great landmasses. Slavery was the essential piece in a triangular trade that brought labor from Africa to work in the Americas, mainly Brazil and the Caribbean. During this period, the slave trade engulfed and destroyed millions of lives and fundamentally transformed both Africa and the Americas. Most of the profits from this slave labor flowed into Europe, enriching the great maritime empires there and providing capital, in Britain particularly, for economic development. This, in turn, would fuel a new round of imperialism. The effects on Africa and the Americas cannot be overstated: although a few African polities thrived on the slave trade, most were depopulated, particularly of their most productive people, with demographic, economic, and political consequences that would last for centuries. During this period, the movement of Africans to the Americas—almost all of it forced—far exceeded European migration, contributing to a complex and often violent racial interaction that defined many aspects of American life.

At opposite ends of Afro-Eurasia, very different models of rulership emerged from this period. At one end, new ideas about sovereignty and legitimacy were taking hold. These ideas spread as Britain took the lead in overseas empire from rivals like France and Spain, but they also challenged regimes across Europe (and European-founded states in the Americas) to find new sources for legitimacy, stability, and power. New ideas of rulership also developed in China, as Qing emperors grappled with the cultural and political diversity of their empire. By 1765, the Qing Empire was at its height, expanding across what is now Mongolia and Tibet. Japan, too, was prosperous and stable. Given the upheaval in Europe and the Atlantic world that continued into the nineteenth century, one might have thought that the next hundred years would be "the East Asian Century," but it was not to be.

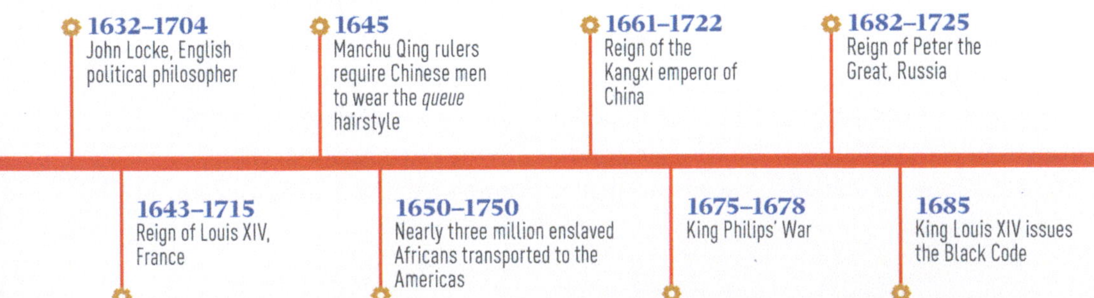
TIMELINE
1632–1704
John Locke, English political philosopher
1643–1715
Reign of Louis XIV, France
1645
Manchu Qing rulers require Chinese men to wear the queue hairstyle
1650–1750
Nearly three million enslaved Africans transported to the Americas
1661–1722
Reign of the Kangxi emperor of China
1675–1678
King Philips' War
1682–1725
Reign of Peter the Great, Russia
1685
King Louis XIV issues the Black Code

A Few Good Books

Daniel Baugh. *The Global Seven Years War, 1754–1763: Britain and France in a Great Power Contest.* London: Routledge, 2011.

David Eltis. *The Rise of African Slavery in the Americas.* Cambridge: Cambridge University Press, 2000.

Jill Lepore. *The Name of War: King Philip's War and the Origins of American Identity.* New York: Vintage, 1999.

Jonathan D. Spence. *Emperor of China: Self-portrait of K'ang-hsi.* New York: Vintage, 1988.

Audrey Truschke. *Aurangzeb: The Life and Legacy of India's Most Controversial King.* Stanford: Stanford University Press, 2017.

William Urban. *Matchlocks to Flintlocks: Warfare in Europe and Beyond, 1500–1700.* London: Frontline Books, 2011.

For instructional resources and study aids, please go to **www.oup.com/us/carter**. *For primary sources connected to this chapter, please see the table of contents for* Sources for Forging the Modern World *included at the back of the book.*

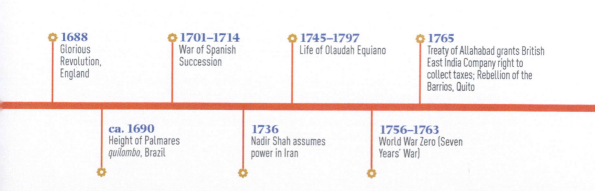

1688 Glorious Revolution, England

ca. 1690 Height of Palmares *quilombo*, Brazil

1701–1714 War of Spanish Succession

1736 Nadir Shah assumes power in Iran

1745–1797 Life of Olaudah Equiano

1756–1763 World War Zero (Seven Years' War)

1765 Treaty of Allahabad grants British East India Company right to collect taxes; Rebellion of the Barrios, Quito

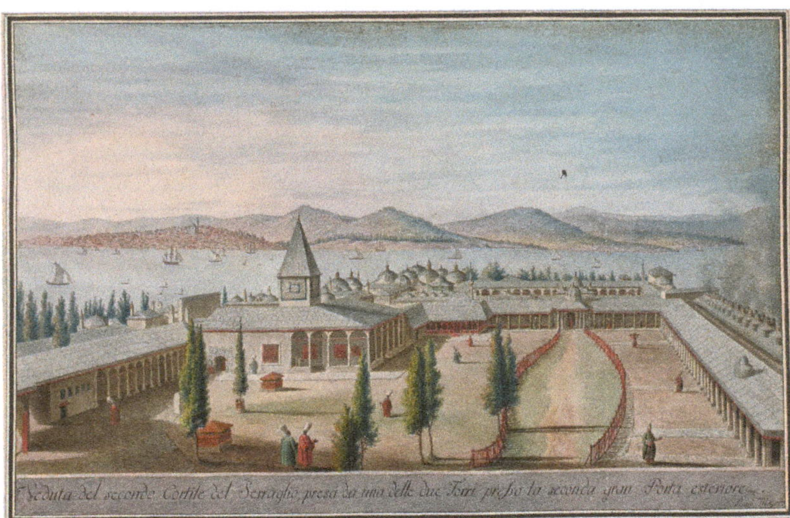

(TOP) The 1755 Lisbon Earthquake. The Lisbon earthquake of 1755 destroyed the Portuguese capital and killed as many as forty thousand people. This 1760 painting by João Glama-Stroberle (1708–1792) depicts a scene in front of the Church of Santa Catarina. The painting conveys religious interpretations of the natural disaster. In contrast, the analysis and responses of many others, from scientists to government officials, lead many scholars to call this the first "modern" natural disaster.

(BOTTOM) Courtyard of Topkapi Palace, Istanbul. The original structures of Topkapi Palace date to the mid-fifteenth century. At its height, the palace complex served as the sultan's residence and the seat of imperial governance, with several thousand people living and working within its walls. By the time the Gulhane Edict was signed there, it was no longer the royal residence but remained an important site for government offices and events. This watercolor, capturing the courtyards of the palace as they appeared in the 1780s, was painted by Luigi Mayer (1755–1803), an associate of Sir Robert Ainslie (ca. 1730–1812), for many years the British ambassador to the Ottoman emperor.

CHAPTER 6

A New Order for the Ages

1755–1839

On November 1, 1755, a devastating earthquake flattened Lisbon, the capital of the Portuguese Empire. The quake, as powerful as 9.0 on the Richter scale, caused damage across the Iberian Peninsula and generated a tsunami that struck islands in the Caribbean Sea, over three thousand miles away. Fires burned in the city for a week, destroying buildings that had survived the initial disaster. Tens of thousands of people were killed, injured, or displaced. Two thirds of the city's housing stock collapsed, and most of its larger buildings, including churches, monasteries, convents, and government buildings, suffered significant, and in many cases irreparable, damage. The Lisbon earthquake is by some measures the largest disaster of this kind ever recorded in Europe.

Responses to the tragedy led some historians to describe this as the first "modern" European disaster. Some contemporaries called the event demonic or a punishment from God, but many others proposed natural and scientific explanations for the disaster and responded to it accordingly. Prime minister Sebastião José de Carvalho e Melo (1699–1782) quickly centralized relief and rebuilding efforts, fighting the spread of disease in the short term and using the opportunity in the longer term to renovate central Lisbon, introducing a new architectural style and "earthquake-proof" construction. The Portuguese Crown rewarded him with noble titles, including marquis of Pombal. The marquis used his power over imperial affairs in the coming decades to impose the Pombaline reforms. Pombal championed broad changes in the Portuguese Empire designed to increase revenue for the royal coffers, subordinate clerical authority to the state, expand economic activity on the empire's periphery, centralize administration, and even raise the quality of Portuguese wines.

In 1839, almost a century after the marquis de Pombal first began his reforms in Portugal, sixteen-year-old Ottoman sultan Abdulmecid (1823–1861) gathered an audience of government officials, clerics, and foreign diplomats in the gardens of the opulent Topkapi Palace to hear the announcement of the Gulhane (Rose Bower) Edict. Frequently attributed to the efforts of foreign minister Mustafa Reșid Pasha (1800–1858), who had been the empire's ambassador to both Paris and London, the edict announced a commitment to reform the administration of the Ottoman Empire and the relationship between the state and its peoples. In contrast to the earthquake in Lisbon, the Ottoman Empire was being shaken during this era by independence movements in Egypt, Serbia, and Greece; unrest in other parts of the empire; and shifting international power relationships. In response, Ottoman rulers created new principles of taxation, military recruitment, and legal administration

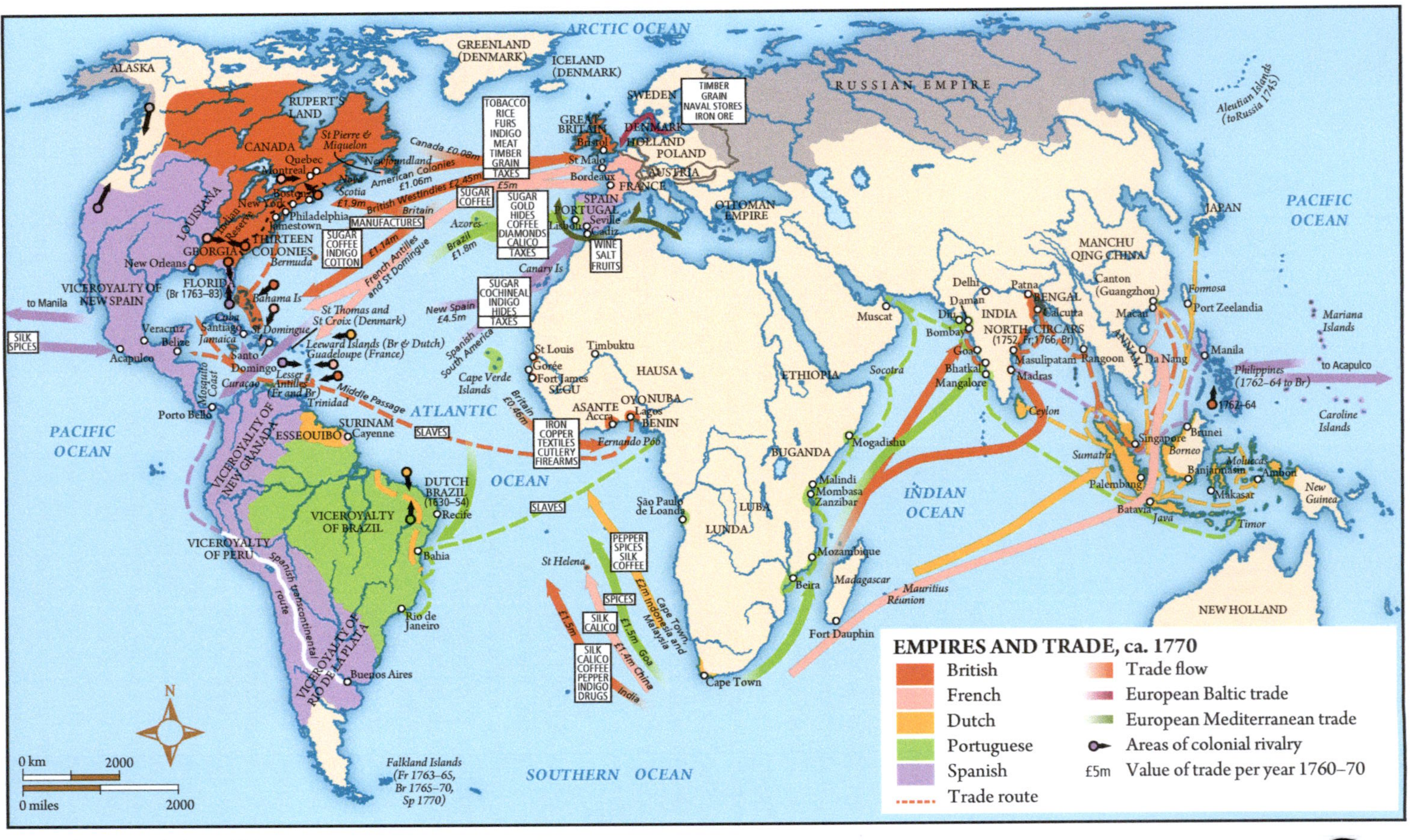

Map 6.1 Empires and Trade, ca. 1770

and applied them universally rather than distinguishing between Muslim and non-Muslim subjects. The Gulhane Edict, paradoxically announcing both "a thorough alteration and renewal of ancient customs," initiated a half century of sweeping changes in the Ottoman Empire known as the Tanzimat (Reorganization).

In this chapter, we analyze transformations in internal structures and global political relations from the mid-eighteenth century to the mid-nineteenth century. We begin by surveying the philosophical and political ferment in the Atlantic world associated with the Enlightenment, focusing on relationships between states and individuals. In the next sections of the chapter, we first explore the US War of Independence and the French Revolution and then examine upheaval in Europe in their aftermath.

After explaining these events, we turn to the relationship between these events and the path to independence in the Caribbean and Latin America. By the 1820s, leaders in regions once controlled by the British, French, Spanish, and Portuguese began building new political regimes, writing constitutions, and fighting over the correct formula to create and maintain nonhereditary, constitutional states. Decades of warfare replaced the formal European imperial presence with independent, liberal, republican constitutional nation-states in most of the Western Hemisphere. These new states struggled for political and economic stability and worked to define justice amid competing rights claims—liberal, national, popular—on both sides of the Atlantic.

In the final section of the chapter, we expand further our geographic and thematic scope. The proliferation of independent states in the early nineteenth century contributed to a burgeoning debate over definitions of nation and citizen and their relationship to territorial states. We describe the terms of these debates and ensuing events as they played out during this era in several regions, including the Ottoman Empire, laying a foundation for subsequent analysis of the challenges to constructing a world of nation-states over the following two centuries.

Questions to Consider as You Read Chapter Six:

1. This era is sometimes called the *age of revolution*. Do you think there are common goals that the different revolutions aspired to? Are there universal rights or values that people are entitled to rebel against their governments to achieve? What are some of these rights?
2. The Pombaline and Tanzimat reforms were, among other things, attempts to apply scientific principles to statecraft. Do you think there are principles that can apply universally to government across different times and places? If they vary, what are some of the reasons why?

What Is Enlightenment?

New ideas and changing circumstances converged in the Atlantic empires during the eighteenth century, spurring changes on the peripheries of those empires but also in the imperial centers themselves. Scholars, authors, and provocateurs used metaphors of light and motion to describe their new ways of thinking about the world.

In English, the term *Enlightenment* came to be associated with these thinkers, who disagreed about many things but shared some assumptions about the world around them. These assumptions included a belief that the methods of natural science could be used to understand all aspects of life, including the principles that govern human behavior as well as interactions among peoples and societies. Enlightenment thinkers generally embraced the idea that the goal of inquiry was not only to discover these principles but also to use this understanding to improve behaviors, structures, and interactions. Furthermore, many believed that properly applying these methods would lead to inevitable and continuous improvement: progress. During the second half of the eighteenth century, these ideas provided both a vocabulary for and an independent impulse toward movements proposing significant change.

Reason and Progress

In the massive *Encylopédie*, an ambitious compendium of human knowledge edited by the Frenchman Denis Diderot (1713–1784), the entry on *political authority* asserted the foundational principle that "no man receives from nature the right to command others." Political power, the entry continues, must be the result of either coercion (fragile and illegitimate) or a social contract (enduring and just). Voltaire (1694–1778), another French Enlightenment thinker, praised the changes, reflective of John Locke's theories, written into the English Bill of Rights at the time of the Glorious Revolution. Voltaire turned this observation into a scathing critique of the French monarchy's absolutism.

The Prussian philosopher Immanuel Kant (1724–1804) tried to summarize the general approach of like-minded thinkers of the era in a magazine article entitled, "Answering the Question: What Is Enlightenment?" In this essay, published in 1784, Kant asserted that the motto of the Enlightenment movement was *Sapere Aude!*—"Have the courage to use your own understanding," or more concisely, "Dare to know!" French writer Nicolas de Condorcet (1743–1794) expressed this faith in progress through reason most fully, writing that "the perfectibility of man is unlimited," dependent only on increasing education and its application. Foreshadowing the attempts to spread European interpretations of Enlightenment values and government across the globe, Condorcet believed these values to be universal and that all human beings—regardless of race, gender, nationality, or religion—would benefit from their implementation and that over time, the stewardship of self-defined modern countries over the earth's peoples and resources would deliver a better world for all.

Even as many, like Condorcet, celebrated the limitless potential of progress, others embraced another Enlightenment value: skepticism. Voltaire was famous for mocking religion—especially Christianity—but he also turned his caustic wit on those who believed that the use of reason would result in inevitable progress. Voltaire's character Pangloss in his 1759 novella *Candide* stands in for overly optimistic thinkers like Condorcet. In the book, while the title character lies beneath the rubble of the 1755 Lisbon earthquake, his mentor and teacher Pangloss ignores Candide's pleas for help so that Pangloss can instead puzzle out the causes of the earthquake.

Enlightenment thinkers also took on key questions about political structures and the distribution of resources. The Scotsman Adam Smith (1723–1790), one of the most influential thinkers in political economy, trained as a moral philosopher. This background strongly influenced the analysis and prescriptions for the way states should create the conditions for prosperity that appear in his dense and lengthy book, *An Inquiry into the Nature and Causes of the Wealth of Nations* (1776). Smith challenged mercantilist views that states should hoard wealth, advocating instead a system of free trade through which individuals would generate wealth and contribute to the betterment of society. A subsequent generation of political economists, including Jean-Baptiste Say (1767–1832), Thomas Malthus (1766–1834), and David Ricardo (1772–1823), considered the role of individual choice in distributing resources, challenging conventional wisdom about the creation and maintenance of wealth and raising questions about how a state could balance competing claims over life, liberty, and property.

The Reform Impulse in Europe

Governments reformed structures and policies across Europe during this era, as many powerful elites accepted the notion that new ideas about human nature could improve society. Although Enlightenment ideals are often associated with aspirations toward democratic and republican forms of government, it was not necessarily so. Voltaire and Kant shared a belief that enlightened monarchs could effectively reform society. Kant wrote in "What Is Enlightenment?" that a sovereign should see "no danger . . . in allowing his subjects to make public use of their reason and to publish their thoughts on a better formulation of his legislation and even their open-minded criticisms of the laws already made." Based on ideas like this, Prussian king Frederick (1712–1786) and Russian empress Catherine (1729–1796) practiced *enlightened absolutism*, borrowing the Enlightenment ideal to make reforms autocratically.

Whether limited in power or absolutist, central governments were revising their views about the rights and powers of individuals within a state. This had an especially strong impact on criminal justice. Across Europe, from Russia to England, attempts were made to discern the purposes of laws and the goals of punishment so that they might be used to improve society. As a result, many European regimes codified legal practices, standardized the operations of the courts, and abolished torture. In 1764, the Italian jurist Cesare Beccaria (1738–1794) laid the foundation, based on Enlightenment principles, for modern European opposition to both torture and capital punishment.

Ideas about the importance of compulsory education for children also circulated. In some parts of Europe, the idea that it was necessary for all children to have some education had roots in the Protestant Reformation of the sixteenth century—if one needed to read the Bible to be saved, one needed to be able to read. But it was only in 1763 that Frederick the Great of Prussia established Europe's first state-mandated system of compulsory elementary education to develop future generations' social discipline and commitment to the state and its sovereign.

Imperial Reform in the Western Hemisphere

Like other European empires, the Spanish and Portuguese monarchies implemented reforms designed to raise revenue and protect imperial interests through rational government that adhered to Enlightenment principles. In the Portuguese Empire, for two decades after the Lisbon earthquake, the marquis de Pombal implemented ambitious political, fiscal, judicial, and military reforms. Even the capital of Portugal's colony, Brazil, was moved from Bahia to Rio de Janeiro in 1763 to improve efficient administration of the empire. The effects of these reforms varied by region and socioeconomic status and were not always welcome: in 1777, Queen Maria I of Portugal, responding to criticism of Pombal's reform measures, stripped him of all political authority.

The Spanish monarchy also instituted policy changes, known as the Bourbon reforms after the ruling family's dynastic name, in the second half of the eighteenth century. The Bourbons reorganized the empire's political and economic structures and changed appointment policies for imperial officials. New officials were deployed from Spain throughout the empire, transforming Spanish America. Over the second half of the eighteenth century, silver production, agricultural output, imperial commerce, and tax collection all grew significantly in Spanish America. There were, however, costs to change. Conflict among colonial elites increased as Crown policies favored those born in Spain (*peninsulares*) over those born in the Americas (*criollos*). Mounting tax burdens and the disruption of entrenched economic, political, and social relations fostered resentment between classes and among ethnic and racial groups. For many, the changed rules and enforcement policies led to greater poverty.

The reforms sparked dozens of uprisings across Spanish America. The Rebellion of the Barrios in Quito, examined in Chapter 5, was just one. The greatest threat to European rule in Spanish America during this time occurred in the Andean highlands, in the viceroyalty of Peru, where the leader of an indigenous community proclaimed the restoration of Inca political and social order, took the name Tupac Amaru II (1738–1781), after the last Inca ruler from the time of the conquest, and called for the overthrow of the Spanish Empire. The Tupac Amaru Rebellion (1780–1782) and others like it frightened most Europeans and split the indigenous elite. Both groups had complaints about the Bourbon reforms, but fear of what would ensue if imperial order were overthrown outweighed those concerns. The rebels lost and were harshly punished.

These responses to the Bourbon reforms highlight an important contrast between British America and Spanish America. In Spanish America, indigenous peoples were a primary labor force and tax base, and their souls were still perceived by many important actors in the empire as one of the primary treasures of imperialism. In British North America, however, indigenous peoples were seen and treated increasingly as outside the political body of the British Empire.

Britain emerged from the global conflict of the Seven Years' War as the dominant European power in the Atlantic and Indian Ocean regions. By defeating the French at Québec in 1759, Britain could dominate North America, including the immensely profitable Caribbean Sea. Spain still claimed most of western North America but the Spanish Empire's centers of power were far from British North America. Vast expanses of the continent were still controlled by sovereign indigenous groups. To secure the advantages it had won in the war, the British government needed to reform how it governed its empire.

In North America, one of Britain's primary goals was to gain more revenue to help pay down the large war debt. The thirteen colonies that would become the United States were already an economic engine that Britain intended to take greater advantage of. Northern colonies produced timber and manufactured goods. Southern colonies produced cotton, tobacco, rice, and sugar, largely with enslaved labor. Colonial cities like Boston, Philadelphia, New York, and Charleston, South Carolina, were markets for goods manufactured in England. From Britain's perspective, taking revenue from the colonies to pay down the debt that had been accumulated to secure the colonies' survival was fair, but the colonists did not see it that way. Taxes that raised additional revenue for the imperial center provoked angry and violent responses. Tensions between and among colonies—coupled with social, economic, and political differences within colonies—meant that any organized collective action was slow to materialize. But the new laws helped to overcome internal divisions and create a stronger sense of unity within the colonies.

Revolution and Reaction

Historians debate the relationships between Enlightenment ideas and the political changes that gripped the Atlantic world between 1750 and 1850. Some argue that the driving forces behind revolution were demographic and economic change. Others challenge the very idea of a coherent movement called the Enlightenment, arguing that it cherry-picks a small number of thinkers and texts from the many philosophical and political debates occurring over a longer period across a wider area. Nonetheless, as the political geography of the Atlantic world changed during this era, the main actors and groups debating and influencing these outcomes generally embraced the framework of Enlightenment ideas and aspirations.

The Breakup of British North America

Popular protests against government economic and administrative changes are already a familiar story in this book. Some things were different in the eighteenth-century Atlantic world, however. Both sides of the Atlantic buzzed with challenges to the foundational logic of Europe's political systems. Locke, Rousseau, Condorcet, and other Enlightenment thinkers argued that individuals had rights independent of their governments, that human society was moving toward perfection, and that government could only rule with the consent of the governed. Although much more slowly than in our own day, these ideas circulated back and forth across the Atlantic Ocean in books and pamphlets. Moreover, the people developing these ideas could themselves travel great distances more quickly and reliably than ever before.

The British colonists' protest slogan, "No taxation without representation," was not a refusal to pay taxes; it was a demand to be included in the decision-making process. The few additional cents that colonists would pay for tea or newspapers wouldn't necessarily cause economic hardship, but opposition to British rule rallied around the idea that London was not consulting the colonists before making decisions. The first armed confrontation between local militia and British troops took place at Concord and Lexington, in Massachusetts, in 1775. A year later, the Declaration of Independence invoked Locke's social contract, asserting that humans have "inalienable" rights—rights that they have simply because they are human—and that governments are put in place to secure these rights, not to grant them, and certainly not to deny them. Because the state (i.e., the British Crown) had violated this contract, the colonists had the right to make a new state. Out of this conflict emerged the United States of America, but the rebellion's success was far from certain at its start. The war lasted almost ten years.

By 1783, when a treaty signed in Paris settled the terms of peace between Britain and its former colonies, tens of thousands of people were dead, tens of thousands more headed into exile elsewhere in the British Empire, and leaders of the new United States of America were left to form a government. The first try—the Articles of Confederation—didn't last long; but the articles' weaknesses point out some important features of modern states. The articles strictly limited central authority and emphasized the power of the individual states that comprised the union. When a rebellion broke out in 1786—again in Massachusetts over economic grievances—the new government could not easily raise troops to put down the insurgency. Unable to levy taxes, regulate commerce, or maintain an army, the US government had little power to exercise sovereignty. Many observers, including officials of the British Empire, expected the weak new state to fail entirely, which would open new opportunities for European empires to return to the region.

The new state survived. Conceding the failure of the Articles of Confederation, a new document refounded the nation-state, strengthening and more clearly defining the nature of its sovereignty and its relationship to its citizens. The Constitutional Convention that began in 1787 was originally convened to revise the Articles of Confederation, not to construct a completely new basis for a national government, but the Massachusetts uprising known as Shays's Rebellion, as well as other events, prompted a more comprehensive effort to strengthen the central government so that it could enforce rules and maintain order while still protecting the prerogatives of state governments and safeguarding individuals from tyranny. Long debates and great compromise were at the core of the convention.

The US Constitution, finally adopted in 1789, was an early example of a literal social contract, containing both Enlightenment aspirations and the painful contradictions that reflected the social and economic realities of its day. It established the idea that the state guarantees and protects (but does not bestow) rights. This was a triumph of Enlightenment principles, but contradictions remained. For instance, if the state is guarantor of the rights of its citizens, what happens to people who are not included in that category? The new Constitution left many millions of people without a voice in politics or even basic rights, because they were defined as "not citizens." Women, for instance, would not get the right to vote in national elections until the twentieth century. Even more egregiously, the new Constitution accepted slavery as a basic condition of the new nation.

Historians Explore How Radical Was the American Revolution?

Historian Gordon Wood argued that the War of Independence "created a society fundamentally different from the colonial society of the eighteenth century. It was in fact a new society unlike any that had ever existed anywhere in the world," overthrowing privilege and making a new category of independent men. Wood saw the revolutionary nature of American independence not in immediate socioeconomic transformation but in ideological change. Doing away with hereditary privileges and social standing as the basis for political authority, the revolutionaries had fundamentally changed society and embraced Enlightenment values in a way no society had done before.

Wood's book, *The Radicalism of the American Revolution*, first published in 1992, contains one of the more well-known interpretations of US independence. Wood's views were popular—his book won the Pulitzer Prize—but controversial. Some historians rejected Wood's narrow focus on elite sources. Many asked how a section of the book titled "Equality" could ignore the issue of slavery. Others wrote that Wood exaggerated the power of the British monarchy before the revolution and understated the importance of social class and privilege after it. How, some asked, could Wood claim that the revolution had made the United States the most egalitarian society in the world when he himself noted that income distribution in the new country was more unequal after independence than before?

The colonists protesting British imperial policy in North America in the 1760s and 1770s generally were not poor. They were not enslaved. To the contrary, some of the men who played crucial roles in the American Revolution, such as Thomas Jefferson and George Washington, owned slaves themselves. Many lived on estates with servants. Subsequent upheavals in the Caribbean, Europe, and Spanish America would entail much larger numbers of poor, oppressed, and marginalized people. Many historians have even questioned whether the US War for Independence can really be called revolutionary. Revolution, after all, must be a radical step. By this logic, only extreme disruptions and extreme outcomes characterize true revolutions. Economically, the conditions in the American colonies weren't much different after Independence. Add to this the fact that those who held positions of power after independence were the same kinds of people who held power before it. An image emerges in some historical works that independence was more a change of administration than a radical transformation.

Supporters of the revolutionary change thesis respond that, in the context of the 1770s, what happened in British North America was indeed radical, even if not a complete break with the past. The (mostly) men who organized the revolution and the new state—despite being wealthy and white—felt oppressed, drawing on the new Enlightenment doctrines that were redefining politics. They asserted that they were governed without their consent and stood on the principle that English rule over the colonies violated the social contract. Building alliances between wealthy gentlemen and the common farmers who composed much of the colonial population might have seemed impossible, but the ideals of the Enlightenment provided common cause for New England farmers, Virginia plantation owners, and others who fought against the British.

A rich debate continues over the nature of the US War of Independence, enhanced by new research that focuses on previously neglected populations and issues. Tens of thousands of colonists remained loyal to the British Crown and established their base in New York. Most left the new country after the war and dispersed throughout the British Empire, bringing ideas about the implications of their experiences with them. The royal governor of Virginia and other officials offered manumission to slaves who took up the Crown's cause; approximately twenty thousand African Americans joined units such as the Ethiopian Regiment and the Black Pioneers. The war split the indigenous population as well. Some Native American nations formed alliances with the patriots and others allied with the loyalists, with repercussions for these communities long after the Treaty of Paris was signed. How would these populations assess the radicalism of the American Revolution?[1]

From the perspective of world history, in both conception and execution, the new United States was a bold experiment that sparked debate and action across the Atlantic world. In hindsight, the creation of a new nation that would become the world's dominant economic, military, and cultural power within two centuries was a watershed moment. At the time, however, the continuities of the new nation were as important as its differences. The same class of people—and sometimes the same individuals—held power. Many institutions and practices rooted in the empire still governed and regulated the new nation, without a monarch atop them. Women remained disenfranchised. Slavery persisted. And the Revolution did not spread immediately: not even all British North America revolted, because Canada remained part of the British Empire. The successful revolt of thirteen colonies against Europe's most powerful empire was impressive but was not perceived as a threat to the global order.

Revolution in France and Haiti

A more comprehensive and violent revolution occurred in France. The French Revolution, like the American one, had mundane roots: eighteenth-century wars, including support for the American independence cause, had drained France's treasuries. A complex and antiquated tax system contributed to fiscal malaise;

---

1 Gordon Wood, *The Radicalism of the American Revolution* (New York: Knopf, 1992). Many of the leading historians of the United States debated Wood's book in the forum, "How Revolutionary Was the Revolution? A Discussion of Gordon S. Wood's *The Radicalism of the American Revolution*," *William and Mary Quarterly* third series 51, no. 4 (October, 1994): 677–716. Recent works that have examined the revolutionary era from the perspectives of different groups include Alan Taylor, *The Divided Ground: Indians, Settlers, and the Northern Borderland of the American Revolution* (New York: Alfred A. Knopf, 2006); and Maya Jasanoff, *Liberty's Exiles: American Loyalists in the Revolutionary World* (New York: Vintage, 2012). A good overview of the changing nature of historical investigations and interpretations may be found in Alfred F. Young and Gregory H. Nobles, *Whose American Revolution Was It? Historians Interpret the Founding* (New York: New York University Press, 2011).

by 1788, the French government was spending 50 percent of its annual revenue on debt service. Population growth and rising prices squeezed peasants who by 1788 were spending half of their income just on bread. At the same time, a class of *nouveau riche* ("new rich") grew wealthy through trade and finance, fueling inequality and simultaneously challenging France's traditional socioeconomic order, still medieval in many aspects.

France had fewer overseas colonies to generate revenue than Great Britain, a situation made worse by losing many colonies *to* Britain. So, the French Crown looked within France itself to finance wars and other government ventures, but the French royal debt grew so large that an exasperated and desperate King Louis XVI (1754–1793) needed to find additional ways to raise revenues. He decided to convene a traditional consultative body, the Estates General, to gain support for his plan. This institution, which had not met since 1614, was rooted in medieval notions of the distinct social classes (estates) of the political body: the clergy; the nobility; and commoners (the "Third Estate"). By custom, the Estates General organized the three estates into three voices of equal weight to offer advice and consent to the monarch on important state matters, like taxation. But as Louis XVI and his advisers set into motion the revival of this cobwebbed institution, many observers, and then some delegates themselves, argued that this new meeting of the Estates General should be reorganized to better reflect Enlightenment principles, taking into account the fact that each of the first two estates (clergy and nobles) numbered in the thousands, but the third estate represented millions of people. Supporters of change called on the delegates assembling at the Versailles Palace to meet as one body, a National Assembly, and to take for themselves a mandate to consider fundamental changes in France far beyond the king's fiscal agenda.

Thus began a series of confrontations between delegates and the monarchy. In the summer of 1789, after winning the battle to meet as one body, the National Assembly crafted the Declaration of the Rights of Man and Citizen, with similarities in Enlightenment language and principles to the US Declaration of Independence and other revolutionary documents. A moderate constitution issued in 1791, retaining the monarchy but limiting the king's powers, lasted only a year. More radical proposals emerged in the National Assembly, which created another new constitution (1792) embracing universal male suffrage and a republican government that stripped the king and all nobles of titles and privileges. The new state was to be based solely on reason: laws were passed to change religious practices and subordinate the clergy to the state because the Catholic Church and its practices were seen as irrational and detrimental to the revolution's goals. Time itself was rationalized: the government declared that days would be ten hours long and that a new calendar would be adopted to eliminate all references

Olympe De Gouges. Frustrated by the exclusion of women from the French revolutionary agenda, Olympe de Gouges wrote a counterpart to the Declaration of the Rights of Man titled Declaration of the Rights of Woman and the Female Citizen. This document, which quoted the Declaration of the Rights of Man and then asserted that they applied to women as well, and de Gouges's other writings were deemed treasonous by the revolutionary leaders, who had her executed. She was one of just three women known to have been executed by guillotine during the French Revolution.

to religion and royalty in the names of days and months. Although changes to the calendar did not survive, a new system of weights and measures—the metric system—was one of the enduring rational innovations that emerged from the revolutionary era.

Violence escalated along with debates over the future of France. Surrounded by hostile monarchies and beset by internal conspiracies against the revolution, leaders of the republic grew more extreme. In 1792, France declared war on Austria, ruled at the time by the French queen's brother. Prussia joined the fight against the revolutionary regime. King Louis XVI was stripped of his authority and then executed as a traitor in January 1793. Summary justice was meted out against others accused of opposing the revolution, even as factions within the revolutionary movement struggled to define their principles and establish a functioning government. An estimated fifty thousand people were killed and five hundred thousand imprisoned during a time of extreme violence and disorder that came to be known as the Terror, which peaked in 1793–1794.

One institution that appeared to be functioning well was the army. Mass conscription, a military draft, created a French army of hundreds of thousands marching off to defend the nation. They achieved success on the battlefield against the armies of surrounding monarchies. Astute observers saw in this the future of warfare: the citizen soldier.

Weary of war and internal chaos, a new coalition formed to oppose the most radical leaders of the Revolution. Its members wrote another constitution and increasingly relied on a young military officer to assist them in reestablishing order. Napoleon Bonaparte, a dynamic general and charismatic leader, outmaneuvered his civilian mentors and took power in a coup d'état in 1799. By 1804, Napoleon was crowned emperor and France was again ruled by an autocrat.

On the eve of the French Revolution, the western region of the island of Hispaniola—Saint-Domingue, later Haiti—was the most productive of France's sugar–slave colonies. The colony's half-million enslaved Africans produced more than 130 million pounds of sugar annually. It was also home to a much smaller but important population of free persons of color and a still smaller number of whites, some wealthy and some not. The emergence of the National Assembly in revolutionary France linked local issues of rights and exclusions to empire-wide debates about citizenship. But while the colony's white population resisted any move to create equality for all free peoples, let alone abolish slavery, the National Assembly in France vacillated on both issues. Unwilling to await the outcome of debates in a distant and disintegrating imperial center, people of color, both slave and free, began a war for their equality and Haitian independence in 1791.

As the French National Assembly moved slowly on abolition and racial equality, antirevolutionary Spain, seeking to undermine its French rivals, supplied arms to Haiti's people of color. When the revolutionary government in France finally agreed to abolition, internal dissent divided Haiti's people of color. In the ensuing civil war, François Toussaint Louverture (1743–1803), a former slave, emerged as a political and military leader able to secure control over Saint-Domingue. Suspicious of Napoleon's intentions as the new leader of the French Empire, Toussaint issued a new constitution in 1801 proclaiming autonomy from France and appointing himself governor general for life. A subsequent French invasion captured Toussaint, who died in a French prison in 1803, but could not reconquer Haiti. Toussaint's successor, another former slave named Jean-Jacques Dessalines (1758–1806), defeated the French and declared Haiti an independent state. In sum, the second independent nation-state in the Western Hemisphere emerged from beneath the yoke of European colonialism only after a massive self-manumission movement of slaves and a long bloody war. The United States, the Western Hemisphere's first independent nation-state, did not establish diplomatic relations with Haiti until 1862, primarily due to their divergence on issues of race—one slave state and one at the vanguard of freedom for enslaved peoples.

The Collapse of Iberian Empires in the Americas

Napoleon dreamed of building an empire to compete with England based on his Continental System, an enforced isolation of England from affairs on the European mainland. Attempting to implement this, Napoleon arranged the abdication of the Bourbon monarch of Spain and deployed the French army to the Iberian Peninsula. In 1808, he placed his brother Joseph on the Spanish throne, fanning the flames of a popular uprising in Spain.

Throughout Spanish America, populations had to decide how to respond to this crisis. In some regions, elites moved swiftly toward autonomy from Spain. In others, elites vowed loyalty to the empire, meaning they wanted to see little change in daily life. Rebellions proliferated, with some claiming that imperial elites had allied with the French and others that the time had finally come to overturn an unjust social order. Forces loyal to the Spanish Empire were most successful in holding their ground where material, military, and cultural resources were most highly concentrated and where indigenous populations appeared to pose the greatest threat to power structures rooted in empire. Independence forces excelled in regions that had the shallowest political and cultural roots in empire and whose elites calculated they had the most to gain from greater autonomy. The regions around the cities of Buenos Aires (Argentina) and Santiago (Chile) achieved effective autonomy from the empire relatively quickly, while military forces loyal to the empire maintained control over the central regions of New Spain (today's Mexico) and Peru.

Over the next decade, loyalists in the Americas struggled to manage both rebels and the fragmenting Spanish Empire. In Spain, the resistance government meeting in the port city of Cádiz created a liberal constitution for the empire in 1812. When Napoleon was defeated and monarchy restored in 1814, this constitution was rescinded, but unrest inside Spain led to its reimplementation in 1820. Even ardent monarchists tired of Spain's instability. In New Spain, the heart of the Spanish Empire in the Americas, military officers who had defended Spanish rule for years turned against the empire in 1820, helping win the independence of Mexico the following year. In 1826, a military unit loyal to Spain surrendered the Real Felipe fortress in Callao, Peru, leaving the islands of Cuba and Puerto Rico the only formal remnants of three centuries of Spanish colonialism in the Americas. More than a decade of warfare depleted the region's resources and

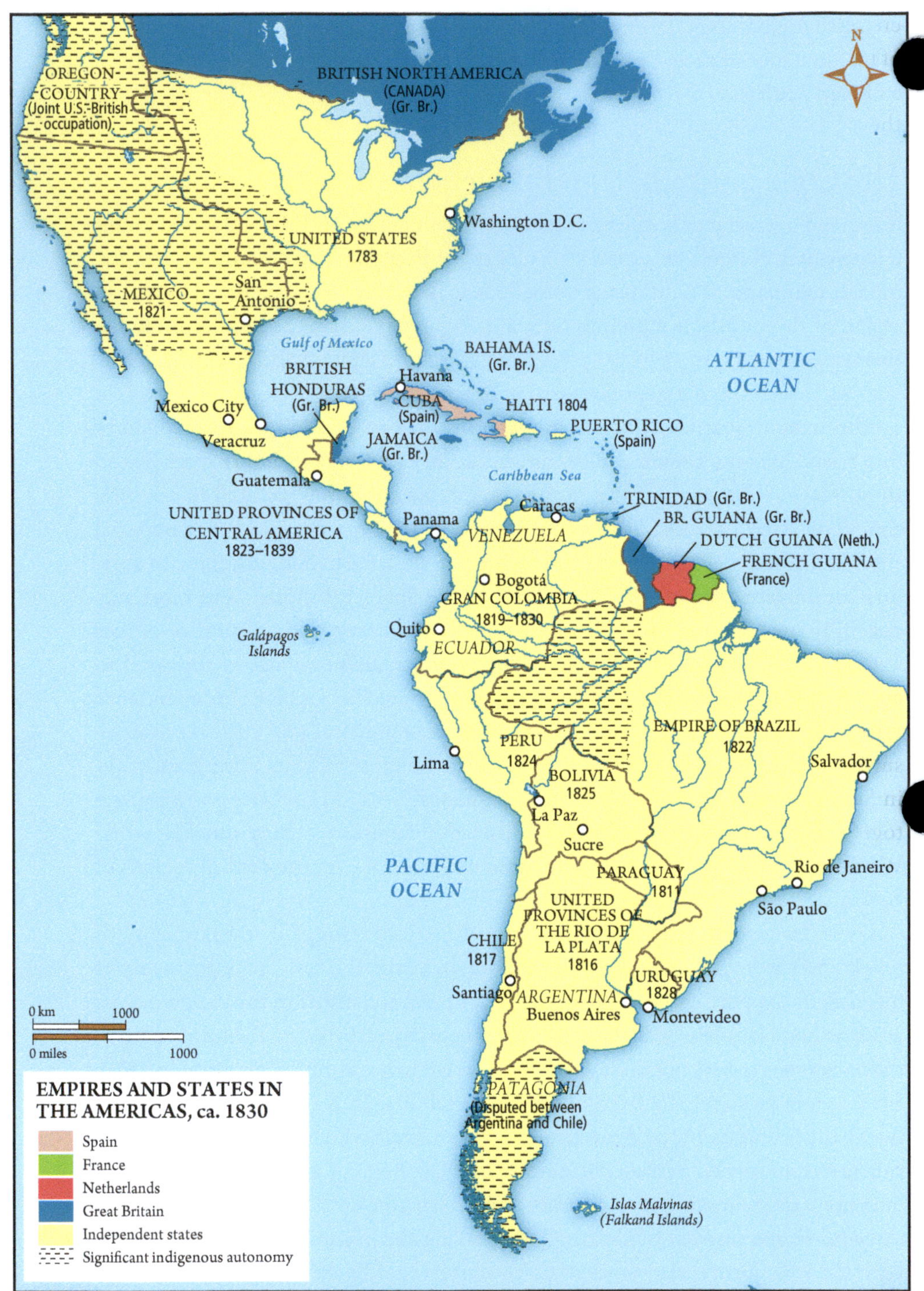

Map 6.2 Empires and States in the Western Hemisphere, ca. 1830

created regional military and political factions that would fight over the meaning of independence into the middle of the nineteenth century.

Brazil's path to independence from Portugal also culminated in the 1820s, but the road and the destination were different from Spanish America. The Pombaline reforms, like the Bourbon reforms, attempted to rationalize the relationship between colony and metropolis but did not have the same disruptive effect. One important reason for this was that distinctions between those born in Europe and those of European descent born in the Americas were never as important in determining political privilege in the Portuguese Empire as in the Bourbon-era Spanish Empire. Another key factor in Brazil's path to independence was the Portuguese response to Napoleon's invasion of the Iberian Peninsula. Facing a French invasion, the Portuguese royal family, with more than ten thousand supporters and the royal treasury, was ushered to safety in Brazil by a British naval escort, becoming the first European royals to set foot in the Americas. There, they established Rio de Janeiro as the temporary new capital of the Portuguese Empire, leaving a governing assembly and an anti-French resistance movement back home. After the Napoleonic Wars, the Portuguese king returned to Portugal, seeking to reassert his authority in Europe, but he left his son Pedro in Brazil. Brazilian elites, unhappy with Portuguese legislators' efforts to subordinate Brazil to Portuguese imperial interests, persuaded Pedro to proclaim Brazil an independent constitutional monarchy. Some fighting ensued, but soon both Portugal and Great Britain signed treaties confirming Brazil's independence, ensuring the survival of a large, Portuguese-speaking, slave-dependent monarchy in South America. Both institutions—slavery and monarchy—remained intact together in Brazil until the end of the 1880s, longer than anywhere else in the Western Hemisphere.

New Challenges of Political Organization

These decades of upheaval transformed power relationships among the European empires, as well as between these empires and their (former) colonies. Most of the Western Hemisphere became untethered from the political and economic relationships with Europe that had defined the Atlantic world for almost three centuries. A radical armed movement destroyed one of Europe's most powerful monarchies from within and exported revolution to its neighbors, as mass citizens' armies marched across the continent. Revolutions spurred reactions as well: people across the political, economic, social, and cultural spectrum attempted to halt, divert, or mitigate the potential damage of the era's dislocations. Those searching for internal and international political stability in the nineteenth century therefore had to take new factors into account.

Defining the Nation

The first phrase of the US Constitution—"We the People"—raised one of the most compelling and challenging questions of modern political organization: Who exactly is the *we*? In other words, to whom does the social contract apply? State builders and political philosophers in this era began to answer the question with the idea of nation. Defining this term is vital—it may be the single most important concept in the rest of this book—but it is a slippery idea. What is a nation? Most nineteenth-century nationalists sought to identify nations based on "common-sense" markers of communal identity like language, religion, physical features like skin and hair color, or geographic homeland. Nationalists placed great value on a population's relationship to iconic spaces like major cities or natural wonders, as well as on collective experiences of violence or trauma, especially in warfare.

Johann Gottlieb Fichte (1762–1814) argued that the nations to which people belonged manifest themselves throughout history and can therefore be readily identified. In his *Addresses to the German Nation* in 1807, Fichte wrote that the eternal spirit of nations transcended time and circumstance; modern states needed to be built to reflect and protect these timeless nations. Ideally, modern states should encompass all—and exclusively—the members of one nation: a nation-state. To use Fichte's example of Germany, all Germans should live in Germany and be governed by fellow Germans, and everyone living in Germany should be German. Italian nationalists made similar claims. In 1831, Giuseppe Mazzini (1805–1872) created Young Italy, a secret society to promote "One, Independent, Free Republic" on the Italian Peninsula.

The fact that both German and Italian nationalism intensified at a time when Napoleon sought to place all of Europe under French domination hints at some fundamental problems with such an idea of nation. Defining what it means to be German (or Italian or any other nationality) turns out to be neither simple nor obvious. Both Fichte and Mazzini knew this, but they were attempting to find a way to overcome cultural, geographic, and economic obstacles to achieve their political goals. It would take decades for unified German and Italian states to emerge. Imagine trying to apply the idea of an eternal nation, grounded in an ancient homeland to the disintegrating empires of the early nineteenth-century Atlantic world, and you can see the complexities inherent in defining the relationship between nations and the states into which they should be fitted.

Yet, feelings of nationalism, and the actions associated with such feelings, became a defining feature of nineteenth-century world history. If nations are neither natural nor unchanging—and the evidence overwhelmingly suggests that they are not—can historical inquiry help us to understand where nations come from? The scholar Ernest Gellner put it bluntly: "Nationalism is not the awakening of nations to self-consciousness: it invents them where they do not exist." Another influential scholar of the history of nationalism and the nation-state, Benedict Anderson, argues that nations are created when individuals join an *imagined community* based on notions of a history and culture shared with hundreds, thousands, or millions of other people, few of whom they will ever meet. These insights do not suggest that nations are not real or unimportant—they are both and shape human history in profound ways—but that they are malleable.[2] In other words, Fichte, Mazzini, and other nationalists were imagining a national community, not reviving or identifying a preexisting thing.

A crucial, and controversial, idea of Anderson's is that the modern concept of nations, as described by people like Fichte, had traction because of historical circumstances that began to emerge in Europe beginning in the mid-fifteenth century. He sees it as deriving from *print capitalism*, that is, the circulation of printed materials in vernacular languages along commercial routes. These materials promoted nationalist visions because a common identity could form over time for people like Fichte through the shared experience of reading particular texts in the same language—books on religion and history as well as fiction and myth.

Freedom and Equality

Enlightenment thought and the rise of nationalism raised additional questions about how social contracts could structure relationships between people and the state. Debates raged about how, when, and why political, social, and economic change can and should be implemented and at what cost. Women like Olympe de Gouges (1748–1793) and Sophie de Condorcet (1764–1822) greeted the early days of the French Revolution with great hope and then lambasted its hypocrisy when the revolutionary ethos of equality was denied to women. Olympe de Gouges advocated the application of Enlightenment principles across gender and racial lines, challenging laws denying women and blacks economic and political rights. She also protested social norms that restricted women to narrowly defined roles. When the Declaration of the Rights of Man and Citizen did not extend equality to women, she penned her own treatise, Declaration of the Rights of Woman and Citizen. An ardent opponent of the death penalty who objected to the execution of the former king, she was herself guillotined during the Terror. On the other side of the English Channel, Mary Wollstonecraft (1759–1797)

---

2 Ernest Gellner, *Thought and Change* (Chicago: University of Chicago Press, 1964). Gellner elaborates on his theories of nationalism in *Nations and Nationalism* (Ithaca, NY: Cornell University Press, 1983). Benedict Anderson, *Imagined Communities*, rev. ed. (London: Verso, 2006).

published *A Vindication of the Rights of Woman* in 1792, arguing that there were no natural distinctions between men and women, only social ones that could be ameliorated through changes in public policy and educational practices.

The age of revolution also inspired political thought that would coalesce into modern "conservative" thinking. Critics of the French Revolution like Edmund Burke (1729–1797) saw it as a lesson in why political change should always be approached with caution and why calls to rewrite the social contract should be greeted with skepticism. Otherwise, argued Burke, the risk of chaos and the complete collapse of institutions built over generations was too great. The question of slavery and abolition was one of the key tests of the nature and limits of the era's changes.

The movement to abolish the transatlantic slave trade connected conscience, international rivalries, and the agency of millions of African-origin peoples. Wealthy Quakers in England pursued this goal relentlessly in Parliament. While slavery pricked the consciences of these Christians, others attacked slavery on philosophical, political, and economic grounds. Opposition to the slave trade grew in England after the US War of Independence and then again during the Napoleonic Wars, although this often had more to do with the chance to damage the economic prospects of rivals than with moral values. Be that as it may, people of conscience used those tactical political openings to expand their campaign for the much more difficult goal of general abolition: elimination of slavery itself, not just the slave trade. Great Britain abolished its slave trade in 1807, but the British Empire still included millions of enslaved laborers. It would take a further two decades to abolish slavery throughout the empire.

In most of the Western Hemisphere, abolition was intimately connected with the wars of independence and the creation of new nation-states. For Haiti, this is clear, as independence and abolition became virtually synonymous. In parts of Spanish America, many slaves freed themselves by fighting in wars of independence; free people of color often linked the cause of abolition to their own participation in independence struggles. Upon achieving independence, new states anxious to gain the recognition of Great Britain were asked to join the campaign to eliminate the slave trade and most did so rather quickly. Nonetheless, whereas Mexico and Central America abolished slavery by the end of the 1820s, the entrenched interests of slaveholders delayed abolition in most Spanish American republics until the middle of the century, as slaveocrats and resource-deprived governments contemplated and negotiated over the obligations that states had to compensate property owners (i.e., slave owners) if they were to confiscate their property (i.e., free their slaves).

Abolition was delayed even longer in the United States and Brazil, as we will see in a later chapter.

Building New Nation-States in Post-Independence Latin America

After independence, the Portuguese Empire in the Americas remained largely intact, and British America split in two. But the collapsing Spanish Empire splintered. Central America, the narrow land bridge between the former viceroyalties of New Spain and New Granada, first separated from New Spain and then fractured into five small, independent states. Armed disputes pitting the port cities of Buenos Aires and Montevideo against each other and both of them against the interior fragmented the former viceroyalty of Río de la Plata. Simón Bolívar (1783–1830), a leader of the independence movement in northern South America, envisioned a single republic, Gran Colombia, stretching from the Atlantic Ocean across the Andes down to the Pacific, from Caracas to Quito and beyond. Gran Colombia was established, with Bolívar as its first president, but the country was beset by conflict. Frustrated in his plans to build and lead a large, unified nation, Bolívar wrote shortly before his death that he was certain of only a few things in

Simón Bolívar and His Generals Plan an Attack against Spanish Commander Pablo Morillo. The revolutionary wave that began with the American Revolution in the 1770s continued across North and South America into the nineteenth century. In South America, Simón Bolívar led the war for independence from Spain. In this painting by Erwin Ochme, Bolívar and his generals are portrayed planning the 1819 surprise attack on the city of Bogotá. Bolívar achieved a series of decisive victories over the Spanish that led to the creation of an independent country (Gran Colombia) with Bolívar as President. Despite these successes, Bolívar's dream of one united country in northern South America did not last. The union disintegrated into three separate republics in 1830, one year before Bolívar died.

life, among them, "America is ungovernable" and "Those who serve a revolution plough the sea."

Historians have struggled to understand why Spanish America remained so unstable for so long. First, it is important to recognize that this vast area was geographically, ethnically, and economically diverse, encompassing tropical rain forest, glaciated mountain ranges, deserts, farm and ranchland, and cosmopolitan cities. Generalizations are difficult. Spanish America had never been a single unified political entity, either before or after the Spanish conquest. After independence, this region became a living laboratory for experiments in constitutional nation-state formation. To understand why, let's do a thought exercise with some issues that the peoples of Spanish America faced after independence. Imagine that your job is to create a new political and economic system, to write a social contract. Familiar questions arise: How should the head of state be chosen? What should be the relationship between the legislature and the executive branch? How should power between the national, state, and local governments be balanced? What kind of economic development policies are you planning? Do you want a national bank or not? Will you protect your local artisans or allow imported goods to enter your country? There is much room for dispute, as we saw in the United States when its first constitution, the Articles of Confederation, failed. Indeed, as we mentioned, many Europeans predicted that the United States would not survive as a unified country. (It almost did not, falling into civil war less than a century after it was founded.)

Now remember that you're not starting to build a new political or economic system from scratch—no state does. You're trying to reengineer an existing set of relationships in the former Spanish Empire after more than a decade of intense civil war and social upheaval. Do you think owning private property is the key to holding office or voting? Do you think that private property is an important principle at all? If you do, what are you going to do about a countryside that is filled with peasants who have access to land as members of a community rather than as individuals? What about former slaves who fought to help achieve independence: do they get to vote or not? If you decide to restrict voting (based on literacy, income, property holding, etc.), how will you tell people who fought to have more control over their own destiny that they don't get a say in determining the country's future? Are you ready to go to war with them? They still have their arms.

Then, there are other questions that are less apparent from our twenty-first-century vantage point. What if government revenue used to come primarily from special "Indian" taxes on indigenous peoples? Would you abolish them as unjust and watch the state collapse for lack of revenue? Or would you try to keep collecting that tax and alienate a population that won't see the difference between you and the former officials of the Spanish Empire, whom you condemned as tyrants?

These are precisely the kinds of questions that created roadblocks to the consolidation of stable nation-states in Spanish America until the middle of the nineteenth century, when constitutional republics began to emerge that more closely reflect the political geography and country names that are more familiar to us today.

Reforming Empires in Western Eurasia

After the defeat of Napoleon, many leaders of European nations hoped to return the political map and rulebook back to the time prior to the French Revolution. This proved impossible. Nationalist uprisings also occurred across western Eurasia in the 1820s and 1830s, but there the most important factor determining the nature of new states tended to be the interaction of empires and not the claims of nationalists. In that context, most new nineteenth-century nation-states emerged at moments of political crisis in larger political structures. Belgium, a predominantly Catholic, French-speaking region that separated from the United Provinces of the Netherlands in 1830, and Greece, which separated from the Ottoman Empire in 1832, are two good examples. Nationalist movements worried the great empires of western Eurasia. The Russian, Austro-Hungarian, and Ottoman Empires all worked to suppress them within their own territories and were even cautious about promoting such movements within rival territories for fear they would threaten the entire international system that they hoped to build after the Napoleonic Wars. The idea of nationalist movements among Serbs or Egyptians might appeal to the Russian tsar and cause the Ottoman sultan to lose sleep; but in the case of Poles or Finns, the sleepless nights would be reversed. Aware of this arrangement, most imperial rulers defended the status quo.

Nonetheless, rivalries among the European empires played a role in shaping the nature and outcomes of nationalist movements. Western European empires worried about Russian imperial expansion in Asia if the Ottoman state were to collapse. In its interest to check tsarist ambitions, England aided the Ottoman Empire in its war with Russia in the mid-nineteenth century, repeating a pattern of Anglo-Ottoman cooperation during Napoleon's invasion of Egypt from earlier in the century. Conversely, Russia saw Great Britain as an expansionist threat, particularly as British interests in India and China grew.

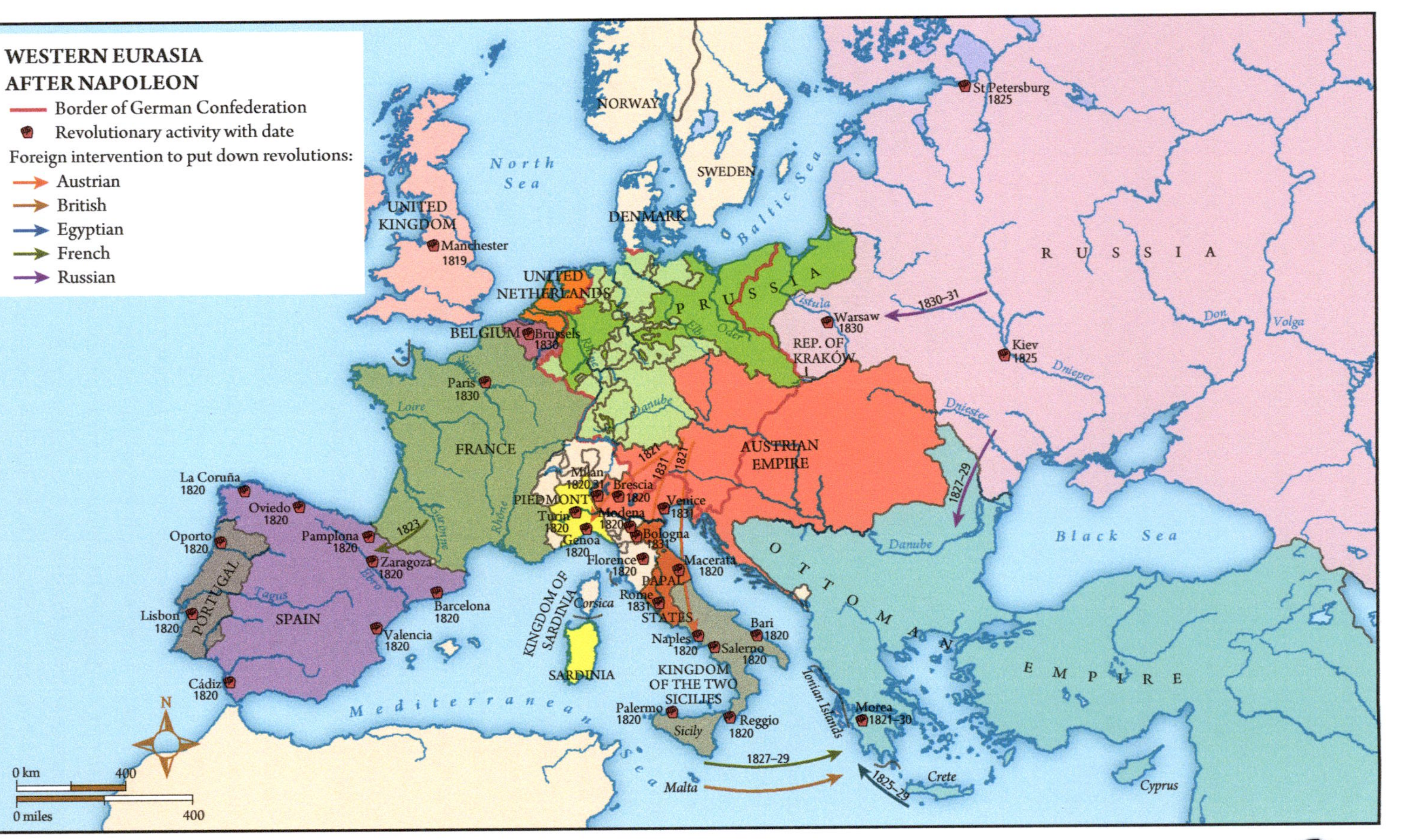

Map 6.3 Western Eurasia after Napoleon

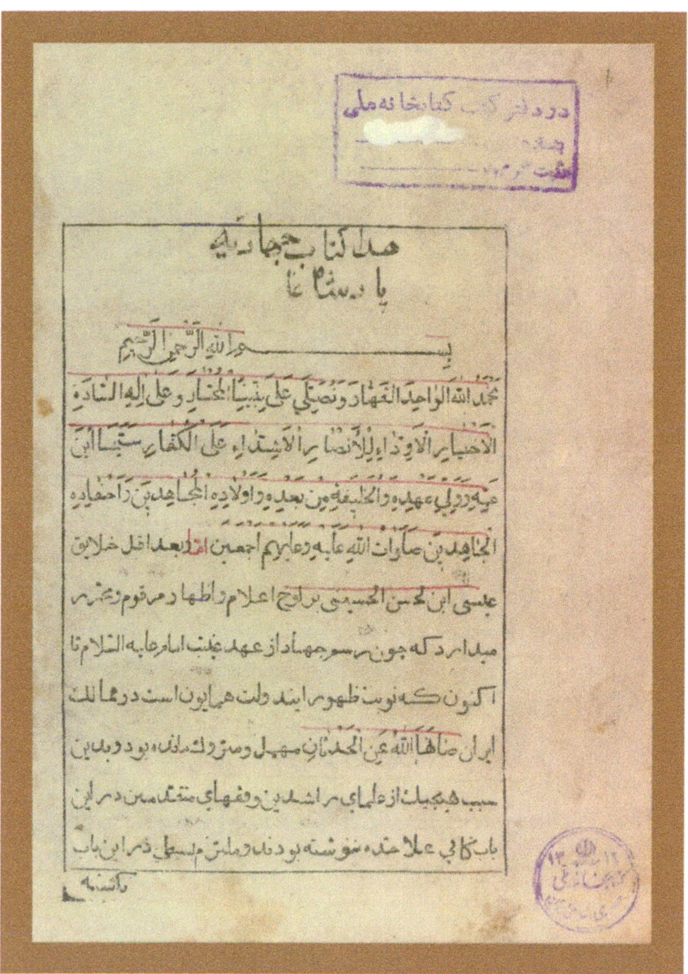

A Treatise on Holy War. Written by the prime minister of Persia in 1817, this book, printed with a Persian language printing press, analyzes the justifications for conducting jihad against Russia for its invasion of Persia during the Russo-Persian War of 1804–1813.

The Anglo-Russian rivalry led each of these empires to play a "Great Game" of intervention in central Asian affairs over the course of the nineteenth century. The tsarist regime attempted to spread the Russian language, culture, and loyalties across a broader empire; and the British used fear of a Russian invasion of India to pressure the rulers of Afghanistan, which the British saw as an important *buffer state* rather than a nation-state. In sum, the rulers of Eurasian empires cautiously viewed nationalist sentiment as a powerful force within their own realms, but at times fanned its flames when it served their self-interests. The solutions that Eurasia's major powerbrokers devised to manipulate or short-circuit nationalist movements often backfired, as nationalism continued to feed political upheaval through the nineteenth century and contributed to global warfare in the twentieth.

Emperors and their advisers faced the dilemma of finding a balance between accommodating concerns of the era and inadvertently damaging regime legitimacy. As we noted in earlier chapters, early modern empires functioned on the recognition and maintenance of difference among subject peoples for judicial, fiscal, and other reasons. One of the questions raised during this era for new states, as well as existing ones, was that of majority–minority relations. Equality before the law may strike a minority group as tyranny if democracy is defined simply as majority rule. Nationalist efforts to promote greater identification with the state, its leaders, and cultural or political practices could threaten distinct cultures or undermine the logic by which an empire was constructed over generations. Majority populations, in contrast, might resist reform efforts that would diminish their power and privilege in the pursuit of greater equality.

The Ottoman Empire provides an excellent example of the variety of challenges that empires faced on this front. Having lost control of Greece completely, facing the growing autonomy of Egypt, and witnessing the disintegration of the Safavid and Mughal Empires, Ottoman rulers attempted to find a new balance in imperial administration. New legislation was designed to eliminate the millet system in which minority populations had managed internal affairs according to their own customs, with their own religious authorities supervising. However, many communities resisted the reforms, seeing them as encroaching on highly valued autonomy rather than an opportunity to be part of a broader, more efficient, more rational, modern political community. The Muslim majority was not always satisfied either; poor Muslims resented that they were now asked to pay taxes traditionally levied only on non-Muslims.

Despite resistance and obstacles, Ottoman rulers invested time and energy in the Tanzimat over the next decades. They established a new legislative body and a Ministry of Education, overhauled legal codes, abolished slavery, and adopted a new flag and national anthem. These actions resonate with broader trends that we have presented in this chapter, as the last surviving, early modern Islamic "gunpowder empire" attempted to create something like a national identity through an anthem and flag and to overhaul the relationship between the state and the residents of the territory over whom the sultans claimed sovereignty while not conceding that an entirely new social contract was necessary to survive in the new order.

Conclusion

French revolutionaries marched to the cry of "Liberty, Equality, and Brotherhood." In the United States of America, it was "Life, Liberty, and the Pursuit of Happiness." These goals were imperfectly realized, but the ideals reshaped politics across the Atlantic world and beyond. Revolutionaries and reformers enacted versions of these goals with wide-ranging implications for society. In the 1750s, European monarchs ruled most of the Atlantic world and slavery was the foundation for the Atlantic economy. A century later, slavery was abolished, or soon would be, across the region, and just a fraction of the Americas remained governed by European powers.

Enlightenment principles undergirded much of the political and social change of this period. Equality—the idea that all human beings share rights based on their capacity to reason and not on their social status, wealth, or political power—was a foundation of those beliefs. Striving for equality sparked many of these revolutions, but it became quickly apparent that not everyone agreed on what equality meant. The American Declaration of Independence asserted that "all men are created equal," but this did not include enslaved peoples, who were treated as property. Many who argued against monarchy insisted at the same time that women were not fully rational human beings. The right to vote was seen as crucial to constructing a government that was responsive and representative, but most democracies reserved that right for men who owned property and, often, only those of a particular skin color. In the first elections under the US Constitution, it seems that only about 5 percent of the population voted.

The new states that proliferated in the late eighteenth and early nineteenth centuries grappled with fundamental questions of political order in their constitutions. The meaning of equality was one, but equally important was the debate over difference. What kinds of difference were acceptable, or important, to the state? What kinds of difference mattered to political and social order, law, or economic activity? What was the proper relationship between the state and individuals and between citizenship and other identities that individuals might have, for example, as members of religious or ethnic groups?

Of course, these questions were important not only in Europe and the Americas. The nation-state, in idea and practice, would become the keystone of global political order in the following centuries. Ideas about equality, difference, and political power, often articulated with extraordinary passion and clarity during this period, set many of the parameters by which modernity would be defined and its achievements measured. In Chapter 7, we will examine a concomitant transformation—industrialization—which contributed additional dislocating tremors to the global order.

A Few Good Books

Elizabeth Covart, host. *Ben Franklin's World: A Podcast about Early American History*. Podcast. http://www.benfranklinsworld.com.

Robert Ekirch. *American Sanctuary: Mutiny, Martyrdom, and National Identity in the Age of Revolution*. New York: Pantheon, 2017.

Ada Ferrer. *Freedom's Mirror: Cuba and Haiti in the Age of Revolution*. New York: Cambridge University Press, 2014.

Caroline Finkel. *Osman's Dream: The History of the Ottoman Empire*. New York: Basic Books, 2006.

TIMELINE

1755
Earthquake devastates Lisbon

1776
Adam Smith, *An Inquiry into the Nature and Causes of the Wealth of Nations*; American Declaration of Independence

1783
Treaty of Paris ends war between Britain and thirteen colonies

1789
US Constitution adopted; Declaration of the Rights of Man and Citizen, France

1793
King Louis XVI of France executed

Lynn Hunt. *The Family Romance of the French Revolution*. Berkeley: University of California Press, 1993.

Nicholas Shrady. *The Last Day: Wrath, Ruin, and Reason in the Great Lisbon Earthquake of 1755*. New York: Penguin, 2009.

Charles F. Walker. *The Tupac Amaru Rebellion*. Cambridge, MA: Harvard University Press, 2014.

For instructional resources and study aids, please go to **www.oup.com/us/carter**. *For primary sources connected to this chapter, please see the table of contents for* Sources for Forging the Modern World *included at the back of the book.*

1799
Napoleon assumes power in France

1804
Haiti gains independence

1807
Johann Gottlieb Fichte, *Address to the German Nation*; United Kingdom outlaws slave trade

1826
Last Spanish Empire troops in South America surrender to independence forces in Callao, Peru

1832
Greece wins independence from Ottoman Empire

1839
Gulhane Edict, Ottoman Empire, initiates *Tanzimat* reforms

FITCH'S STEAMBOAT.
On the Delaware River, opposite Philadelphia.

ARRIVAL OF THE FIRST LOCOMOTIVE IN CHINA.

(TOP) Fitch's Steamboat *Perseverance* on the Delaware River at Philadelphia, 1787. Although it would not be profitable for many years, a demonstration of the new technology of the steam engine was a perfect companion to discussions of how to build a new state at the Constitutional Convention in Philadelphia. Steam would power the expansion of the United States across North America over the century to come.

(BOTTOM) Arrival of the First Locomotive in China. Eight years after the first steamship in China was launched at Shanghai, the first locomotive arrived in the city. Shanghai was the smallest of the five Chinese ports opened to foreign trade in 1842, after the first Opium War, but it soon became the most prosperous. Its central districts included a French concession and an International Settlement run by British and American businessmen, but Shanghai maintained a mostly Chinese population. The city served as a key point for the exchange of ideas and technology between China and its overseas trading partners.

CHAPTER 7

The Engines of Industrialization

1787–1868

Suffering through the heat and humidity of a Philadelphia summer, delegates gathered in 1787 to work on a new constitution for the United States of America. Now independent from Great Britain, the new nation was struggling to build a sovereign central state that respected regional autonomy and the competing rights claims of different individuals and groups, issues that had undermined the nation's first constitution, the Articles of Confederation. Adding to the heat in the Old State House (today's Independence Hall), the doors and windows remained closed to prevent the public from hearing—or jumping into—the deliberations. Many delegates escaped the heat on the afternoon of August 22 to trek about a mile down to the Delaware River where they observed an exhibition that foreshadowed the global economic transformation that would move in tandem with the political changes the delegates were pushing forward.

At the riverbank, inventor and entrepreneur John Fitch (1743–1798) met the delegates with a boat called *Perseverance*, an odd vessel, about forty-five feet long, with banks of paddles on either side. A steam engine ran the paddles, propelling the boat at a rate of about five miles per hour, not nearly as fast as a sailing ship with a stiff wind behind it, maybe not even as fast over a short distance as a rowboat with an experienced crew. The demonstration proved, however, that steam could propel a boat across the water, free from the vagaries of wind or the limits of human muscle. Fitch received a patent for his steam engine from the new US government but never managed to create a profitable business based on the technology. Decades would pass before steam-powered engines would be broadly and profitably utilized in mining, manufacturing, and transportation.

In 1868, a much larger, more sophisticated steamship was launched on the Huangpu River near Shanghai, China. The *Tianqi* ("Auspicious") was the first

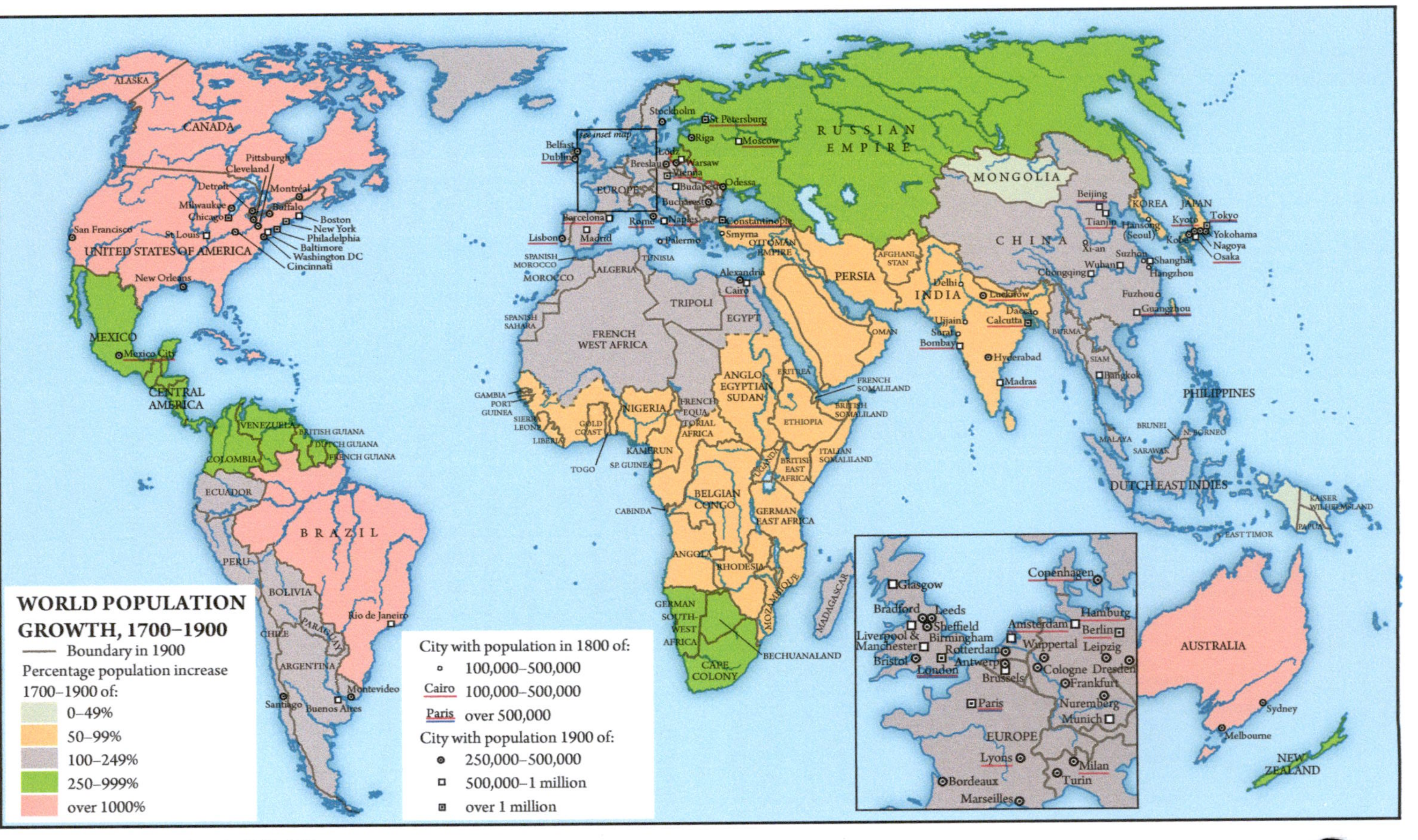

Map 7.1 World Population Growth, 1700–1900

steamship to be built in China, with engines and other parts manufactured in the United States and Europe. It was the brainchild of Zeng Guofan (1811–1872), a long-serving government official who had played an important role in winning the Taiping War that devastated China in the middle of the nineteenth century. In some ways, Zeng epitomized a traditional Chinese official, loyal to the imperial dynasty and steeped in the ways of the Confucian scholar. However, challenged by the simultaneous threats of European armed aggression and civil war, Zeng and his allies wagered the long-term survival of the Qing dynasty on modern factories to build munitions, steamships, and other industrial goods. He also sought to reform the imperial bureaucracy. As part of his plan, Zeng advocated sending Chinese youth abroad to study applied mathematics, science, and business. Not everyone in the Qing imperial elite agreed with Zeng Guofan's proposals, and an intense struggle over China's future ensued. Like people around the world, Chinese elites recognized that industrialization was dramatically changing the world. There was, however, little consensus in China, or anywhere else, about the best ways to respond to these changes.

The events just described help us to identify key aspects of what industrialization was—and wasn't—about: technology, experimentation, risk-taking, failure, war, and government policy decisions around the world. It is difficult to pinpoint the exact start or direct cause of political revolutions; this is even harder with a phenomenon like the Industrial Revolution. Important changes in global economic organization began before 1787, and the transformative effects of industrialization remain key components of our own time.

Industrialization will be part of the essential framework for understanding the rest of this book. In this chapter, we focus on the first wave of industrialization that occurred from the late eighteenth to the mid-nineteenth century—the key events, decisions, interactions, and consequences. We begin with a fundamental question: What is so revolutionary about industrialization? The answers to this vital question are often taken for granted, but we think it's important to understand exactly why industrialization is so crucial to the modern world. Understanding the revolutionary nature of industrialization, however, does not tell us much about how or why it happened the way it did; that's the question we turn to next. By comparing the world of production, distribution, and consumption in some of the world's most prosperous and productive regions in the late eighteenth century, we can better understand the dramatic and unpredictable subsequent changes in the relationships between peoples and resources. We then specify some of the policies and decisions that contributed to the way industrialization began and its early impact on people's lives. Finally, we will offer a series of cases that show the shifting power relationships within and between states and empires that resulted from early industrialization.

Questions to Consider as You Read Chapter Seven:

1. What role did technological change play in the Industrial Revolution? What other factors contributed to the changes in patterns of production and consumption that we associate with the Industrial Revolution?
2. Zeng Guofan considered industrialization an essential process for China to undergo, but Zeng, like many of his contemporaries, also considered industrialization a Western phenomenon. What led Zeng and others to define industrialization this way? What does the historical evidence suggest about this characterization of the Industrial Revolution?

What Is Revolutionary about Industrialization?

The question, what is the industrial revolution, is often answered with a string of dates related to inventors and inventions. But this parade of information misses the point of the question. Although all the inventions associated with the onset of the Industrial Revolution—the cotton gin, the spinning jenny, the steam engine, and so on—are important and remarkable, they don't explain what industrialization really means, why it matters, or what brought it about. To answer these questions, we need to understand basic distinctions between industrial and pre-industrial society, challenge some common assumptions about how the Industrial Revolution happened, and engage with one the most contentious historical debates of the past several generations.

Leaving the Biological Old Regime Behind

Industrialization was a revolution because it enabled human societies to break free from the biological old regime, described in Chapter 1 as a set of constraints on human productivity that had been in place for thousands of years. Beginning in the Middle East around ten thousand years ago and in China, Africa, and the Americas around eight thousand years ago, some societies made the transition from hunting and gathering to sedentary agriculture. By farming and domesticating animals, they were better able to transform potential energy into working energy than if they had remained hunter-gatherers. The ability of people to harness more energy for themselves and others allowed labor to specialize, cities to grow, and surplus to accumulate. For thousands of years, societies around the world made little further progress in tapping into the potential energy available on the earth. They simply did not understand how or have the means to do it. Because of this, fairly strict limits on growth in population and labor productivity prevailed, and societies remained vulnerable to even slight, short-term changes in their environment.

Industrialization changed the relationship between people and the natural environment. Slowly at first, humans began to unleash more of the energy stored in fossil fuels. For example, experimental steam engines, predecessors to the one developed by John Fitch, were designed in the sixteenth century in the Ottoman Empire, in seventeenth-century Italy, and in eighteenth-century England. This phenomenon accelerated with remarkable speed in the nineteenth century, changing the material conditions of human life in ways that were—wait for it—revolutionary. Railroads and steamships (and later automobiles and airplanes) did not rely on favorable winds or currents to reach their destinations. New machines for planting and harvesting brought more land under cultivation, and fertilizers produced in factories raised the land's productivity. Electricity enabled refrigeration, keeping food fresh for longer periods. Combining these technologies, food could be brought from greater distances, preserved long after the harvest, and introduced in greater quantities and varieties in more places.

New technologies also made places once uninhabitable by large populations fit for denser settlement. New transportation infrastructure enabled easier movement from place to place, temporarily or permanently. Electric lights could create a perpetual, artificial daytime. The sheer variety and amount of goods—and the energy used to create them—are mind-boggling compared to that of preindustrial societies.

Industrialization altered human attitudes toward the natural environment. Floods, droughts, and storms continued to remind humans that they did not control nature, but fewer people organized their days or lives according to the constraints of local environments, thanks to massive amounts of energy unleashed from long-dead life forms compressed into coal, petroleum, or natural gas. But now that we know what is revolutionary about industrialization, how did it happen?

Spinning the Industrial Revolution Story

Be forewarned that in the pages that follow, we'll undermine in many ways the story we're about to tell in this paragraph and the one that follows, so be prepared to rewrite your notes! The Industrial Revolution is often explained in terms of the machines themselves. For example, the rural workforce in preindustrial India, makers of those fine and highly desired cotton textiles described in earlier chapters, took about fifty thousand worker-hours to spin one hundred pounds of cotton yarn by hand. In other words, it would take one worker fifty thousand hours, or fifty thousand workers one hour, to produce one hundred pounds of yarn. To put this in the context of how most of us organize our lives, if a single spinner worked eight hours a day, every day—no weekends, no holidays—spinning yarn, it would take more than seventeen years to produce one hundred pounds of yarn.

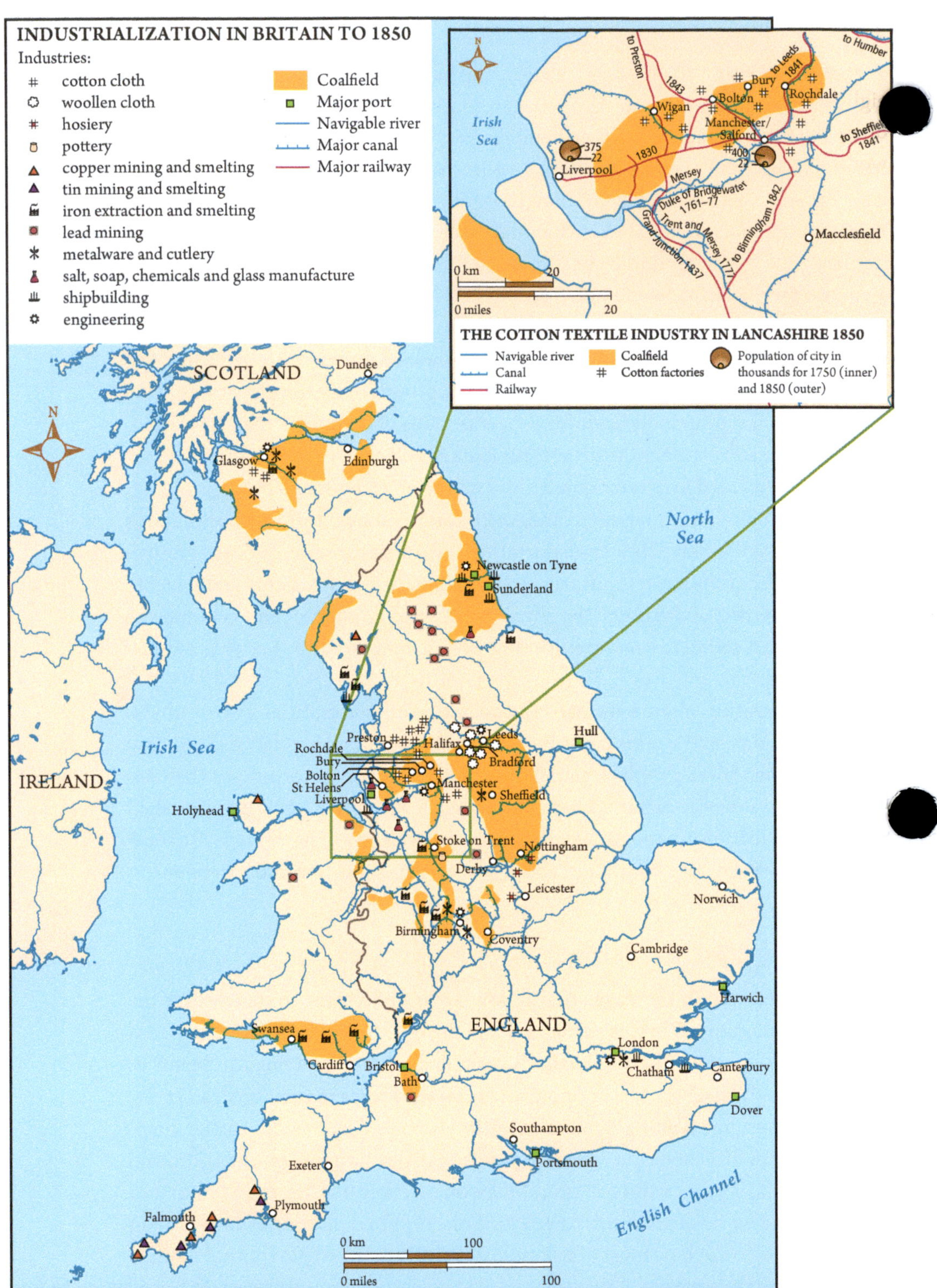
INDUSTRIALIZATION IN BRITAIN TO 1850
Industries:
cotton cloth
woollen cloth
hosiery
pottery
copper mining and smelting
tin mining and smelting
iron extraction and smelting
lead mining
metalware and cutlery
salt, soap, chemicals and glass manufacture
shipbuilding
engineering
Coalfield
Major port
Navigable river
Major canal
Major railway
THE COTTON TEXTILE INDUSTRY IN LANCASHIRE 1850
Navigable river
Canal
Railway
Coalfield
Cotton factories
Population of city in thousands for 1750 (inner) and 1850 (outer)
Irish Sea
to Preston
to Leeds 1841
to Humber
to Sheffield 1841
1843
Bury
Bolton
Rochdale
Wigan
Manchester/ Salford
375
22
400
22
Liverpool
1830
Mersey
Duke of Bridgewater 1761–77
Grand Junction 1837
Trent and Mersey 1777
to Birmingham 1842
Macclesfield
0 km
20
0 miles
20
SCOTLAND
Dundee
Glasgow
Edinburgh
North Sea
Newcastle on Tyne
Sunderland
Irish Sea
IRELAND
Holyhead
Preston
Halifax
Leeds
Hull
Rochdale
Bury
Bolton
St Helens
Liverpool
Bradford
Manchester
Sheffield
Stoke on Trent
Nottingham
Derby
Leicester
Norwich
Birmingham
Coventry
Cambridge
Harwich
Swansea
ENGLAND
London
Cardiff
Bristol
Bath
Chatham
Canterbury
Dover
Southampton
Portsmouth
Exeter
Plymouth
Falmouth
English Channel
0 km
100
0 miles
100
Map 7.2 Industrialization in Britain to 1850

Advances in textile spinning technology began to change this equation in eighteenth-century Britain. By the 1760s, spinning mules enabled one person to operate eight spindles at once. This number doubled in the 1770s. By then, British workers using these mules could produce that same one hundred pounds of yarn in just two thousand hours—fifty weeks of work at forty hours per week. More innovations followed; by the 1820s, it would take only one hundred thirty-five hours to produce one hundred pounds of cotton yarn. A single worker could now produce in a little more than three weeks (working only eight hours a day, five days each week) something that previously took seventeen years. Steam-driven machinery soon led to even greater productivity: more goods, of more consistent quality, at a lower cost. In this way, England, the pioneering center of productivity growth, became the workshop of the world. Other countries to emulated England's success, as fast as they could, if they could. The essential ingredient appeared to be human creativity, based largely in Britain, that created ingenious labor-saving devices.

The description above of increases in labor productivity is accurate, but to suggest that the force behind the Industrial Revolution was a search for this increased labor productivity is inaccurate. Certainly, machines transformed how things were made, and in turn this helped to transform the world. Humans could, as a result of industrialization, make a lot more stuff with a lot less labor. The problem with this as an explanation of how and why the Industrial Revolution happened, however, is that this is only one small part of the equation. These labor-saving devices did not solve any pressing economic problem in the eighteenth century. For one thing, labor was not in short supply in England, so saving it was unlikely to have revolutionary effects in and of itself. And as important as these machines were, they were only part of a system. Textiles machines needed raw materials. Where did the cotton come from? It wasn't grown in England. Where were the textiles sold? The domestic market could not absorb all the new cloth being produced. And Britain, of course, was not the only country in the world. How did other states respond to changes in the productive capacity of the British textile industry? These are the kinds of questions we need to answer to better understand the nature and impact of industrialization.

Historians Explore The Industrial Revolution

Until the middle of the twentieth century, most publications agreed that the Industrial Revolution was a sudden, sharp break with pre-modern economies, that it originated in Britain, and that it was caused largely by major technological breakthroughs. In the past half century, historians have challenged all these assumptions. The global textile industry did change rapidly, and British technological innovation illustrates that change clearly, but contributions to industrialization from other parts of the global economy were less obvious and had little to do with machines. A new picture of industrialization emerged based on the accumulation of many changes rather than a few crucial inventions.[1]

Comparing different parts of the world to see how they changed over time has helped reframe our understanding of industrialization. Numerous scholars have compared China and Europe during the 1700s, for example, examining the relationship between culture and industrialization. Some have concluded that the Industrial Revolution started in Europe, not in China, because of distinct values in European culture, including, in the words of historian David Landes, a "Judeo-Christian" ethic, "respect for manual labor," "the subordination of nature to man," and "a sense of linear time." Historians who are persuaded by this line of reasoning place great emphasis on the idea that conditions existed in Europe generally, or in England specifically, under which innovation and risk-taking were rewarded. They see this as a key to explaining industrialization.[2]

Other historians disagree with this cultural explanation for how and where industrialization first occurred. William McNeill, a pioneer in the study of world history, argued that explanations based on cultural advantage ignore medieval technological and economic leadership in China and the Islamic world. McNeill asserts that these explanations often dismiss achievements by non-Europeans as aberrations, while singling out European innovations in earlier eras as signs of an industrial revolution to come, when that outcome was in fact unpredictable.[3] Other historians note that more careful study provides a corrective to some claims of precocious or exceptional European economic institutions or structures. In the past two decades, scholars have suggested that early modern Chinese markets were larger, more open, and more globally integrated than those in Britain during the same era, undermining the claim that uniquely free British markets made entrepreneurship and invention possible. Primary sources reveal Asian societies that valued rationality, innovation, and, as Peter Vries notes, "love of profit" in ways similar to European ones. In sum, a good case may be made that economic institutions and behavior—culture—in China and Europe were not so different on the eve of the Industrial Revolution.[4]

---

1 For a concise overview of this transformation, see Kenneth Pomeranz, "Is There an East Asian Development Path? Long-Term Comparisons, Constraints, and Continuities," *Journal of the Economic and Social History of the Orient* 44, no. 3 (2001): 322–362.

2 David Landes, *The Wealth and Poverty of Nations: Why Some Are So Rich and Some So Poor* (New York: W. W. Norton, 1998).

3 William McNeill "How the West Won," *The New York Review of Books* 45 (April 23, 1998), provides an accessible overview of McNeill's perspective.

4 Peer Vries, *Via Peking Back to Manchester: Britain, the Industrial Revolution, and China* (Leiden, the Netherlands: CNWS Publications, Leiden University, 2003), 35; R. Bin Wong, *China Transformed: Historical Change and the Limits of the European Experience* (Ithaca, NY: Cornell University Press, 1997); and Andre Gunder Frank, *ReOrient: Global Economy in the Asian Age* (Berkeley: University of California Press, 1998).

If it wasn't culture, what prompted the Industrial Revolution? Kenneth Pomeranz offers an intriguing and thorough answer using the techniques of comparative historical research. Analyzing both the English midlands and China's Yangzi River delta, Pomeranz found that the standard of living in China may have been higher in the 1700s than it was in western Europe. He also found that China's markets were just as free as Europe's, its labor force just as skilled and diversified, and trading networks just as extensive. For Pomeranz, the divergence between Britain and China was due mainly to the relationships these societies had with key resources. Some of the relationships were about policy, but some were also about luck.

One of these resources was coal, a fuel source long known to societies around the world. It was not the only source: wood, peat, animal fats, and other fuels also provided energy for humans to light and heat their worlds. For any energy source to be cost-effective, the energy it produced had to exceed the cost of obtaining it (both in energy and in labor). Wood is not a terribly robust fuel (it doesn't produce a lot of energy), but it is easy to get and easy to burn. It's also renewable (though not inexhaustible). Coal can produce a lot more energy, but it varies greatly in quality and can be costly to obtain. It is usually found deep underground and is hard to dig up. Because pre-modern societies did not see coal as an essential resource (and because it was hidden underground), they didn't build cities to be near coal deposits, though sometimes this happened by accident.

In England, such an accident led to manufacturing centers, port facilities, and sufficient water supplies being near high-quality coal deposits, and this in turn facilitated continued experimentation in practical applications of coal to provide steam power, first for drainage pumps in mines and then in manufacturing and transportation. A similar situation existed in the Ruhr valley in Germany, another center of early industrialization. China had lots of coal too, but it was of poor quality and far from population and manufacturing enterprises. This factor, not under any individual's or group's control, must be brought into the story of why, when, and where industrialization began. Once industrialization began, Europe suddenly possessed readily accessible supplies of one of the world's most valuable resources. Coal had been of limited worth before, but now it could drive the fortune of empires.

Pomeranz also notes that Europe's relationship to Africa and the Americas added human productivity and natural resources to the energy equation of the early modern Atlantic world, permitting parts of western Europe to expand beyond the regional constraints of the biological old regime through the subsidies of conquest and colonization. Colonies in the Americas provided raw materials and markets for manufacturing enterprises, profits for risk-takers, and a destination for European populations displaced by economic changes and government policies. For Pomeranz and other members of what is now called the

California School of world history, it was colonies and coal—not culture—that created the conditions for industrialization.[5] A robust debate continues on these questions.

Life during the Industrial Revolution

As we can see, many factors contributed to where, when, and how industrialization began. This approach does not negate the fact that, beginning in the late eighteenth century, dramatic changes ensued. New inventions produced goods for just a fraction of what they had cost only decades before. New modes of transportation moved goods farther at lower cost. Inexpensive goods of more uniform quality, produced and moved on a massive scale, contributed to a tripling of global trade between 1820 and 1850. In the following section, we analyze the political and economic relationships within which early industrialization occurred and the impact of industrialization on the lives of workers in new industrial centers.

Industrialization, Protectionism, and Slavery

As the British industrial economy took off in the nineteenth century, government officials and economic elites became leading advocates for global free trade. Adam Smith and others had articulated the principles supporting free trade in the eighteenth century, so one might get the impression that free trade practices contributed to Britain's industrialization. On the contrary, Britain relied on protectionist policies to build up its manufacturing base as it began to industrialize. The growth of the British textile industry, for instance, occurred only after Parliament had banned Indian textiles from the British marketplace to protect British manufacturers from competition. This growth accelerated after the British asserted increasingly direct sovereign control over India itself, which meant that British policy influenced the cost of living and availability of goods for millions of people in South Asia. The free trade often supposed to have fueled British industrialization was not so free, even after Britain started to industrialize and became a leading voice for a global free trade regime.

Slavery also played an important role in early industrialization. In the early modern era, enslaved labor worked British colonial plantations, inflating profits beyond what would have been generated with paid labor. British interests also earned significant profits from the slave trade itself. Ships flying the British flag

5 Kenneth Pomeranz, *The Great Divergence* (Princeton, NJ: Princeton University Press, 2000). A good introduction to the ongoing debate may be found in Patrick O'Brien, "Ten Years of Debate on the Origins of the Great Divergence," *Reviews in History*, http://www.history.ac.uk/reviews/review/1008.

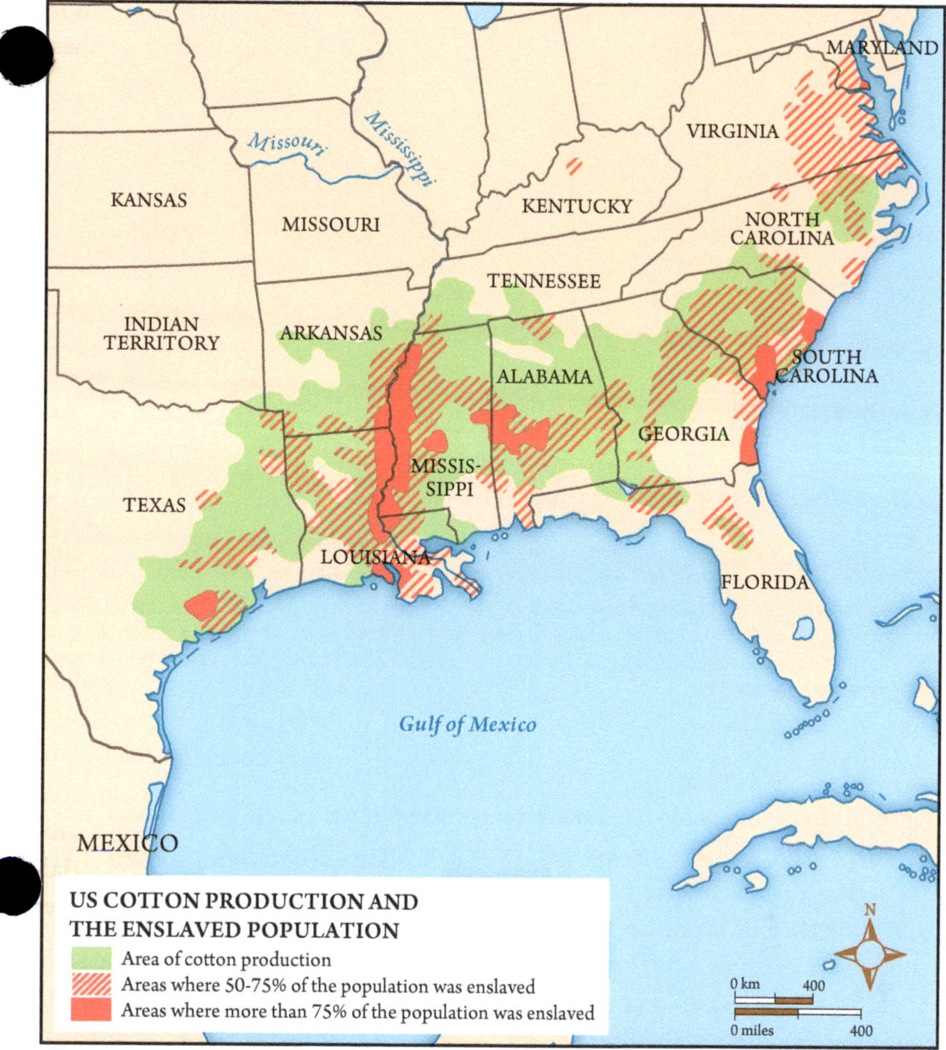

Map 7.3 US Cotton Production and the Enslaved Population

carried more than half of the enslaved Africans bound for the Americas during the eighteenth century. Historians debate just how profitable slavery was for individual slave owners or shipping interests, but the transatlantic system enabled a vast and systematic transfer of wealth from Africans and indigenous Americans to Europeans.

Britain outlawed the slave trade in the empire in 1807, but its markets did not reject resources produced with enslaved labor. The plantations (in the American South, for instance) that produced raw materials for Britain's factories and

Factories at Le Creusot in Burgundy, France, Nineteenth Century. France did not industrialize as early or as rapidly as Britain or Germany, but this image shows the extent to which new factories could transform the environment, as smoke from the chimneys darkened the skies above the Loire River valley. Le Creusot was one of France's first industrial centers, noted especially for its ironworks.

agriculture products for its population continued to rely on slave labor. One of the machines that had a great impact on inputs for the British textile industry was the cotton gin, invented in the United States by Eli Whitney (1765-1825) in 1793. The assistance of machines spurred a dramatic expansion in North American cotton production while the labor force in the cotton fields remained enslaved. Gene Dattel estimates that slave labor produced as much as 80 percent of the cotton spun for use in the English textile industry. Cotton textiles accounted for 40 percent of British export earnings at a time when the British government was the world's leading enforcer of a ban on the transatlantic slave trade.[6]

Factory Work

Factories, the epitome of industrialization, changed the nature of work in fundamental ways. Factory workers did not produce goods the way artisans did. An artisan might produce a chair, for instance, handcrafting each part over a period of weeks or months. When the chair was complete, the maker could sell it and earn

6 Gene Dattel, *Cotton and Race in the Making of America: The Human Costs of Economic Power* (Chicago: Ivan R. Dee, 2009).

money. In a factory, workers contributed just a part of the manufacturing process, and they were paid either for how long they worked or for how many pieces of a larger product they contributed. People were paid for their labor, and working together they made amazing things, but it was difficult to point to anything that any individual worker had "made" in the way the chair-maker did.

A second change had to do with the nature and location of the workplace. Clearer boundaries emerged between the home and the place of work, typically a factory. *Going to work* became a thing, replacing the integrated home and workplace that defined most preindustrial economies. And because workers had to go to work, they needed a way to get there. Many factories were in residential neighborhoods—or sometimes housing grew up around factories—so people could walk to work, but the change also increased demand for public transportation and other infrastructure.

Finally, factory employment crossed gender and age lines. Preindustrial manufacturing or artisan labor usually required some combination of long training as an apprentice, formal education, and/or physical strength. Since women or children were less likely to possess these, or have access to them, men were more commonly artisans, frequently supported by women or children who maintained the household. Factory work, though, required neither great physical strength nor lengthy apprenticeships. Children and women were sometimes preferred as factory workers because they were considered easier to control in the workplace. And they were generally paid lower wages than men.

Life in the Industrial City

Industry needed population centers that could provide a labor force and transportation networks to deliver raw materials and distribute finished goods. The cities that industrialization created became the hallmark of the modern world. Manchester, in England, grew from about forty thousand people in the 1770s to six hundred thousand in 1900, becoming the world's most industrialized city and one of its most populous. Philadelphia's population grew by twenty times in the years this chapter covers, from about twenty-eight thousand to more than five hundred thousand. And as nations industrialized, they became more urban. In 1750, the population of Great Britain was 80 percent rural; by 1900, it was nearly 80 percent urban. The rest of Europe followed this trend, although more slowly. In 1800, 83 percent of the European population lived in rural areas; a century later, only 40 percent did so.

As the nature and location of work changed, other aspects of life changed alongside it, although historians usually find puzzles to analyze rather than a tidy narrative. Studying changes in the family is one example of this. For generations, historians assumed that the movement of many social and economic roles from the household economy to the workplace transformed the average size of families, yet emerging scholarship challenges these assumptions. Research suggests that family size in France and England did not shrink dramatically after industrialization, defying expectations that industrializing economies yielded smaller, nuclear families, as wage labor replaced the rural farm family or the artisanal workshop's multigenerational household economy. In fact, the surprising research results on the size of families in nineteenth-century Europe have pushed scholars to reassess their assumptions about families in preindustrial societies as well. Industrialization clearly transformed society, but it is less clear exactly how, where, and when family structures and relationships changed.

The industrial city had new sorts of infrastructure. Sewers and power lines (gas and later electric) were installed. Trolleys, streetcars, and buses—horse-drawn at first in many cases—filled the streets. The world's first subway system, the London Underground, opened with steam-powered locomotives and gas lighting in 1863. By the end of the nineteenth century, underground or elevated rapid transit systems—now a defining feature of many modern cities—were open

Woman Working a Grindstone. This engraving from 1859 shows two German women working in a factory to produce nibs (pen points or dip pens). In the early days of industrialization, it was common for women to work in many sectors of the economy, including mines and factories. The mass production of durable, inexpensive writing implements was another dramatic innovation of this era. Though early dip pen production was dominated by firms in Birmingham, England, a German competitor (Heintze & Blanckertz) opened its doors in 1842.

or under construction in Athens, Berlin, Budapest, Chicago, Glasgow, Boston, Istanbul, Liverpool, Paris, New York, and Vienna.

Economic output increased and, by many measures, so did the standard of living, although this is another difficult outcome to measure precisely. It does appear that overall life expectancy in Europe rose markedly during the nineteenth century and infant mortality dropped.

The Debate over Industrial Capitalism

The accelerating pace and consequences of industrialization and urbanization ignited contentious debates about the quality of life in the nineteenth century and posed real challenges to many people living through the dislocations of rapid economic and social change. On one side of the debate were people like Andrew Ure (1778–1857), a Scottish professor who wrote *The Philosophy of Manufactures* (1835). Ure acknowledged—but applauded—that modern manufacturing deskilled workers to the point where human laborers might become "mere overlookers of machines"; men, women, and children might be interchangeable in the workplace. Ure responded to critics of the modern factory system by suggesting that the nature of modern work freed the minds of workers and often provided them with moments during the workday to contemplate things other than their labor, which was difficult to do under preindustrial conditions. Ure also made the case that the productivity of British factories generated wealth for the benefit of the entire nation through trade and that industrialization promised an unpredictable but better future because machines "make it possible to fabricate some articles which, but for them, could not be fabricated at all." In other words, machines could make things that people could not make on their own.

Others saw early industrialization less positively. German journalist Friedrich Engels (1820–1895) tried to shatter illusions of a modern utopia springing up through industrialization. Reporting from Manchester, Engels described filthy living conditions and a toxic, dangerous environment, with "heaps of *débris*, refuse, and offal; standing pools for gutters, and a stench which alone would make it impossible for a human being in any degree civilized to live." In his book, *The Condition of the Working Class in England in 1844* (1845), Engels described similar scenes in cities throughout Britain and presented them as visions of a global industrial future. Engels would later collaborate with Karl Marx (1818–1883), another German-speaker living in England, to produce a call to action among workers themselves to change these conditions.

Marx and Engels predicted that the industrial society emerging in the nineteenth century would collapse when workers rose up to overthrow this new system. This did not occur. Coupled with the collapse of communist states in the late twentieth century—the Soviet Union and its European allies—that claimed the Marxist legacy, this might tempt one to skip over Marx's ideas, but they remain important for understanding the modern world in at least two ways. First, Marx's critiques of industrial capitalism and liberal democracy were crucial to debates about their failures and successes in the nineteenth century. Policy and practice changed in response to these criticisms. Second, Marxist ideas define key points of debate in political and economic thinking to this day.

What did Marx think? He wrote more than twenty books, so that's a big question. We will focus on just two of his ideas: his theory of human history and his critique of industrial capitalism. Marx's politics threatened the existing order, but his ideas were born of Enlightenment aspirations to explain human history in rational scientific terms. Marx's theories were rooted in materialism, the idea that economic production and distribution were the foundation of cultural value, political power, and the driving force of historical change. Building on the ideas of German philosopher Georg Hegel (1770–1831), Marx observed that, throughout history, one class held the economic upper hand by controlling the *means of production*, that is, how wealth was produced. At different points in history, this could mean owning slaves, owning land, or—as in nineteenth-century Europe—controlling industry, which Marx related to having investment capital. The class in power tried to maintain wealth, prestige, and political power. It would not yield power willingly but, in time, a new dominant class would always rise up in revolution to establish a new economic and political order. For Marx, the French and American Revolutions occurred because merchants and factory owners sought political power to match their growing economic power and wrote new laws to serve the interests of their class.

Marx admired industrial capitalism as rational and efficient. He argued that it had led to the greatest material progress in human history but, he went on, the keys to industrial capitalism's success would also be its undoing. The system was based on cutthroat competition and an endless search for new markets, continued profit margins, and greater efficiencies. Consider that the goal of any competition is—paradoxically—monopoly: as one factory or company competes with another, the goal is not to continue competing but eventually to win, driving competitors out of business or acquiring their assets. Over time, competition would concentrate wealth in the hands of fewer and fewer winners until society comprised a tiny number of very wealthy owners and an enormous mass of impoverished workers. According to Marx, political power and economic power were one and the same. Factory owners, bankers, landlords, and others like them—the *bourgeoisie* in the language of Marxists—controlled not only the means of economic production, but also political systems, which they used to create laws that would perpetuate their own power and increase their own wealth. Yet, inevitably, thought the Marxists, the motives that fueled the bourgeoisie would destroy it.

Industrialization would drive wages down because, as we saw earlier in the chapter, workers were now being paid for the time they spent working, not for finished goods. Increasingly efficient machines would make more goods in less time, reducing the amount of time workers needed to work and, therefore, reducing their pay. Factory owners would pay workers less and less for the increasingly unskilled labor of the factory. In addition, more efficient machines would require fewer workers, making jobs scarcer. With workers desperate for jobs, wages would go even lower. Eventually, wages would not pay enough for workers even to live on. Revolution would inevitably follow.

The communist revolution Marx predicted did not materialize in his lifetime. Violent conflict involving workers did break out periodically in Europe, and communism emerged to play an important role in defining many workers' organizations and the ideological orientations of workers themselves, but more often workers' movements struggled for marginal political and economic reforms rather than the overthrow of states. And they eventually achieved many of these goals, for example, expanding the right to vote to those who did not own property, establishing the right to form unions and bargain collectively for wages and benefits, and limiting the workday and workweek.

The Transformation of Global Power Relations

Just as industrialization transformed the internal political and economic structures of those societies that industrialized, it also changed international relations, in part because it changed the nature of warfare. The machinery that made clothes, shoes, and housewares also made rifles, cannons, and warships. No major wars were fought in Europe for four decades following Napoleon's final defeat in 1815, but Europeans still fought. In the nineteenth century, especially during its second half, warfare was often tied to commerce, especially global commerce, and illustrated the emerging gap between industrial and nonindustrial powers.

The Opium Wars

The Opium Wars (1839–1842 and 1856–1860) illustrate these trends. China remained the world's most productive economy into and perhaps throughout the eighteenth century. Its Manchu Qing dynasty was expansive and stable, incorporating vast areas of central Asia, including Tibet, Mongolia, and Xinjiang, into its control. The expansion of the Qing dynasty paralleled the growth of the British Empire following its victory in World War Zero. The world's most populous country was an inviting market, and Britain—like other European powers—persistently sought expanded trade with China.

For the Qing, however, the advantages of increased trade with Great Britain were not clear. China had a sophisticated regional economy and well-developed commerce, and Chinese merchants dominated trade in the South China Sea. The Qing state, however, was not active in overseas trade in the way that European states were. In part, this was because the Qing imperial economy was large and productive with few incentives built in for international trade and in part because private merchants conducted commerce without state sponsorship. Furthermore, the Qing state did not routinely participate in a diplomatic or commercial system familiar to Europeans. Foreign regimes, especially neighboring states like Japan, Korea, Vietnam, and Siam, organized periodic, formalized trade missions with China. China also interacted with other states, including Russia, with which the Qing had concluded treaties in the 1600s. But the Qing Empire did not have a single system for foreign relations into which nations like Great Britain could easily fit. Qing statecraft improvised a method for dealing with overseas European visitors, treating them as personal guests of the emperor through the Imperial Household Department.

This system was adequate for the missionaries who began arriving at the Qing court during the seventeenth century. By the middle of the eighteenth century, however, Great Britain was seeking to expand commerce into China and petitioned the court to normalize relations along European standards. The Qing refused and in 1759 established the Canton system, restricting all overseas European trade to the southern city of Canton (Guangzhou), where European traders could reside while they did business with government-licensed Chinese merchants for a few months per year. The British, seeking to open additional markets for its goods, were frustrated by the Chinese refusal to accept their terms.

In 1793, Britain sent a mission to the Qing emperor to ask for more open trade and to establish a permanent trading base on or near Chinese territory. The emperor rebuked this mission, led by Lord George Macartney (1737–1806). In his reply to King George III, the Qianlong Emperor wrote, "Our Celestial Empire possesses all things in prolific abundance and lacks no product within its own borders. There was therefore no need to import the manufactures of outside barbarians in exchange for our own produce." The Canton system remained in place.

The sentiment expressed in this letter to King George was a blow to the British. Britain needed China to buy British goods because Great Britain wanted things that China—and often only China—produced. Silk and porcelain were important, but it was Chinese tea that had become a national obsession after being introduced to Britain in the seventeenth century. Because China purchased little in return, British traders had no choice but to pay in silver, leading to a trade deficit that British politicians and merchants were eager to erase if only they could find something they could sell in China.

While the British position appeared weak, the Qianlong Emperor was confident. The empire appeared prosperous and sound. Yet beneath the surface lay economic, social, and political problems. A growing gap between rich and poor accompanied China's prosperity, which was built largely on interregional commerce and a trend toward urbanization. Cities prospered as commercial centers, attracting job seekers from the countryside. This flow of labor into cities was not a problem as long as the cities could absorb the additional people into productive work; in the event of an economic downturn, underemployed migrants could be destabilizing. At the height of its prosperity, China was vulnerable.

Global events came together with unforeseen consequences. Victories over French forces (discussed in Chapter 5) left Britain the preeminent global trading empire. Britain in the late eighteenth century expanded *company rule* in India. During this period, the British East India Company, a commercial monopoly that oversaw all British trade in Asia, began to take on many characteristics of a sovereign state, collecting revenue and establishing a capital at Calcutta (we saw the company negotiating treaties in the vignette that opened Chapter 5, for instance). Controlling British trade with China and acting as its own government in India, the East India Company began to address its trade imbalance by producing and selling opium. This narcotic had been used in China for centuries, often combined with other substances. Opium grown in China was not very strong, but even so, the imperial government was moving in the direction of outlawing the drug. As early as the 1780s, East India Company directives began promoting the sale of opium in China. By the 1830s, hundreds of tons of opium were being illegally imported to China each year by British traders. As many as ten million Chinese, mainly in coastal cities, struggled with opium addiction.

This was a major problem, but opium sales were not the most important economic factor affecting China at the time. The upheavals that led to independence in Spanish America in the first decades of the nineteenth century severely disrupted the world's supply of silver, diminishing the silver available in China, but also depressing European consumers' demand for Chinese goods. Less silver was available, and less of it was being spent by Europeans to buy Chinese goods. By the 1820s, the flow of silver had reversed and was now leaving China. The Chinese economy contracted, exposing the vulnerability that previously had been masked. Unemployment, social unrest, and economic recession replaced the wealth that the Qianlong Emperor had seen when considering Lord Macartney's request for increased trade in 1793.

British and Chinese interests were now completely at odds. On the one hand, Great Britain wanted to increase trade to China, and opium was its most profitable commodity. The Qing state, on the other hand, wanted to stanch the flow of silver out of the country and the flow of opium in. In 1839, the Qing emperor reiterated the ban on all trade in opium and sent an official, Lin Zexu (1785–1850) to confiscate the opium stored (illegally) at Canton. Lin was partially successful, destroying several tons of opium by burning it and dumping it in the sea, but British traders objected to the seizure and refused to cooperate with the Qing dynasty official. Lin then blockaded foreign merchants in Canton, holding them virtually hostage. After extensive debate in Parliament, the British Crown intervened on behalf of its subjects: war.

The war lasted three years and ended with a decisive British victory. This was largely due to one of the fruits of industrialization: *Nemesis*, the first ocean-going ironclad steamship. *Nemesis* arrived on the Chinese coast in 1840 with watertight compartments, six large guns, and a rocket launcher, in addition to steam power and iron plating. The ship decimated the Qing navy, steaming far upriver with its shallow draft, nearly impervious to opposing firepower. The supremacy of the British navy forced China to accept harsh peace terms. The 1842 Treaty of Nanjing opened five Chinese ports to trade, permitted foreigners to reside permanently in China, and established Hong Kong as a British colony. The treaty said nothing about opium, but it permitted free trade (that is, trade on British terms) in those ports. Disputes over interpretation of the treaty contributed to the Second Opium War, after which the trade in opium was explicitly legalized.

The Treaty of Nanjing also legalized Christianity, which had been outlawed since the 1720s. Merchants and missionaries from Europe and the United States flowed into China. Among the recipients of the new Christian message was a student named Hong Xiuquan (1814–1864), who in the 1830s received in Canton a Christian tract that he later interpreted to mean that he was the younger brother of Jesus Christ. Sent by God to eliminate the evil (the Manchu Qing dynasty) that had enslaved his homeland, Hong launched a war to replace the Manchus with a Kingdom of Great Peace—Taiping.

The Taiping War lasted from 1850 to 1864, brought the Qing dynasty to the brink of collapse, and caused the deaths of more than thirty million people. Many cities took decades to recover from the destruction; some never did. At their height, Taiping forces controlled nearly half of China. That the Qing did not fall was largely due to visionary regional leaders like Zeng Guofan, introduced at the start of this chapter, who raised a militia and allied with British and American generals whom the Qing had enlisted to fight the rebels. These regional leaders, championed by a faction at court that supported their policies, set out to modernize China. *Self-strengthening*, as this movement was called, focused first on the military and education. From the 1860s to the 1880s, armories, shipyards, and military academies appeared in coastal cities.

The Price of Industrialized War in Europe

Industrialization changed military technology quickly and on a grand scale. Seemingly overnight, armies had stronger steel, more reliable and more accurate breech-loading rifles, faster communications and transportation, and more powerful explosives at their disposal. The strategic, tactical, and ethical implications of these changes became clear much more slowly. In the mid-nineteenth century, an alliance of France, Britain, Sardinia, and the Ottoman Empire successfully deployed new weaponry to defeat Russia in the Crimean War (1853–1856). The Crimean War was significant in numerous ways. It rebalanced power in Europe. France appeared to have the most powerful army on the continent, and Russia appeared in decline. But, more broadly, the conduct of the Crimean War forced a reconsideration of the battlefield. What we might now call *weapons of mass destruction* became a necessary part of any state's arsenal. Long-range, high-explosive artillery made it possible to inflict casualties miles from the front lines. Whereas earlier muskets were only accurate at very close range, new rifles—*rifling* in the barrel of the gun spins the bullets as they are fired—improved accuracy and range. In the past, war casualties on the battlefield were relatively few and usually fatal, but the new technologies of explosives and rifles meant many more casualties,

"A Hot Night in the Batteries." Soldiers Loading and Firing Cannons during the Crimean War. Fought between Russia and an alliance of French, British, and Ottoman armies, the Crimean War (1853–1856) was one of the first to use industrial weaponry like machine guns and high-explosive artillery. This 1855 painting by William Simpson shows soldiers far from the front lines, loading artillery to be fired at an enemy miles away. Technology transformed warfare, making it deadlier, less personal, and with a much wider reach.

often far from the front, perhaps not immediately killed, but permanently disabled or otherwise debilitated, and maybe condemned to a slow, excruciating death.

Four years after the end of the Crimean War, Swiss businessman Henry Dunant (1828–1910), traveling through Austria, stayed in the northern Italian town of Solferino. There, a battle between French and Sardinian armies—the largest battle in Europe since Waterloo in 1815—killed or wounded some thirty or forty thousand soldiers, with many of the casualties left on the battlefield. Touring the battlefield the next day, Dunant was so appalled by the extent of suffering, enhanced by the new industrial model of warfare, that he was moved to action. Dunant's experience at Solferino led directly to the creation of the International Red Cross—now the world's largest humanitarian organization—and the Geneva Conventions, an attempt to create more humane rules for modern warfare. Dunant was awarded the first Nobel Peace Prize for his work.

The US Civil War

Images of men marching to battle with new types of weapons became familiar across several continents during the second half of the nineteenth century, both because it was happening with frequency and because new technology, like photography, provided viewers with these images. Some of the most famous early photographs of industrial warfare were produced by Matthew Brady, who documented the US Civil War in thousands of photographs. This war was fought over many things, including the power of states relative to the central government and each other, but at its heart was slavery. The US Constitution permitted slavery, but most Northern states had abolished it by the early nineteenth century. Some contended that the US slave economy was on the verge of a crisis of sustainability by then, as arguments about free labor and the morality of slavery gained momentum across the Atlantic world. After ending its slave trade, Great Britain made slavery in the empire itself illegal in 1833. Slavery was outlawed in most Spanish American republics in their early decades of independence. But in the United States, industrial innovations—especially the cotton gin—gave the "peculiar institution" new viability. The cotton gin increased the profitability of the American cotton industry, as Southern plantations sold great quantities to the increasingly productive textile mills of both Britain and the Northern United States. Slavery boomed. Slaveholders from the United States expanded the cotton frontier into Texas, destabilizing a Mexican government that had already committed to abolition and contributing to the tensions that led to war between the United States and Mexico in the 1840s. By 1860, about 12 percent of the US population—four million of the total population of thirty-one million—remained enslaved, and in some Southern states nearly half of the total population was enslaved. (For comparison, in Brazil, enslaved people comprised approximately 15 percent of the population, but slaveholding was more regionally diversified there).

The US Civil War cannot be separated from global industrialization and empire. Although the international slave trade had ended, much of the Atlantic economy still relied on slavery to subsidize the global expansion of industry and commerce. Bloodshed, rather than diplomacy, resolved the matter. The war repeated the pattern of industrial slaughter that Europeans had seen in the Crimea and Solferino. Many battles saw more than twenty thousand casualties and some twice that many. In four years of war—from April 1861 to May 1865—more than six hundred thousand soldiers were killed and almost as many wounded. The South's economy and infrastructure were destroyed; in contrast, the North ramped up its industrial capacity.

Emerging from the Civil War, the United States faced the daunting political, social, and economic challenges of Reconstruction—the reintegration of the Southern states into the nation—but it was also poised for rapid economic growth. The New England states, especially, became world leaders in the manufacture of locomotives, steamships, clocks, and other industrial goods. Munitions companies that had armed the Union Army during the war—including Remington, Colt, Smith & Wesson, Sharps, and Winchester—became global leaders in the world firearms market.

Arming the Nation

New industrial technology was used to expand, create, and defend states. One particularly consequential example of this process was the role played by Alfred Krupp (1812–1887) in the formation of a larger, unified Germany. Krupp had turned his father's steelworks to creating innovative weaponry, replacing bronze muzzle-loading cannons with steel breech-loaders, which he promoted as more accurate and faster than the standard he hoped they would replace. Few in the military shared his view and, unable to find a buyer, Krupp gave his first steel cannon as a gift to the Prussian king. In 1859, impressed by the weapon, the king's brother, Wilhelm, ordered the Prussian army to purchase more than three hundred of Krupp's cannons. Krupp's weaponry became an instrument of Prussian state-building. Within twelve years, Prussia had led the way in establishing a unified German Empire, with Wilhelm as its emperor. During the process, the German army defeated France, the continent's largest military power. By the 1880s, Germany would also play a central role in accelerating a new, even more destructive round of imperialism in Africa and Asia.

It was this same spirit of state building that led Zeng Guofan, in 1863, to send his protégé Yung Wing (1828–1912) to the United States seeking industrial technology and expertise. China's survival was largely due to the ability of Zeng and others to rally local militia to counter the Taiping cause and to the decision by European states that enforcing current treaties against a weakened Qing Empire would be preferable to negotiating new deals with a new state. Yung Wing's mission to the United States succeeded: he returned with machinery and materiel to establish the arsenals, factories, and shipyards that were at the forefront of China's self-strengthening campaign.

Born in China, Yung Wing became a naturalized US citizen. He was the first Chinese-born graduate of an American university (Yale, 1854) and had two children with his American-born wife, Mary Kellogg. When he returned from China to the United States in 1863—in the midst of the Civil War—he offered to enlist in the Union Army. His offer was refused. Years later, in a feverish display of anti-Chinese xenophobia, his US citizenship was rescinded, and he was barred from returning to his adopted country.

Conclusion

There's no question that industrialization changed the world. But many events—wars, plagues, assassinations—change the world without being called revolutions. The Industrial Revolution was a revolution because it changed, directly or indirectly, everything: where people lived; how they worked; how they traveled; how they communicated; how many people lived on the planet; how the globe's resources were distributed; and how states related to each other.

We cannot catalog every element of change, even in the narrow time frame of this chapter. We've tried to focus on some of the most important causes of the Industrial Revolution, including the importance of chance and the roles of colonialism and slavery. We documented some of the most fundamental changes that industrialization wrought in the first societies to industrialize. We've also tried to demonstrate the early connections between industrialization and warfare because this theme recurs again and again as one of the more important in modern world history.

TIMELINE

1759
Canton system restricts trade with Europe to one port in China

1770s
British workers can produce one hundred pounds of cotton yarn in two thousand worker hours

1787
Philadelphia: John Fitch's *Perseverance* demonstrates potential of steam power

1793
Macartney mission to China; Eli Whitney invents the cotton gin

1820s
British workers can produce one hundred pounds of cotton yarn in one hundred thirty-five worker hours

1820–1850
Global trade triples

1835
Andrew Ure, *The Philosophy of Manufactures*

1842
Treaty of Nanjing ends First Opium War, opening China to European trade and establishing Hong Kong as a British colony

With industrialization, the global importance of western Europe and the United States became magnified. This is because these states leveraged industrialization to expand far beyond their early nineteenth-century borders in pursuit of territory, markets, and labor. Industrialization provides another key to understanding modernity as we described it in the introduction to this book. In Chapter 8, we will explore how changing global economic relations fueled by industrialization dovetailed with the concept of an international political order based on a new hierarchy of nations.

A Few Good Books

Sven Beckert. *Empire of Cotton: A Global History*. New York: Knopf, 2014.

Mark Bostridge. *Florence Nightingale: The Making of an Icon*. New York: Farrar, Straus and Giroux, 2008.

Peter Gran. *The Rise of the Rich. A New View of Modern World History*. Syracuse, NY: Syracuse University Press, 2009.

Emma Griffin. *Liberty's Dawn: A People's History of the Industrial Revolution*. New Haven, CT: Yale University Press, 2014.

Tristram Hunt. *Marx's General: The Revolutionary Life of Friedrich Engels*. New York: Macmillan, 2011.

Julia Lovell. *The Opium War: Drugs, Dreams and the Making of China*. London: Picador, 2012.

Stephen R. Platt. *Autumn in the Heavenly Kingdom: China, the West, and the Epic Story of the Taiping Civil War*. New York: Knopf, 2012.

For instructional resources and study aids, please go to **www.oup.com/us/carter**. *For primary sources connected to this chapter, please see the table of contents for* Sources for Forging the Modern World *included at the back of the book.*

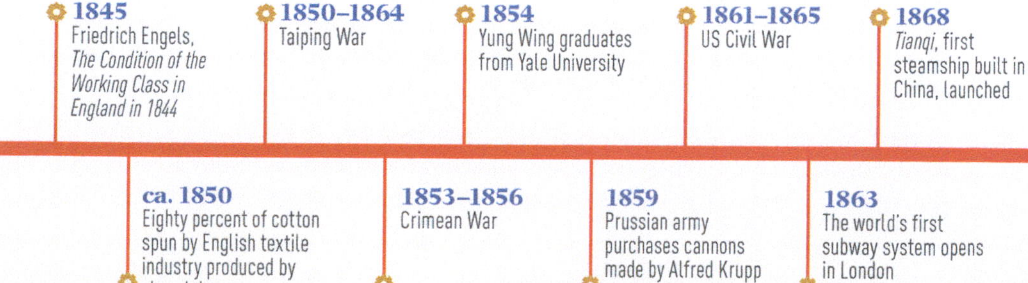

1845
Friedrich Engels, *The Condition of the Working Class in England in 1844*
ca. 1850
Eighty percent of cotton spun by English textile industry produced by slave labor
1850–1864
Taiping War
1853–1856
Crimean War
1854
Yung Wing graduates from Yale University
1859
Prussian army purchases cannons made by Alfred Krupp
1861–1865
US Civil War
1863
The world's first subway system opens in London
1868
Tianqi, first steamship built in China, launched

(TOP) A Forcible Appeal for the Abolition of the Slave Trade. Richard Newton, 1792. This satirical print, suggesting the undeniable cruelty of slavery if one would only consider its realities, was published in London on the eve of a parliamentary debate over a bill to ban the slave trade. A ban did not pass into law until 1807. Richard Newton (1777–1798) produced this print at the age of fifteen for the radical London publisher William Holland (1757–1815). The following year, Holland was jailed for publishing a work by Thomas Paine, who wrote *Common Sense*, the influential 1776 pamphlet that advocated independence for the British North American colonies.

(BOTTOM) Four Young Javanese Dancers, Paris Exposition, 1889. The creation of *living museums* was a popular feature of the world's fairs of the late nineteenth century. These dancers lived alongside other villagers, including artisans and musicians, who simulated life on the island of Java for fair-goers. The dancers performed with a live Javanese orchestra, drawing large crowds to the colonial pavilion.

CHAPTER 8

Modernity Organized

1840–1889

In the spring of 1840, Elizabeth Cady Stanton (1815–1902) took a seat at the first World Antislavery Conference in London. Stanton, an American, was in London on her honeymoon, attending the conference with her husband. Although Parliament passed legislation to abolish slavery in the empire in 1833, the act called for gradual freedom for most enslaved persons. Slavery remained in South America, the United States, and French and Dutch colonies around the world. This conference took as its goal, in part, "the universal extinction of slavery and the slave trade."

But the first day of the conference spent little time on abolition, as delegates instead focused on whether women would be permitted to participate. A majority decided that the several dozen women in attendance could remain only if they sat silently in a segregated area, out of view of the main proceedings. It was there that Stanton met and befriended Lucretia Mott (1793–1880), a Philadelphia Quaker. Stanton and Mott began to plan a different meeting, one that would focus on women's rights and equality. They organized a convention on women's rights eight years later, near Stanton's home in Seneca Falls, New York.

A much larger, and very different, gathering took place in 1889. In that year, Paris, just across the English Channel from where Mott and Stanton first met, hosted the *Exposition Universelle*, a world's fair, the crowning achievement of a generation of international exhibitions that began in the 1850s. Trade fairs and the competitive exhibition of goods had deep historical roots; but during this era, fueled by the Industrial Revolution and progressive ideology, these international gatherings combined commerce with arts, athletics, education, advertising, and propaganda, all on a grand scale. Today's readers, accustomed to sorting through and selecting merchandise from around the world at the touch of a screen or the push of a button, would perhaps find the global-marketplace aspect of the fair familiar. Other elements would seem bizarre and abhorrent: the most visited attraction in Paris was reputed to be the *Negro village*, which housed four hundred Africans brought to Paris to live "as natives" in the French capital under the gaze of visitors to the exhibition—a human zoo.

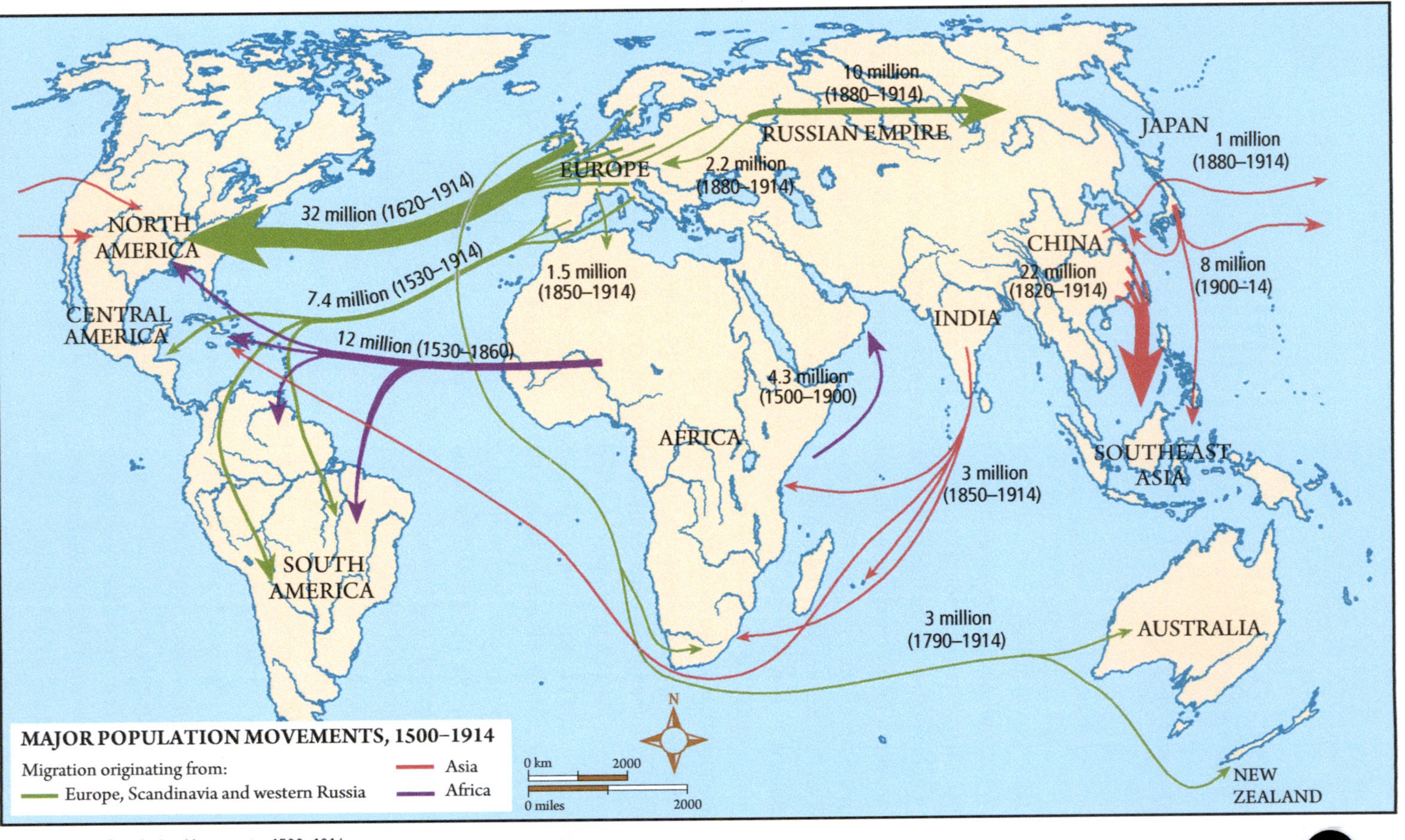
MAJOR POPULATION MOVEMENTS, 1500–1914
Migration originating from:
Europe, Scandinavia and western Russia
Asia
Africa
NORTH AMERICA
CENTRAL AMERICA
SOUTH AMERICA
EUROPE
RUSSIAN EMPIRE
AFRICA
INDIA
CHINA
JAPAN
SOUTHEAST ASIA
AUSTRALIA
NEW ZEALAND
32 million (1620–1914)
7.4 million (1530–1914)
12 million (1530–1860)
1.5 million (1850–1914)
10 million (1880–1914)
2.2 million (1880–1914)
4.3 million (1500–1900)
22 million (1820–1914)
1 million (1880–1914)
8 million (1900–14)
3 million (1850–1914)
3 million (1790–1914)
N
0 km
2000
0 miles
2000

Map 8.1 Major Population Movements, 1500–1914

The world's fairs showcased the growing military and economic dominance of a small number of states but also held out a promise: all peoples could be organized into nations, and those nations were welcome to show the world what they had to offer. In places like London, Philadelphia, and Paris, nations and their peoples displayed technology, weapons, culture, and food. The central architectural feature of Paris's 1889 fair—coinciding with the centennial of the French Revolution—was the Eiffel Tower, still standing today as a symbol of modern France, as the fairs themselves embodied modernity for nineteenth-century audiences.

The antislavery conference, the Seneca Falls meeting, and the Paris World's Fair highlight major themes of the last two chapters to which we now return. In Chapter 6, we analyzed the search for new internal order in sovereign states, including the proper relationship between state and citizen. In Chapter 7, we focused on how industrialization disrupted and reconfigured economic relationships. Each of these chapters raised enduring questions: How can the number and size of nation-states be determined? How is citizenship defined, and what are the rights that citizens can demand? How would ever-increasing supplies of commodities be matched with markets for their consumption? What would be the long-term costs and benefits of industrialization, and how would they be distributed across the planet? In this chapter, we analyze modern answers that developed in the second half of the nineteenth century to these questions.

We begin the chapter with a review of the nation-state formation process, focusing on places where relationships between individuals and sovereign states changed significantly. In addition, we survey alterations in the relative size and power of states themselves. Events belied the predictions of both optimists and pessimists. The political and economic changes triggered neither consistent progress nor collapse and revolution.

In the second part of the chapter, we analyze the Western Hemisphere during the same period. We pay particular attention to the ways in which economic change and the last phases of abolition reordered the labor market, raising new questions about the political, economic, and social role of former slaves and transnational migrants.

We conclude the chapter by exploring the ways in which messages about new global standards and hierarchies were defined, debated, and displayed. During this era, ideas about order, progress, liberty, efficiency, and prosperity were increasingly framed in reference to the industrializing nation-states of the Atlantic world. Many of the world's elites, regardless of their religious, ethnic, social, or geographic locations, came to equate these definitions and policies with the idea of modernity and associated their embrace with survival.

Questions to Consider as You Read Chapter Eight:

1. During this era, political leaders responded in a wide variety of ways to claims based on the idea of popular sovereignty—rule of the people. What factors influenced the decisions of different leaders? What were the immediate and longer-term repercussions of these decisions?
2. Implicit in both the Antislavery Conference and the world's fair are ideas about equality, which many consider an essential modern value. Yet there is a great variation in how equality—of nations and people—is defined. What are some of the different ways equality was defined by different groups and individuals during this period? What are the implications of these differences for understanding this era?

Reform versus Revolution

Karl Marx posited as a scientific fact that the internal contradictions of capitalism would cause communist revolutions in the most advanced industrial countries of the world. He argued that economic class relationships were the most important driver of historical outcomes. For Marx, factory workers, whether in Germany, France, the United States, or England, shared more in common with workers in other countries than they did with factory owners (or the ruling classes generally)

Universal, Democratic, and Social Republic. Lithograph. Frédéric Sorrieu, 1848. Sorrieu (1807–1887), a French artist, was well known for his illustrations of the reform ideals of the mid-nineteenth century. During the Springtime of Nations in Europe, Sorrieu produced this print of the idealized triumph of nationalism as a pathway to brotherhood, greater equality, and progress.

in their home countries. Once workers realized that the states and industrial economies controlled by the bourgeoisie were both designed to oppress them, they would rise up and replace the existing political system with an egalitarian and transnational communist society. Marx thought nationalism—and religion, too—was designed to distract or deter workers from seeing the world as it really was. In the *Manifesto of the Communist Party*, Marx and his coauthor Friedrich Engels concluded, "Let the ruling classes tremble at a Communist revolution. The proletarians have nothing to lose but their chains. They have a world to win. Working men of all countries unite!" This formula for a global proletarian revolution did not come to pass, demonstrating both the strength of nationalism and the resilience of the dominant economic and political model of the nineteenth century. Great changes did occur, but did not lead at the time in the direction the Marxists predicted.

Britain: The Exception That Proves the Rule

Great Britain in the first decades of the nineteenth century was Marx's model for understanding the link between economic and political power in industrializing societies. Yet, British workers did not lead the communist revolution as Marx and Engels predicted. Why not? It's difficult to explain why historical outcomes don't happen, but examining the history of English reform can help identify some of the resilience of the capitalist nation-state model in the face of crisis.

When the Napoleonic Wars ended in 1815, grain imports to Britain should have increased. Napoleon's anti-British Continental System attempted to exclude Britain from most trade with Europe, and the end of this embargo should have flooded the British market with grain, bringing down its price and providing consumers—especially the urban working class—with cheaper bread. But, declining grain prices would threaten domestic landowners' profits, and large landowners dominated Parliament. Recognizing what might happen, Parliament quickly passed the Corn Laws, virtually prohibiting the import of all grain (*corn* in British usage at the time referred to all grain, not just maize). British landowners could maintain higher prices for their crops, which were then reflected in the price of bread.

Criticism mounted against not only the Corn Laws but also the restrictions on suffrage that enabled legislation like the Corn Laws to pass. At the time, voting in England was restricted to males owning at least £200 in property (equivalent to about $250,000 in 2014). This prevented most people from voting at all, but if you were fortunate to own property of this value in more than one district, you could vote in both of them! Besides that, no one in the House of Lords was elected at all: its seats were inherited by the landed nobility. The other house of Parliament—the House of Commons—was elected, but it didn't accurately reflect the people's will either. In addition to the limited franchise, the geographical distribution of seats there had not changed since the 1600s. Since that time, industrialization had dramatically altered the size and distribution of the British population. Remember the growth of cities like Manchester? In 1819, all of Lancashire—a population close to one million that included the industrial cities of Bolton, Manchester, and Blackburn—shared just two representatives in the House of Commons.

With a government elected only by rich men, laws that protected the profits of wealthy landowners, and rising bread prices, Marx's model appeared to be playing out. Cavalry violently dispersed a rally for electoral reform at St. Peter's Field in Manchester in the summer of 1819. Fifteen people were killed and more than six hundred injured in what came to be known as the Peterloo Massacre. Henry Hunt (1773–1835), the featured speaker and a leading reform advocate, was imprisoned for three years on charges of disturbing the peace. Repression followed, as the government essentially outlawed public meetings and censored newspapers critical of the government.

Beginning in the 1820s, a trickle of social, political, and economic reforms emerged from Parliament, culminating in the Reform Act of 1832, which redistributed electoral seats and doubled the number of eligible voters. Other parliamentary reforms reduced some tariffs, reformed the criminal code, and placed limits on who could work and how long they could work. Still, Britain seemed ripe for revolution. The 1832 Reform Act made Britain one of the most democratic societies in Europe, yet it still enfranchised just 5 percent of the population. Many deplorable labor practices continued, and the Corn Laws remained in effect. Proposals for additional reforms fizzled over the course of the 1830s, feeding political dissent. Threats overseas grew as well. In addition to the Opium War with China, rebellions against British rule roiled Ireland, Jamaica, Canada, and India. France, Germany, and the United States challenged British commercial and industrial superiority.

But conflict did not escalate to revolution. Instead, a wide array of actors—parliamentary delegates, factory workers, intellectuals—pushed for and won a series of compromises. Political leaders repealed the Corn Laws in the mid-1840s. Many workers chose to focus their efforts on improving their ability to negotiate with their employers—commonly referred to as trade unionism—instead of trying to overthrow the state. Defenders of the status quo also discovered the value of nationalism during this era, using it to rally domestic populations in support of government policy, as when the British government took direct administrative control over India in 1858. The move was precipitated by an 1857 uprising—the Great Rebellion, or Sepoy Mutiny, as the British press called it at the time—against the British East India Company. Reports, many of them fabricated, in the British press about atrocities carried out against English men, women, and girls rallied public support for the decision by the British Crown to exercise direct rule in India.

New European States

The establishment of Germany and Italy, both at around the same time, also illustrates the power, promise, and limits of nationalism. The process that led directly to their formation took decades. Although many parts of Germany, and Italy, had been united under empires in the past, neither had ever existed as a nation-state, and cultural differences within the territorial boundaries of these would-be nations were profound. In both instances, over the course of several decades culminating in the 1870s, unification was a process whereby existing states (Prussia for Germany; Sardinia-Piedmont for Italy) expanded to create a larger state.

The year the *Communist Manifesto* was published—1848—Europe was ablaze with unrest. Industrial workers were in the streets, but rather than the dawn of a proletarian revolution, 1848 came to be called the Springtime of the Nations, as wage workers joined others to demand universal (usually, universal male) suffrage or national independence. In Budapest, protesters called for Hungarian independence and recited Sándor Petőfi's *National Song*: "The Magyar [Hungarian] name will be great again, Worthy of its old, great honor." In Prague, the members of the Young Czech movement promoted their language against German domination. In dozens of other cities across Europe, revolutionary movements gained momentum, but they tended to be nationalist, not communist, in nature.

As these uprisings spread across Europe, Young Italy's exiled founder, Giuseppe Mazzini, renewed his call for a unified Italian state. Giuseppe Garibaldi (1807–1882), a Genoese who had served as a naval officer in the South American republic of Uruguay, took up Mazzini's patriotic call, leading military campaigns through the 1850s and 1860s. Hailed as a hero in Italy and abroad, as a man of the people, and as a fighter for the cause of popular self-determination, Garibaldi did not see unified Italy become a republic, but he did serve in the parliament of the new Kingdom of Italy.

In that same year, 1871, Wilhelm of Prussia became kaiser—emperor—of Germany. German speakers had always lived in many different states across central Europe. The idea that a large and artificially divided German nation should be brought under one sovereign state gained traction during the Napoleonic era, from 1804 to 1815, when many German-speaking peoples lived under French control. It was in this period that Fichte and others spoke of their dream to "reunite" the German nation under one ruler.

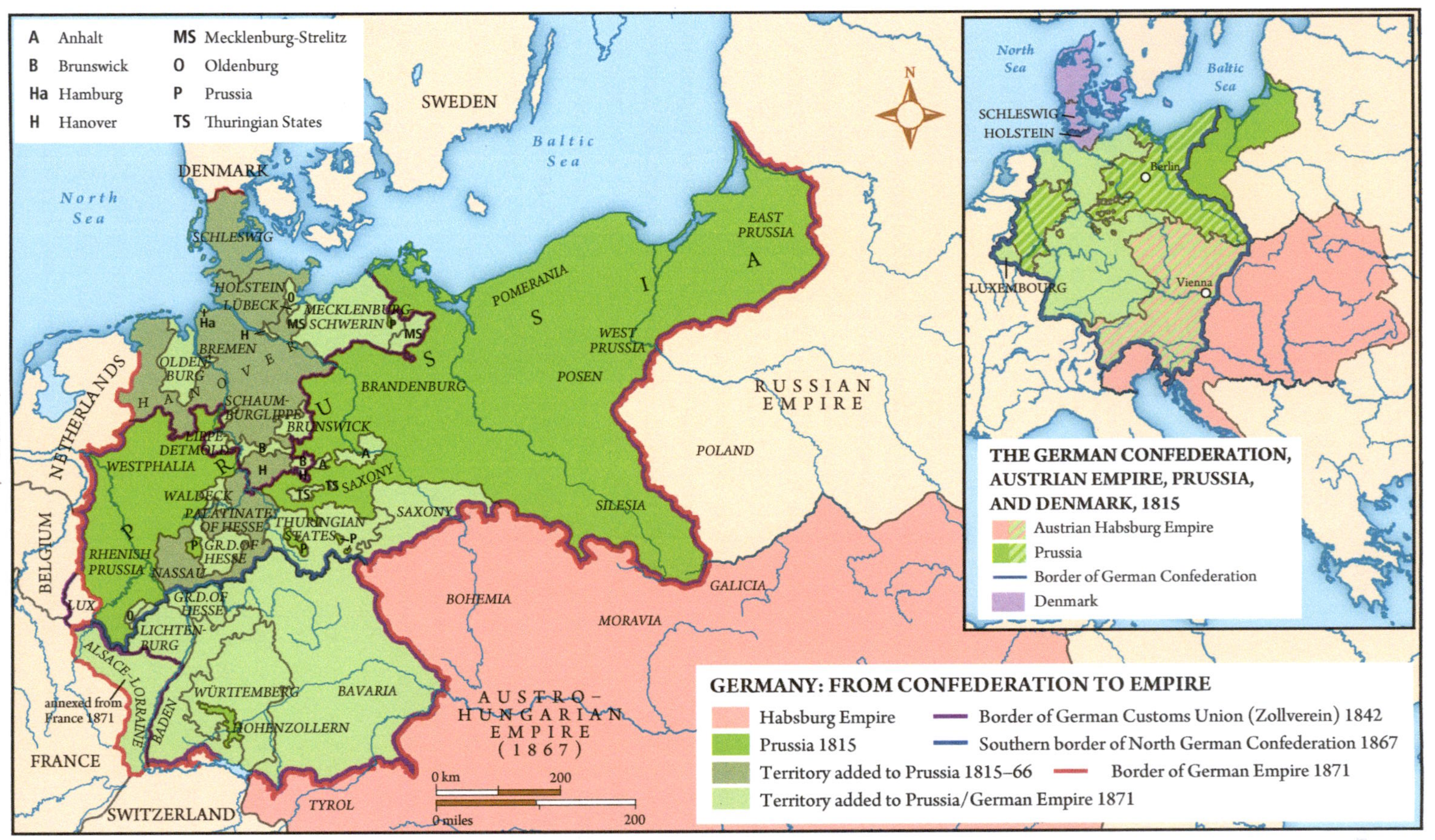

Map 8.2 Germany: From Confederation to Empire

The northeastern state of Prussia, long a formidable military power, became an industrial power as well in the nineteenth century, rivaling Austria as the dominant German-speaking state. When 1848 revolutionaries renewed the call for German unity, Prussian leaders responded, initiating diplomatic and military maneuvers to gain additional territory. Threatened by growing Prussian power to the east, France was drawn into a war in 1870. The resulting Franco-Prussian War brought Prussian armies into other German-speaking states like Bavaria. After defeating France, the Treaty of Frankfurt proclaimed the Empire of Germany, with the Prussian king as its emperor, incorporating almost all European states with a majority of German speakers, except for Austria.

There was no "natural" reason for Austria to be excluded from the nation-state of Germany but Bavaria and Saxony—also mostly German speaking—to be included. And what about Bohemia, which had a mix of (mainly) Czech and German speakers? Or Alsace, where many spoke German, but many also spoke French or Alsatian? The same kinds of questions, with different details, applied to the Italian case. The answers to these questions were rooted in historical contingencies, reinforcing the point that nation-states aren't naturally occurring, self-evident political entities; they are constructed out of circumstances and limited by political possibilities.

In both the German and the Italian cases, nationalism legitimated the new states, but modern technology and the use of force allowed court officers, police, military, and civil servants to make a state and define what a social contract for a modern German or Italian nation should look like. In the two decades after unification, the German government passed laws creating public health insurance, retirement, and disability programs. German leaders, like political elites in other European industrial centers, argued that their political and economic system, based on private property and representative government, gradually improved the lives of their citizens and removed the need for the more radical actions advocated by Marxists.

Challenges to the Ottoman and Russian Empires

The larger, more powerful German Empire profoundly affected states to the east. The Ottoman and Russian Empires were scrambling to outflank each other and to keep pace with their rivals at a time of nationalist ferment and global economic transformation. In response, both empires implemented internal reforms designed to quell potential fragmentation and meet growing military and economic challenges.

In the Ottoman Empire, the Tanzimat (Reorganization), begun in 1839, continued. The government founded a Ministry of Health and Academy of Sciences.

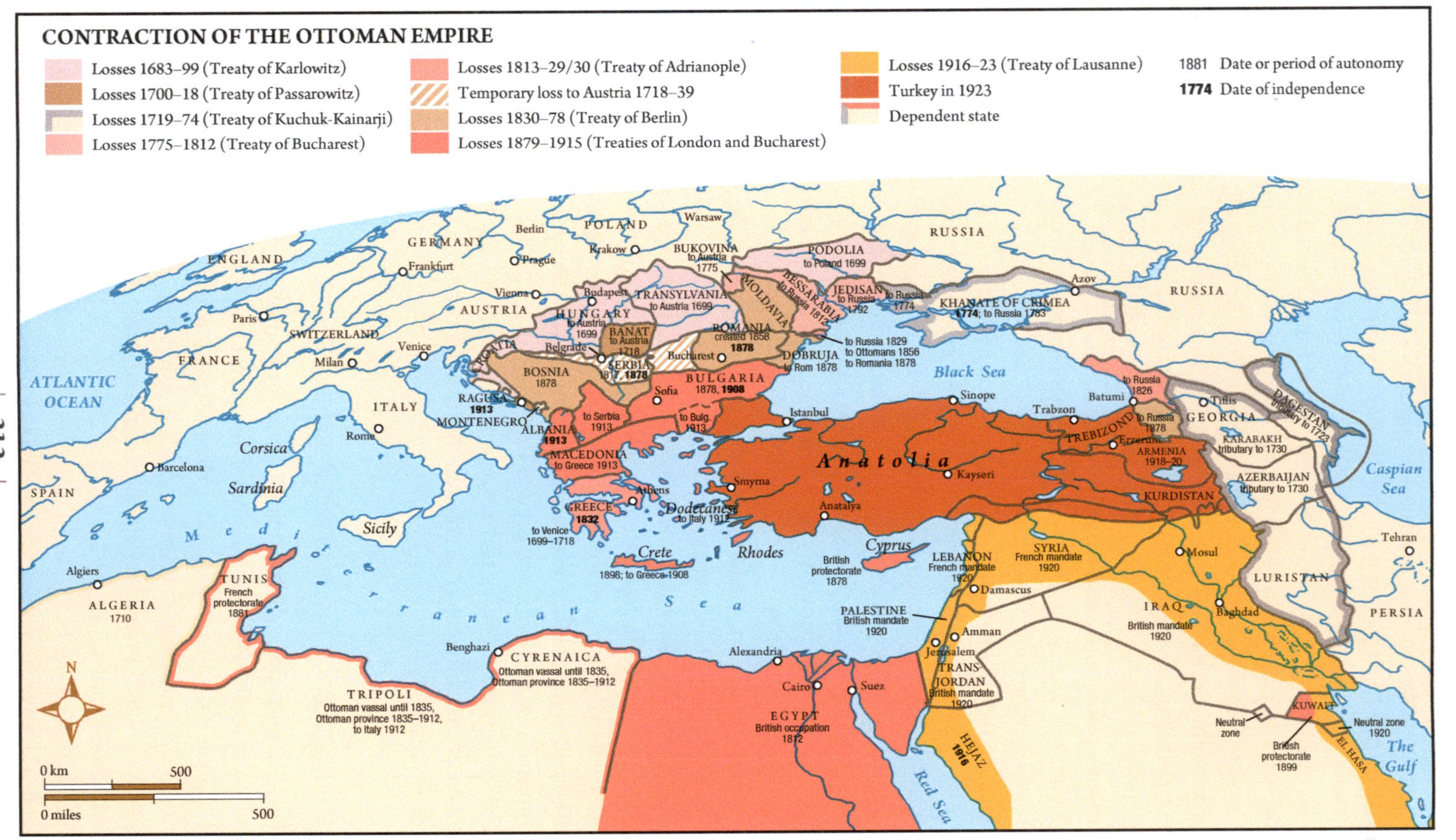

Map 8.3 Contraction of the Ottoman Empire

The first telegraph networks and railroad lines were laid out; steam-powered ferries began to carry commuters between home and work. A central bank and stock exchange contributed financial infrastructure for economic development. Over the next decades, the Ottoman political elite continued to transform military, fiscal, and administrative structures and the relationship between the state and residents of different faiths, all while fighting a series of international wars and separatist movements.

Tsarist Russia launched its own modernization effort, the Great Reforms, which peaked in the third quarter of the nineteenth century. The peasant reform of 1861 abolished the legal ties of serfs to the land. Reforms of the judicial system, municipal government, and military followed. The state used tax policies to protect new industries from competition and tax revenues to subsidize the growth of the railroad network. The state also attempted to manage more effectively the diverse territories and peoples over which it claimed sovereignty, from surveying expeditions to colonization schemes managed through government agencies with names such as the Ministry of State Domains and the Resettlement Authority. In these ways, both empires managed to survive the nineteenth century, although neither would make it past the second decade of the twentieth.

Japan Modernizing

Many people in Europe and the United States saw the "opening" of China at the end of the First Opium War (Chapter 7) as part of an unstoppable march by Western powers through Asia. In July 1853, a decade after that war ended, Matthew Perry led a US squadron into Tokyo harbor. In the preceding four years, thousands of people had streamed to California, when gold was discovered in this territory ceded to the United States by Mexico after the war of 1846–1848. The Gold Rush announced the arrival of the United States as a Pacific nation. California joined the Union in 1850, and the United States was suddenly closer than any western European power to the markets of Asia, made even more accessible by new developments in steam-powered shipping. Turning potential into power required a new type of infrastructure, however: coaling stations for refueling ships along the way. Steamships from the United States heading west from California soon connected a series of islands in the Pacific, including Hawai'i, Guam, and Midway Island. Japan appeared a logical link in the chain connecting the United States to China.

Perry was not the first American to enter Japanese waters. A handful of American traders—often flying the Dutch flag—had been trying to establish trade with Japan since around 1800, but none of them came with the orders—or the fire power—to open trade through military force if needed. Backed by some three hundred marines and some of the US Navy's most advanced guns, Perry refused the Japanese government's order to dock at Nagasaki, for centuries the only foreign point of access to the Japanese market. Defying Japanese protocols for foreign trade, Perry insisted that the Japanese government accept a letter from the US president (with a proposal to open additional ports) or suffer the consequences of war. When officials of the Tokugawa government refused, Perry and his ships conducted target practice in the harbor. The Japanese agreed to accept the letter, after which Perry withdrew from Japanese waters, returning months later with a larger force, including steam-powered frigates and several thousand marines. In March 1854, the Japanese assented to US requests. Within five years, the Japanese government signed similar agreements with European states, igniting conflict within Japan that would dramatically alter its internal political order and its relationship to the rest of the world over the next half century and beyond.

Japan's response to the West is often presented as simple. Japan was supposed to have rationally and quickly perceived the advantages of modernization and transformed rapidly from a feudal to an industrial state. Some elements of this portrayal are true: Japan did accept Perry's demands for open trade in 1853 and within a generation was well on its way to becoming an industrial, imperial power. However, many of the conditions that facilitated this transformation were apparent before Perry's arrival. Japan's population was among the most urbanized in the world, with some of the world's largest cities and a thriving commercial class. Apparent ethnic and cultural homogeneity and natural geographic boundaries gave Japan advantages to state formation described (and sought) by Western nationalists.

In other ways, Japan was not modern: occupations were determined by birth, and law and custom restricted social mobility. Most of the country was feudal in its property relations. Although not as isolated as the seventeenth-century Closed Country Edict (discussed in Chapter 2) would imply, Japan strictly regulated its relations with other countries. Within a generation of Perry's arrival, however, Japanese legislators wrote a constitution and did away with the feudal government system that had ruled the islands since 1600.

The new *Meiji* ("Enlightened Rule") government blended Western and Japanese institutions to modernize the country. The 1868 Charter Oath, although vague, pointed Japan toward Western models of modernization, echoing the US Declaration of Independence ("each be allowed to pursue his own calling so that there may be no discontent") and the Enlightenment ("everything based upon the just laws of Nature"). The oath called for "knowledge to be sought throughout the world," prompting a series of overseas missions to the United States and Europe, gathering information about nearly every aspect of society as Japan tried to modernize. The findings of these missions led Japan to model Western institutions in many critical areas. A conscription law, to build a Japanese national army to replace the feudal samurai, went into effect in 1873. Tokyo University, the first Western-style university in Asia, opened in 1877.

Not everyone embraced change. Saigo Takamori (1828–1877) led an 1877 rebellion to retain a more traditional Japanese government, including a stronger role for the samurai. In a costly war in which both sides were armed with Western munitions, Japanese imperial forces defeated Saigo's samurai, effectively ending the samurai class in Japan and clearing the way for continued Westernization by the Meiji government. The Meiji Constitution, promulgated in 1889, modeled closely the German Empire's constitution.

Nation and Citizen in the Western Hemisphere

Many western European states followed similar political paths during the nineteenth century, as elites gave up some of their wealth and power to maintain order, yet held on to most private and public resources. In these countries, most workers chose to accept reform over armed revolution. Suffrage expanded slowly (seldom including women until the twentieth century), and the relationship between states and citizens expanded to include claims of some social rights in addition to political and civil rights. In the Americas, several factors not present in western Europe lent a distinct character to the consolidation of nation-states. These were states founded through anticolonial uprisings; their populations were characterized by high levels of ethnic and racial heterogeneity; many had sizable and varied indigenous populations; and slavery persisted in much of the region through the middle of the century.

By the end of the nineteenth century, as the trajectory of abolition was finally completed, a second historic wave of migration to the Western Hemisphere accelerated. As a result, concerns over citizenship were not limited to the formerly enslaved. Rising immigration intensified concern across the Americas over identifying, sorting, and preparing responsible citizens and a malleable work force. Economic change and political reform in Europe and elsewhere displaced millions of people. Improved rail and steamship infrastructure moved people to where labor was needed, both within and between countries, including millions of people from throughout the world who came to the United States, Brazil, Argentina, Chile, and other parts of the Americas. The expansion of citizens' political, social, and economic rights claims contributed to an increased scrutiny of who was eligible to enjoy these rights in any given nation-state, a process that continues today.

The Oligarchic Republics of Latin America

Throughout Spanish America, as we saw in Chapter 6, disputes over political and economic order and power drove regional wars in the first decades following the collapse of Spanish imperial rule. Emerging from this era, reformers like Guillermo Prieto (Mexico, 1818–1897) and Domingo Faustino Sarmiento (Argentina, 1811–1888) proclaimed liberalism as the key to progress in their countries. Believers in the transformative power of private property and commerce, Spanish American statesmen in the middle of the century presided over the abolition of slavery in the last of the Spanish American republics where it was practiced. They eliminated special privileges for the Catholic Church and wrote constitutions that emphasized the rights of individuals. Their successors—for example, the Generation of '80 in Argentina and the *científicos* (advocates of "scientific" politics) in Mexico—thought of themselves as adopting the most advanced ideas to bring positive changes to their countries. They encouraged, through additional legislation and their own actions, investment in infrastructure and private enterprise, often partnering with foreign investors.

But the success of these reforms was limited. The political systems that emerged throughout Latin America may be best thought of as oligarchic republics. They maintained periodic elections, separation of powers, equality before the law, freedom of assembly, and other features of liberal democracy; but corruption, fraud, and coercion undermined its practice, as small groups of very powerful men controlled inordinate amounts of political and economic power. In addition, many reformers continued to believe that their states faced "race problems" that could delay or derail progress. As a result, when nation-states were formed, many of the hemisphere's indigenous and African-origin populations remained marginalized.

The Mexican government invited European immigrants to colonize northern Mexico and forced indigenous peoples off their agricultural lands on one side of the country to work in export agriculture on the other. At the southern end of the continent, both Chile and Argentina subdued indigenous populations through military campaigns that inflicted tens of thousands of casualties in the 1870s and displaced many thousands more. As the Argentine general Julio Roca (1843–1914) put it, these campaigns were designed to "put down . . . this handful of savages . . . in the name of law, progress, and our own security."

In 1888, Brazil became the last state in the Western Hemisphere to outlaw slavery when Princess Isabel (1846–1921) signed a law of unconditional abolition. The Golden Law passed without the violent civil war that characterized the end of slavery in the United States, but abolition in Brazil did trigger the overthrow of the last monarchy in the Americas, as key sectors of the nation's elite questioned the ability of the imperial bureaucracy to cope with profound economic and social change.

On November 15, 1889, little more than a year after abolition, a coup d'état laid the groundwork for a constitutional republic. Brazil's new flag proclaimed the aspirations of the nascent regime. Across the center of the flag appeared the optimistic phrase "Ordem e Progresso"—"Order and Progress"—but Brazil's political elite was unprepared to entrust the direction of the republic to the masses, especially those recently emancipated. Voter eligibility rules for the nonslave population had grown more restrictive in the years prior to abolition, and elections remained tightly controlled afterward: less than 2 percent of the population was eligible to vote.

Rebuilding the United States

In some ways, the United States fits the Italian and German models of national unification. United States claims to wide swaths of North America from the Atlantic to the Pacific dramatically increased over the course of the nineteenth century. The vast expansion of territorial claims against Mexico to the south and indigenous states and peoples to the west fueled an increasing debate in the centers of US political and economic power over the defining characteristics of its social contract and economy. As in Italy and Germany, the consolidation of a larger territorial state spurred reconsideration of political and economic relationships within it—a questioning of nation.

In the revolutionary year of 1848, Elizabeth Cady Stanton and Lucretia Mott organized the Seneca Falls Convention mentioned in the chapter's introduction. Conference participants pointed out that the Enlightenment rhetoric of equality and universal rights had been implemented in ways that conspicuously excluded women. The United States, founded on principles of equality and the rule of law, denied women the right to vote, to hold public office, to own property if married, and to serve on juries. Stanton's *Declaration of Sentiments* put the matter in familiar, and revolutionary, terms: "We hold these truths to be self-evident: that all men and women are created equal, and are endowed by their creator with certain inalienable rights."

In the years leading up to the Civil War, the movements to abolish slavery and enfranchise women tended to work together to expand the definition of equality. Frederick Douglass (1818–1895), a former slave, joined other activists like Stanton and Susan B. Anthony (1820–1906) to show the wide gap between the principles of equality that Rousseau, Kant, Condorcet, and others had articulated and their practical realization.

After the Civil War, the federal government declared legal equality for all adult men but would not do the same for women. The nation had determined that its founding phrase, "all men are created equal," included men of color but not women of any color. In 1869, the Constitution was amended to prohibit denial of the right

Indentured Migrants, Jamaica, ca. 1905. Global demand for labor, and its exploitation, did not cease with the abolition of the international slave trade and slavery. Encouraged by the British government, between 1834 and 1916, almost 1.5 million indentured migrants left India and China alone to work in British colonies around the world. More than 35,000 South Asians emigrated to Jamaica as indentured servants between 1845 and 1917. Some returned to India after completing the terms of indenture. Others left to work elsewhere in the Western Hemisphere; about half remained on the island. In this photo, from the early twentieth century, Hindu indentured laborers in Jamaica have gathered for a religious ritual.

to vote based on race or color. Introduced to Congress every year starting in 1878, a similar constitutional amendment giving women the right to vote in the United States was not enacted until 1920, eighteen years after Elizabeth Cady Stanton died.

The Reconstruction era following the Civil War spurred a painful assessment of how the nation-state would fit together and how the government would relate to its population, including former slaves and an increasing number of immigrants from other parts of the world. Creating loyal and useful citizens drove the establishment and expansion of a public school system, as it did in Europe and elsewhere. Lessons designed for use in schools defined national character and the benefits of belonging. Unfortunately, the message sent by government actions suggested that some kinds of people still lacked the proper characteristics to have attained for themselves (yet or maybe ever) the right to full participation in the nation-state. These suspect groups included at one time or another African Americans, Native Americans, Jews, and people from Mexico, China, Ireland, Italy and elsewhere.

This attitude was reflected in territorial, immigration, and social policies. After the Civil War, the US government forced indigenous peoples of the Great Plains on to reservations. Completion of the transcontinental railroad system escalated the conflict over resources as more white settlers moved west. Much of the work on the railroad was completed by immigrant laborers from China, yet in 1882 the US government passed a law prohibiting the entry of Chinese immigrants for ten years out of fear that they posed a threat to order. And, by the end of the century, racial segregation had been ratified as a constitutionally sound practice. In 1890, the state of Louisiana passed a law that required separate accommodations for blacks and whites traveling by rail. In 1896, the US Supreme Court reviewed the case (*Plessy v. Ferguson*) and ruled that the country could endure with its citizens being "separate but equal," a legal standard that survived until the mid-twentieth century.

Historians Explore Abolition, Migration, and the Global Labor Force

Emancipation and abolition ended slavery, but did not end the demand for cheap labor to produce cash crops and other work. African-origin peoples in post-slave societies experienced a variety of working and living conditions. Into the twentieth century, many continued to labor in rural, agricultural settings as sharecroppers or tenant farmers, exchanging access to land in return for a commitment to provide the landlord with a share of the harvest—in cotton, tobacco, or another cash crop. Tenants often relied on their landlords for essential supplies (seed and tools), often provided on credit, to be paid back on unfavorable terms. This created a long-term cycle of debt and dependency. Other forms of labor, including forced labor by convicts, fed the growing demand for agricultural products needed for industry, like rubber and sisal.

In many parts of the world, indentured servitude replaced slave labor. Many migrants moved from China, India, Southeast Asia, and the Pacific islands to work in North and South America, the Caribbean, and throughout the British Empire. The nature of this migration—the terms of labor contracts, the degree to which indentured laborers could exercise any rights, the impact of new racial and ethnic populations in host territories—fueled debates about what it meant to be free and to be a citizen.

Asian laborers—called *coolies* during this era—existed in a gap between the enslaved and the fully free. Recent scholarship has clarified the relationship between the coolie trade and the slave trade. British, and then Spanish, law banned the Atlantic slave trade during the first half of the nineteenth century, so even though slavery continued to be practiced, the labor needs of the sugar-producing colonies in the Caribbean could no longer be met by importing enslaved Africans. The changes were immediate: in 1845, Spanish law forbade trade in slaves; the following year, a Spanish merchant contracted to import Chinese laborers to Cuba. More than 125,000 Chinese coolies were transported through Cuba over the next twenty-seven years, laboring on sugar plantations alongside enslaved Africans in Cuba and other Spanish territories. In the British Empire, where slavery was already illegal, the scale of Asian labor was even greater: 18,000 laborers from China and nearly 500,000 from India worked in the British Caribbean during this same period. British authorities extolled their moral superiority to the Spanish by abolishing slavery, yet many contemporary observers suggested that conditions for coolies and enslaved Africans were not noticeably different.

Asian laborers continued to fill much of the postemancipation demand for labor across South America and the Caribbean. They were crucial to the completion of the transcontinental railroads in the United States and Canada and were generally provided through a contract between owners and agents in India or China. Sometimes paid nominal wages and other times not paid at all, laborers served out the terms of a contract under conditions similar to slavery. During the last half of the nineteenth century in Australia, tens of thousands of Pacific Islanders worked as indentured servants on sugar plantations. As in the western United States, a gold rush in Australia also drew Chinese migrants, and in similar fashion, the growth of this population triggered a backlash. By the early twentieth century, blatant discrimination against Asians was written into law as part of the White Australia movement.

Historians have wrestled to make sense of the relationship between indentured servitude and slavery. Although some argue that indentured Asian labor was in many ways equivalent to slavery, most see it as a third category, neither slave nor free. Asian laborers saw themselves as deceived and mistreated but also saw their position as distinct from slavery. Their employment continued to subsidize the growth of the global economy for many decades after the abolition of the slave trade.[1]

1 Excellent overviews of the historiography of labor, citizenship, and the question of rights in postemancipation societies are contained in David Eltis, Stanley L. Engerman, Seymour Drescher, and David Richardson, eds., *The Cambridge World History of Slavery*, vol. 4 (Cambridge: Cambridge University Press, 2017). Detailed studies of specific societies and populations include Seymour Drescher, *Abolition: A History of Slavery and Antislavery* (Cambridge: Cambridge University Press, 2009); David Northrup, *Indentured Labor in the Age of Imperialism, 1834–1922* (Cambridge: Cambridge University Press, 1995); Frederick Cooper, Thomas C. Holt, and Rebecca Scott, *Beyond Slavery: Explorations of Race, Labor, and Citizenship in Postemancipation Societies* (Chapel Hill, NC: University of North Carolina Press, 2000); Martin Ruef, *Between Slavery and Capitalism: The Legacy of Emancipation in the American South* (Princeton, NJ: Princeton University Press, 2014); Lisa Yun, *The Coolie Speaks: Chinese Indentured Laborers and African Slaves in Cuba* (Philadelphia: Temple University Press, 2008); Moon-Ho Jung, *Coolies and Cane: Race, Labor, and Sugar in the Age of Emancipation* (Baltimore: Johns Hopkins University Press, 2006); and Tracey Banivanua-Mar, *Violence and Colonial Dialogue: The Australian–Pacific Indentured Labor Trade* (Honolulu: University of Hawai'i Press, 2007).

Global Hierarchies Defined and Defied

New flows of international labor migration like the coolie trade draw us to questions about the interplay between global economic change and shifting power relationships among the world's peoples and political structures during this era. Industrialization continued to disrupt global production and consumption patterns. The primary beneficiaries of these disruptions used the power they accrued to imagine a global order that made exchanges—of goods, ideas, and peoples—more efficient and rational. Through events such as the world's fairs, they also offered an idealized microcosm of how they saw the modern world: a place of progress and prosperity, with a clear hierarchy of these goods, ideas, and peoples.

The Second Industrial Revolution

The second half of the nineteenth century saw further change in unleashing the potential energy locked in fossil fuels. Bigger, more powerful engines and new fuels powered military, industrial, and consumer applications. The use of natural gas expanded, first for lighting and then for cooking and heating. Drilling for gas and oil spread across North America and then Europe in the 1850s. By the 1870s, commercial production of internal combustion engines—the kind used in automobiles—had begun. In 1882, the first eighty-five customers lighting their homes through incandescent light bulbs hooked into a New York power station.

Engineering marvels (and spectacular failures) abounded. The Suez Canal linked the Mediterranean and Red Seas in 1869, shaving six thousand miles off a journey from England to India. By the end of the 1880s, both Mexico and Argentina had rail networks of over six thousand miles, in countries where almost no track existed in 1850. In the United States, the transcontinental railroad joined the Atlantic and Pacific coasts in 1869. In Europe, between 1850 and 1890, the German railroad network expanded by a factor of twenty and Russia's by more than sixty. In India, where no railroad existed in 1850, over fifteen thousand miles of track had been laid by 1890, and that number would double again in the following twenty years.

These rails not only facilitated imperial expansion. The global market for industrial consumer goods—bicycles, typewriters, sewing machines—exploded. Goods imported from Asia and Latin America inspired home decorating styles in the United States. Asian elements influenced new trends in art like impressionism and art nouveau. Ordinary consumers had more access to greater quantities and varieties of durable goods and consumables. Entrepreneurs recognized the challenges of profiting from this changing equation and created new sales and marketing techniques to appeal to an ever-broader audience that included both men women. New magazines and newspapers, such as *Ladies Home Journal*, first published in 1883, featured ads for typewriters and sewing machines that showed the convergence of technology and social change.

Along with his sewing machines, Isaac Singer (1811–1875) brought to the table consumer credit, which permitted large numbers of individuals to purchase a relatively expensive and sophisticated machine without having to scrape together the entire purchase price at one time. The retail revolution was also embodied by the rise of department stores, most prominently Harrods in London, which opened with the motto *Omnia Omnibus Ubique—All Things for All People, Everywhere*—in 1849. Like other early examples—Paris's Bon Marché (opened as a department store in 1850), Macy's in New York (1858), Wanamaker's in Philadelphia (1876), Eaton's in Toronto (1869), Mexico City's El Palacio de Hierro (1891), and Moscow's GUM (1893)—Harrods offered a wide variety of consumer goods in one store, at fixed prices, with money-back guarantees and other sales and marketing innovations that turned shopping into a leisure activity, complete with live in-store entertainment. Consumers far from cities could access a wider variety of goods through new mail-order catalogs that took advantage of expanded, faster, and cheaper shipping services in much of the world. Cash registers and adding machines tracked the exchange of money.

Industrialization and the Food Revolution

Techniques for preserving food improved. New metal cans held foods more safely and conveniently for longer periods of time. In 1870, William Lyman (1821–1891) patented the first rotating-wheel can opener. Pasteurization, a process that slowed spoilage, was soon applied to brewing beer around the globe. The growing British rail network made Bass Ale popular across the nation, and in 1876 its red-triangle logo became Great Britain's first registered trademark; soon it was visible across Europe. In the United States, Anheuser–Busch developed a national distribution network out of its St. Louis headquarters, advertising that its Budweiser beer would "keep in any climate." Heineken, shipped from its breweries in Amsterdam and Rotterdam, became the best-selling beer in Paris. A student of French chemist Louis Pasteur (1822–1895), who developed the pasteurization process, cultivated the yeast strain that gave Heineken beer its unique taste; and a mechanical cooling system replaced the use of ice in the company's main brewery in 1881. The breweries that today produce Dos Equis (Mexico) and Sapporo (Japan) also opened during this period.

Other inventions changed the way people ate. Barbed-wire fencing transformed the livestock industry, simultaneously reinforcing new property rights claims over the vast grazing lands of the Western Hemisphere and allowing greater control over herds and breeding. Cattle and hogs began to move from ranch to slaughterhouse to butcher shop on railroads; refrigerated boxcars carried all sorts of perishable goods. Frozen meat moved by ship from Australia and New Zealand to England. Russian wheat reached western European markets. Argentina exported beef and other food products. Processes and applications to exploit natural resources found in limited places, like rubber (footwear and tires, Brazil) and sisal (binder twine, Mexico), brought investment, infrastructure, profit, and tax revenues to new locations or in larger quantities.

The connection between technology and agricultural production is a vital component of modernization and globalization. Before the transportation revolution, few kinds of food could be delivered over such long distances inexpensively and/or without spoiling. Now, a global trade in staple crops like wheat, corn, and rice began to emerge, alongside the chemicals and machines that would lower the costs of their production and raise the productivity of farmland. A new economy of tropical agricultural commodities grew. Bananas, pineapples, and coconuts were still exotic commodities in the mid-nineteenth century, but soon emerging transportation and preservation technologies would link multiple business interests in far-flung places, bringing tons of these products to more tables in the world's temperate zones. The market for more familiar commodities like sugar and coffee was also transformed during this era. Demand and supply for these goods expanded rapidly in the second half of the nineteenth century, creating both opportunity and volatility. Many countries, even entire regions, became increasingly dependent on export revenues from a small number of crops, riding the volatile global commodities market like a roller coaster.

Financiers who risked their capital understood that the marketplace was littered with failures like Dent & Co., the British firm that grew rich on the Chinese opium trade and collapsed just as dramatically in an 1867 Hong Kong bank run. Yet these trends were not simply individual choice, circumstance, and luck interacting on a level playing field. Elites in the United States and Europe leveraged their power to develop global political and economic structures that yielded these spectacular advances but simultaneously constrained the choices available to many individuals and groups, both within their borders and around the globe. The industrial economy enabled men like Cornelius Vanderbilt (1794–1877), Leland Stanford (1824–1893), J. P. Morgan (1837–1913), Andrew Carnegie (1835–1919), Cecil Rhodes (1853–1902), John D. Rockefeller (1839–1937), and others to accrue enormous personal fortunes and political influence around the world. Efforts to keep an ever more integrated global economic system moving forward in a world of distinct nations posed both grand and mundane challenges. Sometimes, both the grand and the mundane were epitomized by the same challenge, as in the question of how to create a way to tell time on a global scale.

Keeping Time in a Connected World

In 1884, the International Meridian Conference convened in Washington, DC. The conference brought together delegates from forty-one countries—the European powers, the United States, many South American states, and Japan—to establish a system for standardizing time across the globe. Time posed vexing problems for travelers. Keeping accurate time was essential to navigation at sea. When sailing near shore, landmarks could guide the mariner; but once out of sight of land, determining position and direction became more challenging. Chinese sailors had used the magnetic compass to determine direction as early as the eleventh century, and these remained in widespread use. Determining one's position and course in open sea required additional aids, however.

In theory, by cross-referencing north–south and east–west positions on the globe, one could derive a precise location at sea even without landmarks. Determining latitude (north–south position) was relatively easy using a simple sighting of the sun at its highest point during the day. Longitude—the east–west position—was harder, a lot harder. The best way was to determine the altitude of the sun, at two different points, at the exact same time of day. Charts recorded the altitude of the sun at different places on different dates, and these could be used for comparison with a traveler's present location, giving longitude. On land, this was easy: just look at a clock. At sea, however, pendulum clocks were unreliable amid the rolling and swaying of a ship. This problem was not resolved until the mid-eighteenth century when Englishman John Harrison (1693–1776) invented a timepiece that could accurately keep time aboard ship.

With this problem solved, navigators could more accurately keep track of their positions at sea, but it did not solve all problems. As one moves east or west across the globe, the time of day (based roughly on the height of the sun in the sky) changes. When the sun is at its highest point, we call that noon and build a cycle of twenty-four hours from one noon to the next. Telling time precisely—within a few minutes or even hours—was not important in the preindustrial world. Each town tended to keep its own time, and everything in the village or city was tied to that time. When traveling to a new place, the voyage was usually slow, and on arrival, you could determine what time it was. Pocket watches, first developed in Europe in the fifteenth century, were expensive and rare.

Industrialization changed the need to tell time in numerous ways. To begin with, factories did not function by daylight like farms had. As workers began to earn hourly wages or demand standard work shifts, keeping track of their hours became important. But the technology that globalized transportation and communication changed the need for keeping accurate track of time across long distances as well. Train travel required different stations to agree, precisely, on the time. Telegraphs and telegrams made it possible to communicate almost instantaneously over long distances. These new modes of transportation and communication revealed the discrepancies among different cities. In 1857, for instance, when it was noon in Washington, DC, it was—officially—12:12 in New York City, 12:24 in Boston, 12:02 in Baltimore, 12:18 in Hartford, and 12:08 in Philadelphia. *Dinsmore's Railroad and Steam Navigation Guide and Route-Book* observed, "The inconvenience of such a system, if system it can be called, must be apparent to all.... Many miscalculations and misconnections have resulted, which have not unfrequently been of serious consequence." The question, of course, was how to standardize time. There are north and south magnetic poles, which serve for setting compass points, but there is no east or west pole; some single line of longitude would have to be agreed on as a standard, from which other lines could be developed to synchronize time around the world. This was the goal of the 1884 Washington Conference.

The Royal Observatory in Greenwich, England, had sponsored the prize to find a reliable and practical method for determining longitude at sea; subsequently, Greenwich Time had become the standard in the eighteenth century for the development of shipboard navigation tables and, later, British railroad timetables. The dominance of British seafaring, and the extensive British Empire, made this the likely choice for the global time standard, a choice the Washington Conference confirmed. Within a few years, most of Europe and the Americas had adopted Greenwich Mean Time as the standard by which to set their clocks. Soon the whole world's day was measured in a standard, universally accepted way—synchronized with reference to a small town on the River Thames.

Keeping Up: The World's Fairs

England was also the site of the first modern world's fair, held in London in 1851. Similar events soon followed in Dublin, New York, Paris, and Vienna. In 1876 alone, the year Philadelphia hosted a US Centennial Exhibition and World's Fair, similar international exhibitions were held in French Algeria, Uruguay, and Scotland. By the early twentieth century, these international exhibits became so frequent that another diplomatic conference was called to establish a Bureau of International Exhibitions. Exploring world's fairs in some detail provides an ideal canvas for understanding the many themes raised throughout this chapter, so we will end it with an exploration of two: Philadelphia (1876) and Paris (1889).

Philadelphia's International Centennial Exhibition was one component of the centennial celebrations of US independence in 1876. The original plan was for one large building divided into ten departments that would represent the stages of human progress. The complex and often conflicting goals of organizers, exhibitors, politicians, and investors rendered this idea unfeasible. Ultimately, 250 individual structures rose on almost three hundred acres of land along the Schuylkill River. Between May and November of 1876, nearly ten million people wandered the grounds. Visitors could snack on exotic foods, like bananas—sold by the slice, wrapped in tin foil—or enjoy substantial meals at one of the restaurants built on the grounds.

Almost fourteen thousand exhibitors from thirty-seven countries competed for both business and recognition; there were juried prizes in twenty-eight different categories. In exhibition spaces around the fairgrounds, small and large enterprises displayed pottery, porcelain, glassware, furniture, mechanical devices, woven goods, carpets, silks, clothing, jewelry, toys, stationery, firearms, ammunition, medicine, medical equipment, hardware, tools, cutlery, vehicles, fresh and preserved food, paintings, sculpture, and other items.

Inventors and companies showcased new products for the marketplace at these international exhibitions—Alexander Graham Bell's telephone caused a sensation in Philadelphia. However, the fair was not ordered exclusively for private enterprises or consumers. The global economic and technological transformation, so much in evidence to visitors, went hand in hand with depictions of an emerging new order of nations at different levels of development. The main hall was ordered "by races," with clusters of displays from Teutonic, Anglo-Saxon, and Latin exhibitors.

Both independent countries and the outposts of European empires brought their goods to display. Some countries, like Britain, Germany, and Brazil, constructed their own buildings, while others shared space. Some countries, like Belgium, Greece, Italy, and Germany, reflected the important changes in European political geography in the decades after the Napoleonic Wars. Others, like the Orange Free State in southern Africa and the Sandwich Islands (Hawai'i), would soon lose their political autonomy to a new wave of imperialism. Latin American participation—twelve countries in total—drew attention to the changes in the Western Hemisphere. As more stable central authorities began to emerge, the nascent national elites of Mexico, Venezuela, Argentina, Nicaragua, and others saw the Philadelphia fair as an opportunity to rebrand their countries as stable participants in modernity, worthy partners in trade, and serious participants in international affairs.

In 1889, Paris hosted its own world's fair to coincide with another centennial, that of the French Revolution. One might have been forgiven for feeling as if time itself had accelerated since Philadelphia's exhibition little more than a decade earlier. Sixteen-thousand machines filled the Gallery of Machines in Paris, housed in the world's largest iron-framed building. The French reserved three-quarters

Liberia Soap and Coffee Display, Agricultural Hall, Philadelphia Centennial Exhibition, 1876. Liberia, a West African refuge for manumitted slaves since the 1820s, created a republican constitution in 1847. Official diplomatic relations between the United States and Liberia were not established until 1862, but Liberia participated in the Centennial Exhibition in the following decade. Like many other participants in the world's fairs, Liberians hoped to introduce the advantages of their products in a highly competitive global consumer culture. The sign in the middle of the display begins with the words, "Liberia offers. . . ."

of the exhibition space in the building for their own products, a reminder of the nationalist motivations driving countries to host these expensive undertakings. Visitors to Paris could see for themselves the first automobile using an internal combustion engine—the Benz *Motorwagen* patented in 1886—and see the first public display of Thomas Edison's motion pictures. The fair's modern aesthetic did not please everyone, however. A group of artists and writers ridiculed the Eiffel Tower as "a gigantic black smokestack," but the majority's enthusiastic embrace of the ambitious iron structure drowned out the naysayers. Originally designed to stand for two decades, the tower remained the tallest structure in the world until it was surpassed by New York's Chrysler Building in 1930.

The notions of progress on view in Paris reveal as much (or more) about the values of the organizers and promoters of the fair as do the machinery and consumer goods. Fair-goers could observe the "natural" habits of "primitive" peoples at a "human zoo," as well as a Palace of the Colonies, where they could see how less developed places on earth were learning how to be modern (or clinging to their "backward" ways). Living displays from Europe's new colonies brought the empire to Paris. A man from Senegal—one of France's African colonies—tended cows, sheep, and goats while crowds watched. The Dutch brought sixty men and women from Java to build a village. The villagers, who also performed (by living their lives!) at other international exhibitions, stayed on the fairgrounds for the duration of the exhibition. A small group of them staged a Javanese opera at regular intervals.

Conclusion

Over the course of the nineteenth century, material conditions and a series of individual and collective decisions led elites in industrializing countries to surrender some of their wealth and power to maintain order. In turn, most members of the working classes chose reform over revolution. A slow, incremental expansion of suffrage occurred in most of these countries, accompanied by social rights legislation. Industrial production provided an ever-expanding cornucopia of goods to be enjoyed by the world's consumers. This was the world of progress on display at the world's fairs in Paris and Philadelphia, idealized versions of a well-ordered global marketplace of abundant, innovative goods and positive change over time.

Yet these displays were distorted snapshots. Some participating countries and groups were navigating the challenges of industrialization and globalization to

TIMELINE

1831 Giuseppe Mazzini founds Young Italy

1832 Reform Act doubles the number of eligible voters in Britain

1833 British Parliament votes to abolish slavery in the British Empire

1839 Tanzimat reforms begin in Ottoman Empire

1840 World Antislavery Conference

1846 First coolies imported into Cuba

1848 Seneca Falls Convention; publication of *Manifesto of the Communist Party* (Marx and Engels); revolutions throughout Europe

1849 California Gold Rush begins

1851 First modern world's fair, London

1853 Matthew Perry leads US naval mission to Japan

1857 Great Rebellion: rebellion against British rule in India emerge with more political, economic, and military power. Others were being undone by the challenges and swept away by change. Careful observers of this era made note of the high costs of order and progress to some peoples and in some places. It is to these concerns that we turn our attention in Chapter 9.

A Few Good Books

Anne C. Bailey. *The Weeping Time: Memory and the Largest Slave Auction in American History*. Cambridge: Cambridge University Press, 2017.

Jean H. Baker. *Sisters: The Lives of America's Suffragists*. New York: Hill and Wang, 2006.

Christopher Benfey. *The Great Wave: Gilded Age Misfits, Japanese Eccentrics, and the Opening of Old Japan*. New York: Random House, 2004.

Ermine Evered. *Empire and Education under the Ottomans: Politics, Reform and Resistance from the Tanzimat to the Young Turks*. New York: Palgrave Macmillan, 2012.

Jill Jonnes. *Eiffel's Tower: The Thrilling Story behind Paris's Beloved Monument and the Extraordinary World's Fair That Introduced It*. New York: Penguin, 2009.

Joanne S. Liu. *Barbed Wire: The Fence That Changed the West*. Missoula, MT: Mountain Press, 2009.

Mike Rapport. *1848: Year of Revolution*. New York: Basic Books, 2004.

Dava Sobel. *Longitude: The True Story of a Lone Genius Who Solved the Greatest Scientific Problem of His Time*. New York: Walker, 2007.

For instructional resources and study aids, please go to **www.oup.com/us/carter**. *For primary sources connected to this chapter, please see the table of contents for* Sources for Forging the Modern World *included at the back of the book.*

1861 Serfdom abolished in Russia
1869 Suez Canal opens; transcontinental railroad completed in the United States
1876 Bass Ale obtains Britain's first registered trademark
1877 Opening of Tokyo University, Asia's first Western-style university
1889 Paris world's fair
1868 Meiji government established in Japan
1871 Unifications of Italy and Germany
1876–1910 *Científicos* influential in Mexico
1888–1889 Brazil abolishes slavery; monarchy falls the following year
1896 *Plessy v. Ferguson* establishes principle of separate but equal in the United States

(TOP) Editorial Cartoon Depicting the "Scramble for Africa" Inaugurated at the Berlin Conference (1884). The new imperialism of the late nineteenth century saw Europe and the United States gain control over 80 percent of the earth's surface. The competition among European states for the resources of Africa is depicted in this cartoon, which shows the manner in which European nations like Germany (here represented by Bismarck, holding the knife) felt it their privilege to distribute African territory as they pleased.

(RIGHT) The Amazon Theater, Manaus, Brazil. Industrial commodities and global markets could bring sudden wealth to producers. In the late nineteenth century, a boom in rubber prices made Manaus, Brazil, deep in the Amazon rain forest, the richest city in South America for a time. To showcase its wealth, the city built a grand opera house—the Amazon Theater—with materials imported from France, Scotland, and Italy. The building was one of the first in the world to have electric lighting; but when the rubber market collapsed, the city's generators were too expensive to operate, and Manaus lost its electric lights for several decades.

CHAPTER 9

Globalization and Its Discontents

1878–1910

Two meetings in Berlin illustrate the ambitions of European leaders in the late nineteenth century. That they were in Berlin showed the importance of Europe's newest power. Germany's capital had grown from four hundred thousand people in 1849 to nearly a million by the end of the 1870s, and its population would double again by 1900. In the first meeting (called the Congress of Berlin), in 1878, German chancellor Otto von Bismarck (1815–1898) hosted diplomats from across western Eurasia to sort out the aftermath of a war between the Russian and Ottoman Empires and redraw the map of southeastern Europe. The results angered many participants. The Ottoman Empire lost territory in its western regions; Russian leaders were frustrated that victory on the battlefield did not translate into even greater territorial gains. Representatives of smaller states felt that the outcome privileged power over principle and served neither the interests of their people nor those of long-term international stability.

In the mid-1880s, diplomats returned to Schulenburg Palace for another meeting, this one referred to as the Berlin Conference, to redraw a different set of borders. This time, the great powers of Europe met to allocate *spheres of influence*, formalizing and giving order to the wave of European imperialism known as the *scramble for Africa*. Over the next three decades, the European states acted on these claims and attempted to exercise sovereignty over much of Africa.

In the same era, Brazilian elites focused on the tropical interior of their own country. Symbolizing their membership in the club of modern peoples, wealthy Brazilians lavished cities like Manaus, the rubber capital, with the latest civic luxuries. Nine hundred miles up the Amazon River, Manaus rose to dizzying heights on income from the sap of the *Hevea brasiliensis* tree, the source of much of the world's rubber. A new industrial process that made rubber easier to shape, stronger, and more durable drove demand. Manaus, a city of several thousand

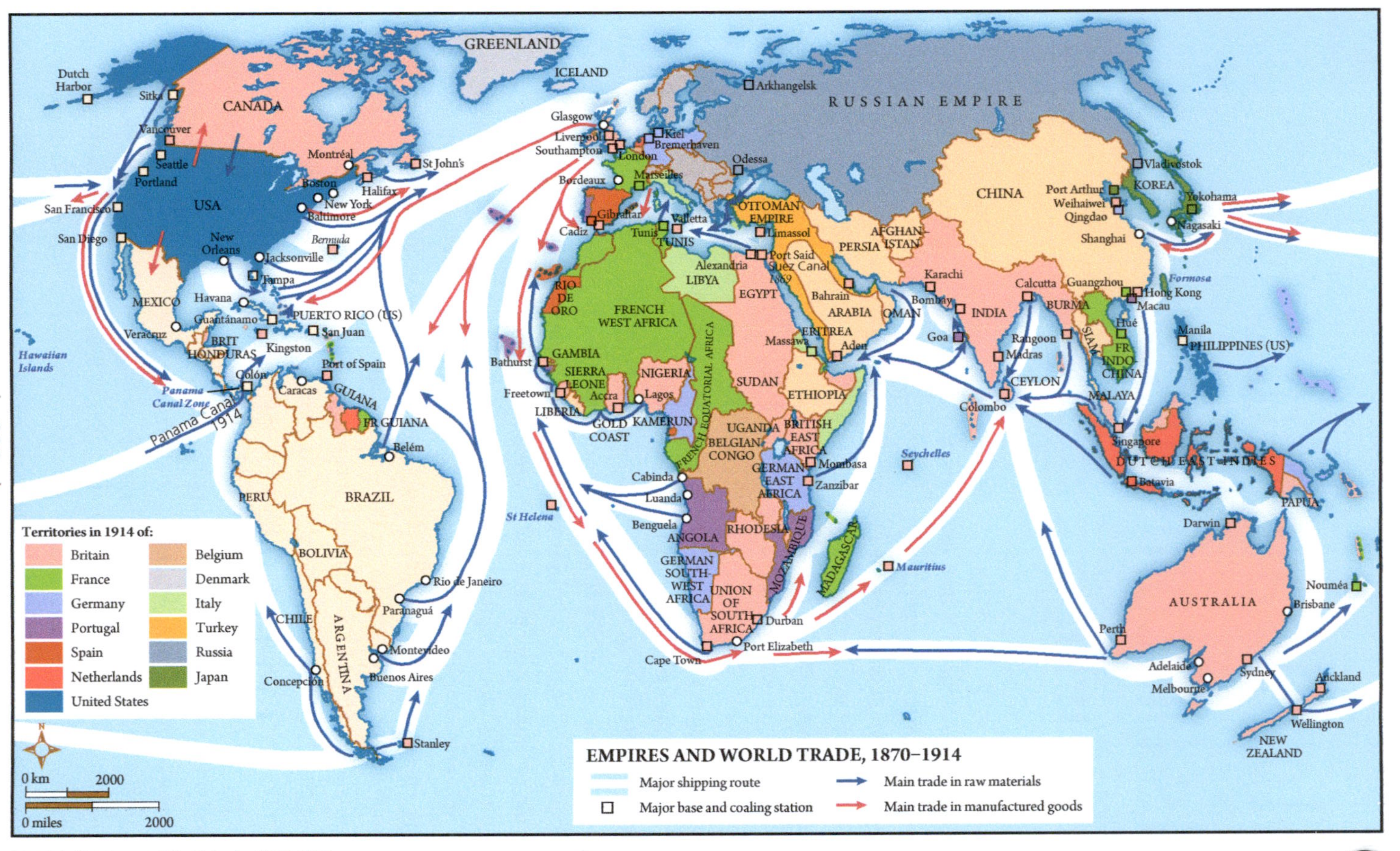

Map 9.1 Empires and World Trade, 1870–1914

people in the 1870s, opened its first bank only in the late 1880s but had one of the first electric trolley systems in Latin America a decade later. In 1897, its lavish Amazonas Theater—a multimillion-dollar opera house designed by an Italian architect and built with materials imported from Italy, England, and France—opened its doors. The population of Manaus reached one hundred thousand as the price of rubber in international markets tripled between 1908 and 1910, when prices peaked.

Elsewhere in Latin America, 1910 marked the year that the governments of Chile, Colombia, Mexico, and others organized lavish ceremonies to celebrate a century of independence from the Spanish Empire. Elites in these countries, like those in Brazil, congratulated themselves on what they saw as their own successful navigation of the path to modernity, including the stability of their political systems and the development of their economic infrastructures, supported by exports of copper, coffee, and other products in demand around the industrializing world. The high costs—wild economic fluctuations, repression of workers, displacement of peasants and indigenous peoples—seemed to them the price of progress.

In this chapter, we analyze global political and economic interactions in the last decades of the nineteenth century and the first decade of the twentieth. We begin by defining the new imperialism, as the great powers of Europe claimed vast territory in Africa and Asia and attempted to consolidate control over a new international political and economic order. We then examine some countercurrents that challenged this impulse. Some states in Africa and Asia maintained territorial sovereignty during this era, and people in both colonies and imperial centers created movements that rejected the principles of political and economic organization by which a handful of European states, along with the United States of America, dominated the globe. In the chapter's last section, we explore changes in the Western Hemisphere during this era.

Questions to Consider as You Read Chapter Nine:

1. What were the most important similarities and differences in the interactions between the European powers (England, France, and Germany) and the peoples of Africa, Asia, and South America during this period? How do these similarities and differences help us to understand power relationships during this era?
2. What kinds of justifications and criticisms of the global political and economic order emerged in the late nineteenth and early twentieth centuries? With whom and where did they originate? What kinds of responses did they trigger?

The New Imperialism and Neocolonialism

We have defined and analyzed empires and imperialism repeatedly in this book, so what is new about this "new imperialism"? Imperialism in this era, driven and facilitated by industrialization, was more extensive and intensive than the imperial dynamics we have described in earlier chapters. By *extensive*, we mean simply that imperial powers claimed more territory than ever before. Between 1878 and 1914, European empires added 8.6 million square miles of territory (more than twice the entire area of Europe) to their empires. At the height of the new imperialism, Europe and the United States claimed more than 80 percent of the earth's land surface. In contrast, European empires of the eighteenth century covered about 50 percent of the world, mostly in the Americas, at their greatest extent.

The new imperialism was also more *intensive* than earlier imperial enterprises. Even the strongest or largest empires of the preindustrial world, by design or necessity, tolerated great variation in political and economic customs and practices. In the nineteenth century, imperialists attempted to penetrate more deeply into local society to enforce decisions made in the imperial center. This reflected the ideals of "order and progress" described in Chapter 8 in which hierarchical, professional bureaucracies were seen as the way to administer modern states, and governments developed more capacity to direct people's behavior and economic practices. So, for example, imperial governments would rewrite property laws or ban cultural practices of indigenous populations in the territories they seized. Although these actions might sound familiar, during the age of the new imperialism, improved technologies and logistics made these practices much more effective. New weapons, communications infrastructure, and transportation systems (including steam-powered navies and merchant ships) contributed to both the expansion and the intensification of empire.

The formal colonialism of European states in much of Asia and Africa demonstrates one aspect of changing power relationships during this era. A more complete understanding of the late nineteenth century needs to include the financial and commercial networks that individuals and institutions in Europe, the United States, and Japan established beyond (or alongside) their own empires. Some scholars have used the term *neocolonialism* to describe this relationship. Others question the term's validity. Rather than review the debates over the merits of the label itself, we think it is important to consider in the pages that follow the question behind the debate: to what extent during this era did some states that were formally independent—for example, in Latin America or eastern Europe—still operate under a compromised sovereignty because they depended on external economic and/or military power to act like a state?

Redrawing the Map of the World

Radiating out from the two Berlin meetings, the European powers reshaped the globe. The Congress of Berlin (1878) remapped the Balkans. This religious, cultural, and political crossroads was coveted by the Austro-Hungarian, Russian, and Ottoman Empires but its residents were energized by the nationalist fervor and rhetoric of self-determination of the nineteenth century. As delegates in Berlin confirmed the independence of Serbia and Montenegro, the great powers determined the size and borders of these new states while denying sovereignty to other territories in the region—Bosnia, Herzegovina, Bulgaria, and other would-be nations all remained parts of empires for the time being.

Although the congress focused on Europe and its immediate borders, the major parties to the treaties that emerged from it were already playing out conflicts on a global stage. Soon after the congress, British troops moved into the Malay Peninsula and Burma in Southeast Asia. Russia continued to expand in central and East Asia, facilitated by an ambitious railroad construction program. France went to war with China in the 1880s to gain territory in Southeast Asia.

Great power rivalries were also plain to see in Africa, where events such as the completion of the Suez Canal and the discovery of diamonds in South Africa sparked further interest in controlling the region's resources. Conflicting claims from France, Portugal, Britain, and Belgium in the Congo Basin motivated the second Berlin Conference (1884). Bismarck noted his primary goal for the conference was solidifying Germany's place in European affairs, rather than solving any particular issues related to Africa.

The diplomats in Berlin settled the Congo crisis by sorting out the claims of European states in the territory, but did so without regard to the indigenous populations, as they agreed with Bismarck that the African settlement was first and foremost an extension of European national rivalries. The outcome established a precedent by which European states had to physically enact claims on African territories if they wished to have other European states recognize them. With this understanding, Europeans accelerated the scramble for Africa using their existing settlements as launch pads to push their claims ever further. By 1910, European empires had transformed Africa into a patchwork of European state-names stitched onto African territorial distinctions and compass directions—German East Africa, French West Africa, Anglo-Egyptian Sudan, Spanish Guinea, Italian Somaliland, the Belgian Congo, and on and on.

Motivations for the New Imperialism

Economic motivations have always been important to empire building, but the new imperialism more completely integrated colonies into an industrial network of extraction, manufacture, and distribution. By controlling how newly colonized regions could participate in the global economy, new imperialist policies contributed to disparities in the distribution of the benefits of globalization. The colonized could neither develop their own internal economies nor participate freely in a global market as producers or consumers.

Historians have long debated why the European powers engaged in the new imperialism and how they benefited from it. Some historians focus on the economic benefits: colonizing powers pursued resources to further their own industrialization and maintain profit margins in the global economy while providing some surplus to industrial workers in the metropolis. Others suggest that domestic politics were paramount, arguing that European governments used imperial expansion to distract or divert potentially disruptive political movements at home or enhance their own popularity by fueling nationalistic fervor for colonies and conquest. Another set of explanations sees acquiring colonies as strategic. Ports for trade and fueling stations for navies were key assets to be used against rival states. In this view, political changes in Europe, such as Germany's unification, drove the new imperialism in the last quarter of the nineteenth century. European imperialism was primarily another venue for competition among European states.

These explanations tend to focus on imperial centers like Paris, London, Berlin, or Brussels, but that's not the only way to understand the logic of the new imperialism. Other historians focus on actions and ideas in the colonies themselves. Local agents of commercial enterprises, even diplomats, sometimes acted without the authorization or consent of superiors back home, perhaps because of the time it would take to receive instructions from the capital. In these cases, what appeared to be government policy might have been just the best guess of the "man on the spot." In other cases, a local agent seeking power, fortune, or glory acted to promote personal goals rather than some preconceived imperial agenda.

Justifying the New World Order

In an attempt to explain and justify such acts and outcomes, many political and cultural leaders, as well as ordinary people, latched onto ideas that came, much later, to be called social Darwinism. The term comes from the suggestion that the new imperialism somehow reflected the scientific theory of natural selection at work among human populations. We'll explain a little later why social Darwinism is not good science and why it does not really reflect the work of British scientist Charles Darwin (1809–1882), but first let's establish Darwin's basic theory and then see what the social Darwinists had to say.

Without exploring in great detail the entire theory of evolution, it's essential to understand that Darwinian theory rests on the idea of natural selection. In struggling to survive, animals cannot change fundamental features about themselves, for example, the length of their necks or the shapes of their beaks. Rather, variations arising from random differences make some individuals better suited to a particular environment or task so they are more likely to survive, reproduce, and pass on these characteristics to the next generation. That is the motor of evolution. The finches of the Galapagos Islands inspired many of Darwin's first ideas on natural selection, and they illustrate the principle neatly. On one island, where conditions led to a collapse of the insect population that the finches ate, the birds turned to eating mostly seeds. Finches with shorter, more powerful beaks were better able to crack the seeds. Birds with longer, narrower beaks, previously useful for catching insects in small spaces, found it harder to eat and survive. The birds with shorter beaks were more likely to live and produce offspring, which were also more likely to have short, powerful beaks. On other islands, where the insects remained, longer, narrower beaks were better adapted, and birds with these types of beaks survived longer and reproduced in larger numbers. In neither case did the birds control the variations in their beaks, yet those variations were the key to individual survival. Fitting an environmental niche led to the proliferation of birds with a particular adaptation. This was called—though not by Darwin—*survival of the fittest*: those members of the species best adapted to their environment would survive.

The term social Darwinism originated in the 1870s, but it was not popularized until the twentieth century, and almost no one who advocated social Darwinist ideas would have used that label. Social Darwinism took Darwin's ideas about natural selection and applied them to conflicts among entire human societies, insisting that the growing military and economic power of some states proved that they were the fittest, winners in a competition to dominate their rivals for the globe's space and resources. Just as the short-beaked finches survived on certain islands, proving their fitness to survive, the European exploitation of Africa and Asia, particularly, was said to prove the superiority of European peoples and societies. It also justified their actions, asserting that the success of certain classes, nations, and races was inevitable. Social Darwinists expected the populations of "less fit" societies to decline over time and saw this as a necessary and appropriate result of natural processes. It's important to note that this view existed in elite and intellectual circles around the world at this time. Many in China, for instance, considered their country's weakness in the face of European imperialism as evidence that Chinese civilization was inferior.

It's also important to understand that social Darwinist ideas are not scientific applications of Darwin's theories. The strategy of an imperial army, or a government's economic policy, is not like the beak of a finch. For one thing, these are not inherited traits; they can be (and are) changed. In natural selection, even if the world's smartest finch knew it needed a different beak, there was nothing it could do about it. The shape of a finch's beak—Darwin's variable of fitness—did not make an individual bird or an entire species that shared this characteristic better or worse, moral or immoral. The very idea is absurd! Yet, social Darwinists often suggested that countries with larger economies or stronger armies were morally obliged to act on and spread their "superiority."

A different, still laudatory, view of imperialism suggested that the imperial powers had a moral duty to instruct and improve those unfortunate persons born in places where Western civilization had not yet taken root. From this perspective, colonial institutions sought to transform these parts of the world by imposing what were claimed to be Western values and methods. Alongside (or even within) rubber plantations, French colonizers in Indochina built schools to teach Catholicism, European history, and the French language. Vietnamese children learned from books that began "Nos ancêtres, les Gaulois" ("Our Ancestors, the Gauls") even though the students were born to Vietnamese parents and were unlikely ever to see France. Advocates of this *mission civilisatrice* ("civilizing mission") brushed aside these absurdities to emphasize the improvements—schools, hospitals, sewers, new ideas—that colonizers brought.

Rudyard Kipling (1865–1936) conveyed this sense of the costs and moral obligations borne by colonizers in "The White Man's Burden," a racist, paternalist poem that described "sullen," "half-devil and half-child" natives who preferred the ignorance of slavery to the responsibility that came from freedom. Only with the guidance of "civilized" (white) men could these societies hope to achieve maturity. One of the most popular writers in the English language in the late nineteenth century, Kipling portrayed imperialism as a difficult and thankless, but necessary, job that included building "Ports ye shall not enter/Roads ye shall not tread" and waging "savage wars of peace" to end famine and sickness in the colonies. Published in 1899, the poem bore the subtitle "The United States and the Philippine Islands" and suggested that the United States, which took control of the Philippines, Puerto Rico, and Cuba after a war with Spain in 1898, could now join the company of mature, European states if it would "take up the White Man's burden" by exercising its imperialist obligations and "have done with childish days." In the sections that follow, we will see in greater detail debates over the causes and consequences on the new imperialism in different regions, as well as responses from those most affected by the robust aggression of this era.

The Impact of Imperialism in Africa and India

Kipling's suggestion that colonizers were the selfless victims of imperialism struck many as ridiculous and insulting. In a biting retort, the African American author and clergyman H. T. Johnson wrote *The Black Man's Burden* (1899), denouncing imperialism as a solution to the "problem" of the world's "red," "black," and "brown" peoples: "in vain ye seek to end it, with bullets, blood or death." Across the regions where imperial powers attempted to tighten their control over political, economic, and cultural affairs, local populations conducted their own assessment of the costs and benefits of imperialism. In many quarters, both elites and nonelites found the imperial balance sheet did not yield a positive outcome, and they fought back in myriad ways.

The Repercussions of the Scramble for Africa

The gap between the rhetoric of European uplift and the reality of colonial exploitation may have been starkest in the Congo River basin, the region that prompted the Berlin meetings of the mid-1880s. The conference delegates created an entity called the Congo Free State, an area of west-central Africa as large as the United States east of the Mississippi River. The region was labeled a free state both because the European powers agreed to allow each other unrestrained travel through the region's river systems and because they agreed to eliminate the international slave trade there. In neither sense did the name fit, as the Belgian King Leopold II ruled with impunity over the Congo Free State.

In contrast to the Congo, in Ethiopia, Emperor Menelik II (1844–1913), who ruled from 1889 to 1913, employed political and economic tactics that reinforced his sovereignty and expanded his territory. He introduced new postal, telecommunications, banking, and electrical systems. He also made shrewd diplomatic maneuvers, building his empire through a strategic marriage and strengthening

Battle of Adwa. On March 1, 1896, an Ethiopian army under Emperor Menelik II defeated invading Italian armies attempting to expand their empire in the region. By defeating the Europeans, Menelik consolidated his own power in Ethiopia and also fueled a variety of interpretations of the event. The Ethiopian victory was an important symbol of Africans' ability to resist and defeat invading armies. Some Europeans, however, dismissed the battle's importance by questioning Italian military skills or by arguing that Ethiopians were not "black."

his relationship with Russia to counterbalance the ambitions of other European powers in the Horn of Africa. It was, however, his military victory against Italy in the mid-1890s, achieved with both nonconventional military tactics (guerrilla warfare) and modern artillery, that proved to be the key event in preserving Ethiopia's independence.

The tactic of indigenous rulers using international rivalries to defeat local opponents was a dangerous game that often backfired, as one sees in many other cases. For example, the competition between Nama and Herero peoples in what is today Namibia led the Nama leader Hendrik Witbooi (ca. 1830–1905) to form an alliance with Germany. Witbooi subsequently altered his position as German ambitions to control the entire region became clear to him. Witbooi died alongside his former Herero enemies in armed resistance to further German expansion.

The Maji Maji Rebellion (*maji* means "water" in Swahili) is another example of indigenous resistance to German expansion in Africa. The rebellion broke out in 1905 in German East Africa, where the colonial regime forced Africans to grow cotton and build roads to facilitate exports. Drought and famine, exacerbated by farmland taken out of food production and given over to cash crops, triggered the uprising. At the heart of the Maji Maji movement was a mysticism that included claims that believers could protect themselves from the violent technologies of imperialists. Kinjikitile Ngwale (d. 1905) emerged to lead anti-German resistance, claiming he had contact with a deity who instructed him to unite the African people against the Germans. Emboldened by a special medicine that was supposed to strengthen its users against German bullets, his followers rebelled. Kinjikitile Ngwale himself was captured and executed for treason in the summer of 1905 but the rebellion continued for two more years. More than ten thousand Africans, but as few as fifteen Europeans, died in the conflict.

The Maji Maji Rebellion was not the first or only revolt against European colonialism in Africa. Like the Wahehe Rebellion (1891–1898) that preceded it and others before and after, the Maji Maji Rebellion provoked brutal reprisals. German military officials encouraged crop destruction to promote famine as a means of subduing the population. Once the revolt was crushed, an even more rigid regime was implemented to monitor conditions more closely and quell potential revolt.

Documenting the Abuses Committed against African Peoples

The Belgian king Leopold claimed that his goal in Africa was to promote trade and eliminate slavery once and for all. Writing in 1890 to George Washington Williams (1849–1891), an African American who had himself been enslaved, Leopold emphasized that his efforts in the Congo were part of his "Christian duty to the poor African," for which he did "not wish to see one *franc* back." Williams was impressed at first, finding Leopold to be "one of the noblest sovereigns in the

Map 9.2 Sovereignty Claims in Africa, Early Twentieth Century

world . . . ruling in wisdom, mercy, and justice." Williams went to the Congo that year, evaluating the new colony as a place where African Americans might seek relief from the legal and social oppression of the post-Reconstruction US South. What Williams found was not Christian charity but what he called "crimes against humanity," employing perhaps for the first time a phrase that would be used, sadly, throughout the next century.

Edmund Morel (1873–1924), a clerk at a Liverpool shipping company, came to conclusions similar to Williams. Forced from his job for calling out Belgian abuses, Morel published numerous books and newspaper articles on the Congo, became a leader of the Congo Reform Association in 1904, and traveled across Europe and the United States speaking out on the situation. His slide show of imperialist atrocities presented shocking images that are still used as primary sources to communicate what was done to African peoples during this era. But, as scholars like Kevin Grant and Nancy Rose Hunt demonstrate, the contexts within which the photographs were captured, and the ends to which they were used, present problems that viewers need to consider. Making sense of these images requires a deeper, more nuanced understanding of their history.

The Baptist missionary Alice Seeley Harris (1870–1970), an influential activist in her own right who spoke at hundreds of public meetings on both sides of the Atlantic Ocean, took the photographs that Morel used. Seeley's photographs, taken with one of the world's first portable cameras, provided damning evidence of Leopold's atrocities. These images shaped the understanding—both in the Congo and outside it—of Leopold's Congo "rubber regime." But Hunt and Grant remind us that using the photos runs the risk of reducing real people's lives to two-dimensional artifacts, depriving them of agency and making them appear passive victims. In this way, the photos can add yet another indignity to what happened.

Other primary sources help us understand the people of the Congo as historical actors rather than as photographic objects. Congolese men and women gave more than 250 statements to a Belgian Commission of Inquiry in 1905–1906. In addition, journalists, missionaries, and diplomats conducted extensive interviews, leading to a report on the Congo to the British government in 1904. In the mid-twentieth century, an oral history project collected more stories from the era's survivors. The detail, nuance, and range of human experience and emotion conveyed in these testimonies remind us of the power of primary sources and the agency of African peoples resisting their oppressors. Boali, a Congolese woman who was among Harris's photographic subjects, testified about her experiences on a Belgian rubber plantation. One day, Boali resisted the sexual advances of a plantation sentry (the guards were used to keep workers and their families in the work camps rather than to keep trespassers out). As Boali reports, the furious guard, named Ikelonda, "fired a gun shot at me. . . . I fell on my back; Ikelonda thought I was dead, and to get hold of the brass bracelet that I wore at the base of my right leg, he cut off my right foot." The weight of evidence suggests that murder, starvation, amputation, and rape at the service of extracting African wealth for European benefit were commonplace, as was resistance.[1]

1 Kevin Grant, "Christian Critics of Empire: Missionaries, Lantern Lectures, and the Congo Reform Campaign in Britain," *The Journal of Imperial and Commonwealth History* 29, no. 2 (2001): 27–58; Nancy Rose Hunt, "An Acoustic Register, Tenacious Images, and Congolese Scenes of Rape and Ruination," *Cultural Anthropology* 23, no. 2 (2008): 220–253. Boali's testimony is quoted on page 225.

Women Captives with Guard, Belgian Congo. This early twentieth-century photograph, by Alice Seeley Harris, was used by the Congo Reform Association in its campaign against abuses of indigenous peoples in the Belgian Congo. Association records tell us that these two women were taken hostage because their husbands fled to the forest to escape the labor demands of the Anglo-Belgian Indian Rubber Company.

The Debate over British Rule in India

The British Crown took over direct rule of India from the British East India Company in 1858. In recognition of the monarchy's larger role in the imperial project, the British Parliament gave Queen Victoria a new title in 1876: empress. Over the second half of the nineteenth century, the economy of India was increasingly integrated into the broader empire. New political institutions were created at the local and provincial level—elected district councils, even a council of Indian elites chosen to advise the viceroy, the Crown's representative in India. Sayyid Ahmad Khan (1817–1898), one of the foremost Muslim leaders of his day in India, celebrated European institutions and sought to educate and elevate Indians through them, establishing a college for Indian Muslims who lacked access to British universities. Jamal al-Din al-Afghani (1838–1897), another Indian Muslim, could not have disagreed more strongly with this line of thinking. While Khan created a Muslim college along British lines, Afghani saw Britain and other European states as plunderers. Afghani, who spent time in Afghanistan, Iran, India, Egypt, Turkey, Germany, France, England, and Russia, attempted to bridge the ethnic and religious differences among Muslims and build a unified Islamic response against European expansionism.

The argument between Afghani and Khan captures the stark differences of opinion on the new imperialism. Some viewed it as a positive development, at least potentially. Others saw it as an unspeakable evil. Dadabhai Naoroji (1825–1917) tried to measure with some dispassion its costs and benefits. In his writings and speeches as the first South Asian—and more generally, the first Asian—member of the British Parliament, Naoroji expressed his admiration of British traditions and institutions. But even in the praise he offered, there was a lament. Naoroji combined economic data, government documents, and personal observation to conclude that India provided enormous direct and indirect subsidies to England from profits and taxes and the exploitation of Indians used to enforce British imperial rule around the world. Naoroji objected to British rule of India because it was "un-British." In the introduction to a collection of his work, entitled *Poverty and Un-British Rule in India* (1901), Naoroji stated that "my whole object in all my writings is to impress upon the British people, that instead of a disastrous explosion of the British Indian Empire" a brighter future would emerge if the rulers would "be true to their British instincts of fair play and justice."

Support for reform within an imperial order began to lose traction in the early twentieth century, as people like Mohandas K. Gandhi (1869–1948) emerged as leading voices critical of British imperialism. Gandhi had been educated in London and worked for years as a lawyer and activist in South Africa, another British imperial outpost. In his 1909 pamphlet "Indian Home Rule," Gandhi wrote, "I have no objection to your remaining in my country, but although you are the rulers; you will have to remain as servants of the people. It is not we who have to do as you wish, but it is you who have to do as we wish." Gandhi represented a rising generation of leaders who questioned both the loss of sovereignty and the institutions being built under the imperial system.

Sovereignty and Conflict in East Asia

Rulers in Asia who were able to maintain sovereign control of territory during this era found ways to back up claims to rule with both skillful negotiation and military force. In Southeast Asia, successive rulers of Siam (Thailand) balanced their kingdom between the ambitions of France and Britain, giving the Europeans some territory and access to resources in return for the recognition of sovereignty. The rulers of Siam also adopted new fiscal policies, built railroads and telegraph networks, reformed the education system, negotiated commercial contracts with European investors, and transformed the military. The cases of

Japan and China, struggling with internal reforms and European threats while competing with each other, illustrate additional complexities of the era of the new imperialism.

Debating the Future in Japan and China

The debates in Japan over how to respond to Western expansion, spurred by the Meiji reforms, continued through the end of the nineteenth century. An 1885 newspaper editorial titled "Goodbye Asia" urged Japan to emulate Western institutions and embrace Western technologies. Published anonymously, but subsequently attributed to author, entrepreneur, and journalist Fukuzawa Yukichi (1835–1901), "Goodbye Asia" argued that Japan should "leave the ranks of Asian nations and cast our lot with civilized nations of the West." Fukuzawa admired the strength of Western technology and values and decried Japan's neighbors (China, Korea, and Vietnam) as weak, both spiritually and technologically. This was not the only view in Japan, of course. Diverse agendas and priorities competed, ranging from the ultratraditional to the completely new—some in Japan even advocated making English the new national language! In the end, Japanese elites undertook aggressive modernization, including the import and development of Western technologies, institutions, and structures. An industrial economy, linked to global markets, rapidly transformed society.

Debate among China's elites about the path forward in many ways mirrored the dispute between Sayyid Ahmad Khan and Jamal al-Din al-Afghani. Did the Western imperial powers have institutional models to be admired or were they predators? The Qing dynasty's leaders decided on a program of *self-strengthening*, a compromise solution embodied in the concept of *ti-yong*, a formulation adapted from ancient texts that called for embracing Western practical ideas (yong) while maintaining traditional Chinese values as the foundation for society (ti). This principle guided investment in modern military hardware and economic infrastructure.

Foreign aggression and internal rebellions continued to threaten China's imperial government as the nineteenth century entered its last decades. The French invaded and occupied Indochina in the mid-1880s. Russia claimed territory in the north, pushing a railway across Manchuria. Germany claimed the city of Qingdao and its environs in the early 1890s (quickly planting hops and building a brewery that still produces Tsingtao beer). Many nations expanded the scope of their activities in ports like Shanghai, Tianjin, and Canton, where they were exempt from Chinese laws. Japan's Meiji government then joined the wave of new imperialists searching for international prestige, strategic advantage, and economic resources at China's expense.

Historians Explore The Sino-Japanese War

Japan's overseas expansion began first in Korea, which offered many of the resources and advantages that Japan sought in an empire just 150 miles across the Straits of Tsushima. At first Japan competed for influence in the Korean royal court with China, as the Qing dynasty still considered Korea a tributary state. Political jostling broke into armed conflict between Chinese and Japanese forces. In September 1894, armies of the two empires fought at Pyongyang, where Japan scored a decisive victory. The next day, Chinese and Japanese warships met at the mouth of the Yalu River, the border between China and Korea. The Chinese fleet was larger, with larger guns. Its battleships, *Dingyuan* and *Zhenyuan*, were both built in Germany and appeared more formidable than anything the empire of Japan could put in the water.

The first barrages from the Chinese battleships had almost no effect—a combination of defective artillery shells and poor targeting—while Admiral Ito's first volley destroyed the flying deck of the Chinese flagship and gravely injured the Chinese admiral. By the time the battle ended, nearly nine hundred Chinese sailors were dead, and five ships had been sunk. Another five hundred Chinese were injured. The Japanese suffered nearly three hundred killed and two hundred wounded, along with two vessels lost. The Sino-Japanese War ended just seven months later in a decisive Japanese victory.

Explanations of the war's outcome often hinged on perceptions of the different Chinese and Japanese responses to modernity. Many observers at the time, and scholars for decades after, attributed the result to Japan's technological advantage, a result of its superior ability to modernize generally and to China's failure to industrialize.[2] This explanation still dominates many popular references that characterize the war as a mismatch between modern Japan and tradition-bound China. Certainly, the outcome of the war illustrates that Japan was the superior military power, but recent scholarship challenged the standard interpretation of what made Japan superior. Benjamin Elman has argued that, overall, China's failure to modernize its military has been exaggerated and that the Qing defeat owed less to a failure of science and technology than to political infighting. Corruption and inefficiency were much greater problems than a lack of technological sophistication. Even where Chinese technology was clearly at fault—for instance, artillery shells that failed to explode when fired—Elman sees explanations in the political corruption that diverted funds from munitions and not from Chinese inability to build

2 For example, the scholar Han Quansheng wrote several articles on the failure of Chinese industrialization during this time period, including "Qingmo Hanyang tiechang [The Late-Qing Hanyang Iron Works]," *shehui xuecong lunwen* 1 (1950): 1–33.

Map 9.3 The Expansion of Japanese Influence, 1870s–1930s

effective armaments. S. C. M. Paine has written carefully of the war itself, demonstrating the importance of training, logistics, and tactical decisions by leaders, rather than simply the number and type of ships and bullets, in determining outcomes. A recent reassessment of the war by Chinese military leaders draws similar conclusions, emphasizing failures of strategy, planning, and organization as keys to the

Woodblock Print of a Naval Battle during the Sino-Japanese War. A traditional medium in Japanese art, woodblock prints like these conveyed the rapid modernization of the Japanese military. Scenes of the Sino-Japanese War (1894–1895) encouraged patriotism and support of the war effort by illustrating the successes of "modern" Japan against "backward" China, but inspection of the scene reveals that both sides in the war attempted to muster the most modern military technologies available.

Qing defeat. Paine also notes that this war, like all wars, was also about the decisions leaders of both states were making to manage their long-term position not only in the international order but also within their own countries. For both Paine and Elman, the enduring narrative of China's failed modernization that emerged out of the war was perhaps the most important outcome of the war itself.[3]

Complex interactions, rather than a single overarching factor, produced the war's outcomes, which transformed East Asian geopolitics. China was vulnerable to further destabilization, as outside powers followed Japan's lead with even greater territorial aggression against China. Japan emerged as an imperial power, annexing Taiwan, formerly a Chinese province, as a colony in 1895. Korean "independence" was just a brief euphemism, as Korea became a formal Japanese colony in 1910.

The Boxer Uprising

In the aftermath of defeat by Japan, Chinese leaders took bolder steps toward reform in the summer of 1898. The Guangxu Emperor (1871–1908) himself was among a group that enacted reforms drastically revising China's government, civil

3 The narrative of failure is described in Benjamin A. Elman, "Naval Warfare and the Refraction of China's Self-Strengthening Reforms into Scientific and Technological Failure, 1865–1895," *Modern Asian Studies* 38, no. 2 (May 2004): 283–326. More general assessment of the war can be found in Benjamin Elman, *On Their Own Terms: Science in China, 1550–1900* (Cambridge, MA: Harvard University Press, 2005) and *A Cultural History of Modern Science in China* (Cambridge, MA: Harvard University Press, 2009); and S. C. M. Paine, *The Sino-Japanese War of 1894–1895: Perceptions, Power and Primacy* (New York: Cambridge University Press, 2002).

service, and educational system. The so-called Hundred Days' Reform were without doubt a response to foreign encroachment but did not reject Chinese models wholesale. The scholar Kang Youwei (1858–1927) titled one of his works *Confucius as a Reformer*, recasting the ancient Chinese philosopher as one who could imagine changes of the scope being attempted at this time. In their efforts on so many fronts simultaneously, the movement's leaders misjudged others in the imperial government, even some who had supported the idea of self-strengthening. After 103 days, the emperor's aunt, Cixi (1835–1908), who had played an important role in China's government for decades, imprisoned her nephew and asserted control over the Qing court. Cixi ended the reform program and reestablished the authority of Qing officials who had opposed reform. The would-be reformers fled into exile.

Intrigue over reform at the highest levels of the Chinese government occurred at the same time that a xenophobic, mystical movement that abhorred all things Western was percolating up from the lower levels of society. Free trade, dominated by British shippers, had exposed Chinese markets to global economic forces. For many rural Chinese at the turn of the twentieth century, the effects were disastrous. These people saw Western power not as something to admire or imitate, but to be feared and destroyed. The Boxer uprising (1899–1901) emerged in poor, rural northeast China, where the new trade regime enforced by foreigners had wrecked local economies. In Shandong Province, imports of foreign cotton (mostly on British ships from India) had undermined the local market, dropping the price farmers could earn from their crops below subsistence levels. Many farmers turned to growing opium poppies, which could be sold for cash, but this came with a risk: with less land given over to growing food, poor harvests produced devastating famine.

The Boxers claimed to channel the spirits of Chinese cultural heroes and deceased ancestors. They practiced traditional Chinese martial arts rituals—called boxing by foreign observers—that they claimed would make them bulletproof or invisible. Economically and socially marginalized, tens of thousands of young Chinese joined the movement to rid China of Western influences. Boxers targeted, persecuted, and killed Christian missionaries and—especially—Chinese Christians. Sweeping across the North China plain, the Boxers reached the capital, besieging the Beijing neighborhood where most foreign legations were located, with many casualties on all sides. An expeditionary force of American, British, French, German, Japanese, Austrian, Russian, and Italian soldiers relieved the foreign diplomats and civilians within the quarter. The empress dowager, who had announced the dynasty's support for the Boxers, remained in power, largely because foreigners again preferred that a Qing figurehead remain in place rather than renegotiate existing treaties and relationships—with China and with each other—if the Qing regime were to be ousted. Loss of territory, coupled with unfavorable foreign concessions, demonstrated that although the Chinese imperial court had avoided a complete loss of sovereignty, it was still irreparably damaged by the new imperialism.

Challenging Modernity at Its Core

Radical resistance to global political and economic changes could also be found in the West itself. Socialist political parties, anarchist movements, Marxist unions, general strikes, riots, and political assassinations showed that even in the wealthiest industrial centers, satisfaction with "the system" was not universal. The most enduring ideas posited as alternatives to global capitalism—a network of nation-states organized to protect private property—were Marxist movements, but none came to power during this era. We will analyze the Marxist regimes that came to power in the twentieth century in subsequent chapters, but bear in mind that Marxism was already a powerful influence during the late nineteenth century.

Concurrent with political activism, other critiques challenged the idea that Western civilization could bring endless progress. Some insisted that humans could not transcend nature; others observed that the seemingly irrational consequences of rational acts raised fundamental questions about what it meant to be human and civilized.

Working-Class Agitation

Taking root among other movements that appealed to the working class with alternative conceptions of international organization, like Marxism, was anarchosyndicalism. This ideology sought to merge the political ambitions of anarchists (the dissolution of any kind of formal state) with the economic goals of syndicalists (worker control of the industrial economy). Anarchosyndicalism gained popularity in France, Italy, Great Britain, the United States, and many Latin American countries, representing a large and radical challenge in the world's most advanced economic sectors.

One of the leading voices of the anarchosyndicalist movement was Emma Goldman (1869–1940), who was born in the Russian Empire and immigrated to the United States in 1885. In 1892, one of Goldman's first major acts was to organize, with Alexander Berkman (1870–1936), the Homestead Strike against the Pittsburgh steel refineries of Andrew Carnegie. Plant managers attempted to use strikebreakers to put the plant back in production. A twelve-hour gun battle broke out between guards hired to protect the nonunion workers and strikers. Sixteen people were killed. Berkman later snuck into the office of Henry Clay Frick (1849–1919), who managed the business for Carnegie, and shot him three times before stabbing and beating him (remarkably, Frick survived).

Berkman served fourteen years in prison for the attempted murder. Goldman was involved in the plot to kill Frick, which she hoped would "strike terror into the soul of his class," but no evidence to arrest her was found, and so she remained free. Goldman was routinely arrested as she traveled the country addressing crowds of thousands and urging workers to take direct, even violent, action to advance their cause. Goldman was even implicated in the assassination of US president William McKinley (1843–1901). Although refusing to denounce the act, she was again cleared of any direct involvement in the crime.

Darwin, Freud, and the Question of Human Nature

Anarchists attacked the premise that the modern nation-state was the preferred form of political and economic organization. At another level, changing perceptions of human nature during this era challenged the premises on which the nineteenth-century global order had been built. For some, the work of naturalist Charles Darwin and other scientific investigations of the natural world posed a challenge. While some imperialists warped Darwin's theories as a justification for expansionism, the universal application of Darwin's theory leads one to conclude that humans are subject to the rules—and limits—of natural selection and evolution, as are all living things. Further, there might not be anything special about any particular group of humans, or humans in general, from a scientific point of view. In reaction, some religious leaders and their followers revived arguments raised by their predecessors in the sixteenth and seventeenth centuries that modern science was not an ally, but an enemy of Western civilization as it should be properly understood.

Darwin's *Origin of Species*, published in 1858, shaped the world in which another influential man of science, Sigmund Freud (1856–1939), grew up. Freud trained as a neurologist, but it was his theories and insights on human psychology that were most important. His first major work, *The Interpretation of Dreams* (1899), laid out many of his key principles about how humans operate. From the moment of their publication, Freud's ideas influenced debates about what it meant to live in the modern world. Freud's conclusions have been challenged; the charge that he looked for sexual symbols and motivations at every opportunity subjects him to caricature and ridicule. Yet, Freud's observations remain foundational to most modern understandings of human nature. Freud emphasized that important parts of the human mind function in ways that are not transparent, so individuals are often incapable of fully understanding themselves and the reasons for their own behaviors.

As different as their subject matters are, Freud's body of work resonates with that of Darwin. They are part of a wave of thinking that challenged notions of an endless forward, orderly, and rational march of progress. Their ideas suggested that human beings—even civilized ones—needed to be understood as animals, and the world they inhabit (whether the world of the mind, of human society, or of the natural environment) is strongly influenced by events that appear irrational, random, and outside of human control. Whereas Isaac Newton had suggested that with enough data and enough time he could predict every action in the universe, Darwin and Freud insisted that the realm humans can rationally control, or even understand, is very limited. Darwin observed that evolution relied on random mutations. Freud argued that our forms of political, social, and economic organization extract a high toll that is paid out in conflict and suffering. The English title of one of Freud's later and most popular works is *Civilization and Its Discontents*. Although many still shared the Enlightenment optimism articulated in the eighteenth century, celebrating and predicting the unlimited march of civilization and progress, Darwin, Freud, and others challenged the position that rationality would yield unlimited progress and increasing "civilization."

The Price of Progress in the Western Hemisphere

Most European colonial claims in the Western Hemisphere were gone by the end of the nineteenth century. An ill-fated attempt to place a European archduke as head of state in Mexico in the 1860s failed, while Spain ceded its last territories in the Caribbean to the United States in 1898. Most elites in the United States rejected Kipling's call to take up the mantle of imperialism, arguing that US goals and methods were different from those of the European powers. Yet, US actions in Puerto Rico and the Philippines would fit most definitions of imperialism. Further, the interactions between modern, expansionist institutions—armies, private property—and indigenous peoples of North America raise interesting opportunities for comparison with the African experience of European imperialism.

In Latin America, during the second half of the nineteenth century, the region's liberal constitutional regimes were controlled by small numbers of elite families. These countries' finance, transportation, manufacturing, and natural resources were all increasingly integrated with the centers of empire. Critics argued that this model of political organization and economic growth served only the elites, while also leaving each country vulnerable to external forces over which domestic actors had too little control.

Contemplating Extinction in North America

The railroad was a product and a cause of both the Industrial Revolution and imperial expansion. Railroads, most of them designed by European and American engineers and built by laborers from across the world, knitted the globe together, transforming the surface of every continent. In North America, the railroads helped settlers push west, through the great disappearing eastern forests to the plains, where they encountered two species in enormous numbers: the passenger pigeon, and the American bison, or buffalo. Although quite different—one weighed just twelve ounces, the other, more than two thousand pounds—the two animals defined the North American environment in the nineteenth century. One flock of passenger pigeons, one mile wide, three hundred miles long, took fourteen hours to pass an observation point in southern Ontario in the 1880s. There may have been five billion passenger pigeons in North America and, beneath them, as many as two hundred million bison grazing on the Great Plains, with subspecies ranging east to the Atlantic Ocean and across the Rocky Mountains, from northern Canada all the way south into Mexico.

As new populations and systems of production, consumption, and distribution covered the eastern third of North America and then pushed westward, the consequences for both these animals were quick and dire. Both had evolved to suit environments that were disappearing in the nineteenth century: the Great Eastern Forest and the Great Plains.

Some environmental historians theorize that passenger pigeons were limited in number until the smallpox epidemics that accompanied European colonization limited demand for them as food; others disagree. What we do know is that by the eighteenth century, the passenger pigeon was the most abundant bird in North America and perhaps the most abundant on earth. Passenger pigeons were considered cheap food—including for the enslaved. The immense flocks and communal nesting sites were easy targets. Hunting and deforestation began to decimate the enormous flocks. By 1900—just fifty years after John James Audubon (1785–1851) reported riding fifty miles in Kentucky, from Henderson to Louisville, under a single flock of passenger pigeons, it was rare to see the bird in the wild at all.

By 1907, just seven passenger pigeons remained in existence: four in a zoo in Milwaukee and three in the Cincinnati Zoo. By 1910, a female named Martha was the last one. Martha became a celebrity for several years as the last of her species, and a reward was offered to anyone who could find her a mate. No one was able to claim the $1,000 prize, however, and on September 1, 1914, Martha died. In less than a century, human beings had driven the most abundant bird species on earth to extinction.

The decline of the buffalo was more closely related to the potential extinction of distinct indigenous societies. Buffalo had provided the native peoples of North America with food, shelter, clothing, and tools for many generations prior to the arrival of Europeans, but the introduction of horses and firearms as part of the Columbian exchange improved the ability of indigenous peoples to hunt the great herds. Bison numbers may have started to decline as early as the 1500s as humans hunted them more effectively. New European settlers prized these animals for their pelts, but also found them an obstacle for the growth of railroads, farms, and ranches. Railroad managers and owners, eager to thin the herds, encouraged tourists to shoot buffalo from the windows of passing trains, even running special hunting trains. Military and political leaders in the United States made extinction a strategy, encouraging the slaughter of buffalo herds to eliminate them as a source of food for Native Americans. By 1884, the American bison was nearly extinct.

The bison obstructed the expansion of a new type of political economy in North America just as much as it sustained the indigenous ones, and its near-destruction was not an accident. It was partly accepted consequence, partly explicit goal of the transformation of the interior lands of North America. In the late 1880s, a Native American named Wovoka (also known as Jack Wilson, ca. 1856–1932) began the Ghost Dance, a ritual that called on the ancestors of the native people for assistance in restoring the bison and resisting the extinction of indigenous society.

After the Civil War ended in 1865, the US government turned greater military attention to the indigenous peoples who still blocked the movement of goods and settlers through the middle of the continent. Treaties signed in previous generations collapsed, and war escalated. By the end of the 1870s, indigenous control over the Great Plains was confined to the limited spaces and compromised sovereignty of reservations.

Wovoka prophesied that the Ghost Dance, along with hard work and peaceful living, could unite Native Americans and return the natural abundance of their lands, which Native Americans would enjoy more fully again in the future. As the ideas and practices of the Ghost Dance spread, some came to believe that they could don special shirts, vested with powers to protect their wearers from harm. The movement spread across the high plains as tensions rose between the US government and the Lakota Sioux over treaty violations. Rumors spread that leaders like the Lakota chief Sitting Bull (d. 1890)—the architect of the indigenous military victory over US cavalry at Little Big Horn in 1876—were using the Ghost Dance ritual to prepare for rebellion. Police were sent to arrest Sitting Bull. Amid confusion and resistance, shots were fired. Sitting Bull was killed, along with other Native Americans and some police officers.

Now connected to the death of Sitting Bull, the Ghost Dance grew as a powerful symbol. Local representatives of the US government feared the indigenous response to Sitting Bull's death, while many Lakota worried about the US military's next moves. Three days after Christmas in 1890, US soldiers massacred 150 Lakota men, women, and children at a creek called Wounded Knee. The shirts that promised the Ghost Dancers protection from such violence did not save them. A week later, the bodies were buried en masse at Wounded Knee. Two weeks after that, on January 15, 1891, the last of 4,000 Ghost Dancers surrendered to US cavalry troops, effectively ending the movement.

The Boom-and-Bust Cycle in Latin America

In making comparative assessments about global political and economic relations during this era, we must be careful to distinguish what was happening in Latin America from the formal European colonies elsewhere. Although Latin American countries received tremendous investment from the centers of empire and exported raw materials to the industrial economies, this does not mean that foreigners controlled domestic elites and decision-makers. Rather, domestic and foreign actors made alliances to pursue their interests. Foreign investors built railroads, mines, and utilities. They also made loans to governments, which built infrastructure and grew their militaries.

Where did the money come from to make these investments? British capital comprised 60 percent of all private foreign investment in Latin America at the turn of the twentieth century. German and French investors also participated in the Latin American economies. Until the early twentieth century, US investment was concentrated in Mexico, Central America, and the Caribbean rather than South America. Foreign investors often competed against one another in individual countries.

What did the Latin American economies deliver to the global marketplace? The Central American republics focused almost exclusively on coffee exports, which made their economies vulnerable to fluctuations in the global coffee market. Mexico, Brazil, and Argentina had more diversified export bases. Overall economic growth under this model could be spectacular. For instance, Argentina, with an economy fifteen times larger in 1914 than in 1885, had one of the largest gross domestic products per capita of any country in the world in the early twentieth century. In addition, like the United States, the southern cone of South America (Argentina, Brazil, Chile, and Uruguay) attracted European migrants displaced by industrialization and pressure on resources in their home countries. Many of these migrants traveled back and forth across the Atlantic Ocean in search of work.

These economic systems did not operate smoothly, however. A series of booms and busts characterized the nineteenth century and economies careened from wild profits to collapse. The Brazilian rubber boom, responsible for the spectacular growth of Manaus described in the introduction to this chapter, ended abruptly in 1910, as demand for Brazilian rubber stagnated and the price plummeted. This happened in large part because European investors seized opportunities to create rubber plantations in colonies like British Ceylon (Sri Lanka), French Indochina (Vietnam), and the Belgian Congo. They no longer needed to buy from Brazil. Brazilian rubber production fell between 1910 and 1920, while global production increased by almost 600 percent during the same period. The Amazon Theater closed its doors and Manaus lost its luster.

Economic crises were sometimes the result of fierce global competition, but they could also result from crop failures, natural disasters, mismanagement, speculative bubbles, or fraud. The Latin American economies suffered routinely from financial panics—wild fluctuations in the value of currency or debt—that often led to economic recessions. During the second half of the nineteenth century, severe economic crises gripped the region in 1857, 1866, 1870, 1873, 1884, 1890, and 1893.

In addition, the wealthy classes in Latin America who benefited from integration into the global industrial economy regularly fought with indigenous groups and peasant communities struggling to retain their economic, political, and cultural autonomy. Labor organizations seeking more benefits for workers met with bloody repression. Critics of these elites and their political systems argued that their countries were so economically dependent on, and militarily vulnerable to, the great powers that their countries might be independent in name, but still colonies in fact.

Conclusion

Although none of the events described in this chapter was secret, none of the speakers at the 1910 centennial celebrations in Spanish America referred to the decline of the passenger pigeon, the atrocities in the Congo, the tottering Qing dynasty, or the seething resentments of Serbs and Bulgarians. One would not have expected this. Nor did they speak of the discontents of their own peoples: the strikes, rural rebellions, and food shortages. Instead, the men in morning coats and top hats spoke with great optimism about the future. Like their brethren

TIMELINE

1858
Origin of Species, Charles Darwin

1875
Sayyid Ahmad Khan founds Mohammedan Anglo-Oriental College in India

1878
Congress of Berlin mediates disputes over borders in southeastern Europe

1884–1885
Berlin Conference mediates competing European claims to African territory; Congo Free State ("the Belgian Congo") formed

1885
Fukuzawa Yukichi publishes "Goodbye Asia"

1889–1913
Reign of Menelik II of Ethiopia

Late 1880s
Wovoka begins practicing the Ghost Dance; American bison nearly extinct

1892
Dadabhai Naoroji elected to Parliament; Homestead Strike, Pittsburgh

around the world, they shared a belief that the future was bright. They believed the civilizing mission of Western culture would go on, that they were a part of it, and that the global economy would continue its bumpy but inexorable expansion.

Those who disagreed with this worldview—groups like the dissident intellectuals of India, the Boxers of China, the Maji Maji rebels of East Africa, and the Ghost Dancers of western North America—faced forces who shared this strong belief that the magic formula of modernization would bring endless progress. The distress signals of a new century did not register as significant to cosmopolitan elites yet, but in the next generation, change came with a speed and intensity that upended the entire global order.

A Few Good Books

Paul Avrich and Karen Avrich. *Sasha and Emma: The Anarchist Odyssey of Alexander Berkman and Emma Goldman*. Cambridge, MA: Harvard University Press, 2012.

Robert A. Bickers. *The Scramble for China: Foreign Devils in the Qing Empire, 1832–1914*. New York: Penguin, 2013.

Joel Greenberg. *A Feathered River across the Sky: The Passenger Pigeon's Flight to Extinction*. New York: Bloomsbury, 2014.

Adam Hochschild. *King Leopold's Ghost: A Story of Greed, Terror, and Heroism in Colonial Africa*. New York: Houghton Mifflin Harcourt, 1998.

Lynn Martin. *Commerce and Economic Change in West Africa*. Cambridge: Cambridge University Press, 2002.

Pankaj Mishra. *From the Ruins of Empire: The Revolt against the West and the Remaking of Asia*. New York: Picador, 2014.

Heather Cox Richardson. *Wounded Knee: Party Politics and the Road to an American Massacre*. New York: Basic Books, 2011

Gene Luen Yang. *Boxers and Saints*. New York: First Second Books, 2013.

For instructional resources and study aids, please go to **www.oup.com/us/carter**. *For primary sources connected to this chapter, please see the table of contents for* Sources for Forging the Modern World *included at the back of the book.*

1894–1895
Sino-Japanese War
1897
Amazon Theater opens in Manaus, Brazil
1898
Hundred Days of Reform in China
1899
Rudyard Kipling, "The White Man's Burden"; H. T. Johnson, *The Black Man's Burden*; Sigmund Freud, *The Interpretation of Dreams*; Boxer uprising begins in China
1904
Edmund Morel becomes leader of the Congo Reform Association
1905
Maji Maji Rebellion, German East Africa
1910
Korea becomes a colony of Japan; peak of Brazilian rubber production
1914
Eighty percent of earth's land surface controlled by Europe and United States; Martha, last passenger pigeon, dies

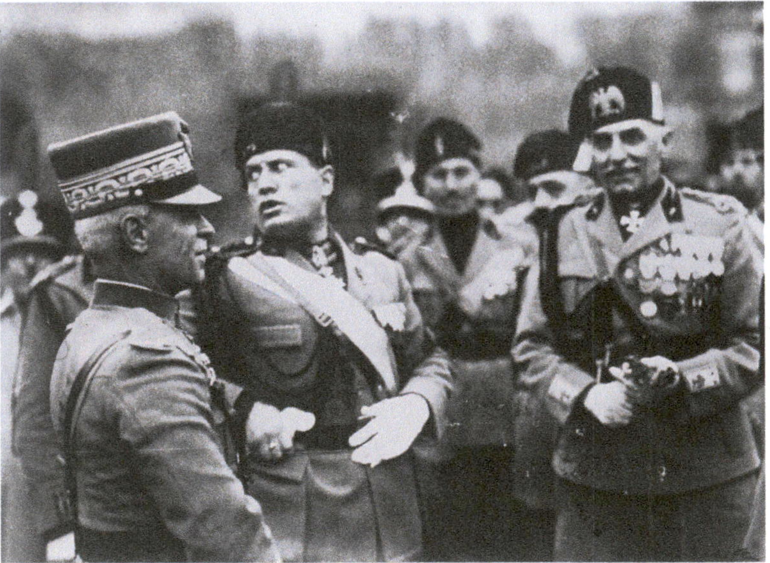

(TOP) Hibiya Riots Illustration, *The Japanese Graphic* No. 66, September 18, 1905. Dissatisfied with the terms of a peace treaty between Russia and Japan, crowds in Tokyo rioted in 1905. The riots illustrated the perils of democracy and social protest as well as the dramatic changes that had taken place in Japan during the preceding decades. A special edition of the magazine *The Japanese Graphic*, entitled "The Tokyo Riot Graphic," appeared in mid-September. This illustration offers an image of Kono Hironaka (1849–1923), a Japanese politician and opponent of the Treaty of Portsmouth, stirring up the crowd at the "anti-peace mass meeting."

(BOTTOM) Benito Mussolini Presides Over the First Anniversary Celebrations of Fascist Rule in Italy, 1923. Mussolini denied fundamental principles of liberal democracy, dismissing majority rule and egalitarian principles as misguided and weak. Fascist movements in Europe emerged in the wake of the Great War, arguing that the failed political and economic systems of the past should be replaced with modern totalitarianism. Fascists often dressed in military garb to symbolize their commitment to physical struggle in support of their cause.

CHAPTER 10

Total War and Mass Society

1905–1928

Nearly thirty thousand demonstrators tried to gather in Tokyo's Hibiya Park in September 1905, upset by the outcome of Japan's recent war with Russia. They were not angered by defeat, however; they were protesting the terms of victory. During the summer, Russian and Japanese delegates had traveled to the US Navy Yard at Portsmouth, New Hampshire. There, they hammered out a deal, congratulating themselves and winning the Nobel Peace Prize for US president Theodore Roosevelt, who had brokered the negotiations. However, the treaty did not confirm territorial gains made by Japan during the war, nor was Russia made to pay an indemnity, historically the price of peace for the losing side. Many Japanese found these terms too concessionary. Informed about the war mainly from government propaganda, the people of Japan had no idea that their government would have been unable to continue the bloody and expensive war for much longer.

To defuse the protest, the government kept the gates to the park locked, infuriating protesters like Yano Fumio (1850–1931), a writer, political activist, and founder of *The Japanese Graphic*, a weekly magazine with illustrated news of the day. In a special issue titled "The Tokyo Riot Graphic," Yano described, in pictures and words, a broad array of people, from many walks of life—shopkeepers, rickshaw pullers, craftsmen, factory workers—taking part in the protest. When the police ordered everyone to disperse, the crowd instead marched on the imperial palace. Unable to enter the palace grounds, the protesters turned on any available symbols of authority, attacking firefighters and police officers and even burning the home of a government minister. For more than two days, crowds marched in central Tokyo, setting fires and attacking public officials. More than 350 buildings were destroyed, seventeen people died, and more than five hundred were injured. Similar protests in other cities broke out as news of the Hibiya riots spread. While foreign commentators and diplomats marveled that an Asian country had defeated

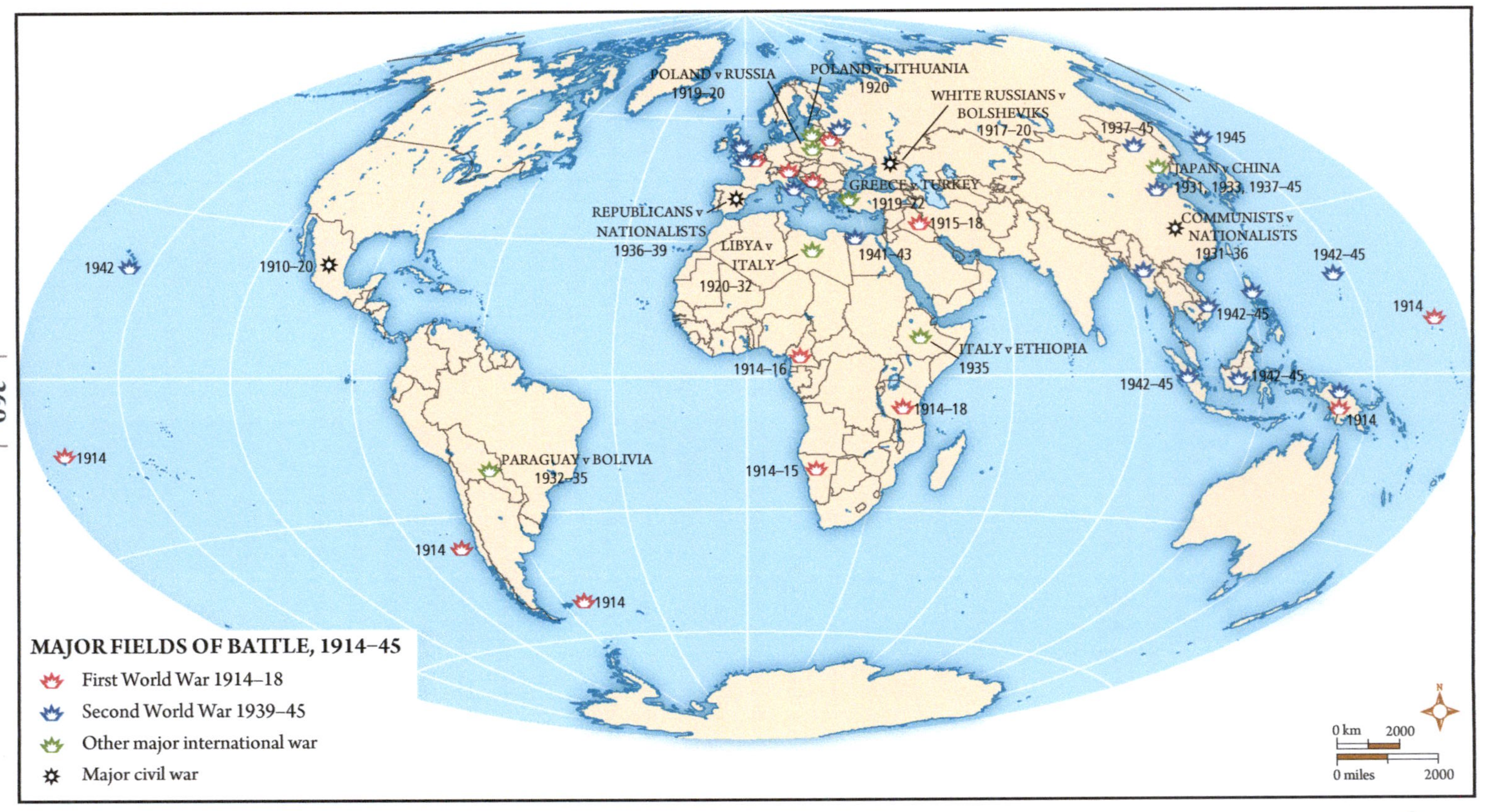
MAJOR FIELDS OF BATTLE, 1914–45
First World War 1914–18
Second World War 1939–45
Other major international war
Major civil war
POLAND v RUSSIA 1919–20
POLAND v LITHUANIA 1920
WHITE RUSSIANS v BOLSHEVIKS 1917–20
GREECE v TURKEY 1919–22
REPUBLICANS v NATIONALISTS 1936–39
LIBYA v ITALY 1920–32
1915–18
1941–43
JAPAN v CHINA 1931, 1933, 1937–45
COMMUNISTS v NATIONALISTS 1931–36
1937–45
1945
1942–45
1942–45
1942–45
1942–45
1914
1914
1910–20
1942
ITALY v ETHIOPIA 1935
1914–16
1914–18
1914–15
PARAGUAY v BOLIVIA 1932–35
1914
1914
1914
0 km 2000
0 miles 2000
N

Map 10.1 Major Fields of Battle, 1914–1945

a European power in war for the first time in centuries, in Japan itself the peace treaty was followed by a declaration of martial law to rein in popular unrest.

A quarter century later, in the fall of 1928, a new law in Italy handed the power of constitutional review, approval of legislative candidates, and the setting of government policy to something called the Grand Council of Fascism, a committee headed by Benito Mussolini (1883–1945), Italy's prime minister since 1922. Mussolini's aggressive supporters, called Blackshirts, used violence and intimidation to promote their cause. Whereas some Italians were coerced into supporting the fascist leader, others enthusiastically embraced Mussolini's ideas and tactics, tired of domestic political disorder and economic stagnation and discontented with the international order of the early 1920s.

Mussolini, a former socialist and military veteran, came to reject not only socialism but also liberal democracy. He promoted a new ideology, called *fascism*, as the politics of modernity, celebrating the interests of the pure nation-state's collective good over the debased and "possibly harmful freedom" of individuals. In Italy and elsewhere, the new political and social order that the fascists were building, designed to match the challenges of the twentieth century, required a new name—totalitarianism—used by both admirers and critics.

These two vignettes introduce the topic at the heart of this chapter: the changing connections among war, the modern industrial economy, ordinary people, and the global political order in the late nineteenth and early twentieth centuries. In this chapter, we cover the shortest chronological period of any chapter in the book, yet it is one of the most complex to understand, as so many events pivotal to the entire twentieth century occurred in this era and were related to each other.

Beginning with the arms and technology race that gripped the world in the late nineteenth century, we then describe three revolutionary movements—in China, Mexico, and Russia—in which growing tensions inherent in these countries' different paths through the nineteenth century erupted in the early twentieth century. This theme of increasing tensions born of nineteenth-century transformations and decisions is context for the Great War of 1914–1918. In the sections that follow, we offer an explanation of the changes in scale and nature of warfare that emerged during the Great War. At the end of the chapter, we explore the aftermath of the Great War, as leaders and common people struggled to make sense of the mass mobilizations for mass destruction that characterized this era.

Questions to Consider as You Read Chapter Ten:

1. How did warfare as it came to be practiced in the first decades of the twentieth century change the way states related to their populations and to other states?

2. How did experiences of the first decades of the twentieth century change the way different individuals and groups understood the idea of modernity and their expectations for the future?

Theory Meets Reality in Modern Warfare

As the nineteenth century waned, leaders across the globe invested heavily in the latest military equipment. Governments also asked their citizens to invest, literally and figuratively, in the use of violence to serve the national interest. Residents of the Ottoman Empire and France ran fundraising campaigns for the purchase of military hardware. Japanese postcards commemorated military victory over Russia. Nationalism and the military were celebrated everywhere, from small tokens like British trading cards, found in cigarette and tea packets, featuring imperial flags and military uniforms, to grand gestures, like military parades during national holidays. These parades were filmed so that audiences across the nation and around the world could witness the awesome spectacle of modern military power at ease but poised for action. Some argued that the altered arithmetic of confrontation born of industrialization would ultimately serve the cause of world peace. The newest battleships had a dozen or more guns that could hit targets more than ten miles away. A single machine gun could replace forty riflemen. Who would risk war on a grand scale against such well-armed rivals?

Many of the world's political leaders maintained great confidence that they could master the balancing act of this new era, but mass uprisings in three distinct regions of the globe provide examples of the many ways nineteenth-century models could unravel. As the twentieth century dawned, Russia, China, and Mexico all experienced the beginnings of revolutionary upheaval that would redefine modern politics. Each revolution was different, and none can be considered typical, but these events provided a counterpoint to the talk of progress and grand strategy that dominated many European capitals and previewed the global conflagration on the horizon.

Military Strategy and the Balance of Power

In the late nineteenth and early twentieth centuries, political elites around the world were drawn to the theories of Alfred Thayer Mahan (1840–1914), a captain and lecturer at the US Naval War College. In his 1890 book, *The Influence of Sea Power upon History*, Mahan argued that navies determined the fortunes of European powers in the early modern period, an idea that resonated with contemporary political elites anxious to enhance their countries' positions in the new global hierarchy of wealth and power. Concerns about sea lanes, choke points, refueling stations, and safe harbors drove states to invest in ever larger, faster, and more heavily armed ships.

These initiatives accompanied a dramatic reallocation of the globe's resources, as the European powers, the United States, and Japan acquired more than ten million square miles of land as colonial possessions, populated by almost 150 million people. By the early twentieth century, the North Atlantic world, led by Great Britain, Germany, the United States, and France, controlled 80 percent of the world's manufacturing output, an almost complete reversal of the situation at the dawn of the eighteenth century when China and India combined were responsible for more than half.

Small wars had become consistent features of this global reorganization. Recognizing this, political leaders around the world spurred an arms race, acquiring new technologies to quell anxiety over the consequences of failing to keep up with current or potential rivals. Military expenditures rose almost 200 percent for Europe as a whole, and over 400 percent for Germany, between 1883 and 1913. Beyond western Europe, governments from the Ottomans to the Argentines commissioned ships, bought weapons, and arranged for European officers to visit their countries on training missions. Ships on both sides in the 1894–1895 Sino-Japanese War had European officers aboard during battles. The Greek and Ottoman navies purchased experimental submarines. Latin American governments invited French and German officers to reorganize their militaries. Japanese officials offered Alfred Thayer Mahan a faculty position at their own Naval Staff College.

The industrialization of the military is one facet of the changing nature of warfare. Another emerged from the changing relationship between individuals and the state. Paralleling the spread of compulsory public education and welfare systems, by the end of the nineteenth century, most nations with aspirations to global power—including Germany, Italy, and Japan—had adopted systems of compulsory male military service. In theory, the new citizen armies could mobilize millions of soldiers if necessary. But even in states that had yet to adopt universal military service, like the United States and Great Britain, going to war became key moments for building ties between states and their citizens. In 1898, US newspapers called on readers to "remember the *Maine*," a US battleship sunk in Havana harbor, to rally opinion for war with Spain. Great Britain's *Daily Mail, The Times, The Guardian, The Morning Post*, and *The Morning Chronicle* all sent correspondents to South Africa to cover the Boer Wars (1880–1881; 1899–1902). Their stories aimed to build patriotic sentiment for the empire and its wars.

Beneath the bravado and optimism, economic and social dislocation, popular mobilization, and modern warfare created a volatility that stretched the capacity of political regimes in the early twentieth century. In China, the collapse of the imperial regime did not surprise observers familiar with the regime's nineteenth-century challenges, from the Opium Wars through the Taiping Rebellion. In contrast, both Russia and Mexico had appeared to have stable political systems at the beginning of the twentieth century. Yet, in all three, unrest became large-scale revolt and then finally the complete collapse of political, social, and economic order.

Unrest in Tsarist Russia

The Russian Empire appeared formidable in the early twentieth century. It was the world's largest state in terms of contiguous territory. In power since 1613, the Romanov dynasty had overseen Russia's expansion across central Asia and Siberia, reaching the Pacific in the mid-nineteenth century and even briefly claiming territory in North America (the state of Alaska today), which it sold to the United States in 1867. The Trans-Siberian Railway, completed in 1904, symbolized the empire's expanse and modernity as it traversed almost six thousand miles from Moscow to the Sea of Japan.

At the same time, however, internal dissent was growing across the enormous empire. Workers seeking labor reforms and better working conditions began striking with greater frequency. Some political dissidents increased their demands for a constitution and a transition away from absolutist rule. Others agitated for a radical break with the existing political order rather than gradual reform. Worsening economic conditions and bad news during the war with Japan fueled protests against the rule of Tsar Nicholas II (1868–1918). On January 22, 1905, a crowd of several thousand approached Nicholas's winter palace in Saint Petersburg to petition for improved working conditions and increased recognition of workers' rights. The protests began peacefully, exalting the tsar with patriotic hymns, but soldiers and police intent on dispersing the crowd moved aggressively, using swords and rifles against the protesters. The government acknowledged the deaths of around one hundred people; unofficial estimates exceeded one thousand killed. Strikes and protests spread around Russia in response to this "Bloody Sunday" massacre. Demands for reform intensified.

In October 1905, the tsar agreed. Unrest ebbed, although the Fundamental Law of 1906 still asserted that the tsar maintained "supreme sovereign power" mandated by God. In 1907, the tsar reconstituted the empire's legislature, the Duma. As the second decade of the twentieth century began, agitation for more radical political reform and additional labor unrest again challenged the empire's status quo. War in the nearby Balkans region in 1912 and 1913 drew the attention of both leaders and common people who cheered the aspirations of their fellow Slavs, seeing the promise of a better future for Russia if larger, independent Slavic-majority states were to emerge in the region. In 1914, events in the Balkans would spark a global war and a more dramatic social revolution in Russia from which the world's first communist regime would emerge.

The Collapse of Imperial China

Revolutions do not occur according to anyone's schedule, not even those who plan them. The revolutionary end to two thousand years of imperial rule in China was no exception. In October 1911, Sun Yat-sen (1866–1925), the most important leader of China's nationalist republican movement, was traveling in the United States, building support and raising money for his planned revolution against the Qing dynasty. On a train from Denver to Kansas City, he read that the revolution had started without him: the accidental detonation of a bomb exposed the conspiracy against the emperor, leading rebellious military units to publicly declare against the dynasty. Sun returned to China as the Qing dynasty collapsed and was sworn in as provisional president of a new Republic of China on January 1, 1912. Conceding defeat, the last Manchu emperor abdicated in February.

By inaugurating the new republic on the Western New Year, rather than China's traditional lunar New Year, Sun made a statement about the future he envisioned. His *Three Principles of the People*—nationalism, democracy, and the welfare of the people—embodied the rhetoric of state formation that had come to define the modern world during the previous century. Sun proclaimed that his goal was "to place China in a respectable place in international society, to follow in the steps of the other powers of the world."

The quick abdication of the Qing ruler gave false hope to advocates of a smooth transition to a democratic republic. Sun Yat-sen had provided the ideological framework for the revolution, but he lacked the military resources to carry out his vision and quickly passed the presidency to Yuan Shikai (1859–1916), a former Qing general who brought his armies with him to the revolution. When Sun's political party, the Chinese Nationalist Party, won the republic's first elections and dominated the new National Assembly, Yuan Shikai betrayed a promise to observe democratic principles and instead proclaimed a new, authoritarian Great Chinese Empire. The return to autocracy failed. Provinces began to secede from the central state amid calls for new revolution. Yuan renounced the new empire in March, but it was too late. By June, Yuan was dead (from kidney disease) and China was entering more than a decade of civil war—often called the warlord era—that divided the former empire among dozens of regional armies. There was no effective central government.

The Mexican Revolution

China and Mexico had little in common in the early twentieth century, yet both countries were plunged into civil war when their political systems collapsed and their militaries fragmented. In 1910, armed rebels called for an end to the regime of President Porfirio Díaz (1830–1915). Díaz had come to power in the 1870s promising a modern centralized state and liberal democracy. Instead, Díaz and his supporters ruled Mexico for four decades through a political machine rigged to guarantee his reelection. Foreign investment had transformed the Mexican economy, building infrastructure to integrate Mexico's exports and imports into an expanding global trading system. This economic strategy had high costs for peasants, who were displaced and impoverished, as well as workers in mining and manufacturing, who were brutally suppressed when they tried to organize for better labor conditions. Some members of the middle class and even certain elites grew increasingly disaffected from the Porfirian regime's principles and performance.

Francisco Madero (1873–1913) had challenged Díaz in the 1910 elections and been imprisoned for his troubles, but was able to flee the country with the help of his influential family. From exile in the United States, Madero made a public announcement of the planned date and time for an uprising to begin. The call to overthrow Díaz resonated with exasperated common folk as well as aspiring elites and regional political operators. When armed insurgents defeated the federal army, the eighty-year-old Díaz chose to leave for Paris. He lived his final years in exile.

Madero served only briefly as Mexico's new leader. His early actions enraged some insurgents who were fighting for broad economic and social reforms rather than just a change in national political leadership. Emiliano Zapata's (1879–1919) peasant army condemned Madero's "treason," while other revolutionaries remained loyal to the new regime. In 1913, reactionaries seized the opportunity created by this split to engineer a coup d'état, installing a military officer from the Díaz regime in the presidency. Mexico then, like China, plunged into more than a decade of civil war, as insurgent forces, including the peasant armies of the south and more heterogeneous forces in the north, toppled the central government but then continued to fight among themselves over leadership and goals for the future.

A Great War

In the summer of 1914, Mexico and China were both in the midst of bloody civil wars with no effective central sovereign authority or rule of law in either country. In contrast, the major powers of Europe had never been more confident in their stability and prosperity. When an act of political violence in southeastern Europe threatened to spark war among the major European powers, few of the potential belligerents recognized that they too stood on a precipice, about to plunge themselves into bloodletting and political transformation. One who did was British first lord of the admiralty (and future prime minister) Winston Churchill, who wrote to his wife as the move to war accelerated: "My darling one and beautiful, everything tends towards catastrophe and collapse." Churchill's forecast was prescient.

Nationalism at the Heart of It

On June 28, 1914, a man named Gavrilo Princip (1894–1918) assassinated the heir to the Austrian throne, the Habsburg archduke Franz Ferdinand (1863–1914), and his wife in the city of Sarajevo. Princip had been active in a movement advocating the removal of Austro-Hungarian rule from the Balkans. The world's empires were full of diverse cultural, linguistic, and religious groups; yet, as we have seen, nationalism increasingly expressed itself in the nineteenth century in movements for self-determination, that is, claims that distinct peoples—nations—had the right to create their own states. Southeastern Europe's Balkan Peninsula had long been the site of agitation by multiple groups that sought independence rather than remain within the Austro-Hungarian or Ottoman Empires.

Serbs were one of many Slavic groups with national ambitions. A Serb kingdom had been a regular, although not constant, feature of southeastern Europe for centuries. At the start of the twentieth century, Serbs lived in both the Ottoman Empire and Austria-Hungary, as well as in an independent Serb principality recognized at the 1878 Congress of Berlin. Many Serb nationalists considered territory still controlled by Austria-Hungary part of Serbia. Other national groups in the Balkans pushed for recognition of their own sovereignty, triggering war in 1912 and again in 1913.

Many predicted that a familiar pattern would repeat itself in 1914: a brief regional war, after which the great powers would restore peace and redraw the borders. These predictions were wrong because the responses of Austria-Hungary, Russia, and their respective allies sprung a trap that had been set by changes in Europe's system of imperial alliances. Unified Germany had become an even more important economic and military power than any of its constituent territories—like Prussia—had been. Since the late 1880s, the German government under Kaiser Wilhelm II pursued a *New Course* of aggressive industrial and imperial expansion. Germany pushed to develop a navy that could challenge Great Britain and secure colonies in Africa and the Pacific. These new policies reshaped diplomatic relations among the European empires. By antagonizing Russia, Great Britain, and Italy, Germany had only one reliable ally, Austria-Hungary, which had an aging leadership and contentious internal politics. In the summer of 1914,

Germany and Austria-Hungary were pledged to defend one another if attacked, while Britain, Russia, and France formed a similar pact.

These shifting alliances tipped the balance toward a broader war rather than a limited confrontation. Angered by the murder of the crown prince and eager to send a message to the nationalists within its own borders, Austria-Hungary moved to punish the independent Serbian state. One month after the assassination, Austria-Hungary declared war on Serbia. Russia, which had the largest standing army in the world, mobilized for war, invoking their long-standing and self-proclaimed role as protector of the Serbs, their fellow Slavs and co-religionists. Almost universally, the other great powers interpreted this move in terms of Russia's strategic interests in the Balkans, which it was pursuing at the expense of the Ottomans and Austria-Hungary. Within days, Germany declared war on Russia. Soon, France and Germany declared war on one another and, after the German army invaded neutral Belgium on its way to France, Great Britain declared war on Germany. All the major European powers were now at war.

The Nature of the Great War

Enthusiasm greeted the declarations of war as nationalism overwhelmed competing allegiances and ongoing tensions within the warring countries. Great Britain, which had not yet enacted a compulsory military service law, found eager volunteers who exceeded Parliament's call for 500,000 recruits. By late September 1914, 750,000 men had volunteered to serve in the military in the United Kingdom of Great Britain and Ireland. By the end of the war, nearly one quarter of the male population of the United Kingdom was in the military, with volunteers supplemented by conscripts beginning in 1916.

All the other major combatants had conscription laws at the start of the war, but they also formed volunteer regiments. Tens of thousands of German university students left school to go to war. Public celebrations feted the soldiers who marched to the front from Berlin, Vienna, Paris, and Moscow. Germany's kaiser was so confident of his troops and their officers, he proclaimed that Germany would have "Paris for lunch, St. Petersburg for dinner." Events of the summer of 1914 showed the tremendous power of the modern world's defining political institution—the nation-state—to organize and inspire.

The war celebrations in the summer of 1914 combined demonstrations of national pride and technological prowess in ways that could evoke the world's fairs discussed in Chapter 8, but the optimism of the summer of 1914 quickly collapsed under the weight of the war itself. Military leaders, trained in nineteenth-century strategies and tactics, had little idea of how to use the massive numbers of often poorly trained troops and their new weapons, so they cobbled together an odd and lethal mix of the old and the new. Human runners, dogs, and pigeons still transmitted battlefield messages; soldiers carried pigeon lofts to the front. And although the futility of cavalry charges on horseback was obvious in the face of machine guns and barbed wire, horses still provided transportation and often were used to move artillery—millions of horses died during the war. Machine guns rendered traditional infantry charges ineffective. Although heavy and unreliable compared to later models, each German Maxim machine gun could fire between four hundred and six hundred rounds per minute, a barrage equivalent to between sixty and one hundred individual rifles. The new weapons were so efficient at firing that shortages of ammunition became a common problem.

British troops in southern Africa and their Russian counterparts in Asia had recent experience of the important role that improvised fortifications like trenches could play in countering sheer firepower. On the opposing side, German strategists studied reports of these same campaigns; they trained and outfitted their troops accordingly. As a result, when Germany's original plan to quickly take Paris failed, the German army began to dig in, literally, as did their foes. Thousands of miles of trenches were dug across the Western Front over the following years. Barbed wire migrated from pasture to battlefield, rolled out to render it impossible to overwhelm an opponent's trenches simply through sheer numbers.

The Western Front was five hundred miles of artillery, machine guns, grenades, barbed wire, and trenches stretching across the French countryside from the North Sea to the Swiss border. The defining image of the Great War may be the trench itself. At the Battle of the Somme, the German army had three lines of trenches, reinforced by an additional seven thousand tons of barbed wire delivered to the front every week. As it became evident that there was no clear or easy way to take opposing trenches, both sides invested in their reinforcement. By the fall of 1916, some trenches on the Western Front were thirty feet deep, with timber beams, concrete reinforcements, and steel doors.

The Great War turned into a nightmare. The poison gas both sides used caused only 3 percent of battlefield casualties, but its psychological effect was much greater than these numbers suggest. Chemical weapons also showed how war twisted the promise of new technologies. The initial stockpile of chlorine gas, the most widely used chemical weapon at the start of the war, was generated as a byproduct of dye manufacturing. What began as a means for German manufacturers to produce cheaper, more brightly colored fabrics ended with a new form of devastation on the battlefield. In another perversion of prewar commerce and industry, British manufacturers continued to pay patent royalties to the German firm of Krupp for fuses used in grenades that British troops then lobbed at their German counterparts.

The increase in firepower, confusion over how to fight this new war, the growing complexity of battlefield injuries, the horrible conditions under which immediate treatment could be administered, and the transportation and communications challenges of wartime trumped improvements in the practice of medicine that had occurred over the course of the past century. Casualties were staggering on all sides. At the Somme, the British suffered sixty thousand casualties in one day, most of them to machine guns firing on troops attempting to advance on the German lines. The battle lasted five months—from July to mid-November 1916—and total losses on all sides exceeded three hundred thousand killed and more than one million casualties total. Yet, no one won; the front line barely moved.

Mobilizing the Population for Total War

From the first moments of the conflict, the *home front* was an important site of struggle. All sides employed propaganda to maintain morale among their own populations (and therefore productivity, the discipline of rationing, and the stability of governments) and to undermine that of the enemy. Newsreels, often produced directly by the armed forces, made their way into movie theaters. Posters appeared on the walls of buildings to remind all citizens of their important roles in the war effort (whether it was as a soldier, worker, mother, or investor) and to remind the people why the nation was at war, often by depicting the enemy as inhuman monsters. Radio, which would come into its own in both governmental and commercial manifestations only in the 1920s, was used on an experimental basis.

Cover of *Hurray! A War Picture-Book.* Published in Germany during the Great War, this book portrays one German and one Austrian boy—Willi and Franzl—on their way to war. The caption on the cover says, "Dear Fatherland, rest assured. We won't let anyone in!" Mobilizing for total war in the early twentieth century encompassed all levels of society, including the nation's future soldiers.

The idea of a home front is misleading, however. The case of poison gas illustrates the fading distinction between civilians and soldiers and the eroding concept of the front as a specific site where battle takes place. Development and production of chemical weapons on a large scale required the resources and cooperation of government planners, university researchers, and private companies. As the war dragged on, strategies to win focused on disrupting the enemy's economic and political engines that drove the war machines. The Great War did not introduce *strategic bombing*—the systematic bombing of targets away from the front lines to disrupt the war economy and demoralize an enemy's population—but it expanded the practice greatly.

Hundreds of German civilians were killed in bombing raids, primarily on munitions factories. About fifteen hundred Britons were killed and another five thousand injured in the aerial bombing campaigns carried out by zeppelins and airplanes against British cities. German U-boats sank more than six thousand commercial ships, taking almost fifteen thousand civilian sailors to the ocean floor. And as with poison gas, the number of casualties alone does not convey the full impact of these tactics, in which an unseen threat menaced everyone. Beyond the numbers, the fact that targets were increasingly far from the fields of military combat and often without direct military roles made clear that entire nations—not just opposing armies—were at war. These tactics also contributed to the transformation of this conflict into a truly world war.

The Global Repercussions of the Great War

As the war dragged on, additional peoples and resources became entangled in the fight. The widespread damage and scope of participation led to debates about how to unravel the mess of the war itself and address its root causes. As the war wound down and peace treaties were negotiated, it was clear that the world was vastly different in 1918 than it had been in 1914, but there was little agreement about the lessons to be learned from the confrontation or a clear path forward.

The Great War as World War

After the outbreak of hostilities, additional states joined the fray. Within months, the Ottoman Empire, which had military connections to Germany and was particularly concerned with its Black Sea rival Russia, was drawn into combat. By the summer of 1915, Italy, despite its historic alliance with Germany, was enticed instead to join the British by promises of territorial gains at war's end. Romania, Serbia, and Greece also lined up on that side, while Bulgaria joined the Germans. These maneuvers alone do not come close to capturing the extent to which the war grew into a global confrontation.

As imperial powers fighting an industrialized war, the antagonists set their sights on control of the globe's resources. The British, whose interests included not only the Suez Canal but also the vital Anglo-Persian oil pipeline, developed a strategy for what was beginning to be called the *Middle East*. As the sultan of the Ottoman Empire declared a *jihad* against nonbelievers when entering the war, the British appealed to the nationalist aspirations of Arab Muslims, who revolted against the Ottomans. The Europeans fighting from Egypt east through Persia made local alliances and implied promises about the future political geography of the region, but the secret Sykes–Picot agreement between England and France (1916) created a blueprint for a post-Ottoman Middle East without input from local leaders. After the war, many actors in the region would feel betrayed by their ostensible allies.

The composition of their forces also revealed the reach of the European empires. Over one million soldiers from the dominions of the British Empire—Canada, Newfoundland, Australia, and New Zealand—crossed the seas to fight. More than one million volunteers from South Asia fought for the British Empire during the war, in Egypt, Persia, and Europe. Over one hundred thousand troops from West Africa joined the French lines. More than one hundred thousand Asian and African troops died in the European trenches alone.

May 4 Protests in China. At the Versailles Peace Conference ending World War I, China expected to regain control of the territory that had been taken by Germany as a colony in the 1890s. When the colony of Qingdao was instead given to Japan, protests erupted against both Western hypocrisy and Chinese government weakness. The largest protests were in Beijing, in what is now Tiananmen Square, and are pictured here.

The global stakes extended the conflict beyond just Europeans and their empires. Japan agreed to maintain sea lanes open for the British alliance and helped to suppress a rebellion of Indian troops stationed in Singapore. The Japanese government also used the war to gain control over the German colony of Qingdao in China and several islands in the Pacific. The Chinese Republican government, struggling to gain international recognition, sent 140,000 workers to support the European war effort. The US government, concerned with maintaining access to the newly opened Panama Canal and its strong commercial and diplomatic ties to England, prevented the establishment of German fueling stations or safe harbors in the Western Hemisphere. Its relations with Germany deteriorated after US citizens died in the 1915 sinking of the ocean liner *Lusitania*, then broke in early 1917 when Germans resumed unrestricted submarine warfare in the Atlantic Ocean and made a clumsy bid to form an alliance with the revolutionary government in Mexico. The United States declared war on Germany in April 1917.

British Empire World War I Recruitment Poster for India. The translation from Urdu reads, "Who will take this uniform, money and rifle? The one who will join the army." Approximately 1.5 million Indian volunteers took part in World War I. India's contribution to the war effort, including a high casualty rate, fueled nationalist demands for Indian autonomy and independence after the war.

The direction of the war shifted after the United States entered. Fresh US troops and materiel bolstered their allies. In 1918, Germany's allies began to abandon the cause while Germany itself started a descent into domestic turmoil. The kaiser abdicated on November 2, and the new German government signed an agreement to end the fighting on November 11. The fight over the peace began immediately thereafter.

Negotiating the Future in the Shadow of the Great War

The statistics are overwhelming. In Europe alone, nearly ten million soldiers and almost seven million civilians died. Great Britain, France, Russia, Austria-Hungary, and Germany all lost more than 3 percent of their total populations. In the Ottoman

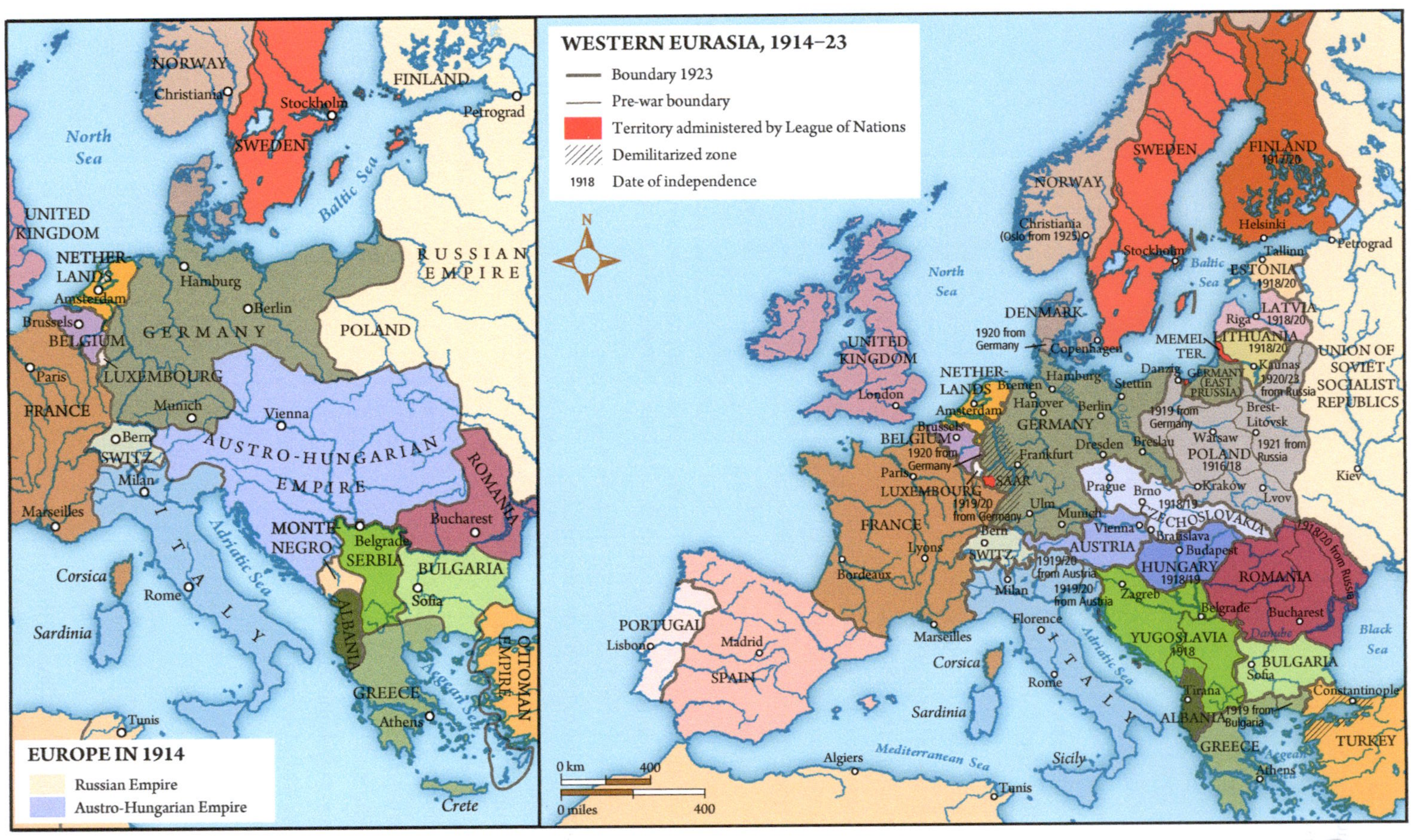

Map 10.2 (a) Europe in 1914; (b) Western Eurasia, 1914–1923

Empire, more than 13 percent of the population died. This number includes Armenians who died as a result of policies designed and implemented by their own sovereign—a genocide that foreshadowed other great horrors to come. A global flu pandemic broke out in 1918, killing another fifty to one hundred million people.

Political regimes were casualties as well. Tsarist Russia, the kaiser's Germany, Habsburg Austria-Hungary, and the Ottoman Empire all collapsed during the war or soon after. The costs to the British monarchy and the French Republic were also great, although both survived the war with their basic political institutions, including their empires, intact. Of the world's industrial powers, the United States and Japan suffered the least damage from the war, accelerating migration of the world's economic leadership away from Europe. Armed factions in China were still struggling to establish their sovereignty over the territory once ruled by the Qing dynasty, as they had been before the war started.

The war's end presented a dramatic opportunity for reimagining the world. The United States, which had become the world's largest economy just prior to the war, was now an international power broker. Its leader, Woodrow Wilson (1856–1924), first articulated the principles of his vision for the postwar world in a speech before the US Congress in early 1918. Wilson advocated a postwar order of liberal, constitutional, sovereign nation-states trading freely in a market-oriented global economy, with disputes resolved by a new "general association of nations." Implementing Wilson's ideas—summed up in his Fourteen Points—bedeviled those who charged themselves with rebuilding global order from the rubble of the war. Wilson's lofty rhetoric was undermined by multiple factors, including the exclusion from the negotiations of representatives of many constituencies with stakes in their outcomes.

The case of a young Vietnamese nationalist illustrates both the hopes for change that Wilson's vision inspired and the undermining of those hopes. Vietnam had been brought under French control in three phases beginning in the 1880s; a movement against French rule had existed for just as long. Many, including a man called Nguyen Ai Quoc ("Nguyen the Patriot"; 1890–1969), saw the peace negotiations as a chance to change Vietnam's relationship to France. Nguyen Ai Quoc, who was living in Paris when the war ended, petitioned the delegates at Versailles to support "equal rights for Vietnamese and French in Indochina, freedom of press and opinion, freedom of association and assembly, freedom to travel at home and abroad, and to substitute rule of law for government by decree." His demands were moderate, seeking not independence but representation for Vietnamese in the French parliament and equality before the law. Despite this, a Vietnamese delegation was refused admission to the talks, and their demands were never considered. Rebuffed, Nguyen Ai Quoc—who later took the name Ho Chi Minh—moved toward more radical anticolonial measures, eventually leading an armed movement in Vietnam against France.

Other cases illustrate further inconsistencies in the application of the Fourteen Points. Japanese and Chinese diplomats both sat at the victors' table. China representatives expected to be recognized as equal partners in the settlement. China had come late to the Great War, entering the conflict on the Allied side a few months after the United States in the summer of 1917, but they had sent more than one hundred thousand men to work behind the lines in Belgium and France as laborers and orderlies and in other capacities. At the very least, China expected to regain territory that Germany had colonized before the war, but the treaty's brokers ignored the Chinese position. German colonies in China were taken from Germany, but then given to Japan, seen as a greater military power and more important potential ally (or threat) to the victorious European powers.

When word of the treaty's provisions reached China, thousands of students from Beijing's universities protested, occupying the space that is now Tiananmen Square, chanting slogans and waving banners. In the following days, the protests spread across China, in a wave of Chinese nationalism directed against the very countries that Sun Yat-sen had claimed China would have as a partner when it had achieved modernity as well as the Chinese government that had been unable to stand up for its interests. The Chinese government refused to sign the treaty, but it made little difference.

These treaties also established several mandates that gave the victors temporary roles in territories taken from the defeated powers with the vague promise of eventual independence. The British took responsibility for Mesopotamia and Palestine; the French presided over Syria. Over the next three tortuous decades, the independent states of Iraq, Lebanon, Jordan, Syria, and Israel were carved from these mandated territories, inciting disputes that would continue through the end of the twentieth century over their borders, political organization, and even their reasons for existing while claims of other peoples to create their own sovereign nation-states were denied.

The future in eastern Europe and the Balkans, the tripwire region for the Great War, involved other thorny challenges. New states like Czechoslovakia and Yugoslavia were created, and existing states had their territories reallocated, but few in the region were satisfied. The war's losers—Austria-Hungary, Germany, and the Ottoman Empire—were excluded completely from the decision-making processes about the future shape of the region. Furthermore, the Allies forced Germany to accept responsibility for the war and imposed punishing conditions, including loss of territory and colonies, compromised sovereignty, and reparations. Many Germans felt that the treaty denied their country the means to recover from the devastation of the war, leaving them humiliated and resentful.

Russia, too, was excluded from the postwar decision-making process because of the dramatic turn of events in the midst of the Great War that we introduced previously. At the start of the war, the Russian Empire fought Germany and Austria virtually alone on the Eastern Front. The Russians scored some important victories, but Russia's industrial capacity and lengthy supply lines could never properly equip its military. Moreover, inflation and food shortages afflicted Russian civilians. Amid bread riots, strikes, and mutiny, the tsar abdicated in February 1917 and was placed under arrest.

The collapse of an authoritarian regime was followed by civil war, as happened earlier in the decade in Mexico and China. In Russia, two main rival groups competed for military and political supremacy throughout the spring and summer of 1917, culminating in an October Revolution that installed revolutionary socialists—calling themselves Bolsheviks—led by Vladimir Lenin (1870–1924). Lenin had agitated for a Marxist revolution since the late nineteenth century and had been exiled by the tsarist government. Slipping back into Russia during the fall of 1917, Lenin's charisma, political acumen, and uncompromising tactics enabled his Bolshevik party to overthrow the provisional government in October and establish what would become the Union of Soviet Socialist Republics. The Bolshevik government withdrew from the Great War and signed a peace treaty with Germany. The new government also repudiated debts accumulated by the tsarist regime to Russia's old allies and released diplomatic correspondence that exposed the postwar colonial plans of these former partners. The Bolshevik government was not offered a seat at the table in Versailles.

Historians Explore Literature as Sources

Historians sometimes use literature—poems, memoirs, or novels, for example—as sources. This can be an especially useful way to convey the *zeitgeist*, or the spirit, of a period. The events addressed in this chapter inspired an impressive output of literature that is both moving and insightful. English poet Rupert Brooke (1887–1915), who volunteered and did not survive the war, captured the idealism of many who welcomed war as an opportunity to win glory for their nation, writing in his poem "1914": "Now, God be thanked Who has matched us with His hour, And caught our youth, and wakened us from sleeping." In another stanza, Brooke celebrated the idea that dying for one's country would not only bring glory to the individual but also consecrate for the nation the earth on which one fell:

> If I should die, think only this of me
> That there's some corner of a foreign field
> That is forever England.

Brooke's fellow English poet, Wilfred Owen (1893–1918), conveyed a very different spirit in his poetry. The terror and anxiety caused by the ever-present threat of gas attack gnawed at troops on the front line, and the gasmask became an icon of the new warfare. Owen—who died in the last weeks of the war—described a gas attack in his poem, "Dulce Et Decorum Est":

Gas! GAS! Quick, boys!—An ecstasy of fumbling,
Fitting the clumsy helmets just in time;
But someone still was yelling out and stumbling,
And flound'ring like a man in fire or lime . . .
Dim, through the misty panes and thick green light,
As under a green sea, I saw him drowning.
In all my dreams, before my helpless sight,
He plunges at me, guttering, choking, drowning.

Owen's narrator sees—through the green-tinted lenses of a gasmask—a man drowning in his own blood as poison gas destroys his lungs. The poem evokes the psychological power of gas: although only one man dies in the attack, the ethereal killer terrorizes the entire platoon and haunts the narrator's dreams.

Some of the most well-known novels of the twentieth century, like Ernest Hemingway's *A Farewell to Arms* (1929) and Erich Maria Remarque's *All Quiet on the Western Front* (1929), are set during the war. Hemingway worked as an ambulance driver in Italy, and Remarque served on the front in Belgium. Both were wounded, and their novels reflect their experiences of the battlefield and beyond. Vera Brittain's memoir *Testament of Youth* (1933) brings another perspective to the same era. Brittain (1893–1970) worked in a field hospital, tending to the wounded while coping with the deaths of her fiancé, brother, and two closest male friends in the war. Brittain's sadness, outrage, and journey to pacifism contrasts poignantly with Brooke's excited patriotism and zeal: both illustrate aspects of that moment.

The era's national revolutions also generated abundant literary output. Between 1915 and the late 1940s, almost three hundred novels regarding the events of the revolution were published in Mexico. *The Underdogs,* written by Mariano Azuela (1873–1952) in 1915, is still required reading in many courses on modern Mexican history. His indelible protagonist, Demetrio Macías, therefore has become synonymous with the prototypical Mexican insurgent leader for generations of readers. With *Cartucho* (1931), Nellie Campobello (1900–1986) provided a fictionalized account of her youth in northern Mexico, one of the few published works of the revolution written by a woman who lived through the upheaval about which she was writing.

As in Mexico, the Russian Revolution yielded a body of literature that was born from and continued to feed polemics about whether the rise of a communist state was the salvation or the death knell of the Russian people. Alexander Serafimovich's pro-Soviet novel *The Iron Flood* (1924) is set in the aftermath of the Bolshevik rise to power. Serafimovich (1863–1949) would receive awards for his writing from the new state, including the Order of Lenin and the Stalin Prize. In contrast, Ivan Bunin (1870–1953), the first Russian to receive the Nobel Prize in Literature, was one of thousands of Russian intellectuals who lived the last decades of his life outside the Soviet Union. Already an esteemed writer at the time the revolution broke out, in works like *Cursed Days,* a diary published in serial form in 1925–1926, Bunin provides a vivid and seething portrait of resistance and exile. Nadezhda Aleksandrovna Lokhvitskaya (1872–1952), who wrote under the pseudonym Teffi, was another well-known Russian writer prior to the revolution who grew alienated from the Bolsheviks and lived her final decades of life in exile. Her word sketches of life before, during, and after the rise of Lenin provide a valuable counterpoint to both Serafimovich and Bunin.

As these examples make clear—Brooke versus Owen; Serafimovich versus Bunin—one must be just as cautious in using literature as with any other sources in making historical generalizations, even when trying to illustrate something like the *spirit of the age.* No single author or work can capture such a thing. In addition, we must also remember that scholarly debates about how to interpret literary sources are just as contentious as they are for other kinds of sources, contributing to the vibrancy of our engagement with the past.[1]

Which Way Forward?

The Great War shook badly, but did not destroy entirely, the nineteenth-century global political order. The colonial empires of France and Britain remained in place, and the mandates of the new League of Nations confirmed their authority over the future of much of the world's territory and peoples. The principles of the

---

1 Rupert Brooke, *The Collected Poems,* ed. George E. Woodbury (New York: Lane, 1916); Wilfred Owen, *Poems* (New York: Heubsch, 1921); Hemingway; Remarque; Vera Brittain, *Testament of Youth: An Autobiographical Study of the Years 1900–1925* (New York: Penguin, 2005); Mariano Azuela, *The Underdogs* (New York: Signet, 1996); Nellie Campobello, *Cartucho and My Mother's Hands,* trans. Doris Meyer and Irene Matthews (Austin: University of Texas Press, 1988); Alexander Serafimovich, *The Iron Flood,* 3rd ed. (Westport: Hyperion Press, 1973); Ivan Bunin, *Cursed Days: A Diary of Revolution* (Chicago: Ivan R. Dee, 1998); Teffi, *Memories from Moscow to the Black Sea,* trans. Robert and Elizabeth Chandler, Anne Marie Jackson, and Irina Steinberg (New York: New York Review Books, 2016); Patrick J. Quinn and Steven Trout, eds., *Literature of the Great War Reconsidered: Beyond Modern Memory* (New York: Palgrave, 2001); Vincent Sherry, ed., *The Cambridge Companion to the Literature of the First World War* (Cambridge: Cambridge University Press, 2005); Katerina Clark, *The Soviet Novel: History as Ritual,* 3rd ed. (Bloomington: Indiana University Press, 2000).

league embodied liberal, progressive ideals that pledged to bring the world away from the darkness and devastation of the Great War.

On another level, important questions and troubling signs coexisted with efforts to move past the crisis. The United States and Japan, the world's newest powers, were not nearly as affected by war as many other places, and the nature of their engagement with any form of rebuilding and reconciliation related to the root causes of the war was uncertain. Further, new political regimes emerged in Russia and Italy that rejected liberal models of political economy all together, but were also rabidly opposed to each other.

The United States and Japan as Global Powers

By the end of the Great War, the United States and Japan had replaced the European empires as the world's economic engines and potentially its dominant political powers. The United States had in fact asserted its place as a guardian of a particular global order in the decades before entering the Great War, deploying troops and battleships repeatedly to the Caribbean, Central America, and Mexico and acquiring colonies around the globe, such as the Philippines, Hawai'i, and Puerto Rico. The opening of the Panama Canal and the outbreak of the Great War the same year led the United States to deploy significant military and economic resources to guard its strategic concerns, such as the sea lanes leading to the canal. In addition, concerns over protecting private investment and racist paternalism also contributed to decisions to occupy Haiti (1915–1934) and the Dominican Republic (1916–1924) and to station marines intermittently in Cuba, Honduras, and Nicaragua. United States troops invaded Mexico twice—in 1914 and again in 1916—during the Mexican Revolution.

The position of the United States in the global economy changed significantly during the course of the Great War. A net debtor in 1914, by 1917 the United States was a net creditor, buying up assets sold by Europeans to pay for the war. Unlike European fields, American farms had not become battlegrounds and US agricultural output rapidly expanded. The United States made a significant contribution—militarily and economically—to the outcome of the Great War. Its leaders expected to play an important role in shaping the postwar world. The intellectual bridge between Europe as the old guarantor of civilization and the United States as the new one was made explicit in the movement to create Western civilization courses at elite universities in the United States. These courses were designed to introduce US students to the idea that such a thing as Western civilization existed and that these students had inherited it and needed to be custodians of it in the twentieth century (prior to this, history classes in the

United States tended to emphasize how distinct the country was from Europe). The nature and direction of US global engagement remained uncertain, however, symbolized by the fate of the Treaty of Versailles. Although US public opinion and many political leaders favored the treaty, including the president who helped inspire it, the US Senate never ratified it, and the United States never joined the League of Nations.

Similar questions could be asked about Japan's future role. Japan had been tasked with maintaining order in the Pacific for the Allied powers during the Great War and had been rewarded for it. From the mid-nineteenth century on, Japan had rapidly industrialized and become an imperial power with overseas colonies (Korea, Taiwan) and a military force that had defeated China (1895) and Russia (1905). The 1889 Meiji Constitution had created Asia's largest democracy (although only about 1 percent of the population could vote), but the Meiji emperor's death in June 1912 had been followed by a political crisis, as rival constituencies vied for power. The military, angered by proposed spending cuts, used its constitutional veto power in the cabinet to prevent the formation of any government whose policies appeared not to suit it. Populist and progressive groups, feeling that the military had too much power over the government and its budget, staged protests, burning progovernment newspapers and occupying public spaces.

The so-called Taisho crisis, named for the new emperor's reign, initiated a period of fitful growth of political parties and public participation but also instability. Prime ministers changed fifteen times during the era of *Taisho democracy*, including one who was assassinated and two more who died in office. Progressive measures, such as the General Election Law (giving all men over age twenty-five the right to vote), were enacted alongside reactionary ones like the Peace Preservation Law (effectively banning public expressions of political dissent). When Taisho's successor, Hirohito (1901–1989), took the throne on Christmas Day 1926, Japan's democracy was functional, although strong authoritarian factions continued to agitate.

While domestic forces in Japan wrestled with how to best implement and define democracy, the Great War presented Japan with an opportunity to grow its economy—the country's exports began to outpace imports during the war—and to expand its international influence. Japan supplanted Germany in East Asia, occupying the German colony of Qingdao in China and taking control of other German outposts in the Pacific. Pressing its advantage, Japan made its Twenty-One Demands on China in 1915, insisting on special economic and military rights there. Japan had taken the opportunity presented by the Great War to confirm its place among the world's powers; but like the United States, the ends to which this power would be asserted remained unclear.

The Enlightenment Model Revived?

After the war, a broader electoral franchise, including women, spread. Only a handful of states gave women the right to vote prior to the Great War, but many of the new states constructed after the war joined existing polities in extending the vote to all adults. Austria, the Baltic states, Czechoslovakia, Germany, Great Britain, Hungary, the Netherlands, Poland, Scandinavia, and the United States all expanded the suffrage in the ten years between 1913 and 1923. Women had earned the right to vote in Belgium, the United Kingdom, and the United States right around the end of the war after long and sometimes violent struggles, including the incarceration of suffragist leaders. This expansion of the right to vote might seem to affirm an earlier generation's faith in progress, despite the catastrophe of the war, but in many places, laws still made voting difficult for the poor, less well-educated, and minority groups. Votes for women were still decades away in France and most of Latin America. Much of the world's population, male or female, had no meaningful formal political representation.

The new European states were institutionally weak, and key groups did not appear fully invested in the maintenance of the new states' integrity or efficacy. The new Chinese state had a severely limited franchise, and voting had little impact in determining who held power. During the Red Summer of 1919, three dozen US cities experienced riots triggered by acts of discrimination against African American veterans coupled with postwar social and economic dislocations. That same year, at the southern tip of the Western Hemisphere, a police unit opened fire on striking workers in Buenos Aires, beginning the Tragic Week, during which a general strike shut down the Argentine economy while violent clashes between civilians, the police, and military continued. President Hipólito Yrigoyen (1852–1933), who had been elected under the most inclusive electoral laws in the Western Hemisphere at the time, declared martial law.

In Mexico, revolutionaries attempted to consolidate their control over the country and navigate the complex challenges of forming a stable state by adopting a new constitution in 1917. This constitution had a specificity lacking in the social contracts of earlier generations—it was four times the length of the US Constitution. Dozens of references to the working class mark it as a document of the industrial age. It was also the first constitution to explicitly guarantee extensive social rights to citizens—such as rights to land, education, and social welfare—beginning a trend that would continue in the formation of new constitutions just after the Great War. The Mexican constitution defined the state as the protector of the interests of the Mexican nation, limiting the terms under which non-Mexicans could own property and empowering the state to redistribute land

and seize other economic assets from private owners if these actions were perceived to be in the national interest.

Passage of the constitution did not end civil war in Mexico. Mexico's revolutionary military leaders finally resolved their disputes over power and policy off the battlefield by the end of the 1920s, but at a cost to pluralism. Revolutionary leaders built a political system that privileged a single party to allocate resources, reward loyalty, and punish dissent. This single political party, eventually known as the Party of the Institutionalized Revolution, would dominate Mexican politics for seven decades.

Italy and Russia Reject the Liberal Model

The Mexican Constitution altered the model of the nineteenth-century liberal state to embrace a greater role for the state in the economy. The Bolshevik state emerging from the ashes of the Russian Empire rejected liberal models of the state–economy–individual relationship entirely. The most important leader of the Bolsheviks, Lenin, was grounded in the Marxist tradition and believed that the liberal state and the capitalist economic system that determined its nature could not be modified but had to be destroyed on a global scale for the world's peoples to enjoy the full benefits of modern life.

Lenin analyzed the global crisis that resulted in the Great War, and his prescription for the future, in a pamphlet, "Imperialism, the Highest Stage of Capitalism." In this document, Lenin incorporated assertions that had already been made by other radicals that Marx's analysis of the path to revolution required some revision. To explain why the socialist revolution predicted by Marx had not occurred in the nineteenth century, Lenin borrowed from the theories of English economist John Hobson (1858–1940). Hobson held that imperialism enabled the production of capitalist economies to outstrip demand if they could conquer—militarily or economically—territories that had not industrialized. By creating modern empires to extract such "superprofits" from the globe's natural and human resources, elites in the world's industrial centers had co-opted political leaders who might otherwise lead revolutions and even for a time marginally improve the lives of workers in the industrialized states without fundamentally changing the political or economic power structures of their countries. Workers who supported the regimes that provided small victories—reductions in hours of the workday or small wage increases—became complicit in both imperialism and their own oppression.

Lenin's description of global capitalism bore little resemblance to Adam Smith's idea that individual actors pursuing their own interests would result in greater efficiency for the benefit of all. Instead, Lenin argued that this image of a

Map 10.3 Revolution and Civil War in Russia

global capitalist economic order enforced by the world's great political and military powers was vital propaganda in the effort to blind the world's population to what was really going on: "the financial strangulation of the overwhelming majority of the population of the world" by "two or three powerful world marauders armed to the teeth (America, Great Britain, Japan), who involve the whole world in *their* war over the sharing of *their* booty."

According to Lenin, the means to break free from this required a highly disciplined organization to cultivate and execute the revolution. This idea led Lenin to carefully organize and develop the Communist Party structure, which gave him and his followers a tactical and strategic advantage once the Russian Revolution began. The Communist Party then became the key institution of the post-tsarist state.

The idea of a tightly organized vanguard with a special claim on political insight and power became a centerpiece of movements across the political spectrum in the twentieth century. In Italy, Mussolini employed this idea in building the Fascist Party (formed in 1921) from the Fascio di Combattimento ("Combat League") he had founded in 1919. Mussolini's hardcore followers adopted a uniform, styled after an elite corps of the Italian military, and became known as Blackshirts. They also gained a reputation for violent attacks on other political groups, union headquarters, and newspaper offices. Mussolini leveraged this reputation in October 1922, calling for a march on Rome from across Italy, promising that the fascists would not stand down until the current government handed over the reins of power. Rather than test the fascist threat and potentially plunge Italy into civil war, King Victor Emmanuel met with Mussolini and invited him to form a government as the new prime minister. The fascists did march into Rome at the end of the month, in celebration of Mussolini's triumph.

Conclusion

The reorganization of global power in the nineteenth century was violent—in some places, such as the Belgian Congo, obscenely so—but underpinning it was the myth of order and progress that we have analyzed in earlier chapters. As the twentieth century began, the myth was buried under wave after wave of violence, accompanied by massive political and economic dislocation. New technologies, including the continual development of more powerful, more accurate, long-distance firepower, aerial bombing, and chemical weapons, transformed the nature of warfare and further dissolved the barriers between military and civilian life. Although atrocities in war were not new, earlier armies had clearer physical limits on the damage they could inflict. Now, artillery shells could hit targets many miles away, aircraft could drop bombs on civilians far from the front, and mustard gas's insidious, mysterious toll on the human body could build over the course of days.

Technology was not the only factor undermining the separation between soldier and civilian. Nationalism encouraged the idea that entire societies, not just armies, went to war, that national solidarity could overflow social and class barriers. The Japanese state, for instance, had worked hard to generate nationalist sentiments among its people so that the victories over China in 1895 and Russia in 1905 would seem like victories not only of the military but also of the entire nation. The Hibiya riots showed both how successful the government had been and how nationalism might turn people against their own governments.

The experiences of the Great War led to questions about fundamental principles of political, social, and economic organization. Billions of dollars had been expended on the latest technology in pursuit of geostrategic interests. Millions of soldiers, workers, and citizens mobilized for their nations' causes. Then, the most advanced industrial economies, the most modern sovereign states, descended into an orgy of destruction. A question haunted the subsequent generation and helped to set the stage for further conflict: What was the point?

Wilfred Owen, the English poet, worried about twentieth-century nationalism's power to mobilize people to fight and die in the ways that the Great War had revealed. He concluded his poem about chemical warfare, "Dulce Et Decorum Est," by addressing the reader directly:

> If in some smothering dreams you too could pace
> Behind the wagon that we flung him in,
> And watch the white eyes writhing in his face,
> His hanging face, like a devil's sick of sin;
> If you could hear, at every jolt, the blood
> Come gargling from the froth-corrupted lungs,
> Obscene as cancer, bitter as the cud
> Of vile, incurable sores on innocent tongues,
> My friend, you would not tell with such high zest
> To children ardent for some desperate glory, The old Lie;
> Dulce et Decorum est
> Pro patria mori.

Owen's concluding line quotes the Roman poet Horace: "It is sweet and fitting to die for one's country." Owen, after seeing the effects of the war that had been rushed into so enthusiastically, decried such sentiment as an old lie.

TIMELINE

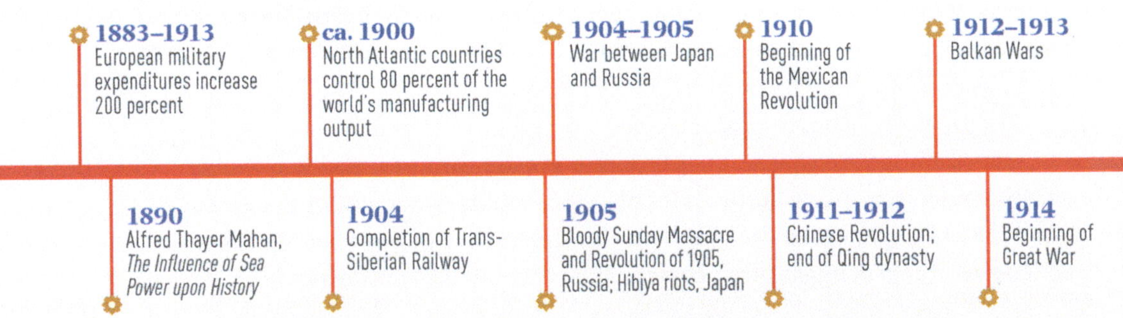
1883–1913
European military expenditures increase 200 percent
1890
Alfred Thayer Mahan, *The Influence of Sea Power upon History*
ca. 1900
North Atlantic countries control 80 percent of the world's manufacturing output
1904
Completion of Trans-Siberian Railway
1904–1905
War between Japan and Russia
1905
Bloody Sunday Massacre and Revolution of 1905, Russia; Hibiya riots, Japan
1910
Beginning of the Mexican Revolution
1911–1912
Chinese Revolution; end of Qing dynasty
1912–1913
Balkan Wars
1914
Beginning of Great War

Mussolini disagreed. He exhorted his followers to believe, "All in the state, nothing outside the state, nothing against the state." After the Great War, both communist and fascist movements in many countries challenged the liberal conception of the state, the relationship between state and nation, and that between state and individual. In Chapter 11, we will follow these conflicts through the ongoing crisis of global order, the economic meltdown of the Great Depression, and renewed global warfare at the end of the 1930s.

A Few Good Books

Sheila Fitzpatrick. *The Russian Revolution*. 4th ed. New York: Oxford University Press, 2017.

Paul Fussell. *The Great War and Modern Memory*. New York: Oxford University Press, 2013.

Robert Gerwarth. *The Vanquished: Why the First World War Failed to End*. New York: Farrar, Straus and Giroux, 2017.

Friedrich Katz. *The Secret War in Mexico*. Chicago: University of Chicago Press, 1981.

Charles King. *Midnight at the Pera Palace: The Birth of Modern Istanbul*. New York: W. W. Norton, 2014.

Michele L. Lauro. *Comrades against Imperialism: Nehru, India, and Interwar Internationalism*. New York: Cambridge University Press, 2018.

Margaret MacMillan. *The War That Ended Peace: The Road to 1914*. New York: Random House, 2014.

Caroline Moorhead. *A Bold and Dangerous Family: The Remarkable Story of an Italian Mother, Her Two Sons, and Their Fight against Fascism*. New York: Harper, 2017.

For instructional resources and study aids, please go to **www.oup.com/us/carter**. *For primary sources connected to this chapter, please see the table of contents for* Sources for Forging the Modern World *included at the back of the book.*

1915 Japan presents China with Twenty-One Demands

1916 Lenin writes "Imperialism, the Highest Stage of Capitalism"

1917 October Revolution in Russia; Mexico adopts a new constitution

1918 Woodrow Wilson issues Fourteen Points; armistice ends Great War

1918–1920 Flu pandemic kills fifty to one hundred million people worldwide

1919 Peace negotiations after the Great War conducted in France

1922 Mussolini marches on Rome

1925 Death of Sun Yat-sen

1928 Grand Council of Fascism established in Italy

1929 Publication of Ernest Hemingway's *A Farewell to Arms* and Erich Maria Remarque's *All Quiet on the Western Front*

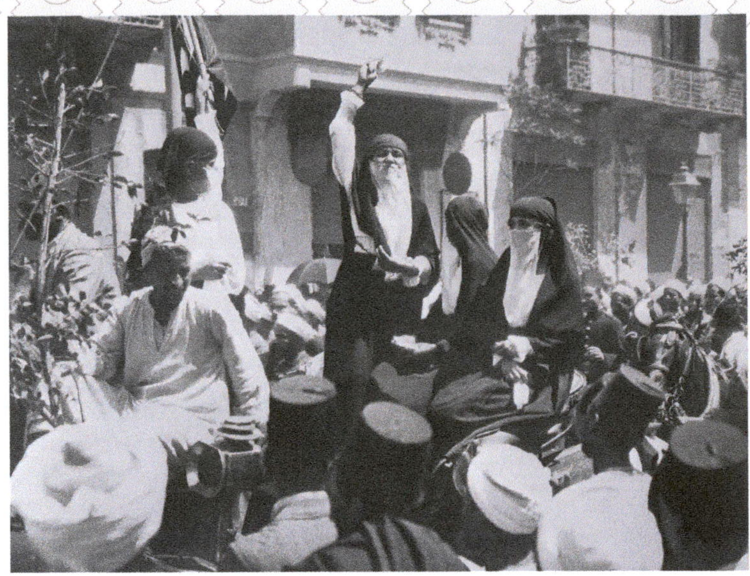

(TOP) Cairo Protests, 1919. Women constituted an important group among the thousands of protesters who filled the streets of Cairo after the Great War, expressing Egyptian nationalism and advocating for independence. The Cairo protests resembled similar anti-imperialist and nationalist protests that took place this same year around the world, including in Turkey, China, Germany, and Korea.

(BOTTOM) Kwame Nkrumah, Ghana's First President, Being Carried by Supporters, April 14, 1957. Born in the Gold Coast (now Ghana) and then educated in Britain and the United States, Kwame Nkrumah returned to Ghana in 1947. He was arrested in 1948 during riots in Accra when Ghanaian soldiers protested the colonial government's failure to deliver promised benefits. Nkrumah was not involved in planning the riots and was soon released, but he used the incident to launch a campaign that led to Ghana's independence within a decade, and he became the nation's first president.

CHAPTER 11

The Ongoing Crisis of Global Order

1919–1948

In the spring of 1919, protests gripped Egypt, a part of the Ottoman Empire since the sixteenth century. British forces had occupied Egypt early in the Great War and made it a protectorate, deploying Egypt's population and resources to serve the empire's wartime goals. At the end of the war, an Egyptian delegation, like many other groups seeking self-determination, was denied access to treaty deliberations. When leaders of the Wafd (Delegation) Party pursued diplomatic and legal maneuvers to end the protectorate, British officers arrested prominent Wafdist leaders. A cross-section of Egyptian society then took to the streets in protest. Huda Sha`rawi (1879–1947), founder of the Intellectual Association of Egyptian Women, emerged as a key figure in the protests, organizing women of means to join the movement. Sha`rawi became head of the Wafdist Women's Central Committee as pressure on the British government mounted, including strikes and acts of civil disobedience. In 1922, the British conceded limited independence and a new constitution for Egypt was promulgated in 1923.

Huda Sha`rawi's subsequent career illustrates the enduring complexities of defining sovereignty, democracy, and justice in the modern world. As Egypt transitioned to independence, women were not granted the right to vote. Sha`rawi resigned her position with the Wafdists in protest and focused her energies on the work of the Egyptian Feminist Union and, later, the Arab Feminist Union. Sha`rawi, who publicly removed her veil as an act of protest in 1923, argued that Egypt, and the Arab world more generally, could only prosper when women's equality became a defining characteristic of independent, sovereign states.

Three decades later, in early 1948, veterans of another world war gathered in the city of Accra, in the British colony of the Gold Coast (today's Ghana). These African soldiers had fought alongside other British troops and been promised an array of veterans' benefits, but they returned home to find these promises ignored. The veterans' concerns dovetailed with a broader protest movement developing in Ghana,

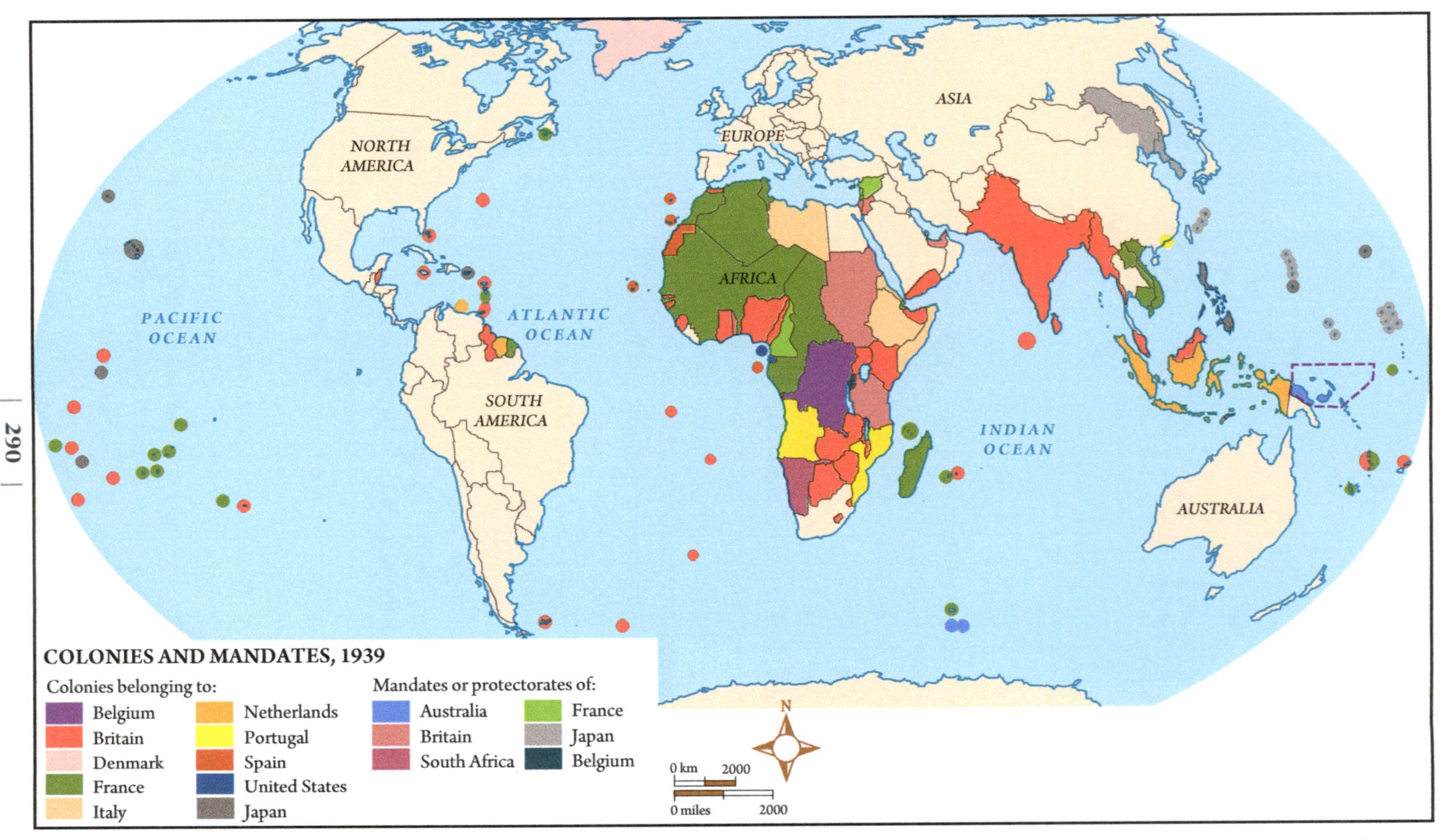
NORTH AMERICA
EUROPE
ASIA
AFRICA
SOUTH AMERICA
AUSTRALIA
PACIFIC OCEAN
ATLANTIC OCEAN
INDIAN OCEAN
COLONIES AND MANDATES, 1939
Colonies belonging to:
Belgium
Britain
Denmark
France
Italy
Netherlands
Portugal
Spain
United States
Japan
Mandates or protectorates of:
Australia
Britain
South Africa
France
Japan
Belgium
N
0 km 2000
0 miles 2000

Map 11.1 Colonies and Mandates, 1939

fueled by high unemployment and rampant inflation. In 1947 protest leaders organized an economic boycott as their primary tool. When businesses agreed to lower their profit margins in response to the boycott, the movement announced a date for the boycott's end. On the last day of the boycott, Ghanaian veterans approached the colonial governor's offices to demand their promised benefits. The police blocked their way and eventually fired into the crowd, killing at least one veteran and wounding dozens. Five days of riots followed.

In the aftermath of the disturbances, imperial authorities arrested six political leaders, including Kwame Nkrumah (1909–1972), for masterminding the protests. Nkrumah was not one of the veterans, but a leading decolonization advocate and organizer. This action exacerbated the situation in Ghana, and the men were soon released. Nkrumah then organized a political party, the Convention People's Party, in 1949. The party became the dominant institution negotiating the transition of Ghana from colony to member of the British Commonwealth (1957) to independent republic (1960). Kwame Nkrumah served as the first prime minister of the self-governing commonwealth country and later first president of the republic, proving to be both a staunch advocate for African independence and unity and an increasingly authoritarian ruler.

These events offer an intriguing introduction to the goals of this chapter. During these three decades, political revolutions, economic catastrophes, and global wars obliterated nineteenth-century promises of order and progress. When the Great War ended in 1918, optimists labeled it a *war to end war*, hopeful that lessons learned from its causes and conduct would prevent future conflicts. Yet, the Great War was only a prelude to even greater destruction. New political and economic experiments proliferated in the 1920s, and enduring resentments festered. A decade after the Great War ended, the global system of production and consumption—what many had come to see as the symbol of modernity itself—collapsed. Economic hardship followed by another bloodletting characterized the 1930s and early 1940s. At the end of the Second World War, individuals and groups vowed not to repeat the perceived errors that precipitated and perpetuated the Three Decades' Crisis, yet the similarities between events in Cairo in 1919 and Accra in 1948 demonstrate the challenges that accompanied this commitment.

In the first section of the chapter, we analyze the struggles over territorial reorganization in the Middle East and Asia after the Great War. We then survey the emergence and consolidation of communist movements, followed by an explanation of the economic events in the 1920s that culminated in the Great Depression. Next, we examine the political and economic fallout of the 1930s, focusing on the spread of fascism and the outbreak of global war. In the last sections of the chapter, we explain the nature of the Second World War and the challenges facing the global community in its aftermath, as the victorious Allies in the war attempted to reconcile competing ideas about property, equality, democracy, and citizenship while much of the world's population clamored for seats at the negotiating table.

Questions to Consider as You Read Chapter Eleven:

1. The protests in Cairo and Accra described above are separated by three decades, yet appear rooted in similar concerns. How did changes in the relationship between Europe and other parts of the world between 1919 and 1948 affect anticolonial protest movements and the responses to them?
2. How did the events described in this chapter change the global political and economic structures and relationships that had been central to constructing the modern global order that emerged at the end of the nineteenth century? What implications would these changes have for the future?

Eurasia after the Great War

As we saw in Chapter 10, the Great War ended with a theoretical commitment to national self-determination embodied in the League of Nations Charter. This commitment, however, quickly clashed with the goals of the war's victorious powers. These states—primarily Britain and France—redrew the map of the postwar world according to their own interests. This could be seen most clearly in the Middle East, where the former Allies worked to squash or marginalize other ideals or organizations. France and Britain, given control of much of the Middle East and North Africa, claimed that they would navigate this part of the world on a path toward independence now that the Ottoman Empire was dissolving. The League of Nations also determined that Great Britain would facilitate a "national home for the Jewish people" in Palestine while simultaneously protecting the rights of the territory's Arab population. The people living in the region were barely consulted; popular unrest, like that in Egypt, greeted the new rules and rulers, as the contemporary forms of the states of Turkey, Iran, Iraq, Jordan, Syria, Lebanon, Cyprus, Saudi Arabia, Armenia, Egypt, Palestine, and Israel began to evolve.

The great powers also failed to implement principles of self-determination and national sovereignty within their own empires. Great Britain remained by far the leading imperial power on the planet at the end of the war, ruling over one-fifth of the world's population and one-quarter of its territory. British leaders expressed little doubt that they were acting with justice and rectitude throughout the empire. Government documents still described British actions throughout the empire as being for the uplift of subject peoples. Challengers to the imperial order, like those in India, consistently exposed the contradictions between the victors' high principles and their questionable practices.

The Republic of Turkey

In the short term, the most prominent independent state to emerge from the former Ottoman lands was the Republic of Turkey. Mustafa Kemal Ataturk (1881–1938), the first president of the Republic of Turkey, enshrined secularism in the country's 1924 constitution and introduced both profound and mundane reforms to distinguish Turkey from the Ottoman Empire. Ataturk liquidated the connection between political rule and religious authority, doing away with the positions of sultan and caliph. The government established a new alphabet for the Turkish language based on Latin letters rather than Arabic script. Laws required government officials to wear Western suits rather than Islamic religious robes, turbans, or veils. The education system was secularized; classroom instruction in Arabic and Persian was stopped.

Non-Turks living under the Ottoman Empire paid a high price for the construction of modern Turkey. A pattern of aggression against Armenians that

Appeal for Relief. Established in 1915 with the aid of the US State Department, the American Committee for Armenian and Syrian Relief provided humanitarian aid to Armenians forcibly deported from Turkey to other parts of the Ottoman Empire during World War I. This poster solicited private contributions to the fund, which were distributed by the US Embassy in Istanbul. The term *genocide* was later coined to describe the forced dislocation and murder of Armenians during this era: 1.5 million people were killed.

began in the nineteenth century turned into a systematic policy during the Great War, organized by leaders intent on creating a more ethnically pure population. Scholars estimate that between 1915 and 1923, more than 1.5 million Armenians perished either from direct assault or from the deprivation of the means to survive. Although the treaties ending the Great War called for the prosecution of those responsible for these crimes against humanity, the great powers ultimately opted to accept the expediency of stable government in the region. A small, independent Armenia emerged, and the new regime in Turkey was not held responsible for prior acts committed against Armenians. No individuals or institutions were ever held accountable for the Armenian genocide.

Challenges to British Rule in India

Opposition to British rule in India continued to build after the Great War. One million Indian soldiers had served in the war; more than seventy-five thousand died. Nationalists in South Asia argued that these sacrifices had earned India greater autonomy. British politicians proposed some reforms, but supreme power remained with the viceroy (the top British official in India), including the unilateral authority to define sedition and suppress dissent. Brigadier general Reginald Dyer (1864–1927) horrifically demonstrated the extent of these powers in April 1919 when he ordered his troops to fire on an unarmed crowd in a public square gathered in defiance of his ban on public meetings. Dyer's troops fired for some ten minutes, targeting the plaza's exits. Estimates of those killed range from around four hundred to almost fifteen hundred. The Amritsar (or Jallianwala Bagh) Massacre widened the rift between Indian activists and British officials. At the end of 1919, Parliament passed the Government of India Act, introducing more shared governance between elected Indian officials and appointed British ones; but in the shadow of the massacre, this attempt at compromise found little favor among Indian nationalists.

In this atmosphere, Mohandas K. Gandhi rose to the leadership of the Indian National Congress, a leading nationalist organization. Gandhi played a key role in turning the political consciousness raised through Indian participation in World War I and the 1919 massacre into action. His success was even more remarkable because of his radical approach to political action: he opposed violence, without exception, in the pursuit of Indian independence. At times, Gandhi's uncompromising commitment to his own vision frustrated both allies and opponents, as opinions among South Asians hardened after the war between supporters of a single independent Indian nation-state and those who believed that multiple independent states would better serve the interests of the region's peoples. These divergent perspectives defined the following two decades in South

Asia. British officials argued that policies like advisory councils and expanded suffrage laid the groundwork for eventual autonomy. South Asian nationalists saw these modest reforms as delaying tactics by an empire desperate to hold onto the region, but the nationalists continued to struggle over their own goals for the long term and tactics for the near term.

A Communist World Future?

Marxists around the world debated various political strategies and tactics after the Great War. After the Bolshevik success in Russia, hopes among communists for global revolution against capitalism had been high. The new Union of Soviet Socialist Republics (USSR), with Russia as its core, tipped the balance in power struggles of bordering countries, incorporating Ukraine and Belarus. Mongolia became a Soviet client state, the Mongolian People's Republic, in 1924. Beginning in 1919, a new *Communist International* (Comintern) became an arm of Russian (after 1922, Soviet) foreign policy that advised communist groups around the world on the correct path to global revolution. Marxists, either in association with the Comintern or independent of it, attempted to organize communist parties and mobilize politically. The success of communist movements in seizing control of states was limited, however. Uprisings in Hungary and Germany failed, and no other communist states emerged in the immediate postwar years, although the Soviet Union continued to advocate an alternative model around which an international order might emerge. At least fifteen countries in the Western Hemisphere alone had communist political parties by 1929, and communists continued to work to gain political influence in China.

Nationalists versus Communists in China

Disappointment over the Great War's political outcomes rattled China. As we saw in Chapter 10, news that the great powers, meeting in Versailles, had turned Germany's former colonies in China over to Japan sparked protests in several major Chinese cities in 1919, especially Beijing. Taking its name from the date of these protests, the May Fourth Movement signaled a fundamental change in China's attitude toward the West. For generations, modernizers in China tended to reject traditional Chinese culture as backward and advocated reform using Western political and cultural models. *Modern* was generally taken to mean Western. Eager to be a modern state, revolutionaries had overthrown China's monarchy. The new republic had sent 140,000 men to Europe in support of the Allies' war effort. The May Fourth Movement expressed a new sentiment: that the great powers had betrayed China as it struggled to constitute itself into a functioning state. Furthermore, the horrors of World War I called Western liberalism sharply into question. Was a civilization that culminated in imperial treachery and trench warfare one that China should emulate?

Communism—neither traditionally Chinese nor liberal—offered an alternative model of modernization. Founded in 1921, the Chinese Communist Party reflected Marxist-Leninist thinking with strong Soviet influence, including an emphasis on China's need to industrialize first before it could proceed to communism. Alternatively, Sun Yat-sen's Nationalist Party remained an important force in China, increasingly divided between one branch sympathetic to socialist ideas and another branch that hewed at first toward liberal democracy and a market economy and later tilted toward fascism. When Sun Yat-sen died of cancer in 1925, disagreement raged over the leader's political agenda and legacy. Even within Sun's family, there was no consensus.

When Japanese-trained, staunchly anti-communist Chiang Kai-shek (1887–1975) succeeded Sun as head of the Chinese Nationalist Party, he moved to unify China and rid the country of communism. In a brutal purge, Chiang massacred most members of the Communist Party in Shanghai in the spring of 1927 as part of the Northern Expedition to reunify China under nationalist rule. The leaders of China's "new" republic, while maintaining many of the formal structures of the state inaugurated in 1912, concentrated power in the office of the president and moved toward fascism, suspicious of multiparty politics and political debate. The surviving members of the Communist Party eventually coalesced around Mao Zedong (1893–1976), who articulated a revision of communist revolutionary doctrine, suggesting that peasant societies like China could stage a successful revolution without having to industrialize first.

From Lenin to Stalin in the USSR

In the 1920s, in the transition from Bolshevik Russia to the Soviet Union, communist leaders constructed a new internal order and sought allies to share their vision of the future. When Lenin died in 1924, Josef Stalin (1878–1953) emerged from a group of would-be successors to gain control of the Communist Party and the future of the USSR. Stalin guided the country through rapid industrialization, centralizing control over production and distribution of resources. The USSR became for a time the world's largest producer of many industrial commodities, including oil, coal, iron ore, and natural gas. Politically, Stalin's Soviet Union denigrated Western liberalism as a tool of the wealthy designed to bamboozle the proletariat. The Soviet Union rejected representative democracy in favor of *democratic centralism*, which held that the Communist Party represented the will of the people and therefore party actions were, by definition, democratic. Anyone who opposed the party's actions could be imprisoned as an enemy of the people. Millions of criminals so defined (including political dissidents but also common criminals and others whose crimes were never fully explained) were deported to a state-administered system of labor camps, known by the acronym *Gulag*. In addition, to achieve rapid industrialization, Stalin implemented a campaign to collectivize agricultural production, taking decisions about production and consumption away from local producers and consumers. Famine gripped some of the Soviet Union's most fertile grain-producing regions. Five to eight million people starved to death in Russia and Ukraine in 1932–1933, and as many as one in four Kazakhs died in this same period in the name of rapid economic transformation.

Historians Explore Famine in the Ukraine

Understanding and interpreting these events challenge researchers. How do we assess the extent of the famine and its toll, its root causes, and their implications for the Soviet political and economic system and its subject peoples in the 1920s and 1930s? Demographic data during periods of trauma are difficult to interpret even when records are detailed and accessible. Many victims of famine do not literally starve to death but succumb to disease or injury because they are already weakened by malnutrition. In addition, birth rates drop in a famine, so some researchers also factor these "missing people" into the toll of the catastrophe.

Record keeping on these Soviet famines was anything but thorough or transparent. Soviet authorities at the time worked to hide the cause and extent of the famine, going so far as to publish deliberate misinformation about harvests and other local conditions. Then, when reports were published suggesting widespread famine had occurred, the Soviet government insisted it was propaganda circulated by its ideological enemies. Access to sources that might aid researchers trying to understand what happened was systematically denied.

Further considerations add to the difficulties of historical research on a topic like this. Many Ukrainians, descendants of those affected by the famine, perceive these deaths to be the goal of a Soviet policy they call *Holodomor*, or "Extermination by Hunger." Historians, each shaped by an overall view of the Soviet Union and global affairs at the time, can minimize, maximize, or even avoid discussion of these events. Robert Conquest, a prominent biographer of Stalin, concluded in his book *Harvest of Sorrow* that the Ukrainian famine amounted to genocide, although he later revised some of his original claims. Scholars Dana Dalrymple, Norman Naimark, and Timothy Snyder also support the view that the famines were the intended result of Soviet policies. Other researchers, such as Mark Tauger and Stephen Devereux, attribute the disastrous outcome more to incompetence and generally bad economic policies than to intentional genocide, defined as policy designed to exterminate an entire people. The debate, hampered by incomplete or inaccessible sources, goes on. The overall evidence, however, indicates that Stalinism was an extraordinarily repressive and ruthless system that delivered industrialization at a very high cost to the people of the USSR.[1]

The Global Economy in the 1920s

The Great War contributed to doubts about the global liberal order. Assumptions about the relationship among free markets, democracy, prosperity, and peace were undone. New models were sought to help the world recover from the catastrophe. Communist leaders proposed a command economy, in which the state controls decisions about the production and distribution of resources, as the best way to manage a modern economy. Some non-communist leaders, like the new revolutionary government in Mexico, also believed that the national state should play a larger role in managing a modern economy for the benefit of the nation. In contrast, ruling elites in the world's largest economies—western Europe, Japan, and the United States—advocated a limited role for government in economic planning and social welfare activities, encouraging individuals and businesses in the private sector to allocate resources and drive growth and prosperity. They tried to put together a system to do that.

Rebuilding Global Commerce

Before the global economic system could be reformed, it had first to be repaired. Although some economies had surged during the war years, the 1920s began with economic recessions in much of the industrialized world, including Europe, the United States, and Japan. Recovery soon followed in some places, but Germany and its allies remained crippled after the war. Monthly inflation rates reached 100 percent in Austria and Hungary and 200 percent in Germany—prices were doubling every few days. Germany defaulted on its foreign debts. World leaders struggled to adjust to the myriad economic consequences of the Great War: ten

1 Some of the important contributions on this question are Robert Conquest, *Harvest of Sorrow* (Oxford: Oxford University Press, 1987); Norman Naimark, *Stalin's Genocides* (Princeton, NJ: Princeton University Press, 2011); Timothy Snyder, *Bloodlands* (New York: Basic Books, 2012); Sheila Fitzpatrick, *Stalin's Peasants* (Oxford: Oxford University Press, 1996); R. W. Davies and Stephen Wheatcroft, *The Year of Hunger* (New York: Palgrave MacMillan, 2004); Mark B. Tauger, "Arguing from Errors: On Certain Issues in Robert Davies' and Stephen Wheatcroft's Analysis of the 1932 Soviet Grain Harvest and the Great Soviet Famine of 1931–1933," *Europe–Asia Studies* 58, no. 6 (September, 2006): 973–984; and Anne Applebaum, *Red Famine: Stalin's War on Ukraine* (New York: Doubleday, 2017).

billion dollars in military spending, devastated infrastructure, denuded agricultural land, nine million dead and twenty million wounded.

Recovery was complicated by a dramatic shift in global wealth and productive capacity. By the end of the Great War, the United States was responsible for nearly half of the entire globe's economic output and financial assets. Agriculture and manufacturing in the United States had expanded to fill the gap left as the other major industrial powers turned their economies into war machines. US financiers supplanted Europeans as the world's bankers. When the war was over, with their economies wrecked and their currencies devalued, European states owed private investors and the United States government about ten billion dollars. The treaties ending the war punished Germany by forcing it to pay the victorious countries over thirty billion dollars in reparations.

These conditions left the United States as the engine to drive the postwar global economy, and both the League of Nations and the US government emphasized international commerce as the key to a peaceful and prosperous future. Political and business leaders concluded that it was essential to address the postwar monetary systems. Who would get paid first? On what terms? Would repaying debts and reparations stifle economic recovery? Or would readjusting their terms trigger financial chaos, political upheaval, or military intervention? Should the amount of cash available in any given national economy be limited to the amount of gold reserves in its national treasury, or would that limit the availability of credit, which was crucial for future growth?

Repairing Financial Systems

Two attempts to answer these questions and address financial uncertainties emerged in the mid-1920s. First, the victorious Allies, led by the United States, implemented the Dawes Plan, reorganizing the German financial and tax system. This plan also revised the war reparations process and encouraged investment in Germany. Second, more than twenty countries returned to the *gold standard*, tying the value of their currency to that of gold. Advocates of this system asserted that fixing the value of national currencies in relation to gold would boost global economic confidence by reducing uncertainties about how individual currencies related to each other.

The postwar economic overhaul was not limited to Europe. Latin American and Caribbean leaders who hoped to enjoy renewed economic growth powered by agricultural and raw materials exports recognized that their primary economic partner now would have to be the United States. Many of them contracted the "money doctor," Princeton University's Edwin W. Kemmerer (1875–1945), who prescribed the gold standard and balanced government budgets to reform the financial systems of Mexico, Guatemala, Colombia, Chile, Ecuador, Bolivia, and Peru. Kemmerer also worked in Poland, China, and South Africa. US bank loans and private direct investment also helped to fuel the economies of Asia and the Middle East.

The money doctor and his policies seemed to do the trick. Confidence in a global economic recovery, fueled by American optimism and cash, soared. So did stock prices. The United States experienced the Roaring Twenties and France *Les Années Folles* ("The Crazy Years"). But as the champagne flowed, structural weaknesses remained. The world's agricultural sector, for example, had changed during the Great War. The farms of Europe had become killing fields, while hungry soldiers and civilian populations still needed to be fed. Producers in other regions—North and South America, Africa, and Australia—had responded by converting acreage into food crops, with the expectation of greater profits. The rapid return to productivity of European agriculture, aided by new industrially produced fertilizers and the dynamic output of newly independent states in east central Europe, overwhelmed the agricultural market in the 1920s. Prices fell as supply increased. Income stagnated for farmers across the world, yet some regions still suffered food shortages, as populations could neither produce enough food locally nor afford imported staples.

Besides the glutted commodities market, the other hidden weakness in the global economy was the increasing use of credit in economic transactions, which maintained an appearance of prosperity with little real wealth to support it. A belief in future economic growth made retailers willing to sell goods on installment plans and consumers willing to buy them. Both buyers and sellers believed that it wasn't important whether you had the money to buy something now, because next year you were sure to have more than enough! This attitude was at its most extreme in the US stock market, where investors borrowed money from stockbrokers for the purchase of stocks, expecting to repay the loan from future profits.

These transactions depended on both economic growth and the belief that this growth would continue indefinitely. When perceptions about the potential for continued growth changed, the value of stocks began to fall. As stock prices fell, the profits that investors were counting on to pay for the stocks they had already bought shrank, then disappeared. Brokers demanded the money they had loaned out, and investors began selling their stocks, even at prices lower than the original purchase price. Instead of getting rich, investors were losing money. As more people lost more money and more people demanded to be paid, investors sold stocks at whatever price they could, driving down the market. "The Crash" came on October 28 and 29, 1929, two days in which the New York Stock Exchange lost more than thirty billion dollars in value. The Dow Jones Industrial

Average—an indicator that measures the market value of large corporations in the United States—declined 89 percent between 1929 and 1932; it would not return to the levels of early 1929 for twenty-five years.

The Great Depression

The great stock market crash of 1929 was itself the result of larger problems in the global economy, but it made clear that the system was in crisis. Panic spread across the globe. "Bank runs" proliferated, as many financial institutions lacked the cash reserves to meet the demands of customers who wanted to withdraw their money. One-third of the banks in the United States closed. The largest commercial bank in Austria shut its doors in 1931, followed by important banks in Germany and Britain. As credit dried up, industrial output fell, and jobs disappeared. Unemployment rose to 20 percent in England, 25 percent in the United States, and 30 percent in Germany.

The effect and duration of the Great Depression varied by country and region. In the United States, over fifteen million people—about 30 percent of the labor force—were unemployed in March 1933, the month President Franklin D. Roosevelt (1882–1945) took office and initiated a series of experiments to address the crisis.

Known collectively as the *New Deal*, these policies changed the relationship between the US economy and the state, based on the premise that the modern state had an obligation and a unique ability to manage the economy and address the social welfare of the population. A flood of initiatives and laws followed. Some, like the Social Security Act of 1935, which established support for senior citizens and aid for children living in poverty, became cornerstones of a new American social contract. Others, like an attempt to directly control wages and prices, were challenged in court and overturned. Economic recovery was uneven—by the mid-1930s the economy was again in recession, and unemployment, even in 1939, was at ten million (around 18 percent)—but the US political system survived the ordeal. The same could not be said everywhere.

In Latin America, responses to the global economic collapse varied. Six major military coups occurred between March and December of 1930 alone. More would come in the following years. Chile, described by the League of Nations as the country most devastated by the global economic collapse, moved in the opposite direction, as a military regime proved incapable of managing the crisis and yielded to an intensely partisan, diverse, democratic political system. In all these cases, new governments wondered how to rebuild political and economic order while the region's traditional economic partners in western Europe floundered. This established a pattern for the future, as

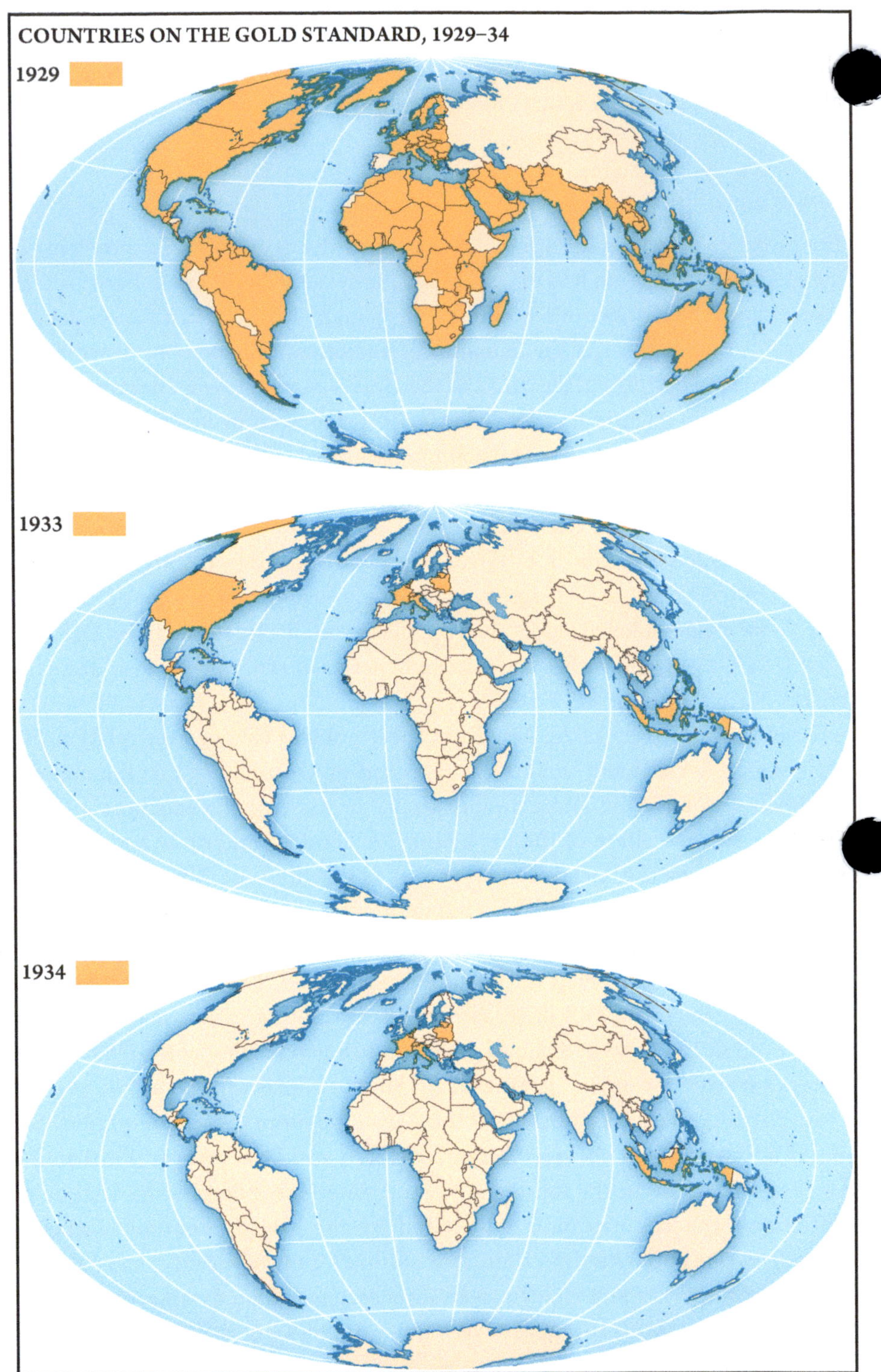

Map 11.2 Countries on the Gold Standard, 1929–1934

South American militaries took the power to determine acceptable political behavior and economic policy away from civilian political systems and reserved ultimate authority for themselves.

German Woman Burning Money on Stove during Hyperinflation, 1923. In the years after World War I, hyperinflation in Germany rendered money all but useless. In this photo, from 1923, a woman burns German marks on the stove because the paper is more valuable as fuel than as currency (at the time, one US dollar was worth about 800 million marks).

Around the world, the Great Depression triggered economic experimentation and reassessment of assumptions about how modern economies work. Several trends predominated in efforts to pull countries out of the malaise. Many, like the reforms in the United States, included an expanded role for the state in managing modern economies. Fiscal and monetary policies were adjusted, with higher tariffs and abandonment of the gold standard common practices. Some countries used deficit spending to initiate public works programs and create jobs. Many countries nationalized foreign-owned businesses, as in the case of the oil industries of Bolivia and Mexico. Other countries also saw some growth in domestic industry as traditional supplies of industrial goods were cut off. Social welfare programs were created or expanded to address basic needs.

Many countries looked to strengthen their regional spheres of influence or colonial economic relations—the shadow of mercantilism. For example, in 1932, the British Empire established a system of lower tariffs for goods traded within the empire than for those entering from outside. The United States pursued new trade agreements within the Western Hemisphere and by 1938 was the major trading partner with most Latin American countries. Germany also pursued trade in Latin America but built its most important international economic relationships through special agreements with Austria, Hungary, Poland, and Yugoslavia. In Asia, Japan strengthened its privileged trading ties with colonies in Korea and Taiwan, as well as the puppet state of Manchukuo, created when Japan invaded Manchuria in 1931.

The Collapse of the Postwar Order

Economic cycles of growth and contraction have always existed in the global economy, but this contraction was particularly severe and long-lasting. For the world's economic elites, the great strength of the global economic system that they were trying to rebuild in the 1920s was its interconnectedness, allowing goods and services to flow easily across borders. This ease of movement meant that the economic crisis in the United States and western Europe spread quickly around the world. General financial chaos erupted, as buyers, sellers, and lenders lost confidence in the economic future. Frightened business people and government officials scrambled to respond. Governments began to abandon the gold standard for their currencies so that they could increase the amount of money in circulation (contributing to inflation). Countries raised tariffs hoping to protect domestic industry and employment at the expense of global integration. The effect was a further economic slowdown, not recovery. Desperate for solutions, fascists, socialists, communists, and liberals traded accusations and proposals in the world's legislative assemblies and the media—and often traded blows on the streets—as the economic crisis deepened.

Fascism Spreads

In the mid-1920s, it appeared that fragile political systems might resist the pull toward fascism that had enveloped Italy (Chapter 10). However, the dislocations of the global economic collapse, lingering resentments of the victorious powers' postwar actions, and a growing collaboration among fascist groups reversed the trend in the 1930s. In Germany, Adolf Hitler (1889–1945) took over the small National Socialist German Workers' (Nazi) Party, which attempted to topple the German government by force. Sent to prison in 1924 for his role in a failed coup, Hitler wrote a manifesto entitled *Mein Kampf* (My Struggle), that promised a future when a *Führer* (this word is rarely translated in this context, but means "leader") would oversee the creation of a new German empire. Beginning in the mid-1920s, a reorganized Nazi Party produced an ultranationalist message, opposing both communism (because it emphasized class over nation) and liberalism (because it emphasized individual over nation). The Nazis also institutionalized Hitler's scapegoating of Jews, blaming a fictitious international Jewish conspiracy for German economic woes. Like other totalitarian groups, the Nazis emphasized military-style organization and mass events to demonstrate that their movement went well beyond that of a political party. Hitler led the Nazis into the 1928 elections, where they attracted only 2.8 percent of the German vote, but Nazi poll numbers grew consistently after the collapse of the global economy. By 1932, the Nazis had become the most popular party in Germany, although still not a majority in the legislature.

Disagreements among Hitler's opponents prevented them from pooling their votes to form a successful coalition against the Nazis. Instead, Hitler convinced nationalist and conservative politicians outside the Nazi Party to support his bid to be appointed chancellor. Within the first month of his term in office in 1933, Hitler blamed a suspicious fire at the German parliament building (*Reichstag*) on the German Communist Party, which held the second largest delegation in the parliament. An emergency edict banned the communists, leaving their seats in the legislature empty and giving the Nazis a majority.

Italy Invades Ethiopia

The fascist idea of a world of warring nations (remember, fascism argued that war was not only necessary but also desirable) contrasted with the League of Nations' vision of a world free from conflict and dedicated to human progress. In the mid-1930s, Italian fascists invaded Ethiopia to realize their vision of a new Roman empire, using chemical weapons—banned by international treaty—to achieve their objectives. Ethiopian emperor Haile Selassie (1892–1975) appealed to the League of Nations delegates for help in a speech, asking, "Have the signatures appended to a Treaty value only in so far as the signatory Powers have a personal, direct and immediate interest involved?" Yet, no coordinated effort to counteract Mussolini materialized, in part because other European states could scarcely object to Italian imperialism in Africa when they had their own African colonies. Besides, thought the leaders of the great powers, the addition of independent Ethiopia to Italy's African empire, which also included Libya, Eritrea, and Somaliland, did not appear to pose a direct threat to any of them.

The Spanish Civil War and Aerial Bombing

Not everyone agreed that the invasion of Ethiopia was unimportant. A young English journalist named George L. Steer (1909–1944) reported on the downfall of independent Ethiopia as part of a worrisome trend, both because of fascist aggression and because of the unconventional methods employed. The next battleground Steer covered, the Spanish civil war between fascists within the military (nationalists) and defenders of the civilian government (Republicans), seemed to confirm his fears. In April 1937, Steer reported on a raid against Guernica, a Republican town in the Basque region of Spain, in which aircraft dropped forty tons of explosives in an unprecedented use of modern military technology to attack a civilian population. Film footage of the bombed-out city spread outrage that civilians had been deliberately targeted. Pablo Picasso (1881–1973) depicted the carnage in an abstract painting that toured the world, bringing attention to the raid and to the war.

Steer reported that German flyers and aircraft had carried out the raid on behalf of the nationalists. Illustrating just how far this attack on nonmilitary targets strayed from accepted morality, Hitler's German government denied any participation in the raid, claiming this was propaganda used by its enemies. Fascist general Francisco Franco (1892–1975), who came to power when the nationalists won the war in 1939—and who presided as Spain's authoritarian ruler into the 1970s—asserted that the damage at Guernica had been self-inflicted by the Republicans to deny resources to the nationalists and to rally international sympathy to a losing cause. Although supporters of Franco's view presented their own films and photographs to support their assertions, the weight of historical evidence clearly demonstrates that the German military was supporting its allies in the Spanish army, turning Spain into a living laboratory for experiments in new military tactics like carpet-bombing. Support from their allies helped the nationalists secure another victory for a fascist movement. The research also suggests that the bombing was part of a broader strategy, not primarily an attack on the civilian population. It is likely that the actual death toll was lower than the first published reports, like those of Steer, suggested. Still, the bombing of Guernica remains an important entry point for consideration of an increasingly common question in modern, industrial warfare: What are the moral and ethical implications of aerial bombing?[2]

Japan Seeks a New Order in Asia

In Japan, the depression hit the industrial economy hard and the agricultural sector even harder when demand for exports and prices for farm goods fell. Although no single leader emerged as in Germany, Italy, or Spain, the Japanese military claimed the authority to act directly on behalf of the nation and its people, arguing that pluralism, with its mess of party politics, electoral conflicts, and rights claims, had failed the nation and betrayed the emperor. Although the army and navy had frequent internal disputes, military officers increasingly controlled public policy and even sanctioned political assassination. By 1936, Japan was in effect a dictatorship, led by a faction within the military that espoused industrialization via a partnership between the state and private business cartels that

2 Peter Monteath, "Guernica Reconsidered: Fifty Years of Evidence," *War and Society* 5, no. 1 (1987): 79–100; James S. Corum, "The Spanish Civil War: The Persistent Myths of Guernica," *MHQ: The Quarterly Journal of Military History* 22, no. 4 (Summer 2010): 16–22; Ian Patterson, *Guernica and Total War* (Cambridge, MA: Harvard University Press, 2007).

would bring domestic prosperity and place Japan in its appropriate position in a new international order.

Informally at first, then with an official pronouncement in 1940, Japan promoted a Greater East Asia Co-Prosperity Sphere, promising to end Western colonial domination of Asia. Under this policy, Japan, which had already demonstrated its ability to resist—and defeat—Western powers in war, would organize and deploy Asia's resources. As part of this movement, the Japanese government promoted totalitarianism as efficient, necessary, and moral. In 1941, the Japanese Ministry of Education produced a pamphlet called "The Way of Subjects," which emphasized devotion to the emperor and the Japanese state and rejected key liberal tenets, arguing that individual freedoms were not keys to progress or goals to be realized, but evils to be fought against.

Even cloaked in the language of benevolence, Japan's imperial rule in East Asia resembled, and even exceeded, the colonial regimes imposed from Europe and America. During the 1920s and 1930s, Japanese rule directed Korean industry and agriculture to serve Japanese expansion elsewhere. Japan invaded Chinese territory in 1931, 1932 and again in 1937. Echoing the gas attacks in Ethiopia and the civilian bombings in Spain, Japanese bombers attacked residential neighborhoods in Shanghai and Japan's advancing armies carried out mass rape and biological warfare.

Japanese Aerial Bombing of Chongqing, China, 1937. For Europeans, World War II began in 1939, but war had started in Asia two years earlier. Driven from their capital of Nanjing—near Shanghai—by Japanese armies, the Chinese government relocated to the city of Chongqing, nearly one thousand miles to the west, where Japanese bombers conducted regular raids on the city's civilian neighborhoods. Aerial bombardment of civilian targets—practiced by the Japanese against Shanghai and Chongqing, or the Germans against London, was widely condemned; but by the end of World War II, all sides employed strategic aerial bombing of cities.

While the Chinese government resisted Japanese aggression, the collapse of the global economy had confounded Chiang Kai-Shek's plans for a unified non-communist state. As both industrial and agricultural production declined in the early 1930s, Chiang increasingly embraced elements of fascism, styling himself generalissimo, and promoted a state-centered ideology—the New Life Movement—designed to subordinate the individual to the nation and public life to the service of the state. Chiang even pursued a military alliance with Hitler's Germany.

War without Limits

By the mid-1930s, Germany's government under the Nazis was implementing its program to create a new *Reich* (Empire), expanding Nazi sovereignty over territory based on extreme forms of nationalism and cultural solidarity. First bending, and then shattering, the restrictions imposed on it at Versailles, the German government rearmed and redeployed its military and then absorbed Austria and part of Czechoslovakia into a Greater Germany. Some objected to German actions, but most leaders in western Europe saw greater threats from the potential outbreak of another global war or communism's spread than from Germany acquiring territory from its weaker neighbors. Germany's anti-communist treaty alliance with Japan (1936) and then Italy (1937) appeared not as a threat but as a buffer zone surrounding the USSR. Imagine the surprise among those leaders when, in 1939, Hitler signed an agreement of nonaggression with Stalin, stating that if Germany went to war, the Soviet Union would remain neutral and vice versa. Other world leaders would have been less surprised by this strange alliance had they known—as documents uncovered after the war revealed—that Hitler and Stalin had formed a secret side agreement to allow each to take control of parts of east-central Europe. On September 1, 1939, soon after signing the Hitler–Stalin pact, Germany invaded Poland. This was, finally, a step too far for Great Britain and France, which declared war.

The Path through the Second World War

German forces, employing planes, tanks, and other motorized vehicles in a *blitzkrieg* ("lightning war"), subdued Poland, Denmark, Norway, the Netherlands, Belgium, and France within ten months of the start of war. By the spring of 1941, Great Britain was the only sovereign European state with its full capacities devoted to war against Germany. The British lobbied furiously for US aid, but the United States would not take on a combat role in the European war through the fall of 1941.

Map 11.3 Japan in China, 1931–1945

In Asia, Japan, already engaged in an undeclared war against China, signed another treaty in 1940 confirming its commitment to a global anti-communist "Axis" with Germany and Italy. The Japanese occupied French Indochina in July 1941. The United States grew increasingly wary of the turn of events in the Pacific and curtailed shipments to Japan of vital resources like rubber, scrap iron, and fuel. In addition, the United States and other countries froze Japanese assets deposited in their financial institutions. In the spring of 1941, the United States began supplying China, Great Britain, and other combatants fighting the Axis.

Demonstrating the contingent, unpredictable nature of history, two decisions made by Axis leaders changed the course of the war during the second half of 1941. That summer, Germany reneged on its pact with Stalin and invaded the USSR. Then, in December, the Japanese launched a preemptive strike against the US naval base at Pearl Harbor, Hawai'i. Neither action delivered a decisive blow to the target country, but they did turn the Soviet Union and the United States into military allies against the fascist states. This would prove decisive in turning the war against the Axis. Although both the United States and the Soviet Union were reeling from these attacks, the two states recovered quickly, ramping up industrial production and pouring troops and materiel into the war.

In the Pacific, Japanese successes continued for several months after Pearl Harbor, defeating British and American forces in the Philippines, Burma, Malaya, Singapore, the Dutch East Indies, and islands across the Pacific. Forced to rely on aircraft carriers after many of its battleships were sunk at Pearl Harbor, the United States (aided by breaking the main Japanese communications code) defeated the Japanese decisively at the Battle of Midway, in the central Pacific, in June 1942. Although many lives would be lost in three more years of fighting, Midway marked the end of Japanese expansion in the Pacific.

In Europe, the war turned in a similar time frame. The Soviet Union seemed on the brink of collapse for many months after the German invasion. The German armies' advance was eventually stopped at Stalingrad in a five-month battle that began in August 1942. This was one of the bloodiest in human history: as many as two million casualties were inflicted on the two sides during the campaign. Defeated at great cost to both sides, German armies never again achieved success on the Eastern Front and were slowly driven back by the Soviet army.

American and British forces opened a second front against the Nazis. Following victories in North Africa, US and British armies landed in Italy in the autumn of 1943 and in June 1944 launched the largest amphibious invasion ever mounted, on the coast of France. In both the east and the west, supported by the enormous industrial capacity of the USSR and the United States, the Allies began to turn back German forces.

Although in retrospect we can see that the war turned in the summer of 1942, the Second World War dragged on into 1945. Ultimately, the Allied forces won, first over the Nazis and then over the Japanese, but these victories came at mind-boggling material and human cost. More than sixty million people—2.5 percent of the world's population—were killed in the war, including unprecedented numbers of civilians. This war encompassed even more territory and combatants, more battlefield and civilian deaths, and more industrial technologies applied to inflicting pain and suffering than the war to end war had done only two decades earlier. The war's scale and conduct cast a long shadow over the following decades.

Mass Killing and the Modern State

During this Second World War, air power continued to erode the importance of physical distance between combatants. Continuing the grim trend seen in Shanghai and Guernica, military strategists, political leaders, and ordinary people blurred the line between acceptable military targets and tactics and morally indefensible abominations. Aerial bombing of population centers became an accepted, even standard, feature of modern warfare. Germany's "blitz" of English cities from September 1940 to May 1941 killed forty thousand civilians, half of them in London. Allied governments protested the deliberate targeting of civilians, but soon all sides employed so-called strategic bombing. Japanese bombs killed more than ten thousand civilians in China's wartime capital, Chongqing. Allied firebombing included the German cities of Hamburg (42,000 killed) and Dresden (25,000 killed in a single night). The systematic firebombing of Japanese cities was even more extensive: one hundred thousand people died in one night's raids on Tokyo, and in total more than three hundred thousand people died in dozens of raids.

The war also accelerated a race to develop a new generation of superweapons using scientific innovations. The new and shocking power of nuclear weapons was introduced on August 6, 1945, when a single atomic bomb, dropped on the city of Hiroshima, killed tens of thousands instantly and more than 150,000 in total. A second bomb was dropped on Nagasaki three days later. The United States did not monopolize this technology for long, as the Soviet Union, through research and espionage, developed its own nuclear weapons program shortly after the war ended. Other countries would follow.

In the First World War, the experience of chemical weapons like mustard gas had been so horrible that international conventions banned their use in combat. But while chemical weapons were removed from the battlefield, they remained one of the deadliest weapons of the Second World War, their victims now civilians targeted for genocide. Adolf Hitler, himself wounded in a gas attack in the First World War, forbade German armies from using chemical weapons in combat, but he oversaw the industrial murder that came to be known as the Holocaust. Hitler's Final Solution was a government policy of genocide: the attempt to kill all the Jews in Europe, whom the Nazis blamed for Germany's defeat in World War I and its economic struggles afterward. Other groups deemed unfit for living under the new Reich were also identified for extermination, including Romani (labeled "Gypsies"), Slavs, homosexuals, communists, and those with disabilities. With dark efficiency, the German state murdered millions of Jews in gas chambers after methods like mass execution by firing squad were deemed too time-consuming and demoralizing to the soldiers. Estimates of the number of civilians killed across Europe and the Soviet Union by the Nazis range as high as seventeen million; at least six million were Jews.

The Holocaust, atomic weapons, and strategic bombing hideously distorted the technologies that had fueled dreams of progress since the dawn of industrialization. They also demonstrated the failings of modern political ideals and structures. Hitler rose to power through democratic processes, although once in power he dismantled them. The civil and military bureaucracies of the German state linked with the industrial infrastructure to support the political system, with catastrophic results. Millions of ordinary people played roles in delivering victims to concentration camps across Central Europe.

The grim realities of the Final Solution, embedded in the broader context of several decades of global crisis, raised challenging questions for the future. Could this war's victors do a better job ensuring peace than those who tried at the end of World War I? What, if any, limits might be placed on state sovereignty in the interests of protecting individuals and groups living within any given state? Could a system of international security respect the principle of self-determination while still safeguarding some broad, enduring global balance of political, economic, and military power? Under what circumstances, if any, could the development or use of weapons of mass destruction, like nuclear or chemical weapons, be controlled and/or general rules of warfare be enforced?

Empire in the Shadow of Another World War

The Second World War brought questions of the relationship between empire and global warfare to the forefront of political debate again. For most of the tens of millions of people resident in the colonies of Afro-Eurasia, the Second World War simply confirmed disillusion with the good intentions of imperialists. This was not only because of the devastation in the belligerent nations but also because the destruction was once again visited on peoples across the globe. In India, beyond the two and a half million soldiers who fought on behalf of the British, the additional political and economic costs of imperial rule achieved further clarity. Some nationalists in the empire argued that support for the war effort should be the most important short-term priority, but Gandhi's Indian National Congress insisted that independence should be paid up front as the price of Indian support. As a result, Congress leaders were imprisoned for the duration of the war.

The wartime economy laid bare, as it had during the First World War, the relationship between colony and colonizer. Production, distribution, and consumption priorities were determined by policy decisions about what was best for the war effort, but these decisions often privileged the metropolis at the expense of the colonies. In India, for example, British war policies contributed to a famine that killed approximately three million people in Bengal Province in 1942–1943. Some of the blame for the famine may be attributed to the Japanese conquest of Burma, which had previously provided significant amounts of rice to the rest of British India. Britain, however, continued to export rice from Bengal to support the war effort even when local officials asked that it be kept back to feed people who were starving.

The situation in Burma provides another striking example of the dilemma for colonized peoples across Afro-Eurasia during the war. Many in Burma had celebrated when Japan, promising Burmese independence as part of its "Asia for the Asiatics" program, moved against British rule there in 1942. Anticolonial forces in Burma, which had been organizing for years, were armed and trained by the Japanese as the Burmese Independence Army. Fighting against them were hundreds of thousands of soldiers from British India, Burma, and West and East Africa. On both sides, the relationship of soldiers to imperial armies was tenuous. The Burmese leader Aung San (1915–1947) came to realize that Japanese promises of independence were as hollow as British ones. Burmese units fighting for national independence rebelled against both the Japanese and the British. Meanwhile, many of the soldiers who fought for the British in Burma came from other regions of the empire. They fought with the expectation that their service would earn economic opportunities and greater autonomy in their homelands after the war. Such was the case of the Gold Coast veterans, whose 1948 protests in Accra introduced this chapter.

Conclusion

At the end of the Second World War, much of the world smoldered in ruins. Many perceived the crisis of the preceding three decades to have been a product of the global political and economic order that had emerged in the nineteenth century. Imperialist and nationalist rivalries had led to war; global capitalism had fueled depression; science and technology had enabled killing, on an unprecedented scale, of soldiers and civilians alike. The survival of the world's increasingly interconnected population depended on reordering fundamental global political and economic relationships. The victorious Allies agreed that, with fascism's defeat, such a project was essential. The problem, clear even before the end of the war, was that these allies did not agree on what those new relationships should look like. In Chapter 12, we explore the debate over a new global political and economic order, the conflicts that emerged between the world's major powers after the Second World War, and the increasing role of claims made against all power holders on behalf of the world's people.

A Few Good Books

Lizzie Collingham. *The Taste of War: World War II and the Battle for Food*. New York: Penguin, 2012.

Lawrence James. *The Rise and Fall of the British Empire*. London: St Martin Griffins, 1997.

Laure Marchand and Guillaume Perrier. *Turkey and the Armenian Ghost: On the Trail of the Genocide*. Trans. Debbie Blythe. Montreal: McGill–Queen's University Press, 2015.

TIMELINE

1909 Mohandas K. Gandhi publishes "Indian Home Rule"

1915–23 Armenian genocide

1919 Comintern founded; Amritsar Massacre, India; May Fourth Movement, China

1921 Chinese Communist Party founded

1922 Egypt achieves limited independence from Britain

1923 Republic of Turkey declared; Huda Sha'rawi founds Egyptian Feminist Union

1924 Dawes Plan reorganizes German financial and tax system

1925 Chiang Kai-shek assumes control of Nationalist Party in China; Adolf Hitler publishes first volume of *Mein Kampf*

1929 Stock market crash, New York; beginning of Great Depression

Rana Mitter. *Forgotten Ally: China's World War II, 1937–1945*. New York: Houghton Mifflin Harcourt, 2014.

Aviel Roshwald. *Ethnic Nationalism and the Fall of Empires: Central Europe, the Middle East and Russia, 1914–23*. New York: Routledge, 2000.

Robert Service. *Comrades. A World History of Communism*. London: Macmillan, 2007.

For instructional resources and study aids, please go to **www.oup.com/us/carter**. *For primary sources connected to this chapter, please see the table of contents for* Sources for Forging the Modern World *included at the back of the book.*

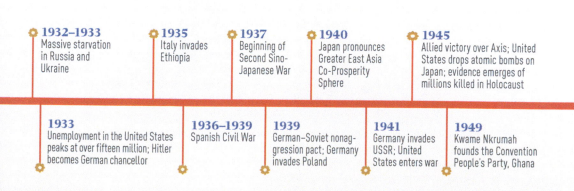

1932–1933 Massive starvation in Russia and Ukraine

1933 Unemployment in the United States peaks at over fifteen million; Hitler becomes German chancellor

1935 Italy invades Ethiopia

1936–1939 Spanish Civil War

1937 Beginning of Second Sino-Japanese War

1939 German–Soviet nonaggression pact; Germany invades Poland

1940 Japan pronounces Greater East Asia Co-Prosperity Sphere

1941 Germany invades USSR; United States enters war

1945 Allied victory over Axis; United States drops atomic bombs on Japan; evidence emerges of millions killed in Holocaust

1949 Kwame Nkrumah founds the Convention People's Party, Ghana

(TOP) German SS Officer Prepares to Shoot a Polish Jew. In this photo, most likely taken in 1942, a member of the German SS paramilitary group prepares to shoot a Polish Jew who is kneeling on the edge of a mass grave almost filled with other victims. Nazi leaders soon thereafter decided a system of industrial death camps should be implemented. At least six million Jews were murdered in the Holocaust between 1941 and 1945. Overall, as many as seventeen million civilians were killed by the Nazis during the war.

(BOTTOM) Poster from the People's Movement for the Liberation of Angola (MPLA), Angola, 1975. The MPLA was one of several armed factions, with roots in the 1950s, struggling against Portuguese colonialism. When a new government in Portugal declared its intention in 1974 to withdraw from its African colonies, the MPLA seized the initiative and declared itself in charge of an independent Angola in 1975. Other armed factions disputed this assertion, plunging Angola into years of bloody civil war fueled by Cold War rivalries.

CHAPTER 12

Hot Wars, Cold Wars, and Decolonization

1942–1975

Feigele Peltel (1921–2012) was in her early twenties in the summer of 1942 when the Nazis began a campaign that killed over three hundred thousand Jews from her hometown of Warsaw in a matter of months. For three years, the Germans had occupied the Polish capital as they waged war to expand their Reich across Europe. As part of their plan to purify the Reich's population, the Nazis had begun to concentrate Jews into a ghetto, building a wall around it to control entry and exit. The Warsaw Ghetto's four hundred thousand residents, nearly 30 percent of the city's population, made it the largest of all the Jewish ghettos in Nazi-occupied Europe. In 1941, the Nazis implemented a plan of mass murder in Poland, at extermination camps like Auschwitz-Birkenau, Treblinka, and several others. These camps' only purpose was to efficiently gather and slaughter human beings and the Jews of the Warsaw Ghetto became a primary target.

Because Feigele Peltel "passed" for a non-Jew in the eyes of the Nazi authorities, she lived outside the ghetto, taking the name Vladka. When Jews in the ghetto organized an armed resistance to the Nazis in response to mass deportations, she smuggled weapons, helped Jewish children to escape, and communicated with groups outside Warsaw. Shocked, then enraged, by the resistance, the Nazis leveled the entire ghetto in the spring of 1943, killing more than seven thousand and rounding up fifty-five thousand others for deportation to work and extermination camps. Years later, from a prison cell, the operation's Nazi commanding officer, Jürgen Stroop (1895–1952), expressed pride in a final act of desecration, demolishing Warsaw's Great Synagogue.

Vladka/Feigele lost her father to pneumonia in the ghetto and her mother and two siblings to the extermination camps, but she survived to see the Germans defeated. After the war, she heard commitments from the victorious Allies that the world could not allow such atrocities to be committed again. However, hostilities within the victorious anti-fascist coalition presented an obstacle to achieving these and other lofty goals for a better world. Her place of birth became an early focus of the deep-seated disagreements between the anti-fascist allies, as the United States, Great Britain, and the Soviet Union fought over the type of

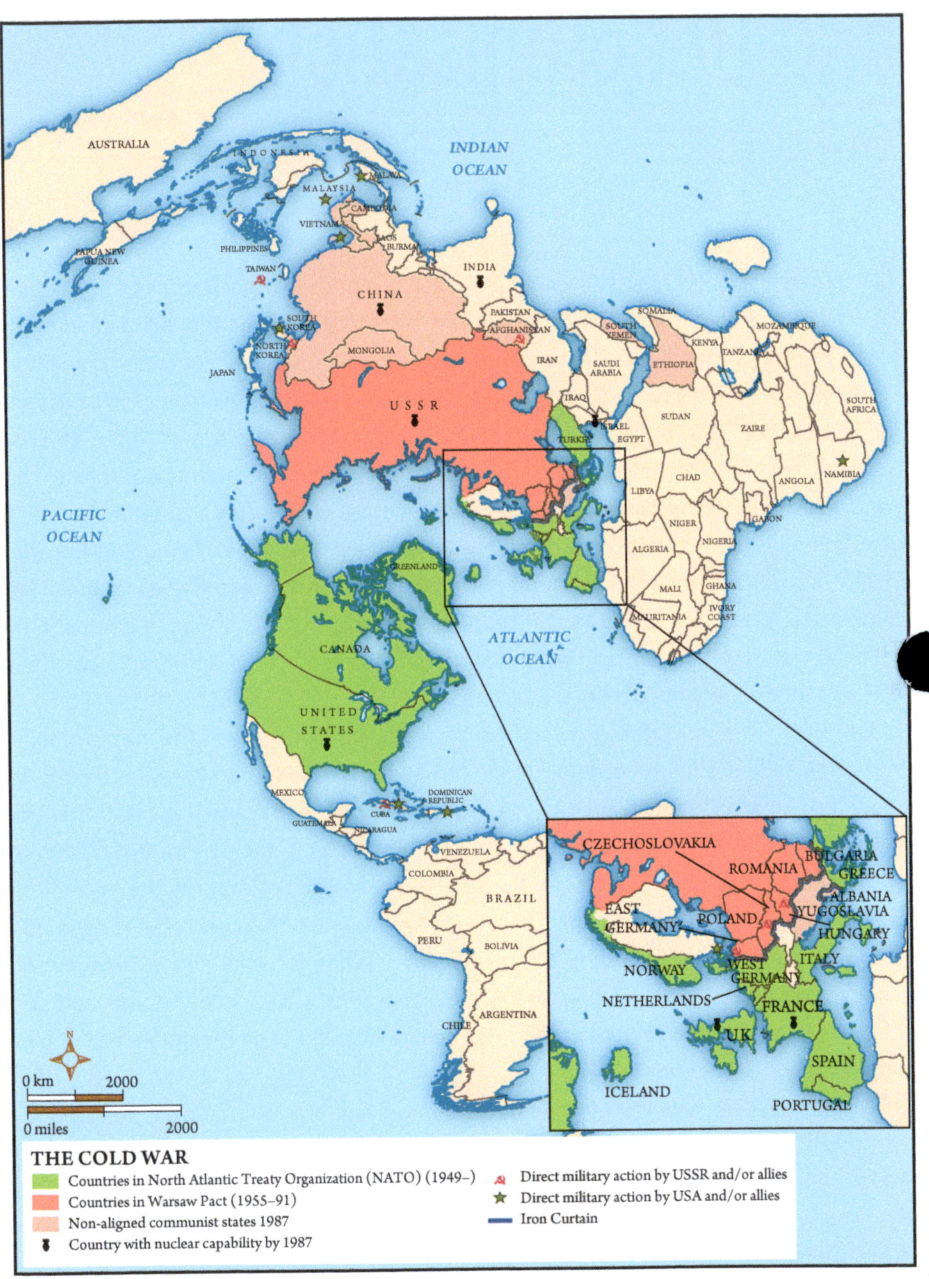

Map 12.1 The Cold War

government and territorial limits that independent Poland would have after the war. Such disputes, played out in a series of meetings between the leaders of these countries, nurtured suspicions that would dominate global relations in the coming decades.

The agonizing history of postwar Angola, in southwest Africa, highlights those suspicions. In January 1975, leaders of three armed factions signed an agreement with the Portuguese government to work together toward a peaceful transition to independence for Angola. Portugal, like Europe's other imperial powers, had moved aggressively to establish colonies in Africa after the Conference of Berlin in 1888. During the first half of the twentieth century, Angola, rich in natural resources, became an important source of wealth for Portugal, whose government encouraged Portuguese colonists to settle there.

After the Second World War, as movements for the self-determination of African peoples accelerated, the Portuguese refused to consider Angolan independence. In the 1960s, armed guerillas forming around regional, ethnic, and ideological affinities created civil unrest. A coup d'état in Portugal in 1974 proved to be a turning point for the relationship with Angola. Leaders of the new regime committed to a transition to independence in Angola and signed an accord with three major rebel groups. Rather than peace, civil war and a refugee crisis ensued.

In the months after the transition agreement was signed, the South African government—controlled by a white minority that had enshrined formal racial segregation (apartheid) into its laws beginning in the 1940s—moved troops into Angola, supporting its own interests as well as anti-communist armed factions in Angola. The US Central Intelligence Agency ran operations out of neighboring Zaire. China and the USSR provided support to competing Marxist groups. In late 1975, Cuban president Fidel Castro (1926–2016) committed thirty thousand Cuban ground troops to support the communist People's Movement for the Liberation of Angola. Factional strife, financed by external aid and the export of diamonds and oil, tore Angola apart for decades.

The Warsaw Ghetto Uprising and the Civil War in Angola, different as they are, reflect important aspects of the dilemmas encountered in rebuilding global relationships in the twentieth century. Extreme nationalism and racialist theories hitched to technologies of destruction produced the Holocaust: mass murder presented as rational progress. Fascist governments in Japan, Germany, Italy, and elsewhere distorted some modern ideals and rejected others, denying political rights to millions of people and glorifying militarism.

The Allies who fought the Second World War to end fascism disagreed on how to rebuild the world after the war. Warsaw had become capital of an independent Poland under the principle of *self-determination of peoples*, after World War I, and Britain entered the Second World War to protect Polish sovereignty. But after the war, Poland became embroiled in the emerging conflict between the United States and the Soviet Union. This face-off recurred frequently as new nation-states, formed through postwar decolonization, became embroiled in the superpowers' conflict.

In the first section of this chapter, we explore how the Second World War Allies began to plan the contours of a postwar world in the midst of the war itself. Determining how the lessons of the first four decades of the twentieth century would be turned into institutions and policies depended to a large degree, but not entirely, on the actions of the dominant military powers that emerged from the war—the United States and the Soviet Union. After World War II, an emerging universal language of human rights, self-determination, democracy, and economic development manifested real actions and outcomes within a global context of persistent inequality in the distribution of material resources, competing interpretations of the lessons from the past, and clashing programs for humankind's future.

In the section that follows, we map out regional variations of how the global superpowers traded arms and economic aid for expressions of loyalty from leaders of other nation-states—or aspiring nation-states—in a *cold war*, simultaneously attempting to undermine rivals through diplomacy, violence, espionage, and even cultural combat. As we have seen throughout this book, however, at times individuals and groups around the globe have used a variety of tools at their disposal to influence events, sometimes out of any proportion to their material resources. In the final section of the chapter, we examine attempts to establish political and economic movements that transcended the bipolar confines of the Cold War.

Questions to Consider as You Read Chapter Twelve:

1. How did the experience of World War II shape ideas about human rights? What actions were taken to protect these ideas, and what limitations prevented these protections from being fully realized?
2. In the aftermath of World War II, numerous international structures and institutions were developed. In what ways did these new institutions represent a break with the past? In what ways did they resemble their predecessors?

Uncomfortable Allies Plan the Future

The closing days of the Second World War in Europe revealed the scale of fascist atrocities. At Nazi death camps like Treblinka and others, Allied soldiers discovered piles of corpses, crematoria, and other evidence of mass murder on an unprecedented scale. These discoveries confirmed for the Big Five allies—the United States, Soviet Union, Great Britain, France, and China—the justice of their war. Even before these discoveries, the Allies began planning for a postwar global order that would oppose fascism and be based on "common principles in the national policies of their respective countries on which they base their hopes for a better future for the world." These words became the core of a Declaration of the United Nations, approved in January 1942 by twenty-six countries, including the major Allies. In addition to reiterating a commitment to the destruction of "Nazi tyranny," the signatories agreed to seek no "aggrandizement, territorial, or other" from the current conflict and that both "victor and vanquished" would be given equal access to economic opportunity after the war. In other words, the Allies were repudiating the victors' justice that shaped the treaties ending the First World War. In the long shadow of the Great Depression, they agreed to bring about global cooperation to secure "improved labor standards, economic advancement and social security." Despite the veneer of unity, deep tensions divided the Allies, especially the United States and the Soviet Union. The two countries agreed that they were fighting against fascism, but they had very different ideas of how to build a future around what they were fighting for.

Origins of the Cold War

In July 1944, delegates from forty-four countries met at a resort in the White Mountains of New Hampshire to lay the groundwork for the economic future. The Bretton Woods Accords, named for the location of the meeting, established a blueprint by which the international financial system would be managed in the coming decades through organizations like the International Monetary Fund, the World Bank, and the World Trade Organization. Although a Soviet delegation participated in the conference at Bretton Woods, the USSR never endorsed the conference agreements and did not join the institutions built on their principles. The vision of a limited state, free trade, and a consumer society was at odds with the Soviets' faith in a centrally directed economy, with state planners determining production quotas and the distribution of resources. Both sides of this divide trumpeted democracy as foundational to their preferred systems, but their definitions and road maps for implementation of this ideal varied greatly.

Different visions of the future also manifested at a series of meetings among the leaders of the United States, Great Britain, and the Soviet Union. In Tehran (1943), Yalta (February 1945), and Potsdam (July–August 1945), the three countries disputed over tactics in the last stages of the war but also over the fate of defeated territories, especially Germany and Eastern Europe. Illustrating the emerging conflict between the United States and the USSR, the American atomic bomb dropped on Hiroshima caught the Soviets completely by surprise. It happened just four days after the end of the Potsdam Conference, but the atomic bomb's existence was not shared with the Soviet delegates. The United States dropped a second bomb three days later, and Japan surrendered just six days after that, much sooner than anyone had expected. With the war suddenly ending, the former allies rushed to secure their interests around the world.

Institutions and individuals escalated tensions between the Soviet Union and the United States. Winston Churchill asserted that communist movements around the world "are established and work in complete unity and absolute obedience to the directions they receive from the Communist center": Moscow. He used the phrase *iron curtain* to describe Soviet machinations that were isolating Poland and the rest of Eastern Europe from the broader world. To prevent Soviet expansion, the states of western Europe, the United States, and Canada formed an alliance: the North Atlantic Treaty Organization.

Stalin responded that the Soviet Union lost many more people in the Second World War than the British and Americans combined and asserted that the communist resistance had been the staunchest anti-fascist fighting force in Nazi-occupied Europe, conveniently ignoring the secret nonaggression pact he had signed with Hitler at the war's beginning. He concluded that it was therefore in the interest of both the Soviet Union and the peoples of east-central and Eastern Europe to establish communist governments that would be reliable allies of the USSR. These allies would later be formalized as the Warsaw Pact, a political and military organization established as a Soviet counterpart to the North Atlantic Treaty Organization.

In response, US president Harry Truman (1884–1972) committed the United States to a policy of containment that would prevent communists from coming to power in additional countries. Thus, Allied unity against fascist aggression had become a bipolar power struggle, embodied most vividly in the ongoing conflicts over Germany. Because the occupiers could not agree on the defeated enemy's future, two separate countries were established in 1949, a communist German Democratic Republic (East Germany), allied with the Soviet Union, and the German Federal Republic (West Germany), supported by the United States and western Europe. The situation was novel and tense (neither state was admitted to the United Nations until 1973), especially in Berlin, where Soviet, American, French, and British forces divided the city itself. Churchill's Iron Curtain eventually took concrete form in 1961 when the East German government erected the Berlin Wall, a militarized boundary nearly one hundred miles long separating the communist from the non-communist sectors of Berlin and the city's residents from each other.

The Search for Common Ground

When the Big Five sat together to figure out how to reorder the world as the fighting drew to a close, they were vastly different in terms of material assets, ideological frameworks, and visions of the future. The two most powerful states—the

United States and the Soviet Union—differed fundamentally on economic and political goals. Great Britain and France were struggling to regain stature in a world where western European military and economic might no longer dominated. By 1946, the battered Chinese republic was again embroiled in a civil war that Chiang Kai-shek would lose to Mao Zedong's communist insurgency. All these countries, except the United States, were physically devastated by the war and struggling to rebuild infrastructure and institutions. The United States, by contrast, had suffered many casualties (though the fewest of any of the major combatants), but its economy was now fully recovered from the Great Depression and embarking on the longest period of sustained economic growth the world had yet known.

Given these vastly different circumstances, defining common interests and the mechanisms to serve them was difficult. The representatives of fifty countries who came together to form the United Nations just two months after the Japanese surrender ended the war claimed multiple goals in the organization's charter, including saving succeeding generations from war, reaffirming the existence of fundamental human rights, the dignity of the human person, and the basic equality of all nations regardless of size or resources. The signatories agreed to work to create a framework of international law that would support these principles, as well as create better standards of living and "social progress" for all the world's peoples.

Early successes bolstered the international community that had committed to these goals. Acting without precedent, special tribunals held in Germany and Japan established new rules for conduct in war and convicted perpetrators of the Holocaust and other crimes against humanity. As further evidence emerged of what had happened in the Nazi death camps, widespread condemnation fueled hopes that such crimes would be impossible to perpetrate in the future. World War I had not turned out to be the war to end wars; but perhaps World War II, which brought the globe to the brink of annihilation, could inspire a new era of international harmony through the United Nations (UN).

United Nations

Three issues—involving power, participation, and principle—demonstrate both the enormous potential and the inherent limitations of forming an international community committed to realizing common ideals. First, power: although the UN Charter asserted that "the Organization is based on the principle of the sovereign equality of all its Members," the five wartime Allies received permanent seats on the UN's most powerful body, the Security Council, and each had veto power over key initiatives. Some have argued that this created an organization that merely served the interests of these most powerful nations; others contended that this created a more durable institution than the League of Nations by reducing the odds that the key actors on the global stage might exit the institution and doom it, as had happened to the League.

Second, participation: although the organization aspired to universality, most of the world's subject peoples were not fully represented when the UN was formed. This was denounced as a concession to the postwar western European powers who wanted to retain their empires, yet others have pointed out that the UN created a space where demands for self-determination could be aired and, in some cases, resolved by the international community.

Third, principles: as we have seen previously, the victorious allies in World War II defined basic political and economic concepts differently. Critics of the UN argued that, depending on the interpretation, the meaning of the concepts expressed by the institution skewed to one side or the other in the growing Cold War confrontation. Supporters of the institution responded that the highest aspirations of the international community were expressed in documents like the 1948 Universal Declaration of Human Rights. Some features of this document harkened back to John Locke and other Enlightenment philosophers, but others responded to the realities of an era more intertwined and more unequal than any in human history. The UN proved to be more durable, its scope of activity much broader, and its accomplishments more tangible than its predecessor. And its membership grew rapidly, as the political geography of the postwar world was transformed by the anguished construction of dozens of new nation-states.

The Global Cold War

The UN Charter reaffirmed "equal rights and self-determination of peoples" as universal organizing principles for the postwar world. Colonialism, which was built on the idea of inequality, was thus ideologically unsustainable, but attempting to turn principle into practice often resulted in bloodshed and displacement. As we have seen, a mixture of cynical politics, philanthropy, racism, and greed had driven imperialism in the nineteenth century, as Western companies and Western products spread alongside Western power. Colonies provided raw materials, markets, and labor. At the end of the Second World War, European countries including France, Britain, the Netherlands, and Portugal seemed in no rush to give up their colonies, even though in principle all were committed to self-determination for the world's peoples.

Violent wars of independence ensued. One million people died in Algeria (1954–1962). One hundred thousand perished in the Dutch East Indies (1945–1949) and Congo (1960–1966). There were dozens of other smaller wars as well. Achieving independence in Africa and Asia drained human and material resources, heightened factionalism among forces fighting for independence, and cast suspicion on the motives of international organizations in which the former imperial powers played important roles. The Cold War complicated the process of decolonization and state formation, as competing nationalist and anti-imperialist factions found ideological (and often practical) support from the Soviets or the United States.

East and Southeast Asia

In East Asia, after the withdrawal of Japanese troops, war resumed between communist and non-communist factions throughout the region, even as European powers returned to their colonial possessions. Chiang Kai-shek's Republic of China was a founding member of the UN and held one of five permanent seats on the Security Council, but in 1949, its wartime ally, the Chinese Communist Party led by Mao Zedong, forced Chiang's government to flee to the island province of Taiwan. In the spring of 1950, it was widely expected that an invasion from the mainland would complete the communist victory. The United States, which had supported Chiang's government throughout the war, indicated publicly and privately that it would not intervene against the anticipated invasion from the newly founded People's Republic of China.

All this changed in the autumn of 1950 when attempts to peacefully reunify the Korean Peninsula failed. Korea, like Germany, had been divided into temporary administrative zones of communist and non-communist influence at the end of the war. North Korean communist troops invaded the south to reunify the country by force, leading the UN to condemn the action and form the first multinational armed force (from sixteen countries) to operate under its auspices. The Soviet Union could have vetoed entry into the war, but at the time it was boycotting the Security Council in an effort to force the UN to seat the Communist People's Republic of China in place of the defeated Republic of China. China's new communist government then entered the Korean conflict, seeing the UN army as a tool of the United States, which provided the largest number of troops. The war resulted in a standoff and an uneasy settlement that divided the peninsula into a communist North Korea and a non-communist South Korea.

More than one million people died in the Korean War, but it was also significant because it reinforced Cold War frames of reference. The containment policy that guided US foreign policy in Europe—driving American aid to anti-communist forces in Greece and Turkey, for instance—was now applied in East Asia. The United States redefined its defensive strategy to stop the spread of communism, reversing its policy on Taiwan and bringing the island within the American defensive perimeter, where it remained a focal point of the Cold

War for decades. In addition to basing thousands of troops in South Korea, the United States also restored formal sovereignty to Japan after years of US occupation. The new Japanese government allowed the United States to develop military bases and station troops on its territory as part of a bulwark against communist expansion.

Throughout Asia, the legacies of colonialism promoted unlikely alliances. National independence movements had grown up against the French in Indochina (today's Vietnam, Laos, and Cambodia); the Dutch in what is today Indonesia; and the British in today's Malaysia, Myanmar, and Singapore. The same factors that spurred Europe's new imperialism motivated the Japanese advance into Southeast Asia, including the search for industrial raw materials like oil, rubber, and metals. The Japanese, however, presented themselves as *anti*-imperialists who would ally against the European colonial powers to create, as their official slogan proclaimed, "Asia for the Asiatics." In Burma, Indonesia, and elsewhere in Southeast Asia, many rebels allied with the Japanese, perhaps taking the Japanese at their word or perhaps simply seeing an opportunity to be rid of their European overlords. Others remained loyal to European colonial governments, hoping to be rewarded with autonomy or independence at war's end. Still others operated in the gaps between the warring powers, hoping to establish themselves as an independent force.

In this context, individuals and groups had overlapping and sometimes contradictory identities and affiliations. Vietnamese nationalist Nguyen Ai Quoc, whom the World War I allies had rejected at Versailles in 1919 (as we saw in Chapter 10), traveled afterward to Moscow, where he trained with the Comintern before finding his way back to Indochina during the 1930s. Despite his time in Moscow, Nguyen Ai Quoc—now called Ho Chi Minh—was ideologically pragmatic, working with American military intelligence and helping to rescue American pilots shot down over Vietnam during the Second World War while still maintaining his connections with the Comintern. Ho seized the opportunity of the sudden Japanese surrender to declare Vietnamese independence. Always aware that to succeed, his movement would need support from at least one of the world's superpowers—but not caring too much which it would be—he drafted a declaration of Vietnamese independence designed to appeal to both the Soviets and the Americans. In it, he quoted extensively from the US Declaration of Independence (a copy of which had been provided by American intelligence agents) while also citing orthodox Marxist theory.

Ho's statement depicts both the long influence of Enlightenment ideals and the extent to which colonialism had exposed their hypocrisy. The Vietnamese Declaration of Independence notes that "for more than eighty years, the French imperialists, abusing the standard of Liberty, Equality, and Fraternity,

Saigon Under Siege, May 1968. During the first half of 1968, North Vietnamese forces and Viet Cong (South Vietnamese communists) launched a major attack on strategic positions across South Vietnam, including Saigon, the capital city. Cholon, the Chinese section of Saigon shown in this photograph, was badly damaged by both the original attacks and the South Vietnamese/US counterattack. The Vietnam War, which grew out of the Vietnamese anticolonial struggle against France, became one of the longest and bloodiest confrontations of the global Cold War. More than a million Vietnamese and fifty-eight thousand Americans died in the conflict.

have violated our Fatherland and oppressed our fellow citizens. They have acted contrary to the ideals of humanity and justice." Ho Chi Minh's observation reflected an important contradiction of the era. The French Revolution promised equal rights to "all men," and France took great pride in its history of "liberty, equality, and brotherhood," yet France aggressively opposed nationalist movements in its colonies that tried to implement those principles. Eager to reclaim its empire, in which colonial subjects were explicitly denied equal rights, France sent armies across Asia and Africa, including Vietnam, Algeria, Cameroon, Madagascar, and elsewhere. Like France, Great Britain took great pride in its tradition of democracy and civil rights. Like France, it feared the demise of its empire, but the British postwar path was different, in large part due to events in South Asia.

Gandhi and the Indian Subcontinent

Mohandas Gandhi, the foremost advocate for Indian independence, was much more than just an Indian nationalist. His role in the Indian home rule movement fundamentally altered the ways that people address power relations. In fact, his tactics and teachings have become an essential part of understanding the modern world. Gandhi's 1909 book *Hind Swaraj* (Indian Home Rule) articulated two crucial concepts: true civilization and civil resistance. Both these ideas rejected common understandings of what the world should look like and how it should work.

Gandhi challenged those who continued to speak reverently of the order and progress that resulted from industrial regimentation. Gandhi rejected the idea that machines held the promise of progress. Quite the opposite, he asserted: "Formerly, men worked in the open air only so much as they liked. Now, thousands of workmen meet together and for the sake of maintenance work in factories or mines. Their condition is worse than that of beasts." And to those who held up Europe as the apex of civilization, Gandhi responded that material

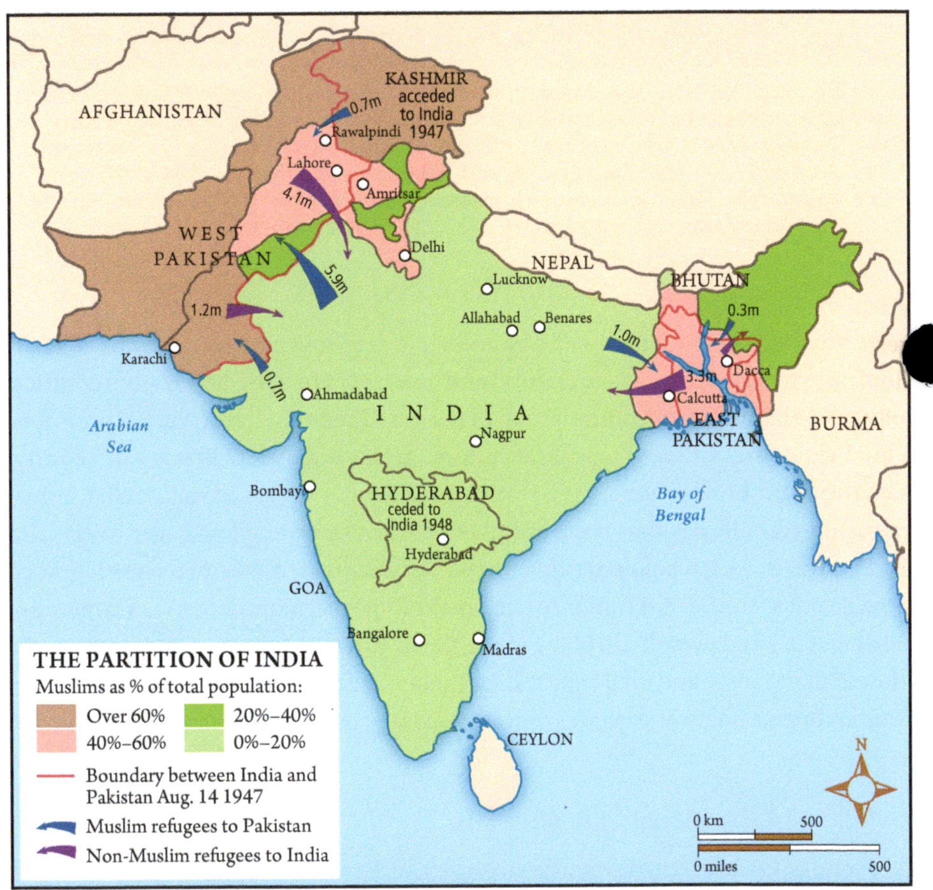

Map 12.2 The Partition of India

obsessions had "taken such a hold on the people in Europe that those who are in it appear to be half mad. . . . This civilization is such that one has only to be patient and it will be self-destroyed."

This belief that Western civilization was morally flawed and unsustainable led Gandhi to reject violence—which he saw as the instrument of imperialism—as a means of achieving independence. This was a radical split from many anti-colonial nationalists in India and elsewhere. Gandhi believed that nonviolent resistance required more courage and moral strength than armed resistance. Even in the wake of atrocities like the Amritsar Massacre, Gandhi was steadfast in his commitment to nonviolence. Rather than military campaigns or violent insurrection, Gandhi opposed British rule by calling on his followers to make their own salt (to undermine a British monopoly on salt production) and spin their own cloth (rather than buy cheap British textiles). When he wished to emphasize his resolute disapproval—of either his supporters or his opponents—he would go on a hunger strike, but he never resorted to violence. This strategy strengthened his stature and frustrated his opponents, who had no effective means of response to someone who, as Gandhi wrote, "will not obey a law that is against his conscience, even though he may be blown to pieces at the mouth of a cannon." Winston Churchill dismissed Gandhi as a "half-naked fakir," but Gandhi's prediction that his strategy and tactics would bring victory proved correct. On January 1, 1947, India became an independent state.

It would be a happy ending to learn that Gandhi's doctrine of nonviolence changed politics forever. Perhaps, after decades of war and genocide, civil resistance had shown the way to a peaceful future. Such was not the reality, however. Even as India was born, it splintered. Over Gandhi's strenuous objections, communal divisions, based on religion, destroyed his dream of a unified, independent India before it could be realized. Promoting such divisions had for decades been a policy of the British in India, who thought they would help prevent nationalists from unifying. Majority Muslim parts of India—the northwestern and eastern border regions—became the independent state of Pakistan. (East Pakistan would later secede from Pakistan, becoming Bangladesh in 1971.) The partition of India was bloody. Many Muslims in Indian territory and Hindus in Pakistani territory began to relocate voluntarily or out of fear. The mass migration led to instability and then violence. More than ten million people moved during 1947, and between five hundred thousand and one million people died. One of those casualties might be said to be Gandhi himself. He was shot at close range by a Hindu extremist who felt Gandhi had been too accommodating of Muslims.

Historians Explore Kenya and Decolonization

Postwar Africa presented the greatest challenge to the integrity of the global commitment to self-determination. Kenya illustrates several important themes for understanding why. It shows that the rhetoric of self-determination accompanying the end of World War I had little impact on European policies outside of Europe. Although significant numbers of Europeans arrived in Kenya in the 1850s and Britain declared it a protectorate in 1895, it did not become a formal colony until 1920, after the peace treaty endorsing self-determination.

From the beginning, indigenous people resisted the European presence, which provoked major rebellions in the 1880s, 1910s, and 1940s. British policy in the region was extraordinarily violent; one member of Parliament remarked in the 1890s that the main beneficiary of Britain's colonization of Kenya seemed to be Hiram Maxim (1840–1916), the inventor of the machine gun. What formerly had been a prosperous, fertile region became increasingly violent and dispossessed of resources, with profits and people—first slaves and later soldiers—extracted for the benefit of Europeans. During the Second World War, while Kenyan soldiers fought for the British Empire, wartime austerity and inflation reinforced poverty at home.

At war's end, violence in East Africa mounted. Winston Churchill worried to aides that the slaughter in Kenya, if widely known, would hamper British policies around the globe. In 1952, a movement called Mau Mau responded by embracing violence of its own. Mau Mau mobilized people from the Kikuyu region of northwest Kenya against policies that took land from Africans and then forced many of them to work this same land—now owned by Europeans—for low wages. The origins of the movement are unclear; even the meaning of the term *Mau Mau* is disputed.

Colonial rulers portrayed the Mau Mau as a terrorist organization of hooligans and savages. Although attacks on Europeans were brutal and highly publicized, most Mau Mau violence was directed at other Africans. The many divisions within African society—some encouraged or even created by the colonial authorities—belie neat categories of resistance fighters or collaborators. Pursuing a strategy to separate loyalists from rebels, the colonial government collected Kenyans into villages surrounded by barricades and booby-traps, similar to the strategic hamlets that the United States would establish in Vietnam a decade later. The colonial state also brought overwhelming firepower to bear against the Mau Mau. By the time the war ended, the Mau Mau had killed about two thousand people (only about thirty of them Europeans). The number of Mau Mau killed is difficult to estimate, but twenty thousand or more seems plausible.

Among those apprehended as part of the Mau Mau movement was Jomo Kenyatta (ca. 1891–1978). Jailed as a leader and manager of the uprising, Kenyatta had studied in London and Moscow during the 1920s and 1930s, becoming

British Police Guarding Mau Mau Suspects, April 28, 1953. Most decolonization struggles were bloody and destructive on all sides. The Mau Mau Rebellion (1952–1960) in Kenya illustrated this. Both the British colonial state and the Mau Mau fighters massacred civilians, including children. British officials implemented a system of concentration camps, designed to isolate the rebels from the population, and used torture to gather intelligence about the movement.

committed to an end to British rule in Kenya. Along with Kwame Nkrumah and others, he was a prominent leader in the pan-African movement and was first president of the Kenyan African Union Party, which advocated for Kenyan independence. He was not involved directly in the Mau Mau movement but was still sentenced to a lengthy prison term. In 1961, after mass demonstrations in the capital of Nairobi, Kenyatta was released from detention. He resumed his position of leadership and was the principal Kenyan negotiator at the talks leading to Kenyan independence in 1963.

The Mau Mau wars offer another chance to view how interpretations and analyses of history change over time and also how questions of politics, perspectives, and sources shape historical debate. Supporters of British imperialism depicted it as more beneficent and humane than what other European powers practiced. In many early historical accounts, the British process of decolonization was presented in similar fashion. Recent scholarship responds with the Kenyan case, offering evidence suggesting the British were just as cruel as the Mau Mau and much more systematic. Historian Caroline Elkins has argued that colonial officials used a system of labor and detention camps, along with strategic hamlets, to carry out "a murderous campaign to eliminate Kikuyu people" that she compares to the Nazi Holocaust. Other scholars reject the comparisons with Nazism and the implications that the Mau Mau and the colonial government were in any way equivalent. Recently, Niall Ferguson ignited a new round of debate with a sweeping and contentious assessment of British imperialism in its entirety. Ferguson, who does not discuss the Mau Mau war, acknowledges that violence was a regular component of the imperial enterprise but concludes that British imperialism was beneficial to the world generally and to the subject peoples of the British Empire specifically.[1]

Superpowers and Decolonization

The European empires—France and Britain especially—were forced to accept a new world in which their international leverage was greatly reduced. In one case, the British and French combined forces to roll back decolonization, invading Egypt in 1956 to reverse Egyptian president Gamal Abdel Nasser's (1918–1970) nationalization of the Suez Canal. Although the British and French forces, aided by Israel, achieved their military objectives, pressure from the United States and the Soviet Union forced them to withdraw. The failure of France and Britain to enforce their interests illustrated the extent to which both had lost power. The new superpowers—the United States and the Soviet Union—considered decolonization important but filtered their understandings of the process through their own confrontation. The United States agreed to formal independence for the Philippines at the end of World War II and reiterated its commitment to self-determination, although it did not enforce this principle consistently: Hawai'i was incorporated formally into US statehood in 1959. Other territories, like Puerto Rico, remained under US control without full political representation for their people.

In Asia, events in Korea reinforced the commitment to the containment policy, which prioritized anti-communism over respect for rights and elections. South Korea and Taiwan developed into anti-communist, single-party police states. Under the umbrella of containment, the United States became deeply involved in the internal affairs of countries in the Western Hemisphere and the Middle East as well. In 1953, the United States and Great Britain covertly funded and supported

1 Judicious historical overviews of the end of the British Empire, which help to situate the debates among scholars, are found in Judith M. Brown and William Roger Louis, eds., *The Oxford History of the British Empire*, vol. 4, *The Twentieth Century* (New York: Oxford University Press, 2001); David Anderson, *Histories of the Hanged: Britain's Dirty War in Kenya and the End of Empire* (New York: W. W. Norton, 2005); Caroline Elkins, *Imperial Reckoning: The Untold Story of Britain's Gulag in Kenya* (New York: Holt, 2005); Daniel Branch, *Defeating Mau Mau, Creating Kenya: Counterinsurgency, Civil War and Decolonization* (New York: Cambridge University Press, 2009); Huw Bennett, *Fighting the Mau Mau: The British Army and Counter-Insurgency in the Kenya Emergency* (New York: Cambridge University Press, 2013); and Niall Ferguson, *Empire: How Britain Made the Modern World* (New York: Penguin, 2012).

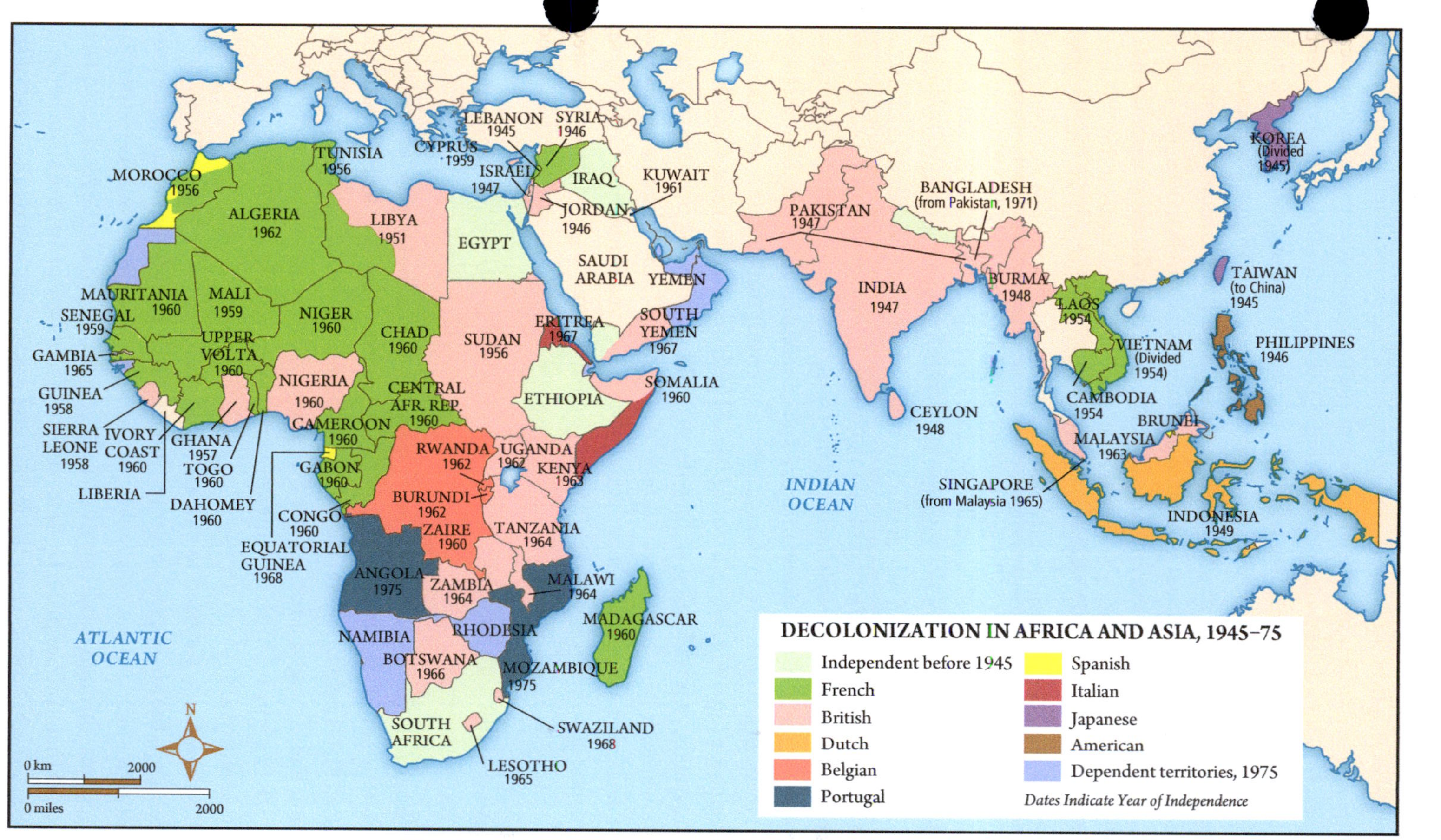
DECOLONIZATION IN AFRICA AND ASIA, 1945–75
Independent before 1945
French
British
Dutch
Belgian
Portugal
Spanish
Italian
Japanese
American
Dependent territories, 1975
Dates Indicate Year of Independence
ATLANTIC OCEAN
INDIAN OCEAN
MOROCCO 1956
TUNISIA 1956
ALGERIA 1962
LIBYA 1951
EGYPT
MAURITANIA 1960
MALI 1959
NIGER 1960
CHAD 1960
SUDAN 1956
SENEGAL 1959
GAMBIA 1965
GUINEA 1958
SIERRA LEONE 1958
LIBERIA
IVORY COAST 1960
UPPER VOLTA 1960
GHANA 1957
TOGO 1960
DAHOMEY 1960
NIGERIA 1960
CAMEROON 1960
CENTRAL AFR. REP. 1960
GABON 1960
CONGO 1960
EQUATORIAL GUINEA 1968
ERITREA 1967
ETHIOPIA
SOMALIA 1960
UGANDA 1962
KENYA 1963
RWANDA 1962
BURUNDI 1962
ZAIRE 1960
TANZANIA 1964
ANGOLA 1975
ZAMBIA 1964
MALAWI 1964
MADAGASCAR 1960
NAMIBIA
RHODESIA
BOTSWANA 1966
MOZAMBIQUE 1975
SOUTH AFRICA
SWAZILAND 1968
LESOTHO 1965
CYPRUS 1959
LEBANON 1945
SYRIA 1946
ISRAEL 1947
IRAQ
JORDAN 1946
KUWAIT 1961
SAUDI ARABIA
YEMEN
SOUTH YEMEN 1967
PAKISTAN 1947
BANGLADESH (from Pakistan, 1971)
INDIA 1947
CEYLON 1948
BURMA 1948
LAOS 1954
VIETNAM (Divided 1954)
CAMBODIA 1954
MALAYSIA 1963
BRUNEI
SINGAPORE (from Malaysia 1965)
INDONESIA 1949
PHILIPPINES 1946
TAIWAN (to China) 1945
KOREA (Divided 1945)
N
0 km
2000
0 miles
2000

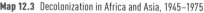

Map 12.3 Decolonization in Africa and Asia, 1945–1975

a coup d'état in Iran, after the elected government had nationalized its oil industry and jeopardized assets of British Petroleum. The following year, using similar techniques, the United States supported a coup against the Guatemalan government, which had enacted an agrarian reform that promised to disrupt the operations of the Boston-based United Fruit Company. The new regimes in Iran and Guatemala supported the United States for much of the Cold War, but the memories of these actions inflamed subsequent generations of anti-American activists. The coup in Guatemala convinced a visiting Argentine doctor named Ernesto "Che" Guevara (1928–1967) that his life's work lay in fomenting revolution against the US imperialists. Che Guevara would go on to lead the Cuban revolution with Fidel Castro, and he stated in his 1967 address to the Tricontinental Congress in Havana that he would work to "create two, three . . . many Vietnams throughout the world."

While Guevara and others railed against US imperialism, Soviet forces brutally suppressed dissent in Hungary (1956) and Czechoslovakia (1968). Although the Gulag system was drastically reduced after Stalin's death in 1953, the Soviet government continued to stifle political debate by defining Communist Party decisions as the people's will. As they sought new allies, the two superpowers found themselves in direct military and economic *aid wars* and indirect conflict through *proxy wars*, sponsoring overt and covert military operations around the globe, as in 1974, when a Soviet-backed military faction took control of an increasingly chaotic Ethiopia. They deposed Emperor Haile Selassie (returned to power with British assistance during World War II), abolished the monarchy, and declared a Marxist-Leninist future. Over the next decade, tens of thousands of regime opponents were executed, imprisoned without trial, or driven to exile.

Economic Development and Nonalignment: Three Worlds?

At the end of World War II, there were several indisputable facts about how global economic power had changed since the start of the Great War in 1914. First, the United States held three-quarters of the world's gold reserves. Second, the Soviet Union had managed a remarkable feat of industrialization since the collapse of the tsarist regime. Third, the European economies were in ruins; the same could be said of Japan.

To these facts, we need to add an assumption shared by most of the world's elites across the ideological spectrum: industrialization was the key to future prosperity. This included not only building factories to make goods but also improving agriculture through mechanization and chemical fertilizers. Beyond these facts and this shared assumption lay fierce debates about how to achieve sustained economic growth, how to avoid the regular and devastating booms and busts of the previous century, how to fairly distribute the world's resources (both within countries and across political boundaries), and how the Cold War would shape responses to these questions.

Khrushchev and Castro, New York City, 1960. Fidel Castro (1926–2016) came to power in January 1959 at the head of a revolutionary nationalist movement that overthrew a staunch US ally and soon thereafter nationalized US-owned businesses in Cuba, triggering a US embargo. In the shadow of the embargo, Cuba began to trade sugar for oil with the USSR. During this era, Nikita Khrushchev (1894–1971) was serving as both first secretary of the Communist Party and Soviet premier. This photo, from September 1960, records the first time the two men met while in New York City for the United Nations General Assembly. Later that month, Castro delivered the longest speech ever delivered at the United Nations, clocking in at almost five hours. At the end of 1961, Castro openly declared his commitment to a Marxist-Leninist future for Cuba.

Rebuilding Global Economic Relations

The policymakers who met at Bretton Woods during the Second World War sought to build a postwar global capitalist economy on predictable transnational financial exchanges and (relatively) free trade. The productive power of the US economy and its stockpile of gold—much of the world's known reserves—would form the bedrock of this new economic order. For the quarter century after the war's end, most of the world's currencies were fixed in relationship to the US dollar, and the value of the dollar itself was pegged to a precise amount of gold. Over forty countries subscribed to an International Monetary Fund, setting aside government assets to maintain monetary stability. Funds were contributed in proportion to the size of a country's economy, and decision-making was apportioned in the same way so that wealthier countries had a greater say in how and when the funds of the International Monetary Fund would be accessed.

A second institution to emerge from Bretton Woods was the International Bank for Reconstruction and Development: the World Bank. Whereas the International Monetary Fund was designed to smooth out hiccups in global currency transactions, the World Bank, through direct loans and guarantees of private loans, would "help in the restoration of economies destroyed or disrupted by war, the reconversion of productive facilities to peacetime needs, and the development of productive facilities and resources in less developed countries."

A third item on the minds of negotiators at Bretton Woods was global trade, but key decisions on trade agreements and tariffs were postponed until after the war. Negotiations to establish an International Trade Organization failed in the face of US opposition. A different treaty, the General Agreement on Tariffs and Trade, which the United States did champion, was signed by only twenty-three countries because many developing countries saw the treaty provisions as blocking their industrialization prospects. In addition to the General Agreement on Tariffs and Trade, regional trade agreements and bilateral treaties, including two in Europe, were designed to facilitate international commerce.

One of the largest factors in shaping the postwar global economy was the European Recovery Program, commonly referred to as the Marshall Plan after the 1947 Harvard University commencement speech by US secretary of state George Marshall announcing the policy. Stalin's Soviet Union forbade its Eastern European allies from accepting Marshall Plan funds, but billions of dollars from the United States helped to rebuild sixteen western European countries between 1948 and 1952. The funds were used to purchase food, fuel, and machines (mostly imported from the United States) as well as to create a pool of money for loans to private businesses.

The United States, which occupied Japan from 1945 to 1952, also played a large role in creating the circumstances under which the Japanese economy would recover. The Japanese postwar constitution (written in English by American lawyers before being translated into Japanese) included a clause forbidding Japan from maintaining a military. With the United States providing security, Japan was freed to invest in infrastructure and industrialization. Through well-coordinated public–private partnerships to manage its postwar recovery, the Japanese economy grew rapidly.

These strategies produced remarkable results. Global economic growth between 1950 and 1973 averaged 5 percent per year. The value of international trade rose even faster, growing at almost 10 percent per year between 1948 and 1973. The marketplaces of western Europe and the United States filled with consumer goods. These numbers hide some underlying problems, however. First, the vast increase in global trade was driven primarily by increases in the value of manufactured goods and less by an increase in the volume of goods traded. Second, the long-term trend in the global economy appeared to favor the economic fortunes of those countries exporting mostly industrial goods rather than primary products like agricultural staples. In this environment, the world's leaders committed their countries to industrialization as the key to future prosperity.

Models for Development

There is no simple formula for industrialization. Two major models emerged in capitalist economies. One, most popular in Latin America, was import substitution industrialization, which focused on developing a manufacturing base to meet domestic demand. Tariffs and other government policies allowed local industries to grow without being undermined by imported goods. Often, the state controlled privileged industries. The other model, export-led industrialization, required countries to hold down wages and domestic consumption to develop industries that could compete quickly in the international marketplace. The so-called Asian Tiger economies—Hong Kong, Singapore, South Korea, and Taiwan—employed this strategy. Both seemed to work in their own way. The growing population of Mexico purchased shirts and shoes produced in domestic factories built with cement produced domestically, with machines fueled by a state-owned petroleum company. Annual economic growth averaged 6 percent for decades. In South Korea, annual growth rates exceeded the projections of government planners, averaging more than 10 percent per year in the late 1960s. In both countries, government policy actively influenced economic planning and resource allocation.

Eastern Europe, China, North Korea, and North Vietnam implemented communist models of political economy. Organizing production and consumption in a centralized manner appeared viable to many and perhaps even superior to or more appropriate in many contexts than the capitalist alternative. Even Western textbooks reported the Soviet "economic miracle" of continuous 6 percent annual economic growth and full employment from the 1930s to the 1960s. In addition to competing with the United States in promising and delivering military aid to client states, the Soviets also provided technical assistance and development aid, a conspicuous example being the Aswan High Dam project in Egypt in the late 1950s.

Examining the period from the Great Depression to the end of the 1970s as a whole, to the extent direct comparison is possible the results are inconclusive. In Germany, after struggling with postwar reconstruction, non-communist West Germany grew robustly; and by the early 1960s, its citizens enjoyed a standard of living far higher than their counterparts in communist East Germany. In Korea, however, the story was at first reversed: the communist north in the 1950s and early 1960s was Asia's second-most industrialized economy, with rapid growth in production and higher standards of living. Many ethnic Koreans living in Japan returned to North Korea in the early 1960s, believing it had better economic prospects than capitalist South Korea. It was not until the end of the 1960s that the south took the lead.

Beyond these countries, Marxist-Leninist guerrilla groups and communist political parties struggled to gain control of additional countries. Some, like Cuba, relied on Soviet commitments for their economic survival, but it would be misguided to think that the communist world marched in lockstep to the beat of a Soviet drum. For example, Cuba's policy of supporting socialist movements in Africa defied Soviet grand strategy. A clearer example of the split among communist states was the growing tensions between China and the Soviet Union, which saw themselves as rivals with divergent visions of Marxism as a global movement.

Trying to Reject the Cold War: Non-alignment

Despite the internal variation within their camps, both the Soviet Union and the United States portrayed the world as a choice between one side or the other, but not everyone accepted that every country had to choose sides in the Cold War. Some powerful voices on the world stage argued that the rivalry was distracting attention and resources from important issues confronting many former colonial states. In April 1955, the leaders of Burma (Myanmar), India, Indonesia, Pakistan, and Sri Lanka (formerly known as Ceylon) organized a conference in Bandung, Indonesia. Delegates from twenty-nine countries, representing half the world's population, emerged from the meeting with a document calling for peaceful coexistence, an end to racism, and economic cooperation. The delegates expressed concern that the Cold War atmosphere had quickly diminished the principles of respect for sovereignty, self-determination, and human rights that guided the foundation of the UN. Two years later, India's first prime minister, Jawaharlal Nehru (1889–1964), summarized the goals of what came to be called the *Non-Aligned Movement*, asserting that most of the world's leaders and peoples would prefer to "maintain friendly relations with all countries, even though we may disagree with them in their policies or structure of government."

The leaders of the Non-Aligned Movement embraced the idea that most of the world's rapidly growing, increasingly urban population lived in the countries of the *Third World*, a place that was part of neither the *First World* of the United States and its military allies in western Europe nor the *Second World* of the Soviet Union and Eastern Europe. Leaders of the Non-Aligned Movement believed that the elusive common ground of the postwar era could be found in serving the interests of the world's majority. Similar sentiments were expressed in 1958 at the All-African People's Conference held in Accra, Ghana, where delegates expressed frustration at the slow pace at which European powers, now organized into Cold War defense agreements with the United States, were decolonizing. The conference fueled agitation for independence across the continent, and a wave of independent states were established over the next decade.

At the Accra Conference, the prominent African American scholar W. E. B. Du Bois (1868–1963), who would spend the last days of his life as a Ghanaian citizen, admonished the delegates to transcend local or regional interests to achieve a greater good. Du Bois echoed the aims of the Non-Aligned Movement, yet this vision proved difficult to realize. In the two decades following World War II, dozens of newly independent states in Africa, like Angola, and Asia, like Vietnam, collided head-on with Cold War schemes and arms. Coupled with conflicts among rival elite and popular factions and fueled by divisive ethnic and religious rhetoric, this drained the political, social, and economic capital of the Third World.

Conclusion

Between the early 1940s and the mid-1970s, the organization of the world changed profoundly. The principle of national self-determination was implemented at an unprecedented pace, as nearly one hundred countries achieved independence during this era. A decades-long economic boom produced extraordinary global wealth and accelerating technological, demographic, and social change. An international organization of nation-states embraced the premise that slaughter like the Holocaust must never again be tolerated and that every human being had rights based solely on his or her humanity and not on membership of a particular national, economic, religious, racial, or ethnic group.

Yet this era was also one of great tensions and enduring conflict. Violent repression of dissent continued to characterize many political regimes, both new and old. Shocking inequalities within countries and among them undermined confidence that growth meant prosperity—or even basic material security—for most of the world's population. Principles such as democracy, self-determination, and human rights too often appeared less as ideals toward which the global community was striving and more as rhetorical cudgels with which opposing sides beat each other. The ever-present threat of nuclear war and the global gamesmanship between the world's superpowers overshadowed every issue of global consequence.

It would have been hard, then, for any of the actors in the Angolan wars of the 1970s to guess that in the next generation, the Soviet Union would disappear and the communist regime in China would embrace the global market economy. Nor would they have predicted that their own civil war would outlast the Cold War. It did, and in its aftermath their country would become one of the world's largest oil producers, yet provide most Angolans with average earnings of only one dollar per day. In Chapter 13, we analyze the surprising path through the end of the twentieth century that yielded these kinds of outcomes.

A Few Good Books

Max Boot. *The Road Not Taken: Edward Lansdale and the American Tragedy in Vietnam.* New York: Liveright, 2018.

Andrei Cherny. *The Candy Bombers: The Untold Story of the Berlin Airlift and America's Finest Hour.* New York: Berkley Trade, 2009.

Frederick Cooper. *Africa since 1940: The Past of the Present.* Cambridge, UK: Cambridge University Press, 2002.

Piero Gleijeses. *Conflicting Missions: Havana, Washington, and Africa, 1959–1976.* Chapel Hill: University of North Carolina Press, 2003.

Meredith Hindley. *Destination Casablanca: Exile, Espionage, and the Battle for North Africa in World War II.* New York: PublicAffairs, 2017.

Timothy Snyder. *Black Earth: The Holocaust as History and Warning.* New York: Tim Duggan, 2015.

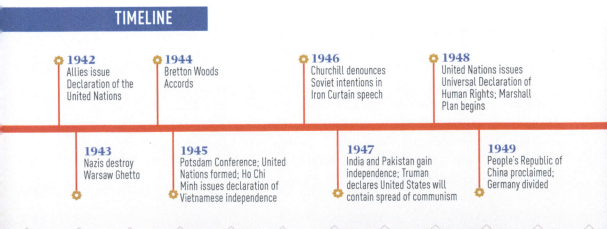

TIMELINE

1942 Allies issue Declaration of the United Nations

1943 Nazis destroy Warsaw Ghetto

1944 Bretton Woods Accords

1945 Potsdam Conference; United Nations formed; Ho Chi Minh issues declaration of Vietnamese independence

1946 Churchill denounces Soviet intentions in Iron Curtain speech

1947 India and Pakistan gain independence; Truman declares United States will contain spread of communism

1948 United Nations issues Universal Declaration of Human Rights; Marshall Plan begins

1949 People's Republic of China proclaimed; Germany divided

Odd Arne Westad. *The Cold War: A World History*. New York: Basic Books, 2017.

Susan Williams: *Who Killed Hammarskjold?: The UN, the Cold War and White Supremacy in Africa*. New York: Oxford University Press, 2012.

Vazira Fazila-Yacoobali Zamindar. *The Long Partition and the Making of Modern South Asia: Refugees, Boundaries, Histories*. New York: Columbia University Press, 2010.

For instructional resources and study aids, please go to **www.oup.com/us/carter**. *For primary sources connected to this chapter, please see the table of contents for* Sources for Forging the Modern World *included at the back of the book.*

1950–1953 Korean War

1952–1960 Mau Mau Rebellion, Kenya

1953 Stalin dies; United States backs coup in Iran

1954–1962 Algerian War of Independence

1955 Bandung Conference sets groundwork for Non-Aligned Movement

1956 Suez Crisis; Soviet invasion of Hungary

1958 All-Africa People's Conference, Ghana

1961 Berlin Wall erected

1963 Kenya achieves independence

1968 Soviet army suppresses Prague Spring in Czechoslovakia

1975 Angola achieves independence; fall of South Vietnam to communist North Vietnamese forces

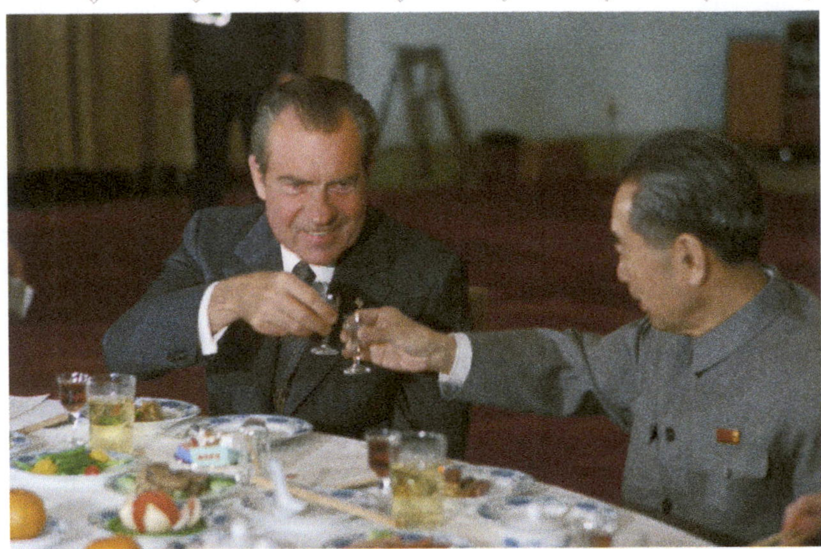

(TOP) United States President Richard Nixon and Chinese Premier Zhou Enlai Share a Toast, February 25, 1972. Nixon's anti-communist reputation made his overtures to the People's Republic of China, in the midst of the Cold War, surprising to many. The new US–China relationship was part of a Chinese reform policy that helped shape the end of the Cold War and laid the foundation for China's reemergence as a major world power.

(BOTTOM) South Asia from Space on a Clear Night. The orange line results from the intense lights that form part of the security corridor on the border between India and Pakistan. India is now the world's fourth largest consumer of energy. In 2012, the country's power grid experienced a massive failure; almost the entire top portion of this image would have gone dark.

CHAPTER 13

The Many Worlds of the Twenty-First Century

1972–2012

In February 1972, Richard Nixon (1913–1994) became the first American president to visit China while in office when he stepped off an airplane in Beijing. At the time, in the depths of the Cold War, the United States still did not have official diplomatic relations with the People's Republic of China (PRC), founded by the Chinese Communist Party in 1949. Few foreigners lived in China; travel there from most other countries was almost impossible. Over the course of a week, Nixon and First Lady Patricia Nixon visited Beijing, Shanghai, and Hangzhou; met with numerous Chinese officials; and toured schools, factories, and the Great Wall. They saw a ballet entitled "The Red Detachment of Women," depicting the transformation of a peasant girl into a model member of the Chinese Communist Party. At the end of the visit, the two countries issued a joint document—the Shanghai Communiqué—committing to the "progressive development of trade between the two countries," which at the time was virtually nonexistent. Since then, China–US trade has become a driving force in the global economy. By 2013, it totaled more than $560 billion annually.

In July 2012, more than six hundred million people in India—almost twice the population of the United States—lost their electricity when the country's power grid failed. In the early twenty-first century, many expected India to surpass China as the world's most populous country and to become one of the most productive regions of the global economy again, as it was in the early modern era. Its technology sector and contentious but resilient democratic government put it at the forefront of global forecasts of countries to watch. Lasting several days, the blackout exposed technical and logistical flaws in India's power grid that were also present in other areas of Indian life. Like many parts of India's infrastructure, the growth of the power grid had not kept pace with skyrocketing demand. Experts estimated that up to 30 percent of the power generated was lost to theft and outdated distribution systems. Advocates of alternative methods of generating power, as well as public- and private-sector

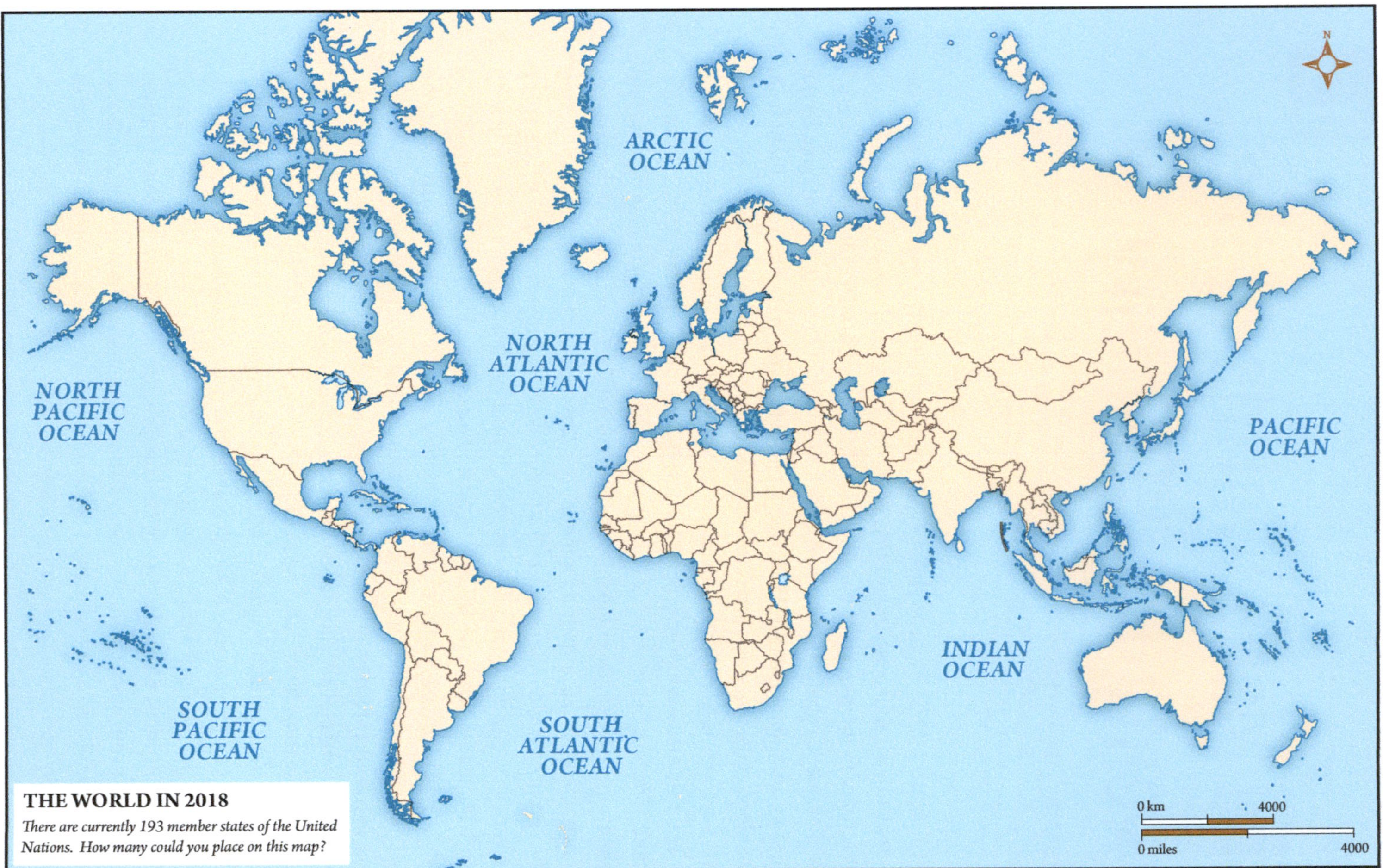
N
ARCTIC OCEAN
NORTH ATLANTIC OCEAN
NORTH PACIFIC OCEAN
PACIFIC OCEAN
INDIAN OCEAN
SOUTH PACIFIC OCEAN
SOUTH ATLANTIC OCEAN
THE WORLD IN 2018
There are currently 193 member states of the United Nations. How many could you place on this map?
0 km
4000
0 miles
4000

Map 13.1 The World in 2018

interests, fought over different economic plans, delaying needed planning and development. The blackout also highlighted the dramatic disparities in the distribution of wealth and resources in our world: one-third of the households in India did not lose power during the blackout because they did not have electricity in the first place.

These brief overviews of Nixon's visit to China and the energy challenges facing India illustrate shifts in economic, political, and cultural power in the last decades of the twentieth century and into the new millennium. In this chapter, we begin with the changing alliances and ideologies that broke down Cold War identities and affiliations and altered the globe's political geography, including the US–China relationship and upheaval in the Middle East, Latin America, and Southeast Asia. In the next sections of the chapter, we explain the factors that contributed to the collapse of the Warsaw Pact nations and the breakup of the Soviet Union.

Then, we present the numerous factors that changed global economic interactions and fueled the growth of economic powerhouses like India and China, along with the major conflicts that emerged in the multipolar, post–Cold War international environment, including ethnic, religious, and other forms of sectarian violence. As the chapter's narrative moves closer to the present day, we sketch the emergent tensions between economic globalization and the enduring model of the nation-state as the primary form of political sovereignty. Finally, we assess some of the costs and benefits of the biological new regime under which all the earth's inhabitants lived in the early years of the twenty-first century.

Questions to Consider as You Read Chapter Thirteen:

1. What motives brought countries like the United States, China, and the Soviet Union to alter their approaches to foreign policy and international relations beginning in the 1970s? What were the short- and long-term consequences of these decisions?
2. The Indian electricity crisis of 2012 tells us important things about the structure of global resource supply and demand. How would you compare these structures in the early twenty-first century with those of the early twentieth century? What are the implications for the future of this system?

Shifts in the Global Political Dynamic

The establishment of relations between the United States and the PRC highlights the complex interplay of strategic interests, economic development strategies, and ideology in the decades following the Second World War. Around the world, alignment with one side or another in the US–Soviet rivalry had been an important feature of global affairs since the war, but it was not the only dynamic.

A series of events and trends, including the growth of Third World economies and populations, the emergence of petroleum as a strategic asset, and the reassertion of religion as a force in politics, shook up global relations in the 1970s.

The US–China Opening

As noted in Chapter 12, neither side in the 1945–1949 Chinese Civil War conceded defeat, and both continued to claim sovereignty over China, even after the defeated nationalists fled to the island of Taiwan. There were two Chinas—although neither side admitted as much. One was the size of the United States and the other the size of the US state of Maryland, yet, for decades, the smaller one was officially recognized by the United Nations as China's legitimate government, thanks to the global clout of the United States.

The absurdity of this position became hard to maintain. In 1970, the government in Taiwan ruled over some fourteen million people and fourteen thousand square miles, whereas the Beijing government ruled over some seven hundred million people and almost four million square miles. In the mid-1960s, the PRC developed and tested nuclear and hydrogen weapons, an expression of power that needed to be acknowledged by the international community. In 1971, a majority of UN members defied US objections and recognized the PRC, giving it the permanent seat on the Security Council that Taiwan had held since the UN's inception. Reassessing its position, the United States began to pursue *ping-pong diplomacy,* which involved US table tennis players visiting China in 1971. Alongside this public cultural gesture, serious negotiations between US and Chinese politicians occurred in secret, establishing the parameters for the US president's visit to China.

This public recognition that the communist world was not a single entity came at a time when the United States was at war in Southeast Asia to stop the spread of communism. However, both the US and Chinese governments understood that the bomb shelters China constructed in the 1960s were designed primarily to defend against Soviet nuclear missiles, not American ones. Border disputes, ideological differences, and personality conflicts between their leaders had driven China and the Soviet Union apart in the late 1950s. By the 1960s, Chinese propaganda was just as likely to depict anti-Soviet as anti-American slogans. Even while the PRC struggled through its radical Cultural Revolution, some in the Chinese leadership began proposing a strategy to reach out to the United States as an ally against the Soviets. The rapprochement between the United States and China showed how political realism could trump ideology in international affairs. But Nixon's visit to China did not mark the end of the Cold War. It remained a high-stakes conflict not only between the superpowers, but also within nation-states and in regional alliances and confrontations around the world.

The Cold War Endures in Latin America and Asia

In Latin America, a brief flourishing of multiparty democracy in the mid-1940s had given way to a bitter clampdown in the 1950s and 1960s. Military coups proliferated, justified in terms of the global Cold War but carrying the distinctive marks of different countries' ethnic, racial, and regional conflicts and histories. In the 1970s, almost every country in the region had anti-communist, authoritarian governments. In response, residents of many of these countries created both peaceful protest organizations and armed guerilla movements in both urban and rural areas to attempt regime change. These homegrown, ideologically diverse movements and their demands were often repressed by governments asserting that Latin America was at the forefront of the global struggle to stop an armed communist takeover orchestrated by Cuba (regionally) and the Soviet Union (globally).

In Southeast Asia, despite US economic aid and direct military intervention, anti-communist regimes in South Vietnam, Cambodia, and Laos all fell to communist armies in 1975. In the same region, however, Thailand, Burma, Indonesia, and the Philippines remained anti-communist. Regimes on both sides of this ideological divide in the region were authoritarian and brutally repressed their own people.

In South Asia, the India–Pakistan rivalry confounded Cold War assumptions. In the first decades of the Cold War, India—a leader of the Non-Aligned Movement—had more cordial relations with communist countries than it did with the United States. However, border disputes with China and concern over Maoist revolutionaries inside India cooled Indian enthusiasm toward China. Ongoing Soviet support for India also expanded the rift between the Soviet Union and China. In contrast, Pakistan had closer ties to the United States for a time after independence, although relations cooled when a left-leaning government came to power in the 1970s and sought development aid from the Soviets. Relations between the United States and Pakistan improved after an anti-communist military regime took power and found common cause with the United States opposing Soviet plans in the region. Complicating international relations during this era, both India and Pakistan developed nuclear weapons technology in the context of their own rivalry, rather than as part of any broader Cold War plan guided by the United States or the Soviet Union.

OPEC, Energy, and Geopolitics

The Middle East, with its enormous oil reserves, played an important role in global political and economic relations. Geopolitics, the Cold War, ethnic and religious tensions, and postwar decolonization led repeatedly to unrest in the

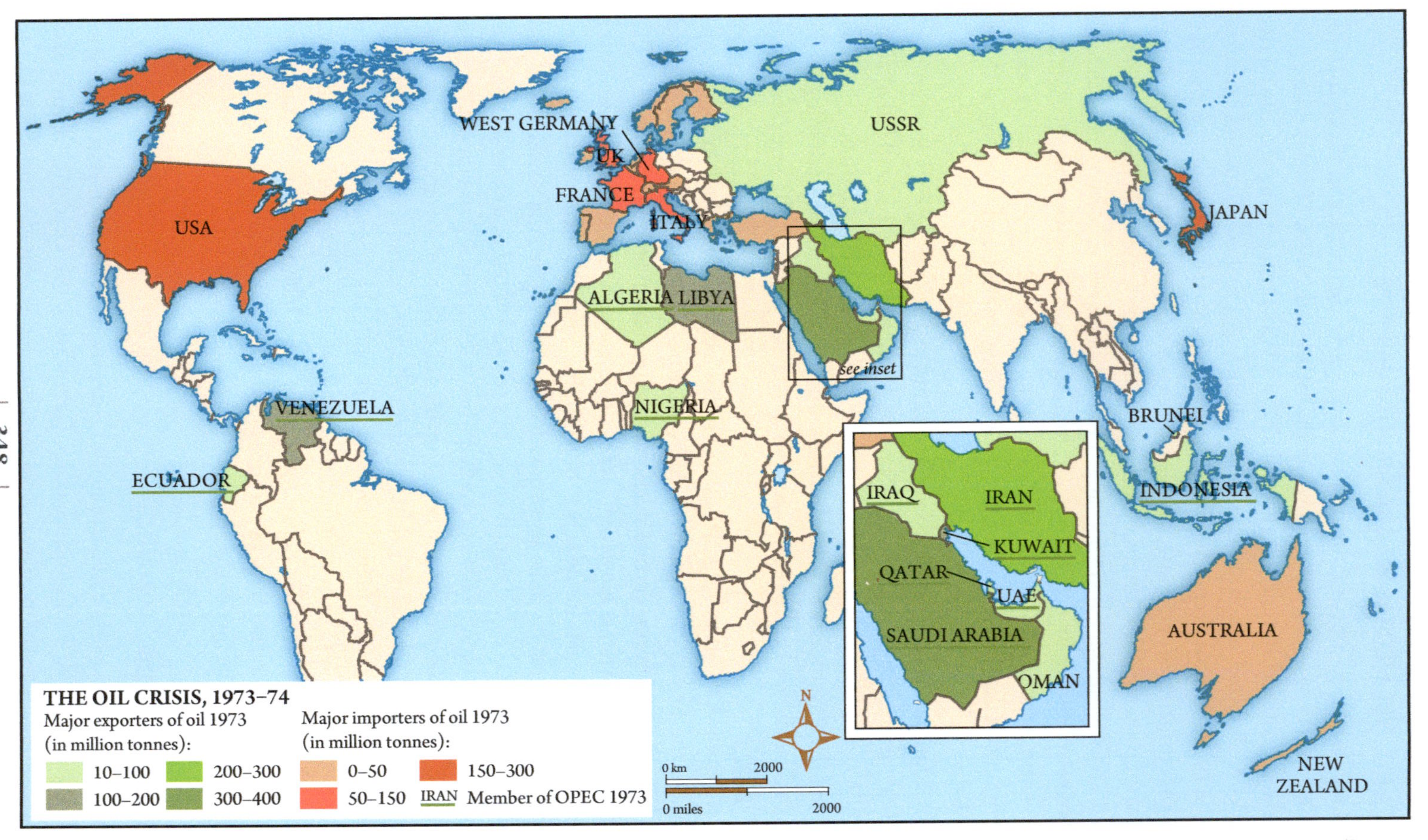

Map 13.2 The Oil Crisis, 1973–1974

region. In October 1973, war broke out for the second time in six years between Israel and neighboring Egypt and Syria. Israel received support from the United States and western Europe. In solidarity with Egypt and Syria, a group called the Organization of the Petroleum Exporting Countries (OPEC) accelerated its plan to shift the relationship between oil producers and consumers, restricting oil production to create shortages and increase prices.

What was OPEC and why did its actions matter? Petroleum was the greatest single difference between the twentieth-century economy and what came before. Oil had replaced coal as the most important power source for global industry. In 1960, four Middle Eastern oil producers—Iraq, Iran, Saudi Arabia, and Kuwait—as well as Venezuela, in South America, joined together to form OPEC. In its founding document, the organization's members agreed to set production levels and coordinate policies to protect "permanent sovereignty over their natural resources in the interest of their national development." Soon thereafter, Indonesia, Algeria, Nigeria, and Libya, all of which had recently won independence from European colonial powers, joined OPEC. By 1973, Qatar, the United Arab Emirates, and Ecuador were also members.

Although founded as an economic organization, OPEC's membership also shared some political interests, many of which challenged the power of Europe and the United States. In retaliation against Western support of Israel in the 1973 war, OPEC drastically curtailed production, restricting global supplies and raising prices. Although the reduction was only temporary, OPEC's actions exposed the dependence of industrial nations. The United States—the world's largest consumer of oil—panicked, government rationing was instituted, and prices rose even more sharply. The global economy soon fell into recession.

This was the first of several "oil shocks" in the 1970s that led industrial nations to reconsider their economic development policies, but the lasting effects of that change have been debatable. Although alternative energy sources—nuclear, solar, wind, and others—and new technologies, such as hydraulic fracturing (*fracking*), have been developed, global industry and transportation still rely fundamentally on petroleum. The global appetite for fossil fuels continued to grow at a rapid pace into the twenty-first century. In addition to the increasing appetites of North America and Western Europe, the economic growth of China and India has ensured that energy demand is greater than ever before.

Revolution in Iran

Another challenge to the Cold War status quo emerged from the Middle East at the end of the 1970s. In Iran, as a mass uprising drove the ruling shah, Mohammad Reza Pahlavi (1919–1980), into exile in 1979, memories of how he had gained autocratic

The Shah's Exile and Khomeini's Return, Hasan Isma'ilzadah, 1979. This poster employs a traditional Iranian storytelling style of painting, popular in coffeehouses. Highly detailed paintings like this were used as storytelling aids, often around national or religious tales. Here, we see the events surrounding the 1979 revolution, with the shah, suitcases packed, leaving the country while the Ayatollah Ruhollah Khomeini returns triumphantly from Paris.

power in 1953—with the aid of the US Central Intelligence Agency—spurred the opposition. Among the most committed activists in the anti-shah movement was a Shi`a cleric, Ruhollah Khomeini (1902–1989), who had spent fifteen years in exile. During his years in Iraq and France, cassette tapes of his teachings—interpretations of Islamic tradition mixed with anti-American and anti-Semitic denunciations—circulated throughout Iran and beyond. Politically savvy, Khomeini reached out to other anti-shah groups, even those whose members did not share his vision of Iran's future but who agreed that any change must start with removing the shah.

Khomeini's faction, committed to a new state where fundamentalist interpretations of Islamic practice would guide all political, economic, and social life, won support when its militants stormed the US Embassy in protest of the decision to allow the exiled shah to enter the United States for medical treatment. The militants took hostages and began to release information obtained in the ransacked embassy files about the ways in which members of rival political groups had "betrayed" the revolution by meeting with US officials. In the version of the revolution's history told by Khomeini, the new regime's political and spiritual leader, the Iranian Revolution was only possible because an alliance between common people and clerics like himself had been blessed by God. The new regime in Iran committed to a policy of nationalization of key resources and full employment for its citizens. One might expect that the emergence of an anti-American oil-producing state in the Middle East would benefit Soviet designs for the region, but the Soviets were themselves fighting an Islamist uprising against the communist regime in Afghanistan.

Afghanistan between Empires, Again

The Soviet invasion of Afghanistan, which began in 1979 (the same year as the Iranian Revolution) evoked past imperialist aggression. The Russian Empire had been deeply involved in Afghanistan and this continued into the Soviet period. Long a strategic crossroads, Afghanistan had repeatedly defied empire-builders' plans to subdue and control it. Its importance to both superpowers grew as its western neighbors, Iran and Iraq, became major oil producers while its southeastern neighbors, India and Pakistan, acquired nuclear weapons technology.

The Afghans faced many of the issues by now familiar to readers of this book: how to modernize the country's economy; what aspects of traditional culture to retain; and how to do all this while facing powerful rivals. Inside Afghanistan, factions disagreed over the country's future. One group attempted to alter many Muslim cultural traditions, including some related to marriage customs and land distribution, as it tried to move the country in a Marxist, secular direction. Unpopular with much of the population, these measures led to civil war, fueled by popular discontent. Foreign governments, including Pakistan and the United States, provided support for antigovernment forces.

Fearing chaos on its border and the loss of a key strategic ally, the Soviet Union sent tanks, aircraft, and more than one hundred thousand troops to support its preferred leadership group. The war, which began in December 1979 and lasted for nearly a decade, was more than a proxy war between Soviet and US allies. The war in Afghanistan also fueled a different international struggle—a pan-Islamist movement. Soviet aggression was denounced by both the United States and revolutionary Iran. Many *mujahideen* (resistance fighters) took as their central goal the overthrow not only of the current Soviet-backed secular government but also of any secular state. From North Africa to Indonesia, the cause attracted Islamist resistance fighters to Afghanistan. Many of these fighters were seeking a broader movement that would transcend what these individuals saw as the artificial territorial boundaries of nation-states imposed on the Islamic world by external forces. After ten years, the Soviets withdrew from Afghanistan without victory and drained of vital resources. In the aftermath, outside forces funded different factions in the struggle for Afghanistan, with Pakistan, Saudi Arabia, and Iran all supporting different groups.

One of the pan-Islamic fighters drawn to Afghanistan was a young Saudi named Osama bin Laden (1957–2011). Born into one of the world's wealthiest families—a fortune made in oil, construction, and banking—bin Laden was a university student when the Soviet Union invaded Afghanistan, but he abandoned his studies to join the fight against the Soviets. Although he saw some combat, bin Laden spent most of the war working with Pakistani forces training insurgents and funneling money to the resistance.

When the Soviets withdrew in 1989, bin Laden returned to Saudi Arabia, intent on spreading the lessons he claimed to have learned in the war against the Soviets. Asserting the need to protect and spread traditional Muslim values against all destructive and immoral secular powers, he urged the Saudi government to reject its alliance with the United States. Bin Laden claimed, like the mujahideen, that he would pursue Holy War against his enemies through a new organization he called *al-Qaeda* ("the Base"), which he had founded in the last years of the Afghan war. As Soviet forces—and American aid to their adversaries—withdrew from Afghanistan, al-Qaeda began to recruit and train a stateless army for global combat and covert attacks on targets it deemed contrary to the interests of Islam, chief among them the United States.

Transitions in the Communist World in the 1980s

While the Soviet Union was fighting in Afghanistan, it faced other challenges as well. Its centrally directed economy could not deliver the quantity and variety of consumer goods as more market-oriented economies. Its most lucrative export was petroleum (the USSR was the world's largest producer), but production peaked in 1987, after which it declined sharply. Economic weaknesses long disguised by oil revenues emerged. The arms race and proxy wars of the Cold War had also drained resources. Sluggish economic growth undermined the legitimacy of communist government. People also had wearied of the authoritarian rule that accompanied Soviet-style communism.

Similar to the situation in Afghanistan, one of the most important challenges to Soviet control in Eastern Europe came from a transnational religious movement, in this case the Roman Catholic Church. Karol Józef Wojtyła (1920–2005), elected Pope John Paul II in 1978, was the first non-Italian leader of the world's largest Christian denomination in more than four hundred years. His Polish ancestry and consistent anti-communist message inspired labor leaders in Poland—which even under communism was overwhelmingly Catholic—and in 1980, a union movement called Solidarity emerged to publicly oppose the communist government. In an earlier era, when dissident movements in east-central Europe challenged Soviet-allied governments, as in Hungary (1956) and Czechoslovakia (1968), their governments unleashed violent crackdowns with Soviet military support. But this did not happen in Poland; instead, the government agreed to hold elections (though with restrictions designed to ensure communist party success). To understand why the situation in Poland developed differently than earlier challenges to Soviet domination, we need to look in large part to changes in Soviet leadership.

In 1982, after almost twenty years as the leader of the Soviet Union, Leonid Brezhnev (1906–1982) died. Two hardline, and elderly, successors died in office over the next three years, destabilizing the leadership and accentuating the

***Perestroika* Poster for the Twenty-Seventh Communist Party Congress, USSR, 1987.** The text states, "The policy is acceleration—perestroika—to work actively, boldly, creatively, competently!" Amid a stagnant economy and political crisis, Soviet head of state Mikhail Gorbachev called for reform and openness (perestroika and glasnost in Russian). Gorbachev's policies contributed to the collapse of communist governments throughout Europe in 1989 and then the disintegration of the Soviet Union itself in 1991.

predicament facing the USSR. Mikhail Gorbachev (1931–) emerged our of the succession crisis as general secretary in 1985. Eager—perhaps desperate—to reshape Soviet society, invigorate its economy, and retain its position as a global superpower, Gorbachev promised *perestroika* (institutional restructuring) and *glasnost* (opening to criticism and debate). Allowing events in Poland to play out without Soviet intervention was one result of these changes in policy.

The outcome of the Polish election was startling. Despite rules designed to prevent Solidarity from winning, the movement took 260 of 261 open seats in the Polish legislature. The communist government could no longer govern without regard for the Solidarity delegates. Single-party communist rule had ended, and this time the Soviet Union did not respond with violence. Tolerance of the changes in Poland signaled to reformers throughout the Soviet bloc what might be possible. In November, protesters tore down the Berlin Wall, which had symbolized the Cold War since its construction in 1961. Communist governments in East Germany, Czechoslovakia, Hungary, Romania, Yugoslavia, and Albania soon followed Poland in collapse. Two years later, the Soviet Union itself dissolved, with fifteen independent states emerging. The superpower relationship that had defined—and threatened—the entire world for fifty years seemed to vanish with unimaginable speed.

Reform and Repression in China

The year 1989 ended with the collapse of communist governments across Europe, but midway through that year events in China made it appear, to the contrary, that communist governments would turn to violence to maintain their power.

Like the USSR, China entered the 1980s facing leadership transition and policy reassessment. In 1976, following the death of Mao Zedong—who had led the PRC since its founding—a brief power struggle opened a path to leadership for Deng Xiaoping (1904–1997). Deng had impeccable military and Communist Party credentials dating back to the 1930s, and his remarkable political skill had enabled him to survive multiple purges under Mao. As China's leader, he charted a radical new course. Instead of ideological fervor and isolation, Deng opened China to the world and embarked on an economic modernization campaign that valued pragmatism and experimentation over communist theory.

Although it is hard to imagine today, when Deng came to power, China made almost nothing for sale in the international marketplace, comprising less than 1 percent of global imports and exports in the early 1970s. This changed abruptly. In 1979, China's foreign trade amounted to under thirty billion dollars. By 1985, it passed seventy billion; and by 2012, the PRC was the world's largest trading nation, with international exchanges valued at almost four trillion dollars, accounting for some 10 percent of all exports worldwide.

Deng moved the country quickly away from Maoist collectivism toward what he called *socialism with Chinese characteristics*. Market forces and private ownership took more prominent roles in a centrally directed economy. State-owned corporations remained powerful, but for the bulk of Chinese society, economic transformation was at hand. Underscoring both the commercial and the international aspect of the changes, Deng left for the United States as soon as diplomatic ties were formally established on January 1, 1979, and signed deals to allow Boeing Aircraft and Coca-Cola to do business with China.

The sweeping changes made the Chinese economy much more dynamic, but also less stable: the lives of millions of Chinese changed, but not continuously or consistently for the better. Global markets put new pressures on wages and prices. Inflation, which had not been an issue in China since the 1940s, rose sharply. Deng's Special Economic Zones brought foreign goods, including luxury goods, into China, but few people could afford them. Corruption, nepotism, and patronage flourished. And what of political change? Would economic changes inspire political change? Perhaps an emerging class of property owners would demand political rights to match its new economic influence?

A crackdown on public protests in the summer of 1989 demonstrated the limits of the regime's tolerance for a movement designed to achieve a political opening to go along with economic change. Inspired by the death of a pro-reform official that spring, protests took place in dozens of cities across the country, but were concentrated in Tiananmen Square, the center of the capital and the symbolic heart of China, where hundreds of thousands of people had gathered.

For weeks, the protesters defied government demands to disperse. On June 4, 1989, Chinese troops cleared the square by force, killing hundreds, perhaps thousands, as they advanced.

Historians Explore The End of the Cold War

The Cold War ended suddenly. Even during the summer of 1989, few predicted the dramatic political changes about to shake Europe, let alone the Soviet collapse. The decades since have seen broad disagreement about what provoked the collapse of the USSR and the end of the Cold War. The Cold War became the realm of historians, who sought out new sources from former communist regimes and declassified documents from the US government and elsewhere. Many explanations emerged to account for this sudden shift in how the world was organized.

Some scholars credit US president Ronald Reagan (1911–2004). In this view, which historian Robert Kagan has called "the standard narrative," Reagan, stridently anti-communist, engaged in tough rhetoric and an arms race, bankrupting the Soviet economy and constantly pressuring the Soviets to reform by exposing the contradictions and falsehoods of communist regimes. More common among historians is the view taken by John Lewis Gaddis and others who give three individuals—Reagan, Gorbachev, and Pope John Paul II—central roles in ending the Cold War. In this analysis, Reagan's insistence that US policy strive to defeat, not contain, communism found a partner in Gorbachev, who rejected the authoritarian model of his predecessors. Gorbachev initiated reforms in the Soviet bureaucracy and refused to suppress antigovernment protesters in Eastern Europe, as his predecessors had done. Catalyzing the people of Eastern Europe was John Paul II, the first Polish pope. When he celebrated mass in Warsaw in 1979, a quarter of a million people attended. His message—"Don't be Afraid"—inspired the creation of the Solidarity movement the following summer.

Other scholars look to changing structural factors rather than individual actors. Joseph Nye, among others, points to the clear failure of the Soviet economy to provide its citizens with the kind of prosperity enjoyed by many Western nations as a critical factor. In this view, the Soviet economy was already in shambles before Ronald Reagan took office, and its political system was unable to respond effectively. The arms race was bankrupting the Soviet Union, but that predated Reagan. In part, these expenditures were the cost of the imperial sprawl of the Soviet Union. Attempting to control disparate and volatile regions and peoples drained Soviet resources, as the invasion of Afghanistan in 1979 demonstrated. Although the adversarial relationship to the United States played a role in this spending, it was not the only factor and could not be attributed to a sudden or important change by one leader or even a trio of them. In this view, economic and ideological rigidity had doomed the Soviet Union before John Paul, Reagan, or Gorbachev stepped on the world stage.

Stephen Cohen rebuts this line of thinking as *retrospective determinism*, arguing that the Soviet Union, like any political system, could and did change over time. Cohen sees the major causes of the collapse as internal to the Soviet Union, including Gorbachev's decisions as leader. The Soviet economy was bad, but large states rarely collapse because of a bad economy alone, Cohen argues. He suggests that the Soviet Union was at its most democratic just before it dissolved and that far from being doomed or evil, the Soviet Union was on the verge of sustainable democratic reform as Gorbachev opened more space for protest and dissent. When Gorbachev also accommodated American demands on arms control and Soviet troop deployments, however, many hardliners within the Soviet establishment saw these two phenomena as linked and threatening. According to this analysis, internal reactions to fluid circumstances, not destiny, and not external actors, brought down the USSR.[1]

Toward a New Global Order

Regime change was also occurring in the non-communist world. Beginning in the 1970s and continuing through the 1980s, dozens of authoritarian governments in Europe, Asia, and Latin America changed their political systems to allow greater electoral competition and to permit civic organizations and political parties to operate more freely. Many factors caused this third wave of democratization around the globe. Exhaustion from long civil wars, bold actions and calls for reconciliation by religious and political leaders, pressure from international organizations and civil society groups, and global economic forces all played a role as Spain, Guatemala, Argentina, South Korea, the Philippines, South Africa, and dozens of other countries built more democratic societies, just as the transformations in the communist world were also a mix of context and contingency. Many of these countries also underwent economic transformations that, although not as dramatic as the turn away from communist authoritarianism, were profound in their own right.

1 Stephen Cohen, *Soviet Fates and Lost Alternatives: From Stalinism to the New Cold War* (New York: Columbia University Press, 2013); John Lewis Gaddis, *The Cold War: A New History* (New York: Penguin, 2006); Robert Kagan, *The Return of History and the End of Dreams* (New York: Vintage, 2009); John Patrick Diggins, *Ronald Reagan: Fate, Freedom, and the Making of History* (New York: W. W. Norton & Company, 2007). A useful overview of these debates is provided by Joseph Nye, "Who Caused the End of the Cold War?," *The Huffington Post*, March 18, 2010, http://www.huffingtonpost.com/joseph-nye/who-caused-the-end-of-the_b_350595.html.

Facing rapid population growth, rising energy prices, low growth in productivity, and high public debt, elites in many developing countries came to believe that prospects for economic stability and development anywhere and everywhere in the world depended on embracing free market open-economy principles. They found common cause with decision-makers in private industry, international organizations, and political leaders in some of the world's most advanced economies, like the Reagan administration (1981–1989) in the United States and the Thatcher government (1979–1990) in Great Britain. The most important of these principles was that future global economic growth required governments to allow markets to allocate more resources, including public goods like drinking water, electricity, and transportation. A corollary principle was that economic well-being required greater participation in international markets and not reliance on and protection of domestic ones. The level of faith in the private sector and commitment to dismantling government programs and services varied, but this trend was evident in policy changes around the world. Tariffs were lowered and government monopolies were sold to private investors. Social welfare programs, public-sector jobs, and public investment in infrastructure projects diminished.

The End of History and Its Quick Return

In the momentous year of 1989, a US State Department official and scholar named Francis Fukuyama published an article titled "The End of History?" The question mark in the title is important because the author's thesis was speculative, but it presented a jaw-dropping idea to those who were living through those moments. Fukuyama mused that the world might be reaching "the end point of mankind's ideological evolution and the universalization of Western liberal democracy as the final form of human government."[2]

The 1990s quickly and violently challenged the End of History thesis that liberal democracy might proliferate. A genocidal war followed the collapse of the communist government of Yugoslavia. Forces of the North Atlantic Treaty Organization, icons of the Cold War, bombed the region in 1995 and again in 1999 to try to curtail the "ethnic cleansing" ordered by Slobodan Milosevic, a politician from the communist era who became the first president of a new Serbian state. Milosevic was later arrested and tried by a UN special war crimes tribunal. Brutal ethnic violence killed or displaced millions of people in Somalia and the central African nation of Rwanda as well. Endemic violence across the Middle East reinforced the notion that ethnic and religious differences were now the primary fault lines precipitating violent confrontations.

---

2 Francis Fukuyama, "The End of History?," *The National Interest* 16 (Summer 1989): 3–18.

From the Cold War to the War on Terror

Like all conflicts, the ones that shaped the post–Cold War world had deep roots that often grew in unpredictable ways. One example of this emerged from the mountains that divided Afghanistan and Pakistan, where Osama bin Laden trained with Pakistani army officers to prepare resistance fighters against the Soviets a decade earlier. The United States, which employed the mujahideen as proxies in the Cold War, partly funded these training camps. Few in Washington (or Moscow) would have predicted that bin Laden's organization, al-Qaeda, would outlast the Soviet Union, but that is what happened.

After the Soviets withdrew from Afghanistan, bin Laden shifted his struggle to a new fight against the United States. He built al-Qaeda on the idea that Western, especially American, values and culture threatened Islam, going so far as to posit a Christian–Jewish conspiracy intended to eliminate Islam. Al-Qaeda embraced religion as its primary identity, but it was rooted also in anticolonialism. For al-Qaeda, the United States was a successor to the European imperialist regimes that had shaped the political geography, economic prospects, and social contours of the world's Muslims for generations. In the worldview of bin Laden and his followers, only by challenging Western cultural and economic hegemony could Muslims succeed.

When challenging overwhelming power, anti-imperial movements have employed many tactics, from nonviolent passive resistance to full-scale warfare. Al-Qaeda, active in more than a dozen countries by 1992, used many tactics, including direct attacks on the American presence in these countries and attacks in Western countries. Both were designed to persuade people and government in Europe and (especially) the United States that maintaining a presence in Islamic countries was not worth the cost. In 1992, al-Qaeda bombed a Yemeni hotel where US troops had been housed. The following year, al-Qaeda operatives exploded a bomb in the basement of New York City's World Trade Center, a failed attempt to bring down the towers. Attacks in Saudi Arabia, Kenya, and Tanzania in the 1990s were all attributed to al-Qaeda.

On September 11, 2001, al-Qaeda transformed itself from just one among many militant groups to the embodiment of the challenges of the post–Cold War world and the central focus of American foreign policy. On that morning, al-Qaeda operatives hijacked four airplanes, crashing one into each tower of New York's World Trade Center and a third into the Pentagon, the headquarters of the US military in Washington, DC. The fourth plane, apparently intended for the White House, crashed in rural Pennsylvania after passengers resisted the hijackers. Nearly three thousand people died in the attacks, and many more were injured. Toxic dust and smoke lingered in the air of lower Manhattan for weeks.

Hopes that the end of the Cold War would deliver a global *peace dividend*—a reduction of violence and shift of government expenditures from military outlays to investments in developing human and social capital—were shattered. In the weeks that followed, US leaders characterized these events as attacks by people who "hate our freedoms" and declared a *war on terror*, invading and occupying both Afghanistan (2001) and Iraq (2003), whose governments were cited as state sponsors of terrorist organizations like al-Qaeda. War shredded both countries, as rivals jockeyed to control territory and resources while the invading coalition attempted to create the conditions under which stable, friendly governments would emerge. Islamic radicals attempted to expand their influence in other countries with majority Muslim populations, from Indonesia to Yemen, while terrorists attacked US allies in London (2004) and Madrid (2005).

Rooted in more than six decades of strife, a fundamental conflict in the region—the tension between the Israeli government and the claims of Palestinians—remained undiminished, while a different wave of demonstrations, protests, and political upheaval, sometimes called the Arab Spring, rocked North Africa and the Middle East in late 2010 and accelerated in the spring of 2011. The long-term consequences of these upheavals remained unresolved as we completed revisions to this book. Violence, often between rival Sunni and Shi`a factions, continued throughout much of the region. In Syria, protests against the government precipitated a violent crackdown and the outbreak of civil war. A radical Islamist group, calling itself the Islamic State, gained control of significant swaths of territory. The war in Syria displaced half of the country's prewar population of twenty-two million, causing a refugee crisis across the Mediterranean and Europe. Regional and global powers, including Iran, Russia, the United States, and Saudi Arabia, continue to provide troops, military hardware, and other resources to support different factions with competing solutions to the ongoing crisis.

Implications for the Global Political Order

These ongoing conflicts illustrate many key points about the post–Cold War world, some of which resonate with lessons of earlier eras. Superior weaponry and troop strength do not determine long-term historical outcomes when violent conflicts arise. Warfare has always been expensive; the costs in "blood and treasure" cannot be borne forever. Long-term sovereignty depends on effectiveness and legitimacy. In a world organized around social contracts and popular sovereignty, these can only be built on local foundations rather than imposed from above or outside. Furthermore, much of the ongoing violence throughout the Muslim world was driven by conflicts between different groups of Muslims split by theological disputes and competing claims over material resources, as well as other religious and ethnic groups with their own differences among them. Finally, states outside the region, including the United States, Russia, China, and the region's most important former European colonial powers (France and Great Britain), all maintained conflicting goals and interests in the region, even though they all agreed in theory that certain forms of Islamic radicalism were a common threat to their visions of the modern world.

This confrontation triggered profound debates about the resilience and potential limitations of the contemporary global political order of nation-states, especially about the extent to which rights claims (including, for example, freedom of speech or proscriptions against cruel and unusual punishment) can or should be limited by sovereign states in the pursuit of national security. Perplexing dilemmas about the rules of war between states and non-state actors lingered as well. During this same era, transformations in the global economy raised additional questions about the nature of sovereignty at the dawn of a new millennium.

Economic Integration

In 1972, the Ford Motor Company launched a secret project named Bobcat. The project's goal was to design, build, and sell a "world car," taking advantage of changes in transportation, communications, and manufacturing to reduce costs and the potential for disruption throughout the supply, production, and distribution chains. Construction workers plowed under onion fields and orange groves in Valencia, Spain, to break ground on a new assembly plant. Engineers in England, Germany, and the United States designed the vehicle. Parts came from factories located in numerous countries. The first Ford Fiesta rolled off the Spanish assembly line in 1976. Subsequent iterations of the vehicle—which became one of the bestselling automobiles in history—have been manufactured and sold in South America, South Africa, South Asia, Southeast Asia, China, and the United States.

Such highly integrated, international processes of production, distribution, and consumption became the norm over the four decades following the introduction of the Ford Fiesta. In many industries, such as consumer electronics and textiles, production could shift quickly and dramatically. Almost one hundred companies manufactured televisions in the United States during the 1950s, but that number declined to zero—none—by the end of the twentieth century. Mexico became the largest exporter of televisions in the world. In the twenty-first century, it became difficult to even define where any single television is made. Most electronics are assembled from parts made in several countries, mostly in Asia. Final assembly of each unit of the same product may occur in any number of countries before being shipped to a warehouse for retail sale.

As we noted previously, opening of economic relations between the United States and China, the collapse of communist regimes, and the reassessment of economic development strategies in non-communist states helped to create the conditions for increasing global economic integration. We must add more pieces to the puzzle, however: the computer and communications revolution, regional economic integration, and the establishment of the World Trade Organization.

The European Union and the World Trade Organization

In 1957, a treaty brought together Belgium, Italy, West Germany, the Netherlands, Luxembourg, and France in the European Economic Community, or Common Market. This charter was one of the first official documents to use the term *supranational*: above the nation. It required individual nation-states to concede to the broader organization power over certain issues formerly reserved for the member states' own governments while retaining full sovereignty in other areas. The steps toward European integration began with agreements on economic issues, such as trade and agricultural production standards, but then moved on to educational and environmental issues, the creation of a common currency—the Euro—and even discussions about foreign policy and collective security. In 1993, the organization changed its name to the European Union (EU) to better reflect its broad mandate. In 2012, Croatia became the twenty-eighth member of the EU, completing a process of application and negotiation that had taken almost ten years. Plans existed for further expanding the organization but, in a remarkable turn of events in 2016, voters in Great Britain elected to leave the EU. While the departure of one country does not doom the organization, EU's future is murkier than it was prior to the vote. Similar anti-EU movements exist in some countries, while sentiment to join or remain is strong in others.

Other regional trading associations emerging in the same timeframe focused mostly on lowering the costs of moving commodities and capital across borders and less on broad issues of political integration and shared sovereignty. Nonetheless, treaties such as the Association of Southeast Asian Nations Free Trade Agreement (1992) and the North American Free Trade Agreement (1994) changed the economic relationships among signatory countries. They also sparked ongoing debate about the nature of sovereignty in the modern world, as individual countries created binding agreements that critics saw as ceding pieces of national sovereignty without the extensive public deliberations that such changes should require. Implementation of the North American Free Trade Agreement sparked a brief armed uprising among indigenous peoples in southern Mexico. Critics in all three countries continue to call for the treaty's renegotiation or even elimination, while supporters point to clear benefits for producers and consumers.

Each of these regional agreements moved in step with the revival of broader global trade negotiations originally envisioned in the days of the Bretton Woods meetings during the Second World War. In 1986, delegates in Punta del Este, Uruguay, began the most ambitious round of trade negotiations ever undertaken, covering global transactions in everything from staple foods, to plastic trinkets, to cutting-edge pharmaceuticals. By the time the negotiations were complete, more than one hundred countries had laid the foundation for the World Trade Organization (WTO), which was inaugurated in 1995. WTO delegates establish the terms by which member states permit goods and services to move across national boundaries. By 2012, more than 150 WTO member states were responsible for 95 percent of international commerce. These negotiations and the organizations that emerged from them created the legal and diplomatic frameworks for further global economic integration. The computer and telecommunications revolutions provided the means by which this integration was carried out.

The Internet

It is nearly impossible to imagine today, but when the Berlin Wall fell, almost no one learned the news via the internet, a system that had its roots in discussions and experiments in data sharing and communications by researchers at universities, corporations, think tanks, and government agencies. The growing availability, capacity, and convenience of personal computers during the 1980s sparked interest in using linked computation for commercial purposes, personal communications, and leisure activities. These trends came together in the 1980s, as closed research networks, often funded by government agencies, yielded to commercial enterprises linking private users to vast and powerful systems of hardware and ever-multiplying packets of data.

In 1990, only 3 million people worldwide had access to the internet, and more than 2 million of these were in the United States. By the start of 1996—the year Larry Page and Sergey Brin began the research that would yield Google—there were still only 16 million internet users, just 0.4 percent of the world's population. In that one year, however, internet use doubled, and it increased at an astounding pace over the following years. By December 2000, the number of users reached 361 million. Five years later, it was more than 1 billion. In 2017, it was estimated that for the first time most of the world's population (51 percent) had access to the internet, approximately 3.8 billion people.

The globalization that accompanied the internet revolution was of such a different quality that it often constituted an entirely new way of interacting. Telephones and telegraphs had made transcontinental communication possible, even instantaneous, a century earlier, but the scale, variety, and declining cost of computing has been one of the great material revolutions in human history, from

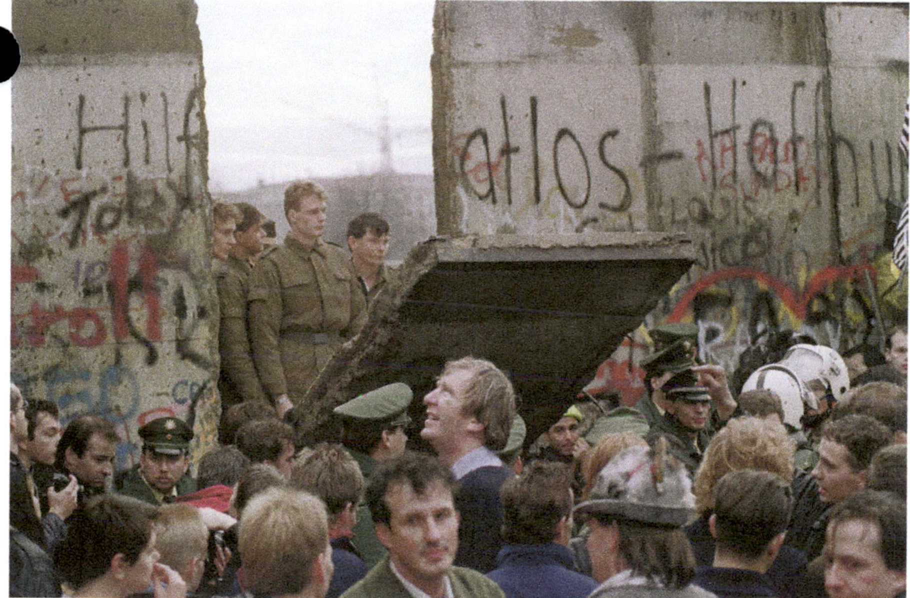

Berlin Wall. From August 1961 until November 1989, the Berlin Wall was the most tangible symbol of the Cold War. The wall was built by East German authorities to prevent movement between the eastern sector and the western sector that had been controlled since the end of World War II by US, British, and French forces. The destruction of the wall in 1989 by private citizens on both sides was among the most dramatic moments in the demise of communism in Europe, culminating in the dissolution of the Soviet Union in 1991.

computer-aided design to massive multiplayer online role-playing games. It is a cliché, but no less true for being so, that the average mobile phone today has more computing power than machines that would have filled a room a half century ago.

The New Global Economy

The three trends of integration, deregulation, and computerization affected the global financial system, just as they did every other piece of the global economy. But in 2008, the system came close to collapse. Fueled principally by risky financial practices in the United States and Europe, many of the world's largest economies fell into deep recession. Lehman Brothers, one of the world's largest and oldest investment banks, collapsed. Trillions of dollars of consumer wealth disappeared, and stock markets shed value. In Europe, many member states of the EU struggled to pay their debts. Governments in Greece, Ireland, and Iceland came close to failure, while the economies of Spain and even Italy—one of the world's ten largest—appeared in jeopardy. Jobless rates approached 50 percent in some European countries. Alluding to the 1929 global crash, some called this the Great Recession. In the United States and Europe, this was termed the global financial crisis.

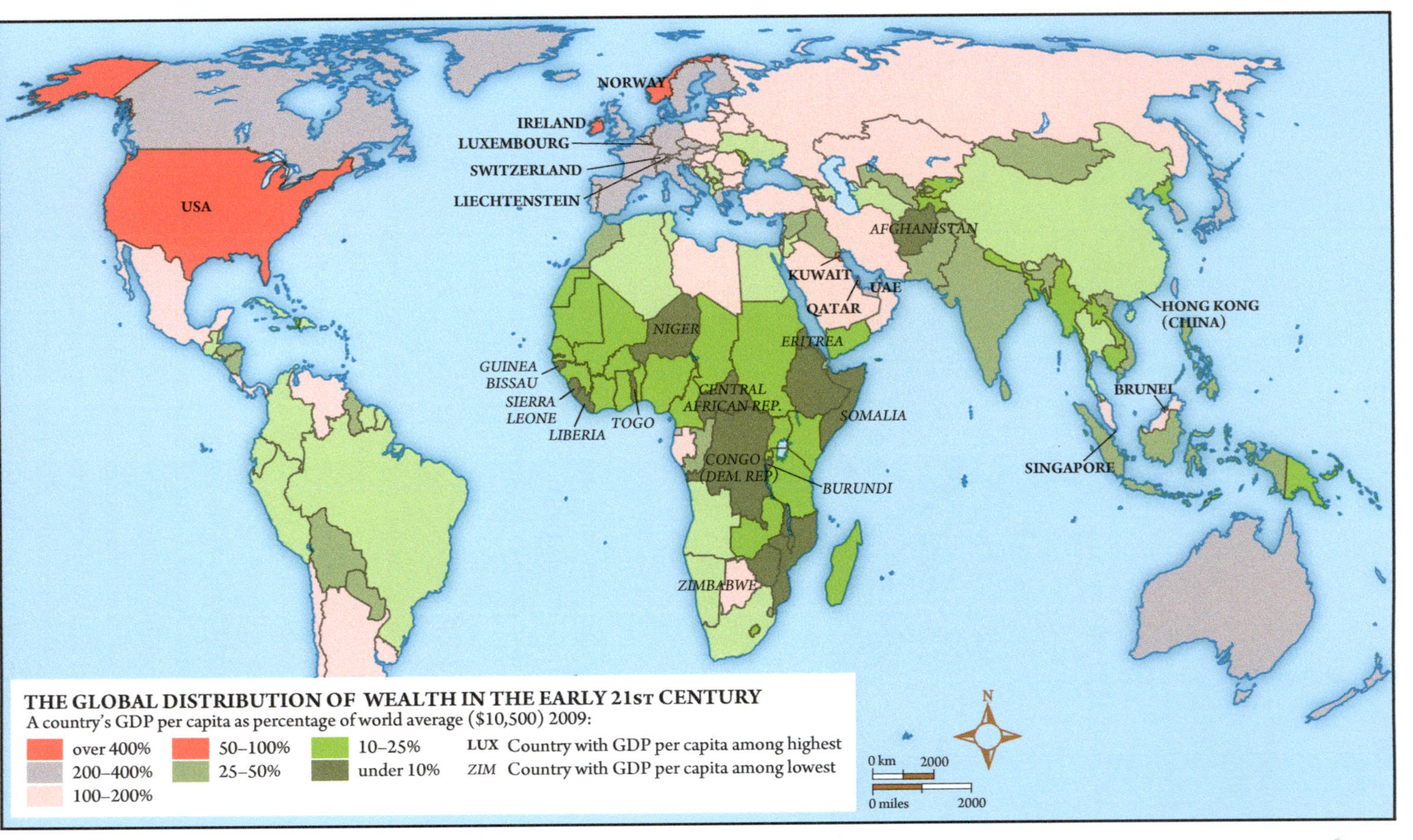

Map 13.3 The Global Distribution of Wealth in the Early Twenty-First Century

However, this global crisis had very uneven impacts around the world. The world's financial system was indeed global, and the downturn in the United States and Europe affected the entire world; but even in 2009—the worst year of the recession—dozens of countries managed economic growth of greater than 4 percent, mostly in Asia and Africa. In 2010, China and India again grew at more than 10 percent per year. In this new decade, half of the world's largest economies were in Europe and North America, but none of the fastest growing economies were. China and India were on both lists: top ten in size *and* in growth. Many observers credited the continued growth in Asia with averting a catastrophe on the scale of the Great Depression.

BRICS

By 2010, after three decades of steady, rapid growth, China overtook Japan to become the world's second-largest economy. It was also the world's largest trading nation, exporting and importing more goods than any other country. All this trade made China wealthy: a favorable balance of trade gave it tremendous cash reserves, enabling it to expand its political influence. China used this influence and cash to satisfy its enormous demand for raw materials. Chinese companies—many of them state-owned or state-supported—invested in Africa, South America, and even the United States. China acquired mineral rights and signed trade agreements in exchange for investment and infrastructure projects.

India also emerged during this period as an economic giant, entering the world's top ten economies in the 2000s. Like China, India relied on manufacturing for much of its growth, but India's experience of British colonialism enabled it to tap into the population's English-language skills as part of its economic plan, particularly in the global service sector, where outsourcing customer support services—help lines and call centers—was now feasible.

These trends and statistics led some analysts to suggest that the global economy, and the power that goes with it, might be moving in a new direction. In 2001, an analyst for the Goldman Sachs investment bank used demographic trends, natural resource stores, and recent economic growth to hypothesize that four national economies—Brazil, Russia, India, and China, or BRIC—would dominate the twenty-first century. As early as 2008, these countries attempted to use the perception of their growing clout to make joint statements and proposals on a variety of global issues on which they had common goals. Subsequently joined by South Africa, the ministers of Brazil, Russia, India, China, and South Africa (BRICS) began to meet regularly at the UN and other global diplomatic gatherings. They issued joint statements on issues ranging from unrest in the Middle East to global climate change. Together, these BRICS states have some three billion people, with a gross domestic product on par with the United States or the EU. Yet these countries have at least as many differences as commonalities, and the global economy continues to change ever more rapidly. Other pundits began to suggest that Mexico, Indonesia, Nigeria, and Turkey (the MINT countries) someday may be the new global vanguard, experiencing economic growth despite serious challenges from forces as diverse as radical Islamists and narcotraffickers.

Are we returning to the world of 1400, when India and China together accounted for two-thirds of the world's economic production? It appears unlikely. While China's economy may already be the world's largest, projections make it unlikely that it could again dominate production as it did in 1400. China and India together account for about one-third of the world's population and are both among the world's ten largest economies, but together they account for just 14 percent of overall global economic output. Europe and North America, however, comprise about one-eighth of the global population, yet still account for well over half of the world's economic output. The North Atlantic dominance that we saw in the late nineteenth century is no longer so striking, but it still exists. At the same time, however, as the stories of BRICS and MINT demonstrate, the modern global economy presents the potential to create wealth around the world. The astonishing economic growth of India, China, and other states in the past four decades has brought unprecedented opportunities—more people have been lifted out of poverty in China alone since 1949 than in the rest of the world in all of history—but also new challenges, both anticipated and unanticipated.

The Down Side of the Economic Up Side

Rapid industrialization in India and China left these two countries reeling from its effects. For many, choking levels of air pollution came to symbolize China's economic growth. In January 2013, conditions became so bad—pollution levels in Beijing exceeded the World Health Organization's recommended limits by 500 percent—that they were labeled the *airpocalypse*. But the airpocalypse was soon repeated, becoming a recurring feature of life in the Chinese capital and other cities. While the dramatic photographs of air pollution captured public attention, experts suggested that water and soil pollution were even more serious problems, with even greater health risks.

In contrast to China's authoritarian one-party state, India, "the world's largest democracy," has competitive, representative politics but endures slowness and inefficiency in its complex, corrupt system. These factors contributed to the 2012 power outages, which affected 9 percent of the world's population. And, although not featured as prominently in international news reports, air pollution in India is even worse than in China.

The experiences of India and China raise crucial points about the environmental costs of economic growth. The scientific evidence supporting human contributions to climate change is robust, yet when considering international solutions, countries like China and India point out that the countries that industrialized in the nineteenth century and remain the world's wealthiest caused much of the damage to the environment, but countries that are industrializing now will bear disproportionately the costs of stricter controls on pollution. They also point out that any global climate treaties might lack sufficient enforcement capacity for all signatories, allowing some countries to delay implementation while others are forced to comply because they are smaller or weaker—not China or India, certainly, but they claim to make this case for other countries playing catch-up in economic development.

Perhaps no country illustrates these dilemmas of the modern global economy better than the Maldives, the smallest country in Asia by population—350,000 residents. The Maldives, a chain of islands off the coast of India that became independent in 1965, is the lowest country on the planet and is slowly disappearing as climate change raises water levels. The Maldives also has the highest gross domestic product per capita in South Asia, a result of the growth in its tourism industry, which provides almost two-thirds of the country's foreign exchange and 90 percent of government income through various taxes. If you were to fly from New York to the islands for your vacation, you would be responsible for pumping almost two and a half metric tons of carbon dioxide into the air. Yet, if everyone decided to forego vacations to places like the Maldives for any reason, even really good ones, much of the global economy would collapse, causing direct and immediate damage to those countries that are pulling themselves out of poverty through tourism. However, without a radical change in our collective behavior, the Maldives might not be here in the next century.

The Maldives illustrate the general trends that characterize this chapter. Between 1970 and 2010, many indicators of human development made tremendous positive strides. Using the UN Human Development Index—an aggregate of health, education, and income—only 3 countries of 135 experienced an overall decline between 1970 and 2010. The average person on the planet was better educated, lived a longer and healthier life, and had a higher income in 2010 than in 1970. The data also show two less encouraging trends. First, the environmental costs of this improvement were high, measured in air pollution, soil erosion, water scarcity, and depletion of resources like forest cover. Second, whereas life for the average person has improved according to the basic indicators used to compile the Human Development Index, the gap between the wealthy and the poor has increased both globally and within many of the world's countries. Both trends appear ominous. One challenge is at the material level, as the planet and its human population test the sustainability limits of the biological new regime that emerged with industrialization in the nineteenth century. The other challenge is political and social, raising questions about the legitimacy of states premised on popular sovereignty and respect for human rights if such inequalities remain entrenched.

Conclusion

The last decades of the twentieth century witnessed remarkable changes to the global political and economic order. The 1970s were in many ways the height of the Cold War. Although still not engaging in direct military confrontation with each other, both the United States and the Soviet Union continued to deploy their own troops and proxies around the world, seeking the upper hand in their long face-off. Authoritarian regimes ruled many of the world's countries, communist and anti-communist. At the same time, bookend events in the 1970s—the change in US–China relations and the revolution in Iran—hinted at the tremendous changes that would emerge in the final two decades of the century.

Political and economic transformations characterized the 1980s. Cold War authoritarian regimes of both the left and the right ceded power to representative governments, while a new push to open the global economy to market forces, accompanied by changes in technology, finance, and other business practices, upended systems of production, consumption, and distribution. Regional and global trade negotiations and organizations attempted to build a rational and stable framework for the new economy.

The end of the Cold War did not deliver on the promise of peace. Religious and ethnic strife gripped much of the world in the 1990s and into the new millennium. The pace of the global economy and the precipitous dismantling of regulation intersected in the broadest crisis in global markets since the Great Depression. Perceptions that the global economy and political structures of the

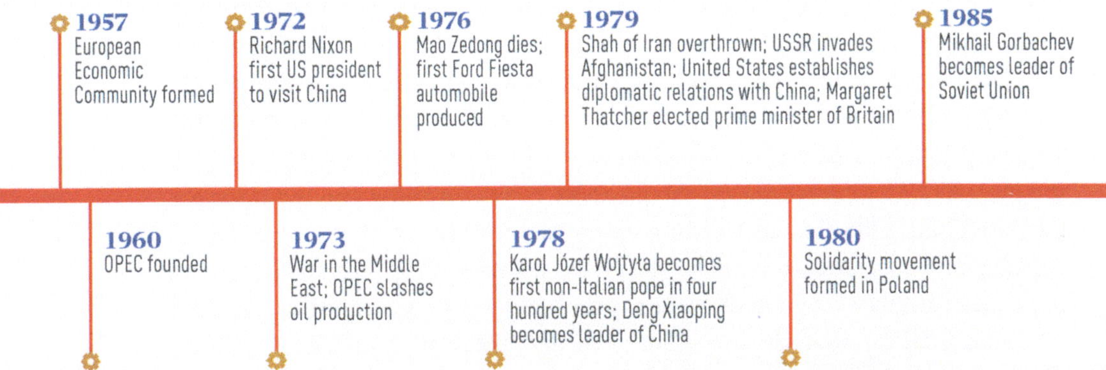
TIMELINE
1957
European Economic Community formed
1960
OPEC founded
1972
Richard Nixon first US president to visit China
1973
War in the Middle East; OPEC slashes oil production
1976
Mao Zedong dies; first Ford Fiesta automobile produced
1978
Karol Józef Wojtyła becomes first non-Italian pope in four hundred years; Deng Xiaoping becomes leader of China
1979
Shah of Iran overthrown; USSR invades Afghanistan; United States establishes diplomatic relations with China; Margaret Thatcher elected prime minister of Britain
1980
Solidarity movement formed in Poland
1985
Mikhail Gorbachev becomes leader of Soviet Union

twenty-first century do not serve the interests of common people continue to drive both peaceful and violent protest among various groups that agree on the problem but diverge radically over proposed solutions.

Overall, the material quality of life improved for most of the planet's population between 1972 and the present, but at a high cost to the environment and an increase in the gap between a wealthy cosmopolitan elite enjoying the fruits of globalization as never before and an anxious majority, a little healthier, a little wealthier, a little better educated, and very uncertain about its future.

A Few Good Books

Timothy Garton Ash. *The Magic Lantern: The Revolution of '89 Witnessed in Warsaw, Budapest, Berlin, and Prague*. New York: Random House, 1990.

Rachel Aspden. *Generation Revolution: On the Front Line between Tradition and Change in the Middle East*. New York: Other Press, 2016.

Christian Caryl. *Strange Rebels: 1979 and the Birth of the Twenty-First Century*. New York: Basic Books, 2014.

Kristen Ghodsee. *Red Hangover: Legacies of Twentieth-Century Communism*. Durham, NC: Duke University Press, 2017.

Philip Gourevitch. *We Wish to Inform You That Tomorrow We Will Be Killed with Our Families: Stories from Rwanda*. New York: Picador, 1999.

Carolyn Merchant. *Death by Nature: Women, Ecology, and the Scientific Revolution*. New York: Harper, 1990.

Orville Schell. *Discos and Democracy: China in the Throes of Reform*. New York: Anchor, 1989.

For instructional resources and study aids, please go to **www.oup.com/us/carter**. *For primary sources connected to this chapter, please see the table of contents for* Sources for Forging the Modern World *included at the back of the book.*

1989
Soviet forces withdraw from Afghanistan; Tiananmen movement in China; Berlin Wall breached; communist governments ousted in central and Eastern Europe; Francis Fukuyama publishes "The End of History?"
1991
Soviet Union dissolved
1991–1999
Yugoslav Wars, widespread ethnic cleansing
1994
Genocide in Rwanda kills over five hundred thousand people
1995
World Trade Organization founded
2001
Al-Qaeda attacks topple World Trade Center in New York
2003
United States invades Iraq
2008–2009
Global financial crisis
2010
China becomes world's second-largest economy
2012
Massive power blackout in India; 2.5 billion people use the internet
2013
Airpocalypse in China
2016
British citizens vote to leave the European Union

Epilogue

We began our story of how the world came to look the way it does with a vignette about fifteenth-century China and the world's largest ship, so we thought it appropriate to make our last vignette, from the twenty-first century, also about China and the world's largest ship. This story does not involve an emperor; its major actors are businessmen associated with the modern Chinese state, a "people's republic." The treasure crossing the seas is not textiles or spices but petroleum.

In September 2014, a Chinese business group supported by the government leased the world's largest ship, capable of carrying more than three million barrels of oil, enough energy to power a Toyota Prius from Earth to Neptune or satisfy the energy demand for all of South Korea for one day. The Chinese buyers did not want this massive ship to deliver oil to the marketplace, however (at least not right away). Their plan was to keep the tanker at sea until the price of oil rose high enough for them to make a better return on their investment and then deliver the crude oil to a refinery. The plan illustrates not only the importance of petroleum in the world, but also global interconnections: the Chinese leased the supertanker *TI Europe* from its Belgian owners (the ship was constructed in a South Korean shipyard) to place crude oil bought from Russia into floating storage off the coast of Asia. The Chinese gave up their lease on the supertanker in 2017. It was subsequently picked up by the Norwegian state oil company, which was storing petroleum from Angola off the coast of Malaysia at the time we completed this text.

One goal we set for this book was to help readers understand how global political and economic organization in our day compares to that of the fifteenth century. This image of the petroleum market provides a useful snapshot of the terrain we have traversed across the pages of this book. When Zheng He sailed the Indian Ocean in the 1400s, he represented an empire whose ruler inherited his position and claimed political legitimacy as the "son of heaven." The Chinese sovereigns who helped sponsor the voyage of the *TI Europe* preside over territory similar to that of Ming rulers, but the modern People's Republic of China is based on a form of political organization that emerged in the eighteenth century and remains dominant in the early twenty-first century: the nation-state. Despite many and constant challenges to the territorial shape and organizational form of individual states, most political movements today accept the claim that sovereignty emerges from a relationship between ruler and ruled, rather than one between ruler and the heavens.

This connection is often expressed through both ideology and performance. In the early twenty-first century, most of the world's nation-states choose their governments by popular vote (though details of these elections vary widely from country to country). Even in states with authoritarian governments and no meaningful popular participation, rulers generally claim the right to rule because they represent the will of the people. The social contract idea may be imperfect or even badly broken, but it still dominates how most people around the world talk and think about government. It also means that interactions among countries take place within a context of rights claims, regardless of any given state's internal political order. In the modern world, war is often justified on grounds that the aggressors seek to liberate peoples who have been unable to exercise their rights claims against the current sovereign ruling over them.

The modern world is also interconnected on an unprecedented scale. It is worth repeating that globalization is not new, but the speed and scale of communications and transportation across the globe have transformed the nature of globalization in the recent past. The Columbian exchange brought global interconnections, but the linkages were slow and intermittent prior to the nineteenth century. In the twentieth century, as steamships, railroads, and telegraphs gave way to airplanes, radios, and automobiles, goods, services, and information traveled still farther and faster. In 1957, the philosopher Hannah Arendt (1906–1975) made the profound observation that the earth's peoples may have had a diverse past, but in the twentieth century, "for the first time in history, all peoples on earth have a common present. . . . Every country has become the almost immediate neighbor of every other country, and every man feels the shock of events which take place at the other end of the globe."[1] In the decades since Arendt wrote that, the links connecting places and people have only become tighter.

The pace of production and consumption sparked by industrialization continues. From the middle of the twentieth century to the early twenty-first century, the world's population grew by approximately two and a half times, but the

1 Hannah Arendt, *Men in Dark Times* (New York: Harvest Books, 1970), 83.

global economy expanded by a factor of ten. This increase in economic activity has not been distributed evenly. Concentration levels of this wealth have fluctuated over time, both within and across states and regions, as has the gap between the world's richest and poorest peoples. However, a sharp contrast between the world's wealthy minority and its poor majority remains a troubling characteristic of the modern world.

Having completed this book, you will have a better idea of the many ways in which the world's fifteenth-century and twenty-first-century political and economic orders differ and some of the ways they may not be so different. We also established another goal, however, which was to provide some understanding of how historical inquiry can be used to explain how and why these changes occurred. Throughout this book, we have explored the ways historians examine the choices individuals and groups had available to them and tried to explain as best we could our understanding of why they made certain choices and not others, as well as how the consequences (intended and unintended) of those choices forged the modern world.

Historians are often asked to explain the relevance of their work. There's a good chance you're reading this book as a requirement for a course at a college or university, and there's a good chance that you (or someone you know) has asked why studying history makes any sense at all. Fair question: Why, in a rapidly changing present, worried about an uncertain future, should anyone take the time to learn about the past?

In a book called *The Idea of History*, the philosopher and historian R. G. Collingwood (1889–1943) laid out various theories about what history was—and what it was not—and how to practice historical inquiry. Collingwood argued that the goal of history was to understand why people in the past acted as they did; it was not enough to know simply what they did. A historian must walk in another's shoes to understand the options that were then available and to make sense of why one choice was made and not another.

To do this requires empathy, creativity, and self-reflection, but it also demands the rigorous analysis of quantitative and qualitative data. The methods of historical inquiry therefore fit the disciplines of both the social sciences and the humanities (even the authors of this book disagree on which side of that divide they reside professionally). Whichever you consider most important, the tools of historians can help us understand how people have evaluated situations, made decisions, and responded to challenges. We can see the consequences of their actions or their failure to act. We can be inspired by people who acted with great wisdom or courage; we can be enraged by those who acted out of spite or hatred. But not all of us will respond in the same way, or take away the same understanding, of every historical era, trend, or event. This is due first to the way that each historian chooses to exercise creativity and empathy in selecting research topics; but it is also because of the data available and the analytical methods applied. As we noted in the introduction, the sum total of all those choices explains how there can be so many different histories.

The task of historical inquiry is now both easier and more difficult than ever before. As we've tried to show throughout this book, historians rely on sources to make sense of the past. Until recently, most archival records resided in a handful of libraries, museums, or government buildings. Few people could reach those repositories; there weren't many of them; and travel was slow, limiting the number of people who could use these sources. But changes that have defined the modern world have also redefined what historians do. New technologies have changed the kinds of sources available to us and the ways historians do their work. Information exists on a scale previous generations could not imagine. Photos and moving pictures have transformed the conduct of historical inquiry, as has the availability of electronic records—emails, tweets, and web pages are now analyzed as part of the historical record.

More and more historical records are available electronically, including reproductions of very old, unpublished documents that archives around the world are making available to the public. The internet gives us instant access to more information than even the largest library could provide just a generation ago. But this is not to say that it is easier to find "the truth." Access to more data does not automatically equate to improved historical understanding, especially because questions of who controls the flow of primary sources—what, how, and where data will be stored and accessed—are as controversial today as they ever have been. The historian's task remains the same, even if the tools and methods are changing.

Marc Bloch (1886–1944), like Collingwood, was a scholar during the tumultuous Three Decades' Crisis we wrote about in Chapters 10, 11, and 12. Bloch was a founder of the Annales school, a group of historians who insisted that the value of historical inquiry did not lie in repeating stories about kings and queens but in analyzing big social structures and socially shared beliefs about how the world worked. Bloch and his colleagues tried to understand how places changed over centuries, even millennia, and how structures shaped the lives of people living in them. This emphasis on structures and underlying conditions led some critics of this approach to accuse these historians of denying the importance of people in shaping their future. But Marc Bloch's life showed just how much he valued individual human agency. When the Nazis invaded France, Bloch left his job as a professor of medieval history to join the Resistance. His book, *The Historian's Craft*, influenced generations of historians but was only published after Bloch was captured and killed by Nazi secret police.

Few of us will confront choices as stark as those Marc Bloch had to make, but this story helps explain why we should all read, and practice, history. We started the book by noting that history is not the same as the past. We'll conclude by asserting that the most important thing about the study of history is really the future. Using all our skills, and mustering the best resources, we can do our best to learn about the choices people made in the past—what constrained their options, why they made their decisions, and what the consequences were. Doing so, perhaps we can learn something about making choices for ourselves, sensitive to the worlds of our fellow inhabitants on this planet. All choices are limited by environment, by technology, and by political, social, and economic constraints, but there are always decisions to be made. Understanding how and why different people made choices in different eras is an essential goal of the historian's craft. And if you believe—as we do—in the importance of human agency and the possibility of free will, then understanding these things might help each of us to make important decisions about the future.

The history of the past six centuries shows that human progress is not inevitable. Some decisions, made by both the powerful and the humble, made the world better. Other decisions helped to impoverish, marginalize, or destroy other human beings. We have at our disposal more tools, more resources, and more ideas than ever before about how to debate and understand world history. Perhaps if more of us engage in these debates, we can imagine and work toward a future that makes the world better for ourselves and others.

Sources for *Forging the Modern World*

Edited by James Carter and Richard Warren

ISBN: 978-0-19-090193-6

Contents

Chapter 3: The Paradoxes of Early Modern Empire, 1501–1661

Chapter 4: Production and Consumption in the First Global Economy, 1571–1700

Chapter 5: Global War and Imperial Reform, 1655–1765

5.3 "Esteem most highly filial piety and brotherly submission." *The Sacred Edict of the Yongzheng Emperor,* ca. 1723-35
5.4 "They were resolved to regain their liberty if possible." William Snelgrave, *A New Account of Some Parts of Guinea and the Slave Trade,* 1734.
5.5 "We fear the damage from a public disclosure." Jorge Juan and Antonio de Ulloa, *Discourse and Political Reflections on the Kingdom of Peru,* 1749.
5.6 "Our hearty thanks for the care you take of us in supplying us with ammunition." *Meetings between a British General and Leaders of the Mohawks, Oneidas and Tuscaroras,* 1755–1756.
5.7 "The Sovereign is absolute." Catherine II of Russia, *Instructions for a New Law Code,* 1767

Chapter 6: A New Order for the Ages, 1755–1839

6.1 "We hold these truths to be self-evident." *The US Declaration of Independence,* 1776.
6.2 "The state ought not to be considered as nothing better than a partnership agreement." Edmund Burke, *Reflections on the Revolution in France,* 1790.
6.3 "Woman is born free and lives equal to man in her rights." Olympe de Gouges, *Declaration of the Rights of Woman and the Female Citizen,* 1791.
6.4 "We will distance forever from this colony the horrible events." Toussaint Louvertoure, *Proclamation,* 1801.
6.5 "I have simply been a mere plaything of the revolutionary storm." Simón Bolívar, *Address at the Congress of Angostura,* 1819.
6.6 "Great revolutions are the work rather of principles than of bayonets." Giuseppe Mazzini, *Manifesto of Young Italy,* 1831.
6.7 "The benefit of a good administration." *The Rescript of Gülhane,* 1839.

Chapter 7: The Engines of Industrialization, 1787–1868

7.1 "The principle of the factory system then is, to substitute mechanical science for hand skill." Andrew Ure, *The Philosophy of Manufactures,* 1835.
7.2 "I have wrought in the bowels of the earth thirty-three years." *The Condition and Treatment of the Children Employed in the Mines and Collieries,* 1842.
7.3 "No exemptions from attacks of epidemic disease." Edwin Chadwick, *Report on the Sanitary Condition of the Labouring Population,* 1842.
7.4 "The statutes of the heavenly dynasty cannot but be obeyed with fear and trembling!" *Qianlong Emperor to King George III,* 1793; *Letter from the High Imperial Commissioner Lin and His Colleagues to Queen Victoria of England,* 1840.

7.5 "To carry the laws of the United States into Turkey and China." Caleb Cushing, *Opinion of the Attorney General*, 1855.

7.6 "All lie stretched in the mud and dust, drenched in their own blood." Henry Dunant, *A Memory of Solferino*, 1859, and Florence Nightingale, *Letter to Sidney Herbert*, 1855.

7.7 "The best adapted to all the crops cultivated in this country." Solon Robinson, *Guano: A Treatise of Practical Information*, 1853.

Chapter 8: Modernity Organized, 1840–1889

8.1 "Working men of all countries, unite." Karl Marx and Friedrich Engels, *Manifesto of the Community Party*, 1848.

8.2 "Paris in America." Herbert H. Smith, *Brazil, the Amazons, and the Coast*, 1879.

8.3 "The history of mankind is a history of repeated injuries and usurpations on the part of man toward woman." Elizabeth Cady Stanton, *Declaration of Sentiments*, 1848.

8.4 "Demand rights for women." Flora Tristán, *Workers' Union*, 1843; Sojourner Truth, *Address to the First Annual Meeting of the American Equal Rights Association*, 1867.

8.5 "Evil customs of the past shall be broken off." *The Charter Oath* (Japan), 1868; *The Emancipation Manifesto* (Russia), 1861.

8.6 "There are endless changes in the world." Zeng Guofan and Li Hongzhang, *Letter to the Zongli Yamen*, 1871; Xue Fucheng, *Suggestions on Foreign Affairs*, 1879.

8.7 "China is just the Opposite." Li Gui, *Glimpses of a Modern Society*, 1876.

Chapter 9: Globalization and Its Discontents, 1878–1910

9.1. "Take Up the White Man's Burden." Rudyard Kipling, *The White Man's Burden*, 1899 and H. T. Johnson, *The Black Man's Burden*, 1899

9.2 "A matter of vital importance for Germany's Development." Friedrich Fabri, *Does Germany Need Colonies?*, 1879.

9.3 "What a pity she wasn't born a lad." Emmeline Pankhurst, *My Own Story*, 1914.

9.4 "One knows the futility of trying to prevent the onslaught of Western civilization." Fukuzawa Yukichi, *Goodbye Asia*, 1885.

9.5 "Civilization is not an incurable disease, but it should never be forgotten that the English people are at present afflicted by it." Mohandas K Gandhi, *Hind Swaraj*, 1909.

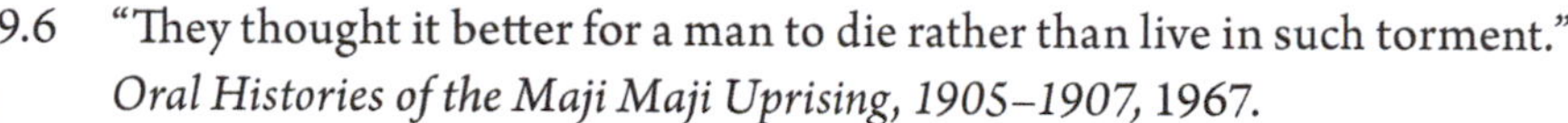

9.6 "They thought it better for a man to die rather than live in such torment." *Oral Histories of the Maji Maji Uprising, 1905–1907,* 1967.

9.7 "Do not tell the white people about this." Wovoka and the Ghost Dance, 1890.

Chapter 10: Total War and Mass Society, 1905–1928

10.1 "The peoples of Asia have cherished the hope of shaking off the yoke of European oppression." Sun Yat-sen, Speech on Pan-Asianism, 1924.

10.2 "Things will never be as they were." Correspondence of Vera Brittain, 1915, 1918.

10.3 "A free, open-minded, and absolutely impartial adjustment of all colonial claims." Woodrow Wilson, Address to US Congress, 1918; and Nguyen Ai Quoc (Ho Chi Minh), Letter to US secretary of state, 1919.

10.4 "The Nation shall at all times have the right to impose on private property." The Constitution of Mexico, 1917.

10.5 "It is proved in the pamphlet that the war of 1914–18 was imperialist." V. I. Lenin, *Imperialism, The Highest Stage of Capitalism: A Popular Outline,* 1917, 1920.

10.6 "Throughout history one of the constant features of social struggle has been the attempt to change relationships between the sexes." Alexandra Kollontai, *Sexual Relations and the Class Struggle,* 1921.

10.7 "The Fascist conception of life stresses the importance of the State." Benito Mussolini and Giovanni Gentile, *The Political and Social Doctrine of Fascism,* 1934.

Chapter 11: The Ongoing Crisis of Global Order, 1919–1948

11.1 "Certainly a government needs power, it needs strength." Adolf Hitler, Munich Speech of April 12, 1921.

11.2 "It is international morality which is at stake." Haile Selassie, Speech to the League of Nations, 1936.

11.3 "They will sweep all the imperialists, warlords, corrupt officials, local tyrants and evil gentry into their graves." Mao Zedong, *Report on the Peasant Movement in Hunan,* 1927.

11.4 "When will it no longer be necessary to attach special weight to the word 'woman?'" Ding Ling, *Thoughts on March 8 (International Women's Day),* 1942.

11.5 "Who is to blame for the condition of China?" Hirosi Saito, *The Conflict in the Far East,* 1939.

11.6 "The work of operating the gas chambers was carried out by a special Commando." Primo Levi with Leonardo de Benedetti, *Auschwitz Report*, 1946.

11.7 "Our forces dare take their position beside any force in the world." General Aung San, *Address to the East West Association*, 1945.

Chapter 12: Hot Wars, Cold Wars, and Decolonization: 1942–1975

12.1 "An iron curtain has descended across the Continent." Winston Churchill, *Address at Westminster College* (Fulton, Missouri), 1946.

12.2 "Mr. Churchill and his friends bear a striking resemblance to Hitler." *Joseph Stalin interview*, 1946.

12.3 "Vietnam has the right to be a free and independent country." *Vietnamese Declaration of Independence*, 1945.

12.4 "The equal and inalienable rights of all members of the human family." *United Nations Declaration of Human Rights*, 1948.

12.5 "We cannot afford even to think of failure." *Kwame Nkrumah speeches*, 1957, 1962.

12.6 "We want to advance in the technological sphere and the scientific sphere rapidly." Jawaharlal Nehru, Convocation Address, *Indian Institute of Technology*, 1956.

12.7 "Some governments still rest on the theory of racist superiority." Indira Gandhi, *Presentation of the Jawaharlal Nehru Award for International Understanding to Martin Luther King*, 1969

Chapter 13: The Many Worlds of the Twenty-First Century, 1972–2012

13.1 "We shall confront the world with our ideology." *Ayatollah Ruhollah Khomeini speech*, 1980

13.2 "Comrade Gorbachev recommended not to be deterred." *Memorandum of Conversation between Egon Krenz and Mikhail S. Gorbachev*, 1989

13.3 "An axis of evil." George W. Bush, *State of the Union Address*, 2002; Hugo Chávez, *Address to the United Nations General Assembly*, 2008.

13.4 "The backward glance leading to self-knowledge." Mary Robinson, *Keynote Address, International Conference on Hunger*, 1995.

13.5 "The deepest roots of the problems of contemporary civilization lie in the sphere of the human spirit." Vaclav Havel, *Mahatma Gandhi Award Acceptance Speech*, 2004; Nigel Farage, *Address to the UKIP Conference*, 2013.

13.6 "People have not become more open-minded." Sri Mulyani Indrawati, *Commencement Address at the University of Virginia*, 2016.

Credits

CHAPTER 1

p. 18: The Philadelphia Museum of Art/Art Resource, NY; p. 18: Erich Lessing/Art Resource, NY; p. 31: Gregory A. Harlin/National Geographic Creative; p. 37: BnF, Dist. RMN-Grand Palais/Art Resource, NY; p. 40: DEA/G. DAGLI ORTI/Contributor/Getty Images

CHAPTER 2

p. 46: MS. Arch. Selden. A. 1 fol. 013r Bodleian Libraries, University of Oxford/The Art Archive at Art Resource. Codex Mendoza, Spanish guide to Mexican culture, early 1540s, The Conquests of Ahuitzol ("Water Animal"). Commissioned by Antonio de Mendoza, first Viceroy of Mexico 1535-1550, for presentation to the Emperor Charles V of Spain. The pictographs, by an Aztec artist, were annotated in Spanish by a Nahuatl-speaking Spanish priest; p. 46: © The Trustees of the British Museum; p. 53: The Fray Angélico Chávez History Library, New Mexico History Museum; p. 61: Courtesy of the Library of Congress; p. 64: Courtesy of the Library of Congress

CHAPTER 3

p. 68: © The Trustees of the British Museum; p. 68: China: The 4th Qing Emperor Kangxi (1654–1722), temple name Shengzu. He is considered one of China's greatest emperors./Pictures from History/Bridgeman Images; p. 74: Historical Picture Archive/Contributor/Getty Images; p. 77: The Walters Art Museum, Baltimore; p. 80: © The Trustees of the British Museum

CHAPTER 4

p. 94: Courtesy of the Hispanic Society of America, New York; p. 94: Villa Rosemaine 2010; p. 103: © RMN-Grand Palais/Art Resource, NY; p. 104: Jar with Handles, Attributed to Damián Hernández, Mid-17th century, Tin-glazed earthenware. Height: 18 1/2 inches (47 cm) accession #1907-295. Philadelphia

Museum of Art: Purchased with funds contributed by Mrs. John Harrison, 1907; p. 116: Frans Hals Museum, Haarlem

CHAPTER 5

p. 120: Collection of the National Foundation-Brazil Library; p. 120: © The British Library Board, Foster; p. 127: © National Maritime Museum, Greenwich, London; p. 133: © The British Library Board, 522.f.23 volume 2, fold out

CHAPTER 6

p. 146: Gianni Dagli Orti/The Art Archive at Art Resource, NY, Location Museo de Arte Antiga Lisbon; p. 146: © The Trustees of the British Museum; p. 159: Heritage Images/Contribution/Getty Images; p. 167: DEA/M. SEEMULLER/ Contributor/Getty Images; p. 171: National Library and Archives of the Islamic Republic of Iran

CHAPTER 7

p. 176: Courtesy of the Library of Congress; p. 176: © The British Library Board, 8235.k.6; p. 188: DEA/G. DAGLI ORTI/Contributor/Getty Images; p. 190: Grafissimo/Getty Images; p. 197: © The British Library Board, 1780.c.6, page 35

CHAPTER 8

p. 202: © The Trustees of the British Museum; p. 202: Courtesy of the Library of Congress; p. 204: Eltis & Richardson, *Atlas of the Transatlantic Slave Trade*, © 2010, Yale University Press; p. 218: Print Collector/Contributor/Getty Images; p. 227: Liberia soap and coffee display, Agricultural Hall, Philadelphia Centennial Exhibition, 1876 (albumen print), American Photographer, (19th century)/ Free Library of Philadelphia/Bridgeman Images

CHAPTER 9

p. 230: L'Illustration; p. 230: Danny Alvarez/Shutterstock; p. 239: Courtesy of the Library of Congress; p. 242: www.antislavery.org; p. 248: Photograph © 2016 Museum of Fine Arts, Boston

CHAPTER 10

p. 258: Courtesy of Andrew Gordon, Harvard University; p. 258: Courtesy of the Library of Congress; p. 270: bpk Bildagentur/Art Resource, NY; p. 273: Imperial War Museum

CHAPTER 11

p. 288: Bettmann/Contributor/Getty Images; p. 288: Bettmann/Contributor/ Getty Images; p. 303: Courtesy of the Library of Congress; p. 307: Central Press/ Stringer/Getty Images

CHAPTER 12

p. 316: Courtesy of the Library of Congress; p. 316: Michael Nicholson/Contributor/Getty Images; p. 327: Bettmann/Contributor/Getty Images; p. 331: Bettmann/Contributor/Getty Images; p. 335: Courtesy of the Library of Congress

CHAPTER 13

p. 342: Everett Collection/Newscom; p. 342: NASA; p. 350: Courtesy of the Library of Congress; p. 353: Courtesy of the Library of Congress; p. 363: GERARD MALIE/Staff/Getty Images

Index

Italicized page references indicate a photo, illustration or timeline reference.

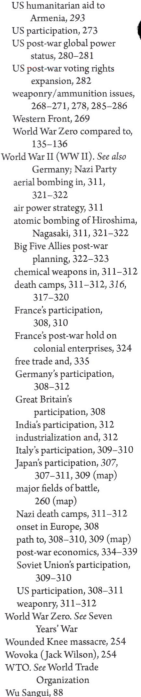